Soul Survivors

A New Beginning for Adults Abused as Children

J. PATRICK GANNON, Ph.D.

Produced by The Philip Lief Group, Inc.

PRENTICE HALL PRESS

New York · London · Toronto · Sydney · Tokyo

Prentice Hall Press
Gulf + Western Building
One Gulf + Western Plaza
New York, New York 10023

PRENTICE HALL PRESS and colophon are registered trademarks
of Simon & Schuster, Inc.

Library of Congress Cataloging-in-Publication Data
Gannon, J. Patrick.
Soul survivors : a new beginning for adults abused as
children/
J. Patrick Gannon.
p.   cm.
"Produced by the Philip Lief Group, Inc."
Bibliography: p.
ISBN 0-13-823642-9
1. Adult child abuse victims—Mental health.   I. Philip Lief
Group.   II. Title.
RC569.5.C55G36 1989   89-31018
616.85'8—dc19   CIP

Designed by Richard Oriolo

Manufactured in the United States of America

10 9 8 7 6 5 4 3 2 1

First Edition

Produced by The Philip Lief Group, Inc.

To my parents and family, whose love nourished my soul

To Weston "Sandy" Jenks—teacher, mentor, and friend,
who helped chart the course of my calling

Acknowledgements

I would like to express my heartfelt gratitude to the many people and organizations that contributed directly or indirectly to the creation of this book. During my research for *Soul Survivors* they unselfishly shared their time and knowledge with me in the hope of furthering our mutual cause: the reduction of child abuse in our society and the recovery of adult survivors everywhere who are still struggling with the long-term effects of their abuse as children. I am especially indebted to the staff of Lutheran Family Services in Portland, Oregon, and particularly Dr. Kao Rhiannon and Annette Selmer, M.S., who provided invaluable assistance. I also would like to thank Dr. Robert Burke and Dr. Jeffrey Kahn of Marin Community Mental Health for their efforts in locating interview subjects. During the course of my research, I interviewed many professionals in the child abuse treatment field who provided me with information, research papers they had written, or their unique point of view about select issues. Among those to whom I would like to express my appreciation are Dr. Kathryn Ridall; Dr. Diane Leroi; Dr. Karen Peoples; Dr. Mary Krentz, director of the Child and Family Therapy Center in Martinez, California; and Officer Sandi Gallant, cult crimes specialist of the San Francisco Police Department.

Over the years, there have been several people who have supported my work as a clinician in the child abuse treatment field who I would also like to acknowledge. I would particularly like to thank Dr. Don Cotton who facilitated our men's groups with me and who generously shared his expertise in the group treatment of adult male survivors. Kathleen Baxter-Stern of the San Francisco Child Abuse Council and Dr. Eliana Gil have always been supportive and encouraging dating back to my work in community mental health. I would also like to acknowledge the training I received from Dr. Graeme Hanson, my consultant during my years as program director for a child and family mental health clinic and Shirley Cooper, L.C.S.W., for her unique clinical perspective on child abuse as well as her thoughtful comments on many segments of the manuscript.

Several people contributed to the preparation and editing of the manuscript who I would also like to acknowledge. First, I want to thank Joanne Harenburg, my transcriber and secretary, who diligently entered the hours of interview transcripts into my computer. In addition, I would like to thank Ms. Jamie Rothstein, my editor, and Philip Lief, my agent, for believing in this project and working to make it accessible to the broadest possible population. I also appreciate the enthusiasm of the people at Prentice Hall Press—PJ Dempsey, Gail Winston, and Marilyn Abraham—who patiently extended my deadline in the hopes of getting this information out sooner rather than later.

The timely help I received from my friends in the form of dinners, advice, and encouragement made it possible for me to plow forward toward completion. I would like to thank David and Teri, Kelly, Ruth, Alan, Bob and Mary, Jeff and Mary, Mark and Sally, and Jeanne and Gary for their unique contributions.

In particular, I would like to express my deep gratitude for the support and encouragement I received from my wife, Dr. Josiane Lismay who is also a psychologist and specialist in the treatment of adult survivors of child abuse. Her understanding and willingness to accept my extended hours at the computer during our most challenging year will be forever valued.

Finally, I would like to thank the many people I interviewed, some of whose stories are contained in this book. Your honesty and courage in detailing your past abuse and subsequent recovery is the backbone of *Soul Survivors* and provided me with the inspiration I needed to complete this work. I hope my words do justice to your experience.

As an arrow pierces the heart,
the pain envelopes my body.
Each breath drawn takes away
Precious moments of a terminating existence.
Beaten eyes slowly close to the realization
of the world around me.
Split lips beg for the sweet surrender
to a fruit-giving life.
Only wrinkles and shame flourish
through years of despair and conflict
Then, the night cries out
with a light of reassurance—
There must be something waiting for me
at the end of this torment.
I am alone now, yet
My soul will live forever.

    –LEIGH ANNE, ADULT SURVIVOR
     (written at age 16)

Contents

Introduction

This book is for the millions of men and women across the country today who, like you, have survived abuse as children. Child abuse—the physical, sexual, or emotional maltreatment of a minor—was a devastating reality for you, coloring many aspects of your childhood and now casting a long shadow over your adult life. Much has been written recently about child abuse—horrible stories reported in the media about the kidnapping, molestation, and abandonment of children. Now, more than ever before, people are waking up to the fact that some 2 million children are being physically, sexually, and emotionally abused each year in the United States.

But what about the past generations of abused children who are today's adults, parents, and workers? What has become of these adult survivors who silently endured their family's dark secret before the media began exposing this ongoing tragedy? Current surveys show that tens of millions of people grew up in dysfunctional families where violence, incest, or emotional abuse caused by alcoholism was an everyday reality. Women survivors were the first to shatter the secrecy of incest and expose the vulnerability of children to sexual abuse outside the home as well. More recently, men have begun to speak about their victimization, challenging the myth that boys don't get sexually abused. We are now recognizing that child abuse is a major social problem, a dark shroud of betrayal and fear that is handed down through the generations.

This book is for those of you who may be questioning whether you were abused as a child, and if so, how the effects of the abuse explain your unhappiness today as an adult. Like the men and women you are about to meet, you too may find yourself struggling through life. Your silence, once an obligation to the family, may now be a barrier to communication. Your solitude, formerly a strategy of self-protection, may now feel more like isolation. Your efforts to forget may now leave you feeling lost and without direction. The physical hurt and sexual stimulation that once left you numb may now have made you numb to the world. For adult survivors, the impact of child abuse is not knowing where to go for love or how to act in your own best interests, burdened by the shame, fear, and betrayal of the past.

Soul Survivors is also written for those of you who are still reconstructing the pieces of your childhood memories. For many of you, these remain blurry images and disconnected scenes from your family's past, recollections that may lie behind a wall of amnesia. You may not recall the specific scenes that link current problems with past abuse. With hard work, courage, and dedication to reclaiming the past, these elusive images will gradually return, and with them, the seeds of your transformation as a person.

Some of you who were not abused as children may want to read this book to understand and help a friend, co-worker, lover, or spouse who was abused as a child. Chapter 8 addresses, in particular, the challenges and questions that you face in your daily relationship with the survivor and what you can do to support this person on the long road to recovery. Some of you may want to give this book to friends and loved ones who are unknowingly carrying on the legacy of their abuse in their self-destructive lifestyle. Your helping hand may rescue them from further victimization.

This book will not be easy to read. Forgetting painful memories may seem like the best way to deal with the past. The problem is that the past will not stay in the past—the fear and shame that you feel most days are present-day relics of your abuse. The powerful feelings, unanswered questions, and unresolved conflicts will have to be faced. Remember that the worst is probably over. You survived the torment as a child who had little control. Now you will have much more control and can learn new strategies for handling your feelings and relating to others.

Child abuse takes many forms that do not always adhere to easy definitions. You may have experienced one particular type of abuse, or more commonly, multiple types of abuse that only you can describe. You may have been continually abused within your family or only once by an acquaintance. You may have been physically abused under the guise of punishment or sexually abused after the pronouncement of love or emotionally abused for the purpose of instilling discipline. You may have been verbally abused for having a certain temperament or bearing some resemblance to a disliked relative. Some of you may have endured aspects of all types of abuse—with a family life like a war zone in which you were the lone soldier operating behind enemy lines. Like the adult survivors' stories you will read in this book, your story is unique to the personalities, circumstances, and heritage that created your family's ordeal. This book will identify and explain these factors so that you will understand and hopefully accept that your parents—not you—were responsible for the abuse.

Those of you abused as children survived by every means imaginable: Some of you avoided home like the plague, getting yourselves "adopted" by friends' families. Some of you became caretakers, devoting yourselves to keeping the rest of the family intact while your parents engaged in their marital warfare. Still others became reclusive, closing yourselves off from everyone by adopting a personal hobby, a secret activity, or even a fantasy life. The terrible shame you felt forced you to suffer your indignity in silence. That silent agony simmered inside for years, eating away at your self confidence.

But now, years have gone by and the silent burden of your abuse has made its impact felt in all aspects of your adult life. Over time, that silence has become like a dam, holding back a reservoir of thoughts, feelings, memories, and resentments. You may think that since you have now become an adult you have little reason to unblock the past. Or you may fear that testing the water beyond the dam will risk a flood of unwanted feelings, washing away your self-identity. These dams inevitably wall off important parts of you—unrecognized parts of your personality, hidden capabilities, and strength of spirit. The tragedy of child abuse is that it leave its victims estranged from the healthiest, most resilient parts of themselves.

Finally, this book will reach out to those of you who are in recovery, working hard to heal the wounds of the past and change the future. As you know, recovery from child abuse is like taking a long journey with many steps along the way. Each of these steps is described in detail with suggestions offered on how to make your journey less intimidating and less lonely. You will no longer have to endure the past alone. Others have blazed the trail for you and their stories can inspire you to move forward toward your new beginning.

INTRODUCING THE
PEOPLE IN THIS BOOK

Before introducing the six survivors whose stories you will read, I'd like to tell you something about myself and why I wrote this book. I am a clinical psychologist who has worked as a therapist with child abuse victims and adult survivors for the last ten years. I am not a survivor of child abuse myself. I had a reasonably normal childhood, although like most families, not without its share of problems. My first contact with child abuse was as a therapist for a small community mental health outreach program operating in a seedy, crime-infested neighborhood in San Francisco called the Tenderloin. Everything was for sale in this area, including children. My work with these abused children and teenagers inevitably led to working with their parents who I discovered had also been abused as children. In fact, I often discovered *exactly* the same patterns of abuse between the child and the parent.

Writing this book was both a challenge and a natural progression of my work as a therapist, teacher, and mental health consultant in the field of child abuse. I hope my perspective is helpful to those of you who have chosen to read it. During the course of researching this book, I interviewed many adult survivors—male and female—who came from a wide variety of dysfunctional families. Each had his or her own story to tell starting from the early years of childhood, continuing through the difficult adult years before recovery, and ending with their triumphs in therapy.

The particular people whose stories I chose to share with you have all experienced one or more types of child abuse: (1) emotional abuse alone, (2) physical and emotional abuse together, (3) sexual abuse and emotional abuse together, or (4) physical, sexual, and emotional abuse together.

An important reason for choosing these survivors is that each of them has faced his or her unhappiness and chosen to reach out and get help. They are at various stages in their recovery and are able to talk about what they have learned and how they have been affected by their abuse as well as to describe their efforts to heal themselves through a comprehensive program of recovery involving self-help and professional help.

Leigh Ann
(Age 37)

When I started therapy a few years ago, I was in the dark about that to expect, what I would feel or how I would change. I could have used a book like this to help me figure out how to deal with the problems I was having. Part of the problem was that I wasn't seeing that I had a problem. I was the one who always survived, who could take anything and still come up standing, if not smiling. I'm a pretty spunky person—I get along with people and am usually well-liked. I thought I got through it pretty well. But the past has a way of catching up with you. My life just wasn't working out for me and making the decision to get help was the best thing I have ever done. I want people to hear my story because I've lived with it for so long and I know what my parents did to me was wrong. Speaking out is my way of saying it wasn't my fault.

♦

Listening to what other people have endured as children and what they have done to overcome the past will inform, inspire, and hopefully motivate those of you who have not gotten help. For others who are in various stages of recovery, reading this book will broaden your understanding of your progress, address specific questions and experiences you might have had, and validate your efforts to heal your body and soul

Jolene
(Age 28)

I grew up in foster homes when I was a kid. My mother, who was living on welfare at the time, had seven kids. I was the unlucky seventh—the one she couldn't handle. If I were the second or third, I might have been raised by my grandparents who were leaders of the black community and ashamed of what their daughter had become. But they already had their hands full with numbers five and six by the time I came around. I got placed in three different foster homes: The first was good, the second was pretty chaotic, and the third was downright weird. My life has been really confusing to me. I'm still trying to sort out what happened and how it affected me. I know that I was abused but there was so much more that happened that I can't get a handle on. I do have strong feelings about the foster care system—it really screwed me over. They took me out of the first home for no reason, left me in the second home when I told them I was being mistreated, and then placed me in this fundamentalist family where the father molested me for three years. For years I have cut myself off from my anger just to get by. Now it's coming back and I don't know what to do with it. Telling my story is perhaps a way to come to grips with my past and do something about it.

♦

Each of the stories you will read will reflect some of the differences in family backgrounds and childhood experiences that make everyone's story unique. Not all of you were raised by your biological families and some experienced child abuse outside the family, which we call *extra-familial* abuse. Friends of your parents, scout leaders, teachers, baby sitters, and other adults in positions of authority are the most likely perpetrators of this type of abuse.

Richard
(Age 30)

I wanted to tell my story because people need to realize how destructive words are—perhaps even more so than fists or weapons. Words can be more piercing than anything else and a child really has no chance against an adult who is a master of the forked tongue. I was never sure that what happened to me was really child abuse. I didn't know if the way my mother hit me or verbally sliced me up really qualified as child abuse. I knew I hated her for it. But I didn't know how that affected me in the long run. In a way, telling my story is kind of validating because I can hear myself describe the worst scenes in my life with my mother and then part of me can sit back and see it more objectively for what it was.

◆

The stories of these six people will touch on many of the issues, concerns, and questions that all survivors have had at one time or another about their struggle with addictions, job problems, and parenting concerns, to name a few. Listening to the stories will give you a framework to recall your childhood and to determine if your family experience was abusive.

Shirley
(Age 38)

I have spoken on radio programs and at conferences about my abuse as a child. It gives me strength to talk about it. I feel validated sharing my past and listening to what other people have gone through. I've gotten a lot stronger during the years of my recovery, first from alcohol and drugs, and later from the molestation and abuse. I am proud of what I've achieved. Talking about it lets me reach out to others and affirm that part of me that feels healthy and alive with myself. I've still got a ways to go. There are still areas of my life—my intimate relationships, for instance—where I get into my old stuff. But I am a survivor. I think everyone who has been abused as a kid has a part of themselves—even just the smallest spark inside—that wants to throw off the past and heal themselves so they can live life instead of fighting it.

♦

Listening to others can play an important role in uncovering the past and helping you to sort out what happened to you. It can also give you some inspiration in starting your own recovery.

Pete
(Age 32)

I thought of writing a book about my childhood, but I knew I would never get around to it. I used to think it was pretty unusual to say the least. What happened between me and my mom and how I got tied up in my parent's sick relationship needs to be understood. They were big lessons for me and perhaps for other people too. I'm sure I wasn't the only boy who was sexually molested by a parent. I've spent the last ten years dealing with the effects one way or another. I think you have to find a part of yourself that wants to be saved and then dedicate yourself to following that feeling. I never thought I would make it. Recently my wife and I moved into our first house, which was really a big thing for me because somehow it represented to me that I had made it—I had changed my life. I could be a healthy man with a healthy family and have a decent life that didn't have to include all the pain that I was so used to. This is what recovery has meant to me and now I'm ready to enjoy it.

♦

It is important to recognize that other people who survived abuse as children are growing stronger by the day and are rebuilding their lives for a brighter future. The past does not need to be avoided forever. If you are willing to invest in your future by reclaiming your past, you can create a new beginning for yourself.

Susan
(Age 34)

I feel like I've come a long way since my days of staying out all night and doing coke—scrambling my way through life. I was in terrible shape and going downhill. I had a kid, not enough money to live on, was getting into these horrible relationships with men that went absolutely nowhere. I really felt horrible—when I wasn't so loaded that I felt nothing. But I'm a survivor—there's no doubt about that. I've worked real hard to change and I've made a commitment to therapy and sobriety, and now, my son. Things are looking up in my life. I may not find the right guy, but I know I can love myself and my kid and be happy in life. For a while I thought that maybe I would never be happy or satisfied. What I have to say will hopefully connect with someone out there who felt as lost as I once did.

♦

Surviving child abuse goes beyond just surviving your family and childhood. It also goes beyond surviving your unhappiness as an adult. Surviving ultimately needs to grow into thriving, when you finally get comfortable with life so that you can make it work for you and you can realize your potential as the unique person you are. Like all major endeavors, it will take a major commitment to make that kind of change.

TAKING THE FIRST STEP

You may wonder what it will take to resolve your childhood pain. The answer, of course, differs with each individual and family situation. Having worked with many survivors during the last ten years, I can attest that each arrived at a point in life at which they felt they had no choice but to change. Life was not happening *for* them; it was happening *against* them. Many were actively thinking about suicide, and those who were not so conscious were risking their physical well-being by driving drunk, or putting themselves in other unsafe situations, or ignoring signs of exhaustion while burning the candle at both ends.

It is my opinion that by making a commitment to a program of personal recovery involving psychotherapy and self-help support groups people *can* change. I have seen it happen many, many times. Seeking help from a therapist or participating in group therapy are powerful antidotes to the problems caused by child abuse. But I admit recovery can be a long and difficult process—one that may take many years and a major investment of time, money, and energy. However, I have never met a survivor in the throes of recovery who was not glad that he or she initiated the first step toward change. Listen to the stories of survivors in this book and you will find that many of them feel reborn as a result of their recovery. They feel reborn in a spiritual sense as well as in a psychological sense. They have found and integrated lost aspects of themselves and have created a new sense of self—one that is far happier and more productive in life. They would never go back to that closed-in feeling and isolated existence of their prerecovery days.

It is hard to pinpoint exactly when change begins, but it usually can be traced back to the decision to take that first step. The first step usually involves some activity that will increase awareness of what you went through as a child and where you are now as an adult. It can then lead to other steps that will create the foundation of your new beginning. Over time, your new awareness will offer a more accurate picture of what really happened to you and how you might be affected by it today. Try not to stumble on the first step just because you feel uncomfortable looking at yourself. Like most other adult survivors, you may have taken on some of your parents' biases and judgments about yourself. It is understandable that you would feel some reluctance to face the conflicts of your past. One of the first acts of change you can make is to avoid making negative judgments about who you are and what your prospects are for change. It is essential that you give yourself a chance to be different and to act differently without the criticism and denigration learned from your parents. Give yourself enough room to get your footing on that first step. You have never been given a chance to discover who you really are. Try not to repeat the mistake your parents made by treating yourself the same way.

You have many different paths to choose when taking your first step of gaining awareness. You may want to talk to a friend, partner, or even family member about yourself, collect mementos from your past, begin a journal or diary, enroll in a class on parenting skills, join a support group, or consult with a professional therapist. I also hope that reading this book may offer you a path toward greater self-awareness. Whatever path you choose, the most important thing is to follow it through. Procrastination, though a trait well familiar to adult survivors, can only deter you from making any beginning effort to increase self-awareness. Remember, the motivation to make that first step will ebb and flow over time. Encourage yourself to explore the walled-off parts of yourself. And support these personal endeavors with respect, commitment, and compassion.

BEFORE BEGINNING YOUR RECOVERY

Before initiating the first step in your recovery process, take a moment to review your support system. Embarking on recovery is not advised for those who are still isolated and without social supports. If your support system needs work, consider joining one of the self-help groups described in chapter 11. Try to meet people who have similar backgrounds and develop some new relationships that will provide understanding and support. If you have an addiction, you can have access to a sponsor and the twenty-four-hour availability of telephone support through membership in one of the 12-Step self-help groups. Talk to a friend or a family member about what you are undertaking and ask if they would be available to provide support as you need it. Another idea is to begin psychotherapy and to use the support of a therapist to help you handle the powerful feelings that will likely emerge. The important message here is, *Do not try to go it alone*. It is essential that you give yourself every consideration to maximize the positive benefits of recovery. If you go only halfway in supporting yourself through this process, you may be setting yourself up for disappointment or possibly continuing the self-sabotage that you learned from your family.

GETTING THE
MOST FROM THIS BOOK

Reading this book may represent your first step, or only one of many steps, in your new beginning. As with any book, remember that not all of the information is relevant to your individual experiences, feelings, and problems. Read and reflect, picking and choosing what fits and dismissing the rest as intended for someone else. Allow yourself to pause for reflection whenever something you read triggers any sort of association to your own experience, past or present. Feel the emotions, recall the memories, reclaim the past.

This book is divided into three sections, each section being a preparation for the next. Like the stagelike process of child development, *Soul Survivors* was organized to be read from beginning to end. However, many of you who are well along in your recovery may want to skip ahead to the chapters that are most relevant to where you are today. For those of you who are just beginning to reclaim your past, take it one step at a time, with ample time for reflection and integration of the information.

Part I is organized to help you determine if you were abused as a child, and if so, to determine the type of abuse and the impact it had on your childhood. You will be supplied with information and questions aimed at helping you to reclaim childhood memories. Factual information will be provided about child abuse that you can use to challenge your misconceptions and family myths about the abuse. Part I will provide the definitions, causes, and consequences of child abuse. It will distinguish between abuse that occurs within the family (*intrafamilial*) and abuse that happens outside the family (*extrafamilial*). It will give you a system for understanding and identifying dysfunctional families and the adult offenders—people within the family and outside the family—who perpetuate the physical, sexual, and emotional abuse of children. It will describe what children do to cope psychologically with the abuse and the personal strengths that grow out of these strategies.

Part II will shift focus from your childhood to your adulthood. It will help you identify problems you may have as an adult that are an outgrowth of your childhood experiences. It will describe in detail the central dynamic of adults abused as children that undermines their happiness and fulfillment as adults. It will bring into focus the overlapping problems of alcohol and substance abuse and what role these addictions play in the lives of adult survivors. It will identify how abuse during childhood affects your life as a parent, a worker, and a spouse or lover. The final chapter is targeted for the partner or friend of a survivor and explains how the issues of abuse get played out in close relationships.

Part III is dedicated to the healing process and will offer a three stage program for overcoming the effects of child abuse. This program of recovery is based on my clinical experience and understanding of current research and theory. Recovery is a long-term process of personal transformation from child victim to adult survivor to self-thriver. As you read and digest, feel and heal; listen to that voice within that will tell you what you need to resolve the past. Trust this voice; it will grow stronger as you recover. If what this voice tells you differs from the model suggested in this book, consider both points of view and make the choice that is right for you.

My earlier suggestion to consider psychotherapy is a serious one. I truly believe that recovery cannot be fully achieved without extended therapy with a trained professional. Selecting the right therapist for you—someone who will become a partner in your recovery and is a caring, warm, and interested person—may be one of the biggest decisions you can make. Considering that some people may have come away from psychotherapy feeling disappointed, I have chosen to include a guide to psychotherapy and a routine for selecting a qualified therapist. A review of self-help groups is also included in recognition of the profound value that such groups have for the recovery process. The final chapter will help you make the right choices in dealing with your family and how and when to confront them with your new understanding of what was done to you as a child.

The appendixes at the end of the book list a variety of resources that you may want to use to understand child abuse more clearly. Also included here is a questionnaire that you can fill out anonymously and send to me after reading this book. This type of information gathered from a large population of adult survivors like yourself would be an invaluable addition to any future editions of this book. Once again, your story may inspire others to get help, but you need not reveal your identity; as always, that is your choice.

THE IMPORTANCE
OF KEEPING A JOURNAL

Writing down your feelings, memories, and experiences is a therapeutic exercise. As abused children, you may have lacked the consistent validation of your experiences, perceptions, and beliefs by your parents. As a result, you often lacked the conviction that what you saw and felt was accurate. If you were subjected to emotional abuse in the form of criticism, rejection, or invalidation, there may be much confusion and lack of confidence about your experience of the world. Writing is a form of personal validation that can help give you what you never got as a child. By expressing a thought, feeling, or memory you can evaluate it and mull it over—both worthy pursuits in building your confidence.

Writing provides many other therapeutic benefits that might not be initially apparent. Going through the recovery process can release powerful feelings that can seem overwhelming. What do you do with these feelings when they arise, especially in the middle of the night after a nightmare? Writing them in your journal becomes an invaluable record of your recovery—a road map of where you have been and the direction toward which you are heading. You can reread your journal and re-experience the feelings, memories, and insights at levels that fit where you are at the moment. You can use it to identify thoughts, feelings, needs, questions, and apprehensions. You can speak to it as if it were the soul of your inner child—the one who never got heard and still suffers in silence inside you. You can control it and choose to share it with others, or keep it private and personal.

Writing engages you in such a way as to stimulate curiosity about parts of yourself that you never knew existed. By writing down your thoughts you are saying, "This might be a piece of my past or a part of who I am." Later you can return to your journal when you are ready to address the material directly. Gradually the repressed memories will filter back, each piece fitting into the puzzle of your life that is being documented by your journal. The process is evolutionary, leading you ever farther toward a more complete picture of who you are.

You will notice that most chapters contain a list of Journal Questions. These questions are designed to stimulate your thinking on particular subjects as you read the book as well as to uncover memories, perceptions, and feelings about the abuse and how it may have affected your life. Some of these questions are close-ended in that they simply ask you to identify or recognize with a yes or no answer whether certain circumstances apply to you. I specifically designed these questions to be helpful even to those of you facing your abuse for the first time and who want to make your way slowly through the discovery process. However, if you can withstand a further delving into the issues discussed, I encourage you to not only answer the close-ended questions in the affirmative or negative but to go beyond those answers to express whatever the questions make you feel at the time.

Use these questions, along with the open-ended ones that require further probing, in any way that helps you to reclaim the memories and lost feelings. If other questions come to mind that are more relevant than those printed in the book, explore where they may take you. Let the words flow—a stream of consciousness writing—to send you on a voyage into your mind, your heart, and your soul. Discover the power of the unconscious mind to educate you as to where you have been and what is ahead. At some point in your life, you will open this journal and feel proud of the beginning effort you made to overcome the abuse. It will be a record of your new beginning—the birth certificate of your new self.

In closing, I want to leave you with a spiritual concept that you can hold as you take your first steps on the road of recovery. As an abused child, you were robbed of an important experience that could nourish your developing sense of self—a warm, nuturing, secure relationship with your parents. Not having this relationship to fall back on is what left you feeling so alone as a child. But you had something else that could give you this sense of security and comfort—*soul*.

Each individual is blessed with a soul that is the unique embodiment of one's presence here on Earth. Your soul is the spiritual side of your conciousness that you may never have met because it was so buried under your reactions to the abuse. However bad your abuse was, your soul never died; it just removed itself from consciousness until you could allow yourself to sense its presence from within. Your soul is the kernel of the real you that can provide a guiding light along the shadowed road to recovery. The soul is the spiritual link to that piece of your true self that is the healthy part of your personality.

If you are reading this book, you must be in touch with the hope for a better existence—an existence that is a true reflection of your purpose and value as a person. This desire is the voice of your soul, which seeks to throw off the shackles of the abuse and find true expression in your conscious experience of life. You may be currently out of touch with its presence, but it is there. The task is to find it within yourself and return to it regularly as you face the challenges of recovery.

Discover the forms that your soul may take—the part of you that can still love, that can give to others, and that can discover how to love yourself. As you work through the pain and horror of your past, you will begin to recognize your spiritual center or soul. Make it larger by paying more attention to it. Allow it to further define who you are as a person. Let it rise to the forefront of your personality where you can experience its guiding light in your everyday life. You have survived your childhood, perhaps damaged, but certainly not defeated. Go forth with your recovery armed with the power of your soul and take the first step toward your new beginning.

PART I

Reclaiming Your Childhood

Chapter One

HOW TO
*D*ETERMINE IF YOU
WERE ABUSED
AS A CHILD

Most survivors in recovery can remember the first time they understood on an emotional level what had happened to them as children. It might have been at a workshop or in a support group, or perhaps, when reading a book like this one. At that moment, the past was suddenly cast in a different light. Memories that you had always regarded in a certain way shifted to incorporate some new understanding of the events in question that changed the frame around the picture. With this shift in perspective you refine the ability to see your past for what it was—abusive or not. By facing the past in a careful, objective manner, you can determine what happened to you and who was responsible, which is also your first step in reading this book—to determine if your childhood experience was abusive, and if so, how the abuse affected you as a child.

It is natural to feel some apprehension at the prospect of resurrecting a childhood filled with upsetting scenes and conflicting relationships. Evoking these memories is likely to stir up the same old feelings that you thought you had forever left behind as a child. Rest assured that I would not be suggesting this course of action unless it were a necessary step in recovering from child abuse.

Remember that as a child you most likely were left alone with your pain. That doesn't have to happen anymore. You will need to be with people who support this healing journey, who understand the pain and fear and anger and shame that has festered for so long inside you and who will support your commitment to heal by giving you a ready ear and an encouraging word. And you will also have the steps outlined in this book to help illuminate this healing journey. Information is power. With the knowledge provided here about child abuse, you will have the strength to challenge your parents' view of reality in a safe and nonthreatening way and at a pace that is decided only by you. The experience of reading this book and reflecting on your childhood will be both personal and shared. Much of what you read may parallel your experiences, but the fine details will have to be filled in as you read along and reflect. Find that courageous part within yourself that is willing to face these powerful memories in the hope of creating a better life for yourself. Talk to the important people in your life about what you want to do and what you will need from them. I can assure you that other survivors have broken the chain of their abuse and have gone on to live more satisfying and productive lives. Healing is not only possible, but with hard work and dedication, it is very promising. Remember that you are not alone in this struggle.

Reclaiming the past means retrieving lost memories and, in a sense, reexperiencing them in order to release them. The process of identifying, facing, and feeling these emotions is what will eventually provide the relief for which you are so desperate. There is a preferred method to this process. First, you will need to look at these memories closely to make sense of their meaning so that you may compare them with the signs and definitions of child abuse to be described later in this chapter. With the memories come the feelings, which are an integral part of your past experience and an essential ingredient of true healing. Facing these feelings now as an adult will reduce their rawness once and for all so that the wounds may begin to heal, granting you some inner calm. Allow yourself to begin sifting through the upsetting events and disappointing relationships, objectively reassessing what was done to you and how you felt about it. Be thorough in your scrutiny of the past; knowing what really happened is the best way to get control of the abuse.

DOES YOUR INTUITION TELL YOU THAT SOMETHING BAD HAPPENED?

Many survivors do not always know that what happened to them may be defined as child abuse. You may have only a prevailing sense—an intuition perhaps—that something upsetting happened to you during childhood that you cannot quite recall or visualize. For those of you who can actually remember being physically hurt or feeling ashamed of some sexual contact, you may still be confused about whether it was wrong or bad for you. Your intuition is a vital clue in understanding the past as well as a starting point for gaining access to the childhood memories. Following the thread of your intuition can provoke anxiety because you are never sure where you will end up. While I can reassure you that with courage, dedication, and faith this process will ultimately bear fruit for you, reclaiming the memories may nevertheless feel especially daunting.

Take each new piece of information gathered by reading this book and relive the memories with nonbiased acceptance. Self-acceptance may be a difficult area for you, but see if you can find that part of yourself that represents your compassionate ally. Be prepared for some internal opposition to this plan. Your psyche, long trained in the art of forgetting, is only too willing to keep the door of conscious awareness tightly closed. One reason why remembering may still be so scary is that you will remember feeling so overwhelmed by the feelings as a child. Like all children who were abused, you felt terrified, alone, and vulnerable. The intensity of these feelings may have simply been too much to handle. Considering that you are an adult now, you can learn new ways to handle these powerful feelings, allowing you to face the past from a position of strength, not weakness.

ARE YOU CONFUSED ABOUT WHAT TO MAKE OF THE PAST?

The meaning that you attach to the specific memories in question may have been shaped by what your parents said about them—how they rationalized, justified, and distorted the circumstances to make them seem right. You may still be suffering from these distortions in not being able to see the past for what it was. To determine if you were abused, you will need to separate the facts from the fiction and use the information uncovered, analyzing it to draw your own conclusions. Ultimately you may come up with a dramatically different understanding—one that exonerates you and implicates your parents in causing the abuse.

Working toward a judgment regarding the quality of your childhood involves a method similar to a "decision tree." By asking yourself the following questions, you can direct yourself toward an understanding of the event.

1. Did your parents' discipline involve corporal punishment, and if so, did their methods result in bruises or injuries?
2. How frequently did this discipline occur and did you ever feel their behavior was out of control?
3. Were any of your interactions with your parents either overtly or subtly sexual or seductive?
4. Were you touched or talked to in a sexual manner and left feeling confused or uncomfortable?
5. How were you emotionally treated by your parents on a day-to-day basis? Were you regularly criticized, threatened, invalidated, or ignored?

Each of these questions should lead to a new memory or thought that in turn produces a new question. Ask yourself whatever questions come to mind as you reflect on the information you are generating. Keep following this question process until you reach a consensus within yourself that answers the critical questions.

HOW WERE YOU
DISCIPLINED AS A CHILD?

Physical abuse often grows out of corporal punishment. Parents mistakenly think that corporal punishment and discipline are the same thing—you punish the child so that he or she learns to behave. Without it, the thinking goes, the child runs amok. Parents who let corporal punishment become abusive do not do so for the sake of the child; they are doing it more out of their own need to discharge their frustration and aggression. The child becomes a target for their own unresolved rage, which has more to do with their personal unhappiness, their inability to deal with stress, and in many cases, their own unresolved childhood. Admittedly, this perspective is beyond the capabilities of most children. But now, years later, you can acquire the facts to help you see the real story of your childhood.

Leigh Anne

I used to think I grew up in a typical Jewish family, although beneath the surface it was far from typical. To begin with, my parents came from very different backgrounds. Their differences caused most of the problems that I remember as a kid. My mother was raised in a well-to-do family and was brought up thinking she was entitled to only the best—a real Jewish princess who had everything she ever wanted as a child. My father, on the other hand, came from a poor peasant family that emigrated from Russia to escape religious persecution. His family was hot-blooded, very high-strung, and incredibly talented, especially in music. My parents never got along; they were like poison for each other. My father was always changing jobs for one reason or another and that meant we had to move a lot. There were also money problems. My mother's parents had a total lack of respect for my father because he couldn't really provide the luxuries that my mother had grown up with—a big house, fancy cars, and three of everything. I think he felt horrible about his lack of success and inability to create a kingdom for his princess wife. They fought constantly and my mother was sick all the time and got hooked on pills, which turned her into a total witch. She would whip him up into a frenzy over something we had done and he would take it out on us.

♦

Child abuse means more than specific episodes of maltreatment. While each abusive episode is harmful in and of itself, the real destructiveness is caused by the *pattern of abusiveness* that gets established in your on-going relationship with your parents and siblings. This pattern is created by the implications of the abuse—"If my parents treat me this way, it means I am bad"—and by the expectations of abuse—"If my parents do this once, it can happen again, which means I have to protect myself." When episodes of abuse occur again and again, the implications and expectations of the abuse cause an ever-widening breech in the parent-child relationship. Even a single episode of abuse, if not quickly addressed and resolved, can set in motion an emotional rift, which may last throughout childhood, leaving the child without a caring, supportive parent figure.

Initially it may help to focus on the individual incidents of abuse to get a handle on the overall experience. By reviewing and dissecting what happened, the more subtle aspects of the abuse may gradually emerge. Take notice of these realizations and write them down in your journal, because they may represent your most personal reactions to a very complex family situation that may not be illustrated in our more general review of the issues. As you continue to move through your storehouse of memories, it is important to broaden your view to understand all of the various ways that the abuse shaped your existence as a child. Like Leigh Anne's experience, you may find that the specific episodes of abuse were only the most obvious signs of a more pervasive pattern of maltreatment that included mental cruelty and verbal abuse as well.

CAN YOU REMEMBER
INCIDENTS OF SEXUAL CONTACT?

Some of you may recall specific interactions with a parent, relative, friend, or caretaker that were sexual in nature, some overtly so, others less defined, that left you confused as to how to understand them. More often than not, when sexual contact occurs between an adult and a child, the adult will justify or explain it in a way that makes it seem acceptable and normal. As a child, you were also vulnerable to accepting rationalizations that seemed normal but were really manipulations designed to maintain secrecy and compliance. One guideline to use in determining what was abuse is to focus on how the interaction made you feel. Did you feel uncomfortable, guilty, ashamed, dirty, or aroused?

Shirley

I was basically raised by my mother and stepfather, and to a lesser extent, my grandmother. We were a white, lower middle-class working family struggling to get by on the salary my stepfather made as a tanker truck driver for an oil company. My mom was divorced from my father when I was four, following an incident where he took a shot at her with a gun. My memories of those early times are of being huddled in a corner witnessing these fights between my two parents who were invariably drunk. For a period of about four years before my mother remarried, we lived with my grandparents—my brother, myself, and my mom—on their farm in the rural Northwest. I would say that this period of my life was the only semblance of a normal family I ever had.

The trouble began when my mom remarried and we moved into my stepfather's home. This is the family environment that had the biggest impact on me because it was very chaotic—they both did a lot of drinking. My stepfather was very domineering and commanding, and when he drank, he got even more so. He would be gone all week driving the tanker and then he would return on Fridays and have three days off. Come Friday afternoons, he would start drinking and demand all this respect and control. He was one of those alcohoholics who would get mean and nasty when he was drunk—kind of a Jekyll and Hyde personality. When I was eight, my stepbrother started molesting me. Later on, when I was eleven, my stepfather started doing the same thing. He would come home on Friday afternoons and molest me before meeting my mom at the bar after she got off work. The weekend would go down hill from there. Tuesday mornings when my stepfather drove away in the tanker, a calm would descend over the family for a few days before the pattern repeated itself again later in the week.

◆

As you unravel the past and try to understand what happened, I want you to keep something in mind that will make this rather formidable task somewhat easier. Remember that despite the horrible reality you were forced to endure, you did your best to cope, to grow up, and to survive your family. You were a child who was legally, morally, and psychologically subject to the power and authority of the adult or parent. In other words, you were at a disadvantage from the beginning and could not be expected to react differently from the way you did. For this reason, any adult who was subjected to abuse as a vulnerable child can be considered a survivor. You survived an experience of physical, sexual, or emotional assault from people who were supposed to comfort and nourish you. In this esssential contradiction lies the seeds for the loyalty conflicts that child abuse creates for children.

WERE YOU PRIMARILY
EMOTIONALLY ABUSED?

There is still much confusion by the lay public about what constitutes child abuse—the specific acts and behaviors by the parent, the legal definitions, as well as the psychological determinants of abuse from the point of view of the child. In the past, child abuse usually meant physical abuse. Outright physical assault on a defenseless child is one of the most extreme examples and the physical evidence in terms of bodily injuries are observable. More recently, parent-child incest and sexual abuse outside of the family has captured the attention of authorities who are now trained in detecting this more hidden type of abuse. The scars of sexual abuse are more psychological than physical. Today, with the increased recognition of damage caused by psychological torment or mental cruelty, a third category of abuse has been added to the list: emotional abuse. Emotional abuse refers to the destruction caused by perhaps the most lethal weapon of all—words. While emotional abuse is always present in physical and sexual abuse (because the child's emotions are being affected by the experience), we now accept that emotional abuse as a prevailing style of relating between parent and child is in itself extremely damaging and constitutes child abuse.

Richard

I lived with my father and mother in South America until I was five, when they divorced. I can recall scenes of this grand old plantation where we lived and of my parents' glamorous parties with their exotic friends who made up the expatriate community down there. Most of my early memories are hazy. I guess it was a lonely time for me because one of the few memories I do have is playing by myself with a bag of toys in the driveway. My parents were gone a lot of the time and servants would watch over me. It all changed later on—very much for the worse unfortunately—after my parents divorced.

My younger sister and I moved back to the States with my mother, who began a slow but steady emotional decline. She didn't do very well on her own and her choice of husbands left much to be desired. She was high-strung and very narcissistic. Her moods would go up and down and when things didn't work out she would blame me for it. She wanted me to do and be everything for her which of course I couldn't. When I "failed her"—which was virtually every day—she would rant and rave. I felt more beat up by her words than anything else she could throw at me. Life was an emotional roller coaster based on my mother's unpredictable moods. She was like that female character in *Fatal Attraction* who would lose it on a regular basis and pull others into her crazy world. Only I wasn't some acquaintance she picked up in a bar, I was her son who had to live with her day in and day out. Although she did hit me, it was the verbal abuse—mental cruelty really—that was more destructive. But I could never figure out if that was really abuse because it's not as dramatic as being beaten black and blue or sodomized in your bed at night. I never really knew it was abuse until I discussed it in therapy.

◆

As is often the case, Richard's abuse was the direct result of one parent's personality problems and stressful life circumstances that were directed at the most convenient target—the child. Although he was physically abused by his mother, it was the emotional abuse—the unpredictability of her actions, her angry moods, and her hateful words—that did far more damage.

Emotional abuse also encompasses physical neglect—the failure to provide food, shelter, clothing, and medical care. Ignoring a child or leaving a child unsupervised is considered emotional abuse. Surprisingly, mental cruelty, physical neglect, and emotional neglect may be the most common and least reported subtypes of child abuse. While physical and sexual abuse may seem more dramatically harmful, emotional abuse may be the most insidious of the three types of abuse. Why? Because the child remembers and often believes the hateful words that parents use to describe him or her, and over time, these words contaminate the development of the child's self-esteem.

ARE YOUR
CHILDHOOD MEMORIES HAZY, SPOTTY,
OR TOTALLY BLANK?

For some of you trying to look back on the past, your family memories may not be clear or accessible. Child abuse has a way of clouding over the past, letting some memories through while blotting out the more painful ones. Consequently, some of you may have only vague recollections of something bad happening while others may have virtually no memories at all. The past may feel like a black hole that stretches to the point when you left home. Other survivors report their childhoods being shrouded in fog. Occasionally, you might picture a scene or an experience before the memory becomes misty, again slipping behind consciousness. Getting a glimpse of a single image may remind you why you wanted to forget although the feelings connected to the memories may still be overwhelmingly painful. As children, you may have survived by putting the horrors of yesterday behind you so that you could face today. Over the years, the habit of forgetting the past has turned into wholesale denial—denial of what was being done to you, denial of how you felt about it, and denial today of how it is affecting your life as an adult.

Pete

There were only three members in my family—my father, mother, and myself. On the outside, we looked like a good, wholesome, Catholic family. Both of my parents worked and they made an effort to present our family as normal and respectable. Inside the house, however, it was a different story. Both of my parents were alcoholics, which meant that the crazy stuff that happened when they were drinking was quickly forgotten or ignored the next day. You couldn't talk about their drinking and you couldn't talk about how you felt about it. The message was, "There is no problem with me, the problem is you." My mother blamed my father for her unhappiness, and when he stopped drinking and she started, she blamed him for not being a good enough man for her. I could not talk about her problems and neither could my father. After a while, I was as good as they were at not seeing what was going on at home.

My father and mother were married when my father was in his early forties and my mom was in her early twenties—a big age difference. This probably played some role in what happened later between my mom and me. My dad's drinking was probably chronic at the time when I was born and it caused a lot of the fighting in their relationship. Then when I was seven, it all changed when he went on the wagon and my mother fell off. The alcohol affected her in a completely different way than it did him. My mom was a raging, out-of-control drinker who was mean and vindictive and she humiliated my father. As she got older, she became more difficult for my father to deal with. I think that had a big effect on me and my life because the way she coped was to focus on me. I was her "little man" who made all the difference in her life. I really felt cherished by her but at the same time, I felt smothered and humiliated because of what I saw her do to my father.

WERE YOU MISTREATED BY ADULTS OUTSIDE YOUR FAMILY?

While most of you will be looking back on your family, many will be struggling to remember incidents that took place outside of your family, with friends' families, stepfamilies, baby sitters, or in foster homes. Many of you may recall incidents that didn't feel right—the gray areas involving someone you liked or respected who may have taken advantage of you in a way that made you feel humiliated. Think back to these past situations that raised questions for you and carefully sort through them. See if you can't come up with more information about these memories. Be prepared to compare them with the actual definitions of child abuse to be provided later in this chapter.

Jolene

My story is pretty different from what other kids went through. In fact, I feel pretty confused about my life in general so I think I've made a point to not think about it much. At the age of three months, my mother gave me up and I was placed with a very caring and hard-working black foster family, the Shepherds, who had moved up from the South and were living in a tenement in the Bronx. The mother worked as a domestic and the father as a chauffeur. They couldn't have kids and wanted to adopt so I became their child. They really loved me and the first six years of my life were happy and filled with all the things a normal family has to offer. There were always good people around—friends from church or the community who took an interest in me. I went to school nearby and had friends. I was especially close to my stepfather who would take me on long drives on Sunday after church.

Then everything went wrong form the age of six on. I don't know what happened, but I was removed from that home and placed down the street with another foster family. I was still able to see the Shepherds at church, but it was never the same. I stayed in this house for the next ten years and had all sorts of things happen to me. This house was run by a scrappy, angry woman who had five foster kids plus three of her own. She really didn't have enough room for us all, but that didn't matter. I think she was in it for the money. She didn't really like any of us foster kids—especially me—and her own kids really resented us being around. She was the only person who I have met that was downright mean. She would do things specifically to make me unhappy, like move my bed out into the hall after I had spent days arranging my room in a way that I liked. She would play her kids off of us, which I think later set the stage for her son to molest me.

When I was sixteen, she got in trouble with my social worker for using our expense money for herself. I got moved again, this time out of the city to this small rural community way up north. The foster family that took me in was into a fundamentalist religion—Seventh Day Adventists—and they were very strict. The father was fairly high up in the local church and was always spouting verse from the Bible and generally acting holier than thou. This was a real joke because within a few months of my getting placed there, he started molesting me.

◆

WAS YOUR FAMILY PLAGUED BY
OTHER PROBLEMS?

Many of you grew up in families characterized by other types of problems—addictions, job and financial problems, gambling and compulsive activities, as well as chronic illness. Thinking about your family may be the best initial strategy to reclaim your childhood memories.

Identify some of the concerns or problems your parents had, how they reacted to them, and how these problems may have affected their relationship with you.

Susan

I grew up in a lower middle-class, urban family that lived on the fringe both financially and emotionally. My family was composed of my mother, my stepdad, me (the only girl) and my three brothers. We lived right in the heart of Chicago until about the third grade when we moved to the country. It was tough. I remember bill collectors coming to the door and calling on the phone. Meals would sometimes be breakfast for dinner. We all struggled early on. We kids all slept pretty much together in the hall that we made into a room. My mother was an adult child of an alcoholic parent who married numerous alcoholics. I didn't know my real father. My mother divorced my real father when I was two and married my stepfather who was an alcoholic himself. Their marriage was no love match by any means. It was the result of a predictable social dilemma for the single mother of two children during the fifties. She was in a state of panic over how to support her family. And I guess there weren't many choices. It wasn't a loving relationship—it was a very stormy, violent relationship with a lot of conflict and the alcohol, of course, fanning the fire. My mother and stepfather would berate and batter each other on a regular basis. We got used to hiding behind the chairs and watching them fight it out. It was awful, frightening, and upsetting.

♦

When families have an alcohol or drug problem, the chance that child abuse will also be a problem soars dramatically. Parents who abuse substances lose their inhibitions and self-control, often committing the abuse while inebriated or during a blackout. The next day they wake up with no knowledge of what they did. Substance abuse problems also trigger other family problems besides the abuse of children. Marital strife may be the most common result, and even when the children are not physically abused, they can be emotionally scarred simply by watching their parents fight. When children witness their parents fighting, they feel scared that their parents will turn on them at some point. Much has been written recently about adult children of alcoholics who are raised by parents whose caretaking is disrupted by their addiction.

BARRIERS TO AWARENESS

After reading about other survivors and their families, you may have registered some of your own thoughts, memories, or questions about your childhood. On what events are you focusing? What feelings arise when you think about certain people and certain situations? As you read, try writing down in your journal your reactions to the questions listed after each section for future reference. Many of these thoughts and memories will be illusory—here now and gone tomorrow. For some of you, reading about child abuse up to this point may not have given you access to the buried childhood memories. What follows are some of the barriers that can inhibit your ability to remember the past. Read each section with an open mind and use the questions to see if these barriers may apply to you.

SELECTIVE MEMORY/PARTIAL AMNESIA

One of the biggest barriers to awareness is caused by the protective function that the mind performs to help children cope with ongoing adversity. Called *selective memory* or *partial amnesia*, it is a semipermanent clouding of hurtful memories and the feelings associated with them. The mind has an incredible self-protective capacity: If a memory is too painful to experience, your mind will shut it out to save you from being overwhelmed or despondent. When old memories are habitually shut out because of an abusive childhood, it is not always easy to unlock these back doors of your mind once you become an adult.

Jolene

My memories of the past are really confused and disconnected. It's like I see snatches of myself as a kid but they are all shuffled in a different order from how they happened. Some of the memories of being sexually abused by these two older girls I had completely forgotten about until recently. It was all too confusing for me with all these foster families—I couldn't keep them straight in my own mind as a kid and I still can't as an adult. A lot of my friends don't even know about all this stuff that happened to me. I keep it to myself and the rest I never think about. The more I go on in therapy, the more I discover how much I've covered up.

◆

You may have partial amnesia surrounding only certain events or times in your life. Or you may have fleeting images that are not quite lucid enough to see them for what they really were. If you allow yourself to reflect on why you avoid thinking about your past, you may have some interesting ideas that could provide a clue to help you reclaim the memories. The amnesia can and will eventually lift if you are sincere in wanting to remember. In many cases, survivors are afraid of remembering because they unconsciously believe they will be destroyed by the feelings associated with the past. Remember, you are looking back from your vantage point as an adult, not a child.

Journal Questions

1. *What general feelings do you associate with your childhood?*
2. *Do you purposely avoid thinking about the past?*
3. *Why is the past uncomfortable to remember?*

Preserving the Myth of a Happy Childhood

Many adults feel a steadfast commitment to the image of a happy childhood, often in the face of growing evidence to the contrary. Childhood is supposed to be a happy time and accepting that it was not may leave you with a sad and empty feeling. No one wants to accept that their parents may have made mistakes or that their family had problems. And yet, accepting that something wrong happened to you is part of seeing the past for what it was.

Richard

When I met my wife, naturally she eventually asked me about my family and parents. I remember telling her without any hesitation that my mother was a saint—a most remarkable woman. How she has raised two children herself and has had a long and distinguished career as a journalist and a writer and how she's a brilliant conversationalist with the coolest wit and the most engaging personality. I used to get caught up in these total fabrications of who my mother was—I was writing a totally different script for my family. And it carried on to the point that I even invited two friends of mine to come to Switzerland for Christmas vacation one year and stay at the chalet that my mom had rented. I cannot say that it was an absolute shock that my mother was her usual critical, moody, and despicable self. But I was surprised when it happened again. I so wanted to have this neat vacation with my friends and show them that everything was normal. But within days, the reality of my mother's personality exploded whatever fantasy I had cultivated.

◆

Accepting that you were abused as a child may raise questions about how "normal" you are, which automatically raises your old anxiety about not being good enough. Many survivors feel stigmatized by what was done to them and preserving the myth of a happy childhood is one strategy in dealing with the feeling of being tainted. The more you learn about child abuse, the more you will see that your personal reactions were a normal response to an abnormal situation.

Journal Questions

4. *How do you feel when friends speak of their childhood?*

5. *Do you have any particular feeling when talking about your family?*

6. *Do you notice yourself creating necessary fictions when you speak of your childhood?*

Denial of What Happened

Denial of child abuse happens on an individual and family basis. If we don't want to acknowledge something, all we have to do is say "no" and then convince ourselves that it didn't happen. If abuse is happening in the family, the abuser will work to justify his or her actions to the child in order to preserve secrecy and maintain the child's cooperation. Eventually, most children start believing what the parent is telling them. Family denial of alcoholism, for example, is not much different than family denial of child abuse. The whole family may deny the abuse ever happened or may minimize its severity and look to each other to reinforce this distortion of reality. While the family may not be ready to accept what happened, that doesn't mean you still have to go along with this charade.

Pete

You know, even now I have to back my way into the facts about my family in order to put the pieces together and tease out the important components of how things really were. As a child, I couldn't see all the facts and what I did see got distorted by the emotions involved. I was in touch with some of those realizations about my family, but I was in no position emotionally or mentally to accurately assess the situation. I had to wait until I grew up and got healthy enough as an adult to see the facts for what they were.

◆

Many adults reexamining their past feel caught in a loyalty bind between the honest part of themselves and the part that identifies with their parents. During the early stage of recovery, these inner parts battle it out with each other over the control of what will be believed. This causes great anguish and many adult survivors will avoid thinking about it in the hope that it will go away. Denial of the problem may seem like a convenient alternative to facing and eventually resolving this inner confusion. Unfortunately, the conflicts and the feelings that are attached to these inner parts will not go away until you take charge to sort them out.

JOURNAL QUESTIONS

7. *What would it mean to you if you decided you were abused?*

8. *What would be your reasons to minimize what happened or gloss over situations that happened only once or twice?*

9. *Have other family members questioned their upbringing?*

FEAR OF FEELINGS

Deciding that you had an abusive childhood is likely to bring up all kinds of feelings—anxiety, fear, sadness, anger, guilt, and shame. Thinking about the abuse as an adult may add disappointment and resentment to the list. You thought you were finished with the past, but these feelings still threaten you. Sometimes adult survivors fear the power and intensity of these feelings and decide it is safer to leave them alone.

Leigh Anne

I never told anybody what happened in my family until now, when I'm almost thirty-seven years old. I kept it all inside because I was so ashamed that this was happening to my family. I was and still am ashamed that this was done to me. Only recently, I am beginning to stop the denial, to talk about what happened and try to resolve it. But it is very difficult to look at all that ugliness, all that sadness, all that pain. It just overwhelms you and makes it hard to get up every morning and face your life. It really helps to have that one person—my therapist—to tell these things to and to be reasonably assured that he will understand and not be disgusted by it all.

◆

Physical and sexual abuse aroused tremendously powerful feelings that threatened to overwhelm you as a child. Today, years later, you may still be concerned about containing and controlling these powerful feelings. But now, seen through the eyes of an adult, these memories may seem less overwhelming than ever before. By facing them directly with the help of a therapist, their intensity can be reduced. You can get a handle on them and learn new ways of controlling their impact on you.

JOURNAL QUESTIONS

10. *Do you consciously turn off your feelings to avoid the pain or does it seem more automatic?*

11. *Do you fear losing control if you let yourself think about the past?*

12. *Is it hard to concentrate when something happens to upset you?*

NOT TRUSTING YOUR OPINIONS AND PERCEPTIONS

Many survivors grew up having their thoughts, feelings, ideas, and perceptions invalidated by their family. You may have been directly challenged, contradicted, and rejected. You may have been made to feel stupid for feeling a certain way. When this kind of perpetual invalidation happens year after year, it is no wonder that adult survivors don't trust their own opinions and perceptions. The lack of confidence that you often feel is related to never having your perceptions validated. This tendency may make it harder to trust your memories and you may dismiss them—something you no longer need to do.

Leigh Anne

When you grow up in a household where there's screaming, and yelling, and fighting, and hitting, you tend to think that this is the way family life is. You think that your parents are the normal ones and that they are acting the way everyone else is. If they are right, then I have to be wrong. And they would tell me all the time that I was wrong and had screwed up ideas about things. You believe them because you never had anything different. How can you trust yourself when no one has ever showed you trust? But now, as an adult, I'm beginning to look back and I'm seeing things so differently. I realize how desperate I was for attention, appreciation, and respect and I would do anything—even accept what my parents would say—just so they would love me. I'm now seeing that a lot of my "crazy" ideas were a lot truer than I ever thought.

◆

Self-doubt reigns supreme in the minds of many survivors. Nowhere is this more likely to occur than when you objectively assess your childhood. If this is a problem for you, keep this tendency in mind as you reclaim the childhood memories and be careful to not throw away any of your ideas simply because you doubt they actually happened that way.

JOURNAL QUESTIONS

13. *Do you constantly doubt yourself—your ideas, opinions, memories, and perceptions?*

14. *Did your family invalidate your ideas?*

15. *Do you feel like you have to keep your opinions to yourself or run the risk of having them be "wrong"?*

ARE YOU READY TO FACE THE REALITY OF YOUR ABUSE?

The next step in facing what happened to you is knowing the definitions, facts, and statistics about the three types of child abuse. It is important to know these things in order to compare your experience with what is now known about child abuse. Ultimately, recovery from child abuse means learning enough to know what is true and what is not. In this next section, we will be facing the reality of child abuse squarely, to illuminate the actual phenomenon in all of its horror and sickening detail. This next step will likely be painful for you and you may not want to proceed until you feel ready to experience whatever feelings may arise. You may want to read this section piece by piece, allowing yourself plenty of time to digest it before moving on. Read it with a friend or discuss your reactions in your therapy or self-help group. Remember that you are an adult now and the feelings that develop will be those of a child. Your ability to understand the complexity of factors involved in your abuse will serve you well in making the past less overwhelming and threatening.

The purpose of this review is not to deny the past but to illuminate it; not to indict your parents but to hold them responsible; and finally, not to blame yourself but to develop a new understanding. Read it with courage and self-compassion.

Child abuse. Child abuse is any act of omission or commission that endangers or impairs a child's physical or emotional health and development including physical, sexual, and emotional abuse.

Physical abuse. Physical abuse is defined as any physical act committed against a child that results in a nonaccidental injury.

An abusive act includes severe hitting, slapping, biting, cutting, pushing, poking, burning, twisting, shaking, choking, punching, pinching, squeezing, whipping, kicking, dunking in water, and pulling of the hair, legs, and arms.

The bodily signs of abusive injuries are bruises, burns, bites, marks, welts, skin punctures, cuts, abrasions, bleeding, broken bones, tearing of the skin, internal hemorrhaging, and loss of hair.

The behavioral signs of physical abuse are extreme vigilance, fearfulness, scanning of the environment for perceived threats, flinching in a self-protective way, either avoiding people or becoming quickly attached to people, hostile or aggressive behavior, self-destructive behavior such as walking in front of cars or falling out of windows, and destructive behavior including setting fires and maiming or killing animals.

Leigh Anne

I now realize that I was physically abused by my father, my mother, and my older brother. But it was definitely the worst with my father. He was so volatile and insecure. He would come home from work, exhausted and frustrated. My mother would be waiting for him with a whole list of what the kids had done and then force him to punish us for all the pain we had put her through. My father's initial intentions, I believe, were to talk to us reasonably about what had happened. But after a few minutes he would get really worked up. Nothing we could say seemed to matter, and then he would explode into a violent rage. He would shout and wail and you could see the veins pop out on his face until he looked like some raging demon. He would move closer and closer to me as I backed away from him. I remember him towering over me as I cowered in the corner, trying to make myself as small as possible. I'd go into what I call "psychotic shock"—like an animal who gets blinded by car headlights. I felt the same kind of immobility. I couldn't even lift my arms to defend myself. I'd open my mouth to cry out and nothing would come out. I was just frozen with terror. When his verbal tirade would peak, he would lose all control and start wailing on me—punching, kicking, slapping me against the walls, just pummeling the shit out of me, all the time shouting at me for being such a miserable kid. I don't really know how long it would last. It seemed like forever, but it was probably only a few minutes. I remember feeling like a broken rag doll—black and blue, bruised and bloody, lying totally spent in a disheveled heap in the corner.

◆

Physically abusing a child under the age of eighteen is now a felony in every state of the union. But that was not always the case. The assault, abandonment, and killing of children has, in fact, been going on since the dawn of civilization. What was referred to in previous centuries as "soul murder" became defined in 1962 as "battered child syndrome" and now, in recognition of other types of child abuse, is referred to as physical abuse. In 1985, the American Humane Society reported that physical abuse was second only to physical neglect as the most common type of abuse reported—some 22 percent of all cases. It occurs in all ethnic, occupational, and socioeconomic groups, although it may be more pronounced in families living in poverty. Economic hardship, racism, and unemployment are stress factors that readily get channeled into family violence. Physical abuse also occurs outside the home in schools, day-care centers, after-school recreation programs, community youth groups, and other well-respected youth organizations.

Boys are more frequently abused than girls between the ages of two and twelve because boys are more likely at this age to present behavior or discipline problems. Boys have a higher activity level than girls at this age, which can irritate a parent and trigger abusive corporal punishment. With adolescence, girls become more of a target than boys because they are physically more vulnerable. Social roles suggest that girls adopt a more passive approach to the world, putting them in jeopardy of being dominated by others.

Physical neglect tends to predate actual physical abuse because most children hate being ignored or neglected and will escalate their attention-seeking behavior to engage their parents. Parents who physically abuse were usually treated in a similar manner when they were raised. Children are typically more at risk for physical and emotional abuse if they remind parents of someone they do not like or with whom they have unresolved conflict. When children have special needs or disabilities, they are also more at risk because they demand more from their parents.

Susan

It was my mother who did the punishing, which I now look back on and realize was abusive. She used one of those wooden paddles you can get in the store today that has a long rubber band on it and a little ball. They are actually some kind of toy, which made it all the more ironic that she used it to hit me. Things would start out where if we were too noisy or she couldn't tolerate something, it was "I'm going to get the paddle"; and then, depending on our playfulness, or her mood, or our judgment of how far we could push her, it would go anywhere from her rattling in the drawer to make the noise that she was searching and we'd shape up, or all the way to, "OK, that's it," and once the paddle was in her hand, that was it. We'd go through begging, "I'm sorry, I'm sorry. OK, we won't do it."

But it would be too late. They were called "sessions in the bathroom" because we would go into the bathroom and then she'd put us over the tub and then just start paddling away. Sometimes you'd get a couple hits and sometimes she just wouldn't stop until you were battered and bruised. I would just shut off and space out. At times, she'd go crazy hitting us. She would not know when to stop. Her frustration and her rage just overwhelmed her and she lost it. My older brother used to get it worse. One time, she started with a belt and lost her grip on the belt, and the buckle ended up hitting him in the face. She just walloped him a good one. It started out fairly structured: We misbehaved, we got warned, and then we got punished. But it wasn't so structured when she was wailing away in the bathroom. It had a different quality—she would lose it with us for a few minutes. I knew that my other friends didn't get hit like that. I just knew this, but not from ever sharing it with them, because there was this family rule to not talk about family business. Later on my girlfriends did know about it because when I was fourteen I had a slumber party and they were able to see what was going on. They got a real eyeful that night. My stepfather was drunk as usual and he just lost it because of some little thing that I did. Seeing my friends' reactions to what for me was a totally normal reality was really important because it told me that my family life was not normal.

◆

Physical abuse often begins under the guise of punishment. What starts out as corporal punishment intended to be purposeful and restrained can often become out of control and excessive—an expression of the parents' personal conflicts. In some cases, physical abuse takes the form of cruel and unusual punishment that the parent imposes on the child for arbitrary reasons. Examples include forcing the child to assume an uncomfortable or physically demanding position for extended periods of time such as kneeling on the floor, ducksquatting, or doing head-stands. Punishments that cause the child extreme terror or humiliation, such as locking a child into a closet or basement is abusive.

Any punishment that calls for the child to do something that he or she cannot physically or developmentally accomplish, such as toilet training prior to one year or taking responsibility for the care of younger siblings, is considered abusive. Hitting a child in sensitive areas of the body such as the face, stomach, and genitals is cruel and unusual punishment, and as such, is reportable as child abuse. Punishment that is meted out to prevent some future behavior before that behavior has actually been initiated by the child should be considered child abuse. An example of this is burning a child's hand as a way of teaching him not to touch the stove. To physically discipline young children before they are able developmentally to understand the connection between the behavior and the punishment is abusive. Corporal punishment that is sudden, arbitrary, or not explained as a consequence of some partic-ular behavior on the part of the child is abuse. In summary, the list of all of the ways and means that parents can physically abuse their chil-dren is almost endless.

JOURNAL QUESTIONS

16. *Did your parents punish you by hitting you with their hand or some implement until you were bruised or injured?*

17. *Were you often slapped in the face, leaving a black eye, bloody nose, or bruised cheek?*

18. *Were you ever punched, kicked or thrown against the wall?*

19. *Were you forced to assume a physically uncomfortable position like squatting or kneeling for extended periods of time?*

20. *Were you ever locked in a closet or basement for several hours?*

Sexual Abuse. Sexual abuse is defined as any sexual act directed at a child involving sexual contact, assault, or exploitation.

Acts of child sexual abuse include fondling, rape, incest, sodomy, lewd or lascivious acts, oral copulation, intercourse, penetration of a genital or anal opening by a foreign object, exhibitionism, presentation of pornographic pictures, telling of sexual stories, and promoting prostitution of minors.

The physical signs of sexual abuse of children include sexually transmitted diseases; genital discharge or infection; physical injury or irritation of the oral, anal, or genital areas; pain when urinating or defecating; difficulty walking or sitting due to gential or anal pain; and stomachaches, headaches, or other psychosomatic symptoms.

The behavioral signs of sexual abuse include sexual behavior with peers or toys, excessive curiosity about sexual matters, overly advanced understanding of sexual behavior (especially in younger children), compulsive masturbation, prostitution or promiscuity, incontinence (in the case of anal intercourse), and excessive concern about homosexuality (in boys who were molested by another male).

The concern about sexual abuse has grown dramatically in recent years with the release of new public surveys showing how pervasive it is. Currently, up to one third of all women and one seventh of all men over the age of twenty-one have been sexually abused as children. Sexual abuse may be the final skeleton in the family closet, obscured for generations behind a veil of secrecy and denial. Only in recent years has the secrecy surrounding sexual abuse lifted due to the emergence of the adult survivor movement—men and women who have suffered from sexual abuse for years as children who are now breaking their silence about their secret.

Shirley

When I was about eight, my older half brother Donnie, who was thirteen, would molest me while he was baby-sitting me. This went on for two or three years. I didn't realize that it was sexual abuse until I got into treatment for it as an adult. I thought it fell under the category of "playing doctor," something that every child experiences. Once I got into treatment though, I realized that it went much further than playing doctor. He would have us both get naked, and then he would place his penis between my legs and ejaculate, and touch me and explore me—those kind of things. That lasted on and off until I was about ten.

Then when I was around eleven, I remember asking my mom some questions about sex. She told me that my dad would explain it all to me and walked out the door. So I told him what Donnie had done, which may have been my biggest mistake, because that was the point that it started all over again except with him doing the molesting, not my brother. He told me that he needed to "check me," as he put it. He would insert his finger into my vagina to make sure that my hymen was intact. I'd beg him not to do it, but he kept saying that he had to know if I got "messed up by it." I remember him getting so angry with me because I would be too tight to permit him to insert his finger inside me.

If I went to any kind of school activity, especially if there were boys there, he would have to check me when I got home. And then he got to the point where he would start disciplining me. I'd have to strip naked so that he could spank me. I was twelve or thirteen at this point. And he would hide whiskey bottles and pornography under my mattress and then confront me with it in front of my mom, trying to break down my credibility with her. I didn't realize what he was doing at the time, but I remember she would never believe me when I told her they weren't mine. She always chose to believe him and then he would punish me the next time we were alone.

◆

Listening to Shirley may evoke your own memories of being molested. Like her, you may have been manipulated, tricked, or forced to engage in the sexual act with your parent. Sometimes abused children think that if they couldn't stop it, maybe they were at least partially responsible for it happening. What the child abuse law says here should challenge this kind of thinking. The law says that when the child victim is under the age of fourteen, *any* sexual contact with an adult is considered sexual abuse, even if consent is purportedly given by the child. When the child victim is over fourteen and appears to be consenting to the sexual contact, the determination of sexual abuse is made by considering other factors including the age of the adult, the nature of the relationship, and the emotional maturity of the child. Clearly some teenagers under eighteen are not psychologically mature enough to give consent in a relationship with someone much older.

There are many factors that place children at risk for sexual abuse, especially in these times of high divorce rates and stepfamilies. Girls are more at risk for sexual abuse than boys, the figures indicating one out of every three girls compared to one out of seven boys. Children are most likely to be sexually abused between the ages of eight and twelve. Girls who have been abused are more likely to live within a stepfamily situation or with a single mother who is employed outside the home. When a natural father is the abuser, often the girl's mother is absent or uninvolved for some reason. She may be disabled, ill, out of the home working, or an alcoholic. The quality of her caregiving suffers and her parental authority is reduced. The marital relationship may be in discord, with the parents avoiding their problems with each other. Ever so gradually, the father may place the girl in the role of wife.

Pete

The incest was something that just happened between myself and my mother. Actually she was very seductive in her dress at a time when I was very vulnerable to that—around when I was twelve or thirteen. She would dress in see-through negligees and baby-doll pajamas. And I didn't know it was inappropriate then but it was obviously inappropriate because I got so turned on by it. I had sexual fantasies about her because basically I was seeing a mature woman's body at a time when I was experiencing puberty. I never understood how inappropriate it was for me to be exposed to this.

The first time that there was sexual contact between us occurred when I was in eighth grade following a wedding reception. I was real drunk and so was she. The memory I have now is that I went into her room and laid down on the bed and exposed myself to her. She touched my penis and started masturbating me. That was the pattern that got established and was repeated later on. Sometimes I would go in the bedroom to take a nap with her and that's how it would happen. It seemed to occur at least four or five times, although it may have happened more, considering my memory for this stuff still isn't so good. I started having blackouts about the same time, which was probably related to my heavy drinking and, of course, the incest. There's kind of like a hazy recollection that I have of one thing she said to me. One time she had masturbated me and I had ejaculated and she said something about her doing this was a way of showing me how much she loved me. I think I felt very confused. It was erotic and I felt it was all my fault because it was gratifying, because it felt good, and because I had some part in soliciting it. And I didn't understand her part in it. It went on for a year or so. It was a crazy and confusing time for me. I think I was torn between the physical urges and knowing that it wasn't right. But I couldn't stop it and neither could she. We never talked about it—it was just something that seemed to happen that was very powerful and overwhelming. I can't remember how I felt afterward. It was too intense to experience whatever feelings might have been there. I mean there was too much conflict to feel. I felt torn apart inside— gratified, and at the same time, evil and dirty.

◆

Sexual abuse also happens to boys, although not to the extent reported for girls. Boys are more likely to be abused by adult males. Given the homosexual implications of the abuse, boys may find it difficult to disclose being abused. When the molestation occurs with a female, the boys are confused about how to interpret the experience. Is it sexual abuse or sexual opportunity? Boys are socialized to want sex and these attitudes often confuse their perceptions of the experience. Because boys are supposed to be "tough" and able to defend themselves, they may be disinclined to speak about being taken advantage of. In many cases, it may be more convenient psychologically for them to interpret the abuse as a conquest rather than as a victimization. But the conflicts do not go away just because the abuse is cast in a positive light. As Pete's story demonstrates, incest between mother and son can be every bit as harmful as it is in father-daughter incest. Pete's case also illustrates another important dynamic in mother–son incest: The incest is usually the outgrowth of a long-established seductive relationship that may have evolved into overt sexual relations when the boy reaches puberty and begins experiencing his own sexual awakening. Although this may imply some complicity on the part of the boy, the responsibility *always* rests with the parent to set appropriate standards of behavior. In cases of mother-son incest, the mother is almost always incapacitated as a parent due to addictions, severe emotional problems, or her own unresolved sexual abuse as a child.

There are many factors involved in sexual abuse that can gauge the degree of impact on a child. When a child has been abused by more than one offender, the degree of trauma is also likely to increase because the repetition of the abuse reinforces the attitude that the child is responsible. The exact nature of the sexual contact can also be significant, with intercourse usually causing more serious consequences than fondling or exposure to pornography. When aggression or violence is used to force sex, the impact is even more negative because the child feels even less control compared to the so-called "seductive" molestation where persuasion and manipulation are employed.

Not all sexual abuse involves actual physical contact. Being exposed to pornography or witnessing adult sexual relations or having an exhibitionist flash his genitals are all examples of noncontact sexual abuse. In most cases, the effects on the child are not as great as with contact sexual abuse, although with some children in can be surprisingly traumatic and will require treatment to overcome.

When children participate to some degree in the sexual contact or are unable (as is usually the case) to find a way to prevent the abuse from happening, the consequences can also be more severe because of the guilt and shame over their involvement. And if there was some pleasureable aspect of the abuse, as there often is when the abuse involves fondling the genitals, children often interpret their feelings as evidence of their culpability. Children do not usually understand that the responsibility for preventing sexual expressions of affection lies with the parent or adult, not themselves. In reviewing your childhood memories, it will be important to ascertain just what reasons you have used to indict yourself.

In cases where the sexual abuse occurs outside of the home, the reaction of the family is paramount in determining the degree of impact on the child. When the family is supportive and gets immediate help for the child and avoids any blaming or stigmatization, the long-term effects can be almost nil. However, when the family is not understanding, or in the worst case, blames the child for the sexual abuse or is unable to accept that the child was victimized, the impact can be truly devastating because the family's reaction confirms the child's worst fears—that they did something wrong. In cases like this, the family becomes an unindicted co-conspirator in the abuse, because in failing to give their child what he needs during a time of tragedy, they may do far more damage to the child than the abuser. It is no surprise that children will feel stigmatized by the sexual abuse if their families treat them with disdain and disgust.

Jolene

I was seventeen when I moved into the third foster home—with the Fundamentalist family. This was a real crazy scene because here I am, a black teenager from the city who gets placed in a white, conservative Adventist family with a father who thinks he is saving the world by taking me in and this cold, submissive mother who silently hates me for it. She didn't want me there but was forced into it by her husband because he somehow justified it on religious grounds. I think she knew what was going on later, but felt pretty powerless to do anything about it. Her resentment just built up to the point where she couldn't even look at me.

He was a strange character because, on the one hand, he tried to educate me about the Adventists and get me converted while, on the other hand, he was having an affair with me. At first, we had this kind of intellectual relationship and he would support my getting more involved with the church. The sex started not long after I got there. I remember us driving home from a meeting and he starts holding my hand. At first I didn't think too much of it, but in the back of my mind, I'm wondering if this is normal or not. I never knew if my friends' fathers did this to them, but then again, I felt like my situation being a foster kid was so weird, I never knew what was normal. Gradually he'd come on to me more often, kissing and touching me. I remember one of the first times he came on to me was when I was sitting in his den typing the church bulletin. He walked up to me and put his hands on my breasts, and I thought, "Here we go again." I thought I was through with that stuff when I left the second home with that foster kid who molested me, but here it was again. I just kind of had that sinking feeling again, that sensation of falling and not being able to do anything about it. My head would start to spin and I would go into this weird state where I wouldn't be able to think straight. I'd get all fuzzy and dazed almost.

Eventually, he started having intercourse with me. I felt like I had to go along with him, even though I didn't like it. There was a short period of time where I think I convinced myself that I kind of liked it because it was the only way I could have any kind of control anywhere. By pretending that it was OK, I didn't have to feel as powerless as I really felt. There was a lot of his coming into my room at night under the pretext of showing me some church papers and him having his hands in my pants. Whenever his wife was out of the house, we would have sex in their bed. Once he took me to a motel, but mostly it took place in my bedroom at night. Sometimes his wife would sneak up to see what was going on and he would start talking more loudly about some phony church business as if nothing was happening. After a while, I just hated him and would try to stay away from him. But this got him really mad and he would accuse me of not wanting to be with the family. I wanted to tell someone but I just didn't know who to tell. Certainly not the mother. And I thought this had to be my fault because I wasn't a child anymore—I was seventeen.

◆

Sexual abuse outside the family may have actually increased during the last twenty years because more children are being cared for in day-care centers, after-school programs, and juvenile institutions. There has been an increase of stories in the media of sexual molestation in day-care centers across the country, although the prosecution of these cases has often been unsuccessful. There are actually three pro-incest organizations operating in North America that dedicate themselves to finding and maintaining sexual relationships with young girls and boys. One group's motto is "Sex before eight—before its too late."

With the explosion of the adult film industry, there is evidence that child pornography rings are proliferating with upward of half a million children involved. Teenage runaways, many of whom end up on the streets hustling for food money, are likely targets for exploitation, violence, and health problems like AIDS. Unfortunately, child sexual abuse is a problem that still occurs, the effects of which will not be fully felt until today's child victims grow up to become tomorrow's adult survivors.

JOURNAL QUESTIONS

21. *Did your parent or another adult purposely expose their body to you?*

22. *Did anyone have sexual contact with you when you were a child that left you confused or feeling ashamed?*

23. *Were you ever shown sexual pictures, films, or photographs by others undressed or provocatively posed?*

24. *Were you exposed to your parent's sexual relations?*

25. *Did you parents say sexual things about you; did they make lewd comments about your body or call you a slut, whore, or hustler?*

> **Emotional abuse.** Emotional abuse is defined as a pattern of psychologically destructive interactions with a child that fits into five categories of behaviors: rejecting, isolating, terrorizing, ignoring, and corrupting.
>
> Physical signs of emotional abuse are malnourishment, small physical stature, poor grooming, and inappropriate attire for the season or circumstances.
>
> The behavioral signs of emotional abuse include constant approval seeking; self-criticism; letting others take advantage of you; excessively timid or quietly aggressive behavior; inability to make decisions; fear of rejection from others; being verbally hostile, provacative, or abusive.

Emotional abuse, more than other types of abuse, must be measured in terms of severity: mild when the acts are isolated incidents; moderate when the pattern is more established and generalized; and severe when acts are frequent, absolute, and categorical. All parents are emotionally abusive to their children at certain times: Parents are not perfect and they too are subjected to stresses and strains of daily living that will cause them to lash out at others. With emotional abuse, it is especially important to determine whether there is an *established pattern* of verbal abuse or mental cruelty in order to label it child abuse. Emotional abuse is the least understood of the three types of abuse because there has been so much confusion as to how to define it and describe it. It was psychologist James Garbarino who recently defined emotional abuse according to the following five components.

> Rejecting involves the adult's refusal to acknowledge the child's worth and legitimacy of the child's needs.

Children experience rejection and abandonment when parents act in ways that minimize the child's importance or value. The child thinks "If my parents don't think I matter, then I must not be very worthwhile. If I'm not very worthwhile, maybe they will leave me." During infancy, this may involve not returning the infant's smiles or misinterpreting crying as manipulation. In later years, it may include refusing to hug the child, placing the child away from the family, "scapegoating" the child for family problems, and subjecting the child to verbal humiliation and excessive criticism.

Richard

When my mother would get angry, she would constantly tell me in so many words that I was a loathesome thing. As I got older, it got worse. She would call me a "repulsive, pimply-faced shit." When she was really in full rage, she would kick me and call me a "cunt." Every filthy word she picked up, she would throw at me when she was enraged. Of course, she would also use the classic rant, "You're just like your father . . . All you ever think of is yourself . . . You're just a selfish, ungrateful, spoiled rotten kid." After hearing it so often, you feel like it's true. The result of all this verbal abuse was that I grew up thinking I was an abomination on the face of the earth—utterly worthless, beneath contempt, the dirt that isn't good enough to spit on.

◆

> Terrorizing includes verbally assaulting, bullying, and frightening the child, thereby creating a climate of fear that the child generalizes to the world at large.

Terrorizing usually involves threatening the child with some kind of extreme punishment or dire outcome—one that is clearly beyond the child's coping abilities. The end result is that the child experiences profound fear and is left to his own psychological devices. Examples of terrorizing vary according to the child's age. During infancy, the parent may deliberately violate the child's tolerance for change or intense stimuli by teasing, scaring, or being unpredictable. As the child grows older, the terrorizing may take the form of verbal intimidation: forcing the child to make unfair decisions such as choosing between competing parents, constant raging at the child, or threatening to expose or humiliate the child in public. In extreme Fundamentalist families, children are terrorized by parents who "put the fear of God" in them or threaten them with the devil's wrath should they not behave.

Richard

The most destructive thing about my childhood was the random violence—the fact that at any moment my mother could unleash an attack. One of my earliest memories of this is as a five-year-old. I had my room—with a desk and some shelves that had books and toys— not incredibly neat but organized in my own way. I would be sleeping and during the middle of the night she would storm into the room and sweep everything to the floor in a fit of rage because she considered the room to be messy. And every object on every shelf and every bookcase would end up in a huge heap in the middle of the room. And there would be no way to predict when she would do that. My life would basically be turned upside down, and I would have to then restore everything; the broken car models would have to be sorted out and either repaired or discarded. The desk drawers—you know, she would take all the desk drawers out and spill them into this heap— would have to be put back and organized.

◆

Ignoring entails depriving the child of essential stimulation and responsiveness that stifles emotional growth and intellectual development.

Ignoring refers to a situation in which parents are emotionally unavailable to the child due to their own preoccupation with themselves. In contrast to rejecting, which is active and abusive, ignoring is passive and neglectful. Ignoring behaviors include not responding to the child's talk or not recognizing developing abilities, leaving the child without appropriate adult supervision, not protecting the child from physical or emotional assault by siblings or friends, not showing interest in the child's school progress, and focusing on other relationships (such as a new lover) that displace the child.

Susan

We were ignored and neglected on a daily basis because my mom and stepdad were so caught up in their own conflicts and daily struggles. My mother's little rule of thumb for raising children was that you provided them a clean house, clean clothes, and fed them three times a day. And she did that, but that was about it. We never really got any good attention. It was always "Just get outta here . . . Go on, get outta here . . . Talk to me later . . . I can't talk to you now . . . I'm busy." Everything they ever did for you was this big effort, and you were sorry you were such a trouble to them. We were home alone a lot. My mother used to write notes to me listing the various chores I had to do. At eight or nine, I pretty much took over the mother's provider role of the family. I did the dishes, I set the table, I did the laundry, I did the folding, I did the ironing, I did the cleaning.

I was never close to my stepdad. He was actually diagnosed as a paranoid schizophrenic, and in retrospect, I think his drinking was his way of medicating himself. There was never any physical affection there. He really paid very little attention to me. Fortunately, he never hit us either: The discipling of the kids was my mom's job. We were just never close. He was just this man that lived in our house and yelled and hit my mom, but there was never any connection with him as a father figure for me whatsoever. I still relate to him as a strange force in my life. He hardly ever spoke to me, although he did to my step-brothers. There was a real dividing line between his natural kids and the stepkids. My memory of this man is of him either sleeping, or yelling, or sitting in a chair watching TV. He was an absolute TV fanatic.

◆

> Isolating is defined as the adult cutting the child off from normal social experiences, thereby preventing the child from forming friendships and resulting in a belief that the child is alone in the world.

Isolating the child from normal opportunities for social relations is another form of emotional abuse because it impedes the essential social development of the child. Included here are efforts by the parents to put the child at odds with friends, to present outsiders as the object of suspicion, to reinforce the child's concerns about peer acceptance, and to thwart the child's attempt to be industrious and self-sufficient. Specific behaviors that isolate are preventing children from seeing family friends, preventing medical care, punishing the child's social overtures, rewarding the child for avoiding social situations, prohibiting the child from inviting other children home, withdrawing the child from school, and preventing the child from joining clubs or dating.

Jolene

The father in the Adventist family got real possessive with me. It got so he wanted to know where I was all the time. He wouldn't want me to leave the house. If I insisted on going, he would take me there and want to wait for me. He would always somehow be around, at the church, at home, at my school. I always had the sense that he was out there watching me. It sometimes made me feel special that he would do all this—devote himself to watching out for me. I thought he was protective of me, which I felt good about at first, but then it started feeling more like he was trying to possess me. It started feeling like I was being suffocated. I tried to get out of the house more. I was also seeing this twenty-eight-year-old guy for a while and the father went nuts, saying he was all wrong for me and telling me how much he loved me and how it hurts him that I can't show it back. The closer he tried to get to me, the more I started avoiding him. It got so that he would spy on me from his car while I went to school and walked home. He would only permit me to see church kids because he didn't want me to "get the wrong idea about things." He was worried that I would tell someone and he would not be able to see me anymore so he tried to control who I saw and who I talked to.

◆

Families of extreme fundamentalist religions are especially prone to isolation and have been known to keep their children out of school because the outside world so conflicts with their personal beliefs and values. The isolation imposed on Jolene is also common in families where father-daughter incest exists. The father wants to keep the child at home to preserve his access to her and to limit the possibility that the child will tell someone. Often, incest comes to light only after several years when the girl, now a teenager, tells somebody in her peer group what is going on. It is far easier to seclude a younger child than an older one.

> Corrupting involves "missocializing" the child so the child engages in antisocial behavior that reinforces deviant social attitudes and renders the child unfit for normal social experience.

Corrupting refers to things that parents do that "missocialize" the child in some way by encouraging and reinforcing more antisocial or deviant patterns of behavior. Most frequently, the corruption has to do with suggesting inappropriate ways of handling aggression, sexuality, or substance abuse. By encouraging antisocial values and behaviors, and discouraging the learning of positive, social attitudes and skills, the parents create a social misfit—a child whose self-identity puts her at odds with the conventions and standards of society.

Leigh Anne

My mother used to get me involved in these insurance scams to make extra money. One time, when I was about eight, I was in the car with my mother and she turned into the driveway as a truck was approaching behind her and nicked her bumper. There was absolutely no sign of any contact on the bumper—no dents, no scratches, nobody was hurt. I felt a slight nudge as the truck went by. But my mother turned it into a very serious accident. Ironically, I am able to walk today because I had to go to the chiropracter three times a week in order to make our case. My father threw me down the stairs on several occasions and my mother fashioned the story to fit the injuries that I supposedly had from the car accident. She would threaten me to go along with it. I was also threatened by the shyster doctor who wrote letters saying it was the car accident that caused the injuries. I ended up crying about all of this and thinking to myself that most parents want their children to know right from wrong, and what is wrong with my parents. I felt incredibly guilty. Eventually I had to go to court and lie through my teeth on the witness stand to support her phony case.

◆

Besides Leigh Anne's example of her parent forcing her to engage in defrauding insurance companies, other examples of corrupting behavior include reinforcing the child for her sexual behavior, condoning drug use, rewarding aggressive behavior, exposing the child to pornography, and involving the child in criminal activities such as prostitution or drug dealing. Some parents force their racist attitudes on their children and encourage them to act on these beliefs in ways that cause problems for them with peers, at school, and with the law.

JOURNAL QUESTIONS

26. *Did your parents frequently rant and rave about what a horrible, stupid, or ugly child you were?*

27. *Would they involve you in some illegal activity?*

28. *Did your parents prevent you from having friends?*

29. *Did they refuse to take you to the doctor when you were sick?*

30. *Would they frequently ignore you by refusing to speak to you or listen to you?*

31. *Were you left alone for extended periods of time before the age of ten?*

32. *Did your parents make you stay home from school to take care of a brother or sister?*

33. *Would they threaten to leave you or kill you if you did not do what they said?*

34. *Did they often make disparaging comments about men or women and predict that you would grow up to be just as bad?*

35. *Would your parents sabotage your efforts to succeed at school, sports, work, or relationships with friends?*

After reading this chapter, you know what constitutes physical, sexual, and emotional abuse. Now you can use this material as a standard to measure what happened to you. If you have some memories that you can determine were abusive, write them down in your journal and see if you can add the fine details to give a more complete rendering of the experience. Jot down all thoughts, feelings, associations, and images that are evoked by this memory. Reclaiming the past is like pulling on a delicate thread: You begin with what you have and follow it wherever it takes you. As you continue to tug on the past, the doors of your perceptive mind will gradually open, giving you additional material with which to work.

If you still do not have many memories from the past, don't despair. You may need more time to prepare to remember. Continue reading this book—it will serve as an unconscious map to the location of your buried memories. As you read the next two chapters on family types and personal coping styles, you may start to gather glimpses of what you did during childhood to survive your family experience. Be patient: More memories will follow when you are ready for them.

Chapter Two

UNDERSTANDING
Your dysfunctional
FAMILY

Your next step in reclaiming your childhood involves understanding how the abuse could have occurred in your family and the role that your parents played in it. As you've already read, children who grow up in dysfunctional families often believe that they are responsible for the problems, not their parents. Nowhere is this dynamic more prevalent than in abusive families where a child becomes the scapegoat for his or her parents' uncontrolled aggression. Blaming oneself for actions taken by one's parents represents the central myth of child abuse and is responsible for much of the emotional devastation that continues into adulthood. This myth of the child's responsibility for the abuse is created by the child's need to protect the image of the good parent, even when the reality shows something very different. Parents are supposed to represent hope, security, and nurturance—everything that the child knows she desperately needs. For a child to accept that her parents are hurtful or bad threatens to sever this essential bond, leaving the child an emotional orphan. Nothing can be worse than the feeling of abandonment, so the child valiantly struggles to construct a different reality—one that offers a sense of control and security over a situation in which she really has none. This myth, undertaken to resolve the uncertainty of a parent fallen from grace, also becomes the faulty corner-stone in the child's developing sense of self. Taking on the responsi-bility for the abuse ultimately leaves the child feeling bad, guilty, and unworthy.

If you listen carefully and with an open heart, you may still hear the words used by your parents to justify their actions. Tragically, somewhere along the line, their words may have become your words. No matter how devastating your childhood was, the words from the past, now used against you, may be even more destructive than the abuse itself. These words may continue to undermine your self-confi-dence today as an adult, just as they did when you were a child. Think about whether you have turned against yourself in this way. Are you self-blaming and negative about aspects of yourself that your parents also criticized? Do you feel sad, guilty, and empty when talking to yourself this way? What can you do to treat yourself with compassion, understanding, and acceptance instead of perpetuating the hurtful words of the past?

These words must be challenged directly for your recovery to pro-ceed. Share these words and feelings with someone you trust and write in your journal about your progress in reinterpreting what happened. Now is the time to challenge this myth by illuminating the dark past with the light of truth—the truth about your family, your parents, and the cause of your abuse.

Leigh Anne

I now know that my parents never should have gotten married. They were not exactly made for each other, as the saying goes. Rather they brought the worst out in each other. The proof of this comes from my father who became a much nicer person after he divorced my mother. My mother manipulated my father with her intelligence and superior upbringing and my father fell for it. He never really felt he was good enough for my mother and his insecurity about himself and who he was as a person somehow weakened him. He fell under her wicked spell in a way. My mother really wore the pants in the family—the wicked witch operating behind the scenes. Unfortunately, my father's personality made him capable of becoming her enforcer. The marriage was a pressure cooker for him—he could never win. We were the only ones he could dominate. And he took it out on me far more than my brother. My brother was the favored child in our family, which explains why he got first crack at everything. There really wasn't much left over for me and I believe to this day that this is exactly what my mother wanted because that is what her family did to her. I always believed that she hated me and now I can see that she probably hated herself just as much. I have always tried to put her out of my mind because she was such a bad presence in my life. Even though I never see her anymore, there is still a piece of her inside me.

♦

You may be starting to recall your own notions about why your parents did what they did. It will be essential to understand what meaning you attached to the abuse as a child and your ideas about your role in it. By establishing what your thinking was as a child, you can compare your ideas to what you are going to learn about the *real* causes of your abuse.

Physical, sexual, and emotional abuse cuts a fairly wide path across the horizon of family life. But these definitions as previously defined illustrate only the end product of abusive parent-child relationships. By the time abuse occurs, the family has long fashioned itself after the personalities of the two parents and the quality of their relationship. Only after years of evolution does the family system become a highly complex web of personalities, roles, alliances, attitudes, tendencies, behaviors, expectations, and beliefs. Out of this mass of human interaction, the potential for abuse is created.

Pete

I think my image of myself as a male came from how I saw my mother treat my father during the years that he was a practicing alcoholic and she was on the wagon. I can now see that she had a lot of resentment and frustration over his drinking and my mom played the co-alcoholic in that she would always nag him, harp on him, and endlessly criticize him. She treated him like he was worthless—a worthless man. I didn't understand how their alcoholism played a part in all of this. Looking back now, I can see that it might have made it easier for me to grow up in this family if I had understood how all of this was related. As a consequence of seeing how my mom treated him, I think I internalized a lot of this negativity about my father. From my perspective as a child, I concluded that my father must be a bad father, a bad husband, and ultimately, a bad man. That's the message that I got from my mother and I took it. But he was my father and I was his son. As a result of all of this, I think I grew up feeling bad about myself as a male.

◆

Unbeknowst to them at the time, children grow up being scapegoated in the family for many reasons—because of their sex, their personality, even the timing of their birth. Others have been abused because they remind their parents of someone they dislike, or in the case of spouse abuse, the children simply get caught in the cross-fire. Alcoholism, personality problems, and overwhelming life stress are the hidden ingredients in the toxic brew of family abuse. No matter what the specific reasons for your abuse, rarely were they ever acknowledged or perceived by your parents. What they told you about why they acted the way they did was as biased as their perspective was limited. Your next step is to understand how your family functioned and the forces that propelled your parents to act in the ways they did.

I cannot stress strongly enough that the responsibility for the abuse always rests with the adults involved, be they parents or other caretakers. Always remember that you were the child and no child can be held responsible for a parent's actions. Where the child is being inappropriate, it is the parents' responsibility to set the standard of behavior and morality. When corporal punishment turns abusive or parents consistently take out their frustrations or sexual urges on their children, they are simply not being good parents. When the abuse is ongoing for several years, the immorality of this crime is even more apparent.

I know that accepting this point of view intellectually is far different than believing it emotionally. It is true that ultimately you will need to accept it both ways. But it may be helpful to keep this intellectual perspective in mind as you uncover the facts and feelings surrounding your family life. The guilt, the shame, and the self-blame that may still implicate you in the jury of your mind needs to be challenged by these facts, however novel they may seem at this time. If you find within yourself some of these feelings and personal indictments, tag them for future reference. You will need to take a closer look at them later in the book. For now, your task is to turn your focus on your parents.

CHARACTERISTICS
OF ABUSIVE PARENTS

For the adult survivor of childhood abuse, the most meaningful question concerning their abuser may be, "How could my father or my mother have done that to me?" Or in the case of extrafamilial abuse,

"Why would an adult turn to a child for sex?" Understanding the motives of child abusers is extremely complex but it is an essential task in order to absolve yourself of responsibility for the abuse. Knowing the facts about offenders and understanding their psychological problems is the best strategy to counteract the adult survivor's self-blame. Fortunately, we can give some answers to the question of why parents abuse their children based on our knowledge of personality development, family dynamics, and sexual deviance.

There are essentially two theories about why parents abuse their children. First, the psychological theory suggests that child abuse is the result of the offender's own personality problems and unresolved, negative childhood experiences. Second, the sociological view attributes the cause of child abuse to the parent's inability to deal with the stress precipitated by social factors such as poverty, unemployment, lack of educational opportunities, and family support. As with many competing theories of casuality, the truth about something as complex as child abuse probably lies with a combination of both. At the same time, we know that abuse tends to be intergenerational, which would suggest that it is related to unresolved psychological problems stemming from the offender's own abuse as a child.

There are some general characteristics of offenders that seem to apply regardless of the type of abuse they perpetrate. Adults who abuse their children either do not understand the result of their actions or deny that it is doing any harm or are simply unable or unwilling to control their behavior. When you look into the background of people who abuse children, many common experiences begin to emerge. Using the casual factors described below, compare the information with what you know about your parents or abuser.

Unresolved Childhood Abuse

Most adults who abuse children have experienced some abuse of their own during childhood that was never treated or resolved. They are also survivors, although still in denial over what happened to them as children. Often they had to grow up, as you did, under the threat of assault and in doing so developed aspects of their personality that predisposed them to acting out their conflicts with someone less powerful—you.

The psychological conditions that predispose an adult—parent or not—to sexually abuse a child are more complex and less understood than those for physical abuse. Abusers who were themselves sexually abused as children sometimes develop a sexual disorder as adults, that determines their sexual preference for children only. These people are called pedophiles. Because their sexual fixation is ingrained in their personality they are not easily treated through ordinary psychotherapy. Pedophiles adopt a predatory approach to obtaining children for sexual relations, often organizing their lives to gain access to new victims, despite the legal prohibitions against it. A pedophile may be a youth club leader, a teacher, a family friend, or a volunteer at a children's program, having the type of job or position that gives them contact with children. Pedophiles sometimes combine other tendencies such as violence, voyeurism, and sadomasochism with their behaviors and activities. The severity of the disorder includes the homicidal pedophile who may kidnap and ritualistically torture a child until committing murder.

The other major category of child molesters includes people who have a more temporary disorder and are referred to as *situational* or *regressed* molesters. For them, the sexual abuse of children represents a temporary regression in functioning due to a combination of factors such as life stress or disappointment in their adult relationships. They can be more easily treated and helped to change their sexual interest from children to adults.

New research on sexual disorders is revealing how troubled people are who turn to children for sex. Although sex offenders are truly sick and in desperate need of treatment, it does not mean that they are any less responsible for what they did to you.

JOURNAL QUESTIONS

1. *Were either of your parents abused during their childhood according to the definitions given in chapter 1?*

2. *If they have never said anything about being mistreated, can you determine how they felt about their parents or how they regarded their own upbringing?*

3. *Do they have contact with their family, and if not, why don't they?*

PERSONALITY PROBLEMS

Most abusers have specific personality problems that contribute to their loss of control over their anger and their sexual urges. They may shirk responsibility, lack a conscience, or be unable to empathize with others. They may have a personality disorder that predisposes them to act in maladaptive ways when they find themselves in particular situations.

Many survivors have been raised by parents who had a full blown psychiatric problem or a chronic medical condition. As a result of their illness, they may have given up being caring parents and became consumed instead by their symptoms and general unhappiness. Anger over their dilemmas may be displaced onto their children. Or they may have such low self-esteem that it causes them to turn to children, instead of other adults, to gratify their needs.

Parents with major personality problems are very vulnerable to stress and losing control of their aggressive and sexual impulses. They may rely on the most rudimentary coping strategies such as denial and aggressive behavior to manage the pressures of daily living. Usually the abuse is triggered by their reaction to some pressing life problem such as marital difficulties, job problems, or financial setbacks. The abuse allows them to feel powerful because they are dominating someone else, when in reality, they really feel defeated by life. These parents often view their children as their possessions, which may help them justify the abusive treatment.

Susan

M y stepfather was a troubled man. He was an ex-World War II veteran who had some real traumatic things happen to him in the war. Early in life he had numerous nervous breakdowns and problems with the law. He even spent some time in prison. He came from an alcoholic home with a father who had physically abused him. All of his siblings have fallen along the wayside too in very sad, traumatic ways. My stepfather was really erratic, and he could never keep a job because of his drinking and he kept switching to new ones. I think he was actually diagnosed as a paranoid schizophrenic. His drinking was his way of holding on. I was sixteen when he had the last breakdown. Because my mother was in the process of divorcing him and we were not his natural children, we couldn't be the ones to commit him. My aunt and my grandmother came up and they committed him into a veterans hospital. As far as I know, he's still alive in a mental institution down South. As I look back on things, I can see where all his behavior was pretty nutty all along, but until recently I felt it was more his alcoholism than anything else that caused his problems. My attitude toward him was "Get him out of our life; get him locked up." All I knew was that this man made everything worse, and because of it, I had to suffer.

♦

JOURNAL QUESTIONS

4. *Did either of your parents have long-standing emotional or physical problems that affected the parenting you received?*

5. *What do you know about your parents' early lives and their adjustment before getting married and having children?*

6. *What signs of personality problems have you seen? Temper, mood swings, phobias, compulsive behaviors, or stress-related illnesses?*

POOR PARENTING SKILLS

Parents who abuse their children often have received little or no training in parenting or child development and instead rely on what they learned from their own parents. They feel unprepared to deal with the constantly changing needs of their children and may resort to the most extreme methods of discipline.

With the breakdown of the traditional family structure, there is often no extended family available to support the young parent and to provide advice, guidance, and reassurance. The social isolation that seems to be the norm for many inner city and rural families places additional burden on the few adaptive parenting strategies they may possess. Under stress, these parents may often repeat the same ill-formed and punitive child-rearing practices with their own children—often with the same results. Physical or emotional abuse often starts as purposeful discipline but ends as a destructive repetition of the past. When this happens, many parents will take their children's normal behavior as a personal insult or challenge to their authority. These parents do not understand or are not sufficiently secure in their identities as parents to see that their children are going through normal stages of development when they try to assert their independence as young toddlers, and later, as teenagers.

Richard

My mother never got along with her mother; they were always in a state of cold war hatred. They could never stay together for more than a day or two without my mother storming out. And it was never clear to me why my mother would complain about her so much because it was difficult for me to see how terrifying my grandmother could be considering how frail she was. But clearly my mother was reacting to her as if she was Thor, the Thunder Goddess. She really felt mistreated by her. My grandmother was a strange person—that much is true. Apparently she was a very critical mother, and nothing my mother could do was good enough. My mother got left with servants a lot because my grandparents were into the social scene. My grandmother wanted a male child and was disappointed with my mother, so she kind of ignored her. When my grandmother turned sixty, she moved into a ritzy hotel in the city and spent my mother's inheritance on living high on the hog. My mother says that my grandmother was that way her whole life. She came first and everyone else didn't matter. It took me a few years in therapy to realize that my mother had done the same thing to me.

◆

JOURNAL QUESTIONS

7. *What kinds of attitudes toward children did your parents have?*

8. *Did they prefer males over females or have peculiar notions of the way children should be?*

9. *Were you ever aware of how their upbringing may have shaped the way they treated you as a child?*

ALCOHOL AND DRUG PROBLEMS

Alcohol and drug abuse is often seen in all types of abusive families. Alcohol abuse alone is a factor in almost three quarters of all family violence cases reported. It is the fuse that ignites wife battering and physical abuse as well as the trigger for releasing inhibitions and internal controls of sexual and aggressive behavior. In some people, it causes a radical personality shift, sometimes provoking unresolved feelings left over from childhood traumas. Parents who seem caring and concerned one minute can turn into abusive offenders after a few drinks. Alcohol blackouts are common triggers of sexual abuse, often leaving the offenders with no memory of their actions upon regaining sobriety. The ranting and raving associated with latter-stage alcoholism is frequently directed at the only witnesses present—the children. The bitter, hateful words that are repeated incessantly and used to avenge past injustices are daily reminders of a family gone awry. Drug abuse, particularly crack and cocaine use, invite irritability, hostility, inconsistency, chronic neglect, and criminality into the home.

Shirley

My parents' drinking pretty much dominated our lives as kids. Because they both drank, we really couldn't rely on either of them. Once when I was with them and my relatives, they ran a red light and we got hit by another car. I needed to have brain surgery and almost died. I used to think my father had the worse problem because he got so controlling and aggressive when he drank. But my mother really neglected us. She was out of the house a lot either working or hanging out at the bar, waiting for him. But she was the mother and we kind of expected more from her. Later when I was in my teens, I can remember that I never really knew what to expect from her. It turned out that she was mixing her pills with the alcohol, which made her almost as violent and abusive as he was.

◆

JOURNAL QUESTIONS

10. *Can you recall if your parents had a drinking or drug problem or were on medication for extended periods of time?*

11. *Do either of your parents' families have histories of alcoholism?*

12. *When your parents drank, did you feel concerned that they might lose control or require you to take responsibility for the house or family?*

FIVE TYPES OF
DYSFUNCTIONAL FAMILIES

Just as there is a wide variety of abusive personalities, there is also a wide variety of dysfunctional families. Families are as complex and varied as the individual personalities that make them up. While it is beyond the scope of this chapter to name and describe them all, it is possible to classify some families according to their dominant styles, which are often related to the specific personality problems of the parents.

There seem to be five major dysfunctional family types that produce child abuse: violent, exploitive, deprived, authoritarian and addictive. Each has a certain set of attitudes, traits, tendencies, behaviors, and limitations that creates the particular climate of abuse. Most abusive families share characteristics of one or more of the five types of family dysfunctions. These categories should not be considered mutually exclusive, but rather, regarded as primary characteristics of a particular family style that may share secondary characteristics from the other four types. Child-abusing families will typically present two or even three of these primary characteristics. It is less important to perfectly categorize your particular family than it is to understand the unique blend of characteristics that make up your family's style. Using these categories, try to identify the type of abusive family style that you experienced.

Violent Families

Violent families are characterized by the physical aggression that is directed toward the most vulnerable members of the family. Constant fighting, wife battering, physical abuse between parent and child and between the siblings are the main signs of a violent family. These families are the most destructive to the well-being of a children because physical force leaves them feeling absolutely helpless. Parents in these families often have highly punitive child-rearing practices and overemphasize control and compliance. They often have alcohol and drug problems that trigger the violence. Sometimes they are pathologically paranoid and suspicious, with a tendency to perceive threat and disrespect where none exists. Their concern with control creates an inability to tolerate individual differences or independence in their children. Extremely low frustration tolerance, quite common in these parents, results in a violent reaction following a buildup of stress. As is so often the case, they may present a history of severe physical abuse and problems with aggression throughout their own childhoods.

The self-repeating cycle of abuse in these families seems to follow a predictable pattern. In general, violent families seem to alternate between periods of neglect or disengagement followed by periods of violence. After the discharge of the aggression, a calm descends over the family and the members retreat to lick their wounds. In the military vernacular, fighting is called engagement with the enemy, and in a way, the members of a violent family also engage with each other through the abuse. Unfortunately, this creates a connection between intimacy and pain that children may carry with them into adulthood and end up repeating in their intimate relationships unless they work through the fear and mistrust that people represent for them.

Leigh Anne

I always felt ganged up against because I was the smallest. I got beat up by everyone at one time or another. My brother and my mother would also get beat up by my father, but I was the main target—I got it the worst. I spent a lot of my childhood hiding under the bed or in a closet when my father came home from work, waiting for things to blow over. But it wasn't just my father. My mother would slap me out of the blue, leaving a bruise on my face. She would grab me by my hair. I had a lot of my hair pulled out. She even had my dog killed when I went away to some relatives for the summer. I felt like anything connected to me was at risk. Even my older brother used to beat me up. He fashioned himself after my father's style—he could get himself all heated up and then start swinging at me or strangling me by the neck. I would have these finger patterns of bruises on my neck. I used to complain to my parents and they would say, "Oh, brothers and sisters fight like that."

◆

Like the personalities of people, the particular personality of a family can run the gamut from extreme to minimal. At the extreme, the violence is severe, constant, and yields multiple victims—spouse, children, even the family pet. Leigh Anne's family would be considered more extreme because she was severely physically abused by everyone in the family and it occurred on a regular basis. She sustained severe injuries that eventually required medical care.

On the other end of the spectrum is the minimally violent family where the violence is usually situational, less frequent and not as severe once it occurs. In these families, the violence is often directed at one child—the family scapegoat—or the spouse who assumes the role of either the passive martyr or the agent provocateur.

Susan

Looking back on my past, I realize now that my mother was abusing us when she took us into the bathroom for the "discipline sessions." The way she would lose control of herself, you could just tell that she became a different person. But, in retrospect, I would say that my mom and stepdad's fighting was far more violent even though it wasn't being directed at us. It was horrible to watch them go at it and see these people get so consumed in their rage. It was really scary to witness this happening again and again. Even when they weren't fighting, there was an atmosphere of fear and trepidation that never really subsided. We were always waiting for the next battle. At the time, my stepdad seemed to be more responsible for the violence, although when I was older, I saw more clearly how my mom would set him off. Back when he became a policeman and started to have access to weapons, things got much worse. When my parents would fight, it was much more serious because he would pull out a gun. I remember being locked in a room with him brandishing a gun. He was clearly out of control. Somebody had to get my grandmother to cool him off before he lost it.

These types of crazy incidents started happening on a more regular basis. I can remember running down the street at two or three in the morning in my nightgown to get my grandmother who lived nearby. My grandmother would get out of bed, come over to the house, and just tell him to knock it off. Even though she wasn't his mother, he would listen to her for some reason. He would calm right down. Later on, when it got even worse, I started calling the police who made our house a regular stop on their beat. I remember sleeping with a croquet mallet under my bed because I was so frightened of him. One time the chief of police came over and told my stepdad, "When the kids have to sleep with croquet mallets under their bed, you have gone to far." He never really did anything to my stepfather. It was sort of understood that he had his problems and everyone—police included—tried to work around them as much as possible. I guess if this happened today, someone would make a child abuse report. Back then, it was dealt with more informally.

◆

Susan's family falls somewhere in the middle of the spectrum because she was both physically abused (although not as bad as Leigh Anne) and was subjected to her parents' fighting and her stepfather's use of guns. The family atmosphere was largely determined by her stepfather's personality problems and the mother's aggressive engagement with him. Alcoholism—the first cousin of family violence—again seemed to play a major role in triggering the marital conflict.

Although Susan was not severely physically abused, it is noteworthy that she experienced the witnessing of the marital violence as more upsetting than the episodes of corporal punishment in the bathroom. When a child sees a parent transformed into an aggressive combatant, her relationship to that parent also undergoes a transformation since the child fears getting too close to someone who can be so aggressive. To witness violence makes a child feel vulnerable not only because she fears for her safety but because she is unable to prevent the violence. Susan felt that she had to physically protect herself from her stepfather, something she felt her mother could not do. Some children attempt to literally step between fighting parents in a valiant but dangerous effort to preserve peace. When this fails—as it inevitably does—the child may feel as if she has failed and blame herself for not being good enough or strong enough or convincing enough.

JOURNAL QUESTIONS

13. *Was your family physically violent? If so, at whom was the violence directed and what form did it take?*

14. *Was the violence triggered by specific situations or did it threaten to erupt at virtually any moment?*

15. *What were your feelings when you witnessed the violence and what, if anything, did you do in reaction to it?*

EXPLOITATIVE FAMILIES

Most families that abuse their children are also exploitative of them in other ways. However, the families that prominently reflect his characteristic have a different feel than other families. Their method of operation is more subtle and manipulative. They need to enlist the child's involvement or cooperation in the abuse rather than dominate him through physical aggression. Families that are characterized by exploitation are ones in which parents typically have a general "user" mentality toward life and see their children as being their personal possessions to service their needs, whatever they may be—emotional support, sexual contact, or a target for their rage. In doing so, they deny their children their rights as individuals and their needs as children.

Taking responsibility for household duties and assuming primary care for younger siblings may be the most typical kinds of family exploitation. Many children were expected to cook, clean, and generally maintain the household, thereby permitting the mother to do something else. Leigh Anne took over household duties because her mother, hooked on prescription pills, spent most of her day in bed. Often this kind of exploitation leads to other kinds of exploitation that are more blatantly abusive. Sexual abuse is perhaps the ultimate exploitation of the children and these families are known for it.

Pete

I think that my father's drinking and my parents' marital problems set the stage for my becoming my mom's surrogate husband. I was, in her own words, her possession. Although that made me feel real powerful and special, I was actually uncomfortable with it because it always seemed that I was getting all this attention at the expense of my dad. I think that this focus on me set in place a lot of what eventually occurred between my mom and me. They never slept together in the same bedroom. When I was real little, I slept in my mom's bed, next to her. At the time, it seemed as though my mom was protecting me from him and his irresponsibility brought on by his sloppy drinking. But it was more than that. At some level, I knew that their relationship was broken and that I was everything to her. And she was always asking me, "What would I do without you?" I think I felt obligated to be this for my mom, although inside, it really tore me up.

A similar type of thing developed with my dad and me around sports. I was my dad's little boy who excelled at sports and he took great pride in it. And I think it became something for him that was not all that healthy. I wanted to be something for him so that he could give me some of the stability that I was so desperate for at home. My mom got to be so out of control with her emotions and needs and demands on me and I looked to my dad to intervene. But once again there was a price to pay and so I tried to become the star athlete that my dad could feel good about. I realize now that I became an outlet for some of his needs and deficiencies as a husband and a man. He could focus on my athletic activities, which would get him out of the house and away from his problems with my mom. What I've learned is that I assumed responsibility for having to be all this for them when actually I was being used by them—a pawn in their battle with each other.

◆

The type of emotional exploitation that Pete describes may be the most subtle kind of all. Parents who have unresolved needs due to unsatisfying marriages often turn to their children for what they are not getting from the adults in their lives. In doing so, they unfairly burden their children with their adult problems and run the risk of playing the child off the other parent. The child—in this case a male—grows up in a sexualized relationship with a parent who has, in effect, given up on her marriage to an alcoholic husband. The child then assumes the father's role, which leads to incest when the child reaches puberty and falls victim to the seduction by the mother. This was certainly the case with Pete who felt so guilty for being his mother's preferred man. What he was not able to see until years later was that in assuming this role for his parents, his own needs were ignored.

Leigh Anne and Richard were exploited by their mothers but to a lesser extent than Pete who was exploited both emotionally and sexually. Shirley's family was also exploitative and shared many similarities with Pete's family. Both were alcoholic families that permitted the level of exploitation to take on new dimensions in the misuse of parental authority.

Shirley

I was very much caught up in a triangle between my parents— my stepdad and my mom. My family was definitely exploitative, but at the time I thought I was being the good kid by doing whatever they wanted. It gave me some meaning and purpose, and I guess, some control. I can see now that they were just using me for their own needs. I was only eight or nine when my mother used me to be the mother that she wasn't—in the sense of being a parent to my younger brother and being the homemaker. My father used me to be his wife in terms of sex. Our family was all set up for it. My mother was absent quite a bit. She made a career for herself and was pretty dedicated to her job. In the evenings, she would go to school. She was absent from the home a lot. I was left to do the cooking and shopping and baby-sitting for my younger brother. I didn't realize it then, but now I can see that I pretty much raised him. He would come to me with his problems. He would come to me with what to wear, how to dress. He'd come to me to help him shop for those things that he needed for school.

My mom would also rely on me to deal with my stepfather when he was drinking. I was the only one that he would listen to—or so she told me. She'd get me up out of bed and take me down to a tavern to go in and get him. As I got older and had my own activities, we started to fight over what she should do and what I would do. With my stepdad, it was more of the same, only different. The pattern was he would return home on Friday afternoon from driving all week. I'd come home from school and that is when he would sexually abuse me. Afterward, he would start drinking. Then he would go meet her at a bar someplace and they would get blasted and start fighting. Since they had their own cars, they would come home at different times, and he would come upstairs and wake me up and want to tell me about the evening, confide in me who my mom was screwing around with or tell me about his girlfriends. So I would become his confidante. Then my mother would come home and they would get into a physical argument and there would be flying dishes, flying fists, screaming and yelling. My mom would come to my room or holler for me to come down and help her out. And I would. I used to step right in the middle of them and try to separate them. Sometimes she would come to my room and that would be her hideaway. But then, of course, he'd come too. So the argument just moved from downstairs to upstairs.

It went on that way for years until I became a teenager and began to want a life of my own. But the three of us were so enmeshed. Part of my recovery was pulling myself out of that triangle, and to see that it was real unhealthy.

◆

JOURNAL QUESTIONS

16. *Did you become the caretaker, housekeeper, confidante, or scapegoat of your parents?*

17. *Did your parents use you to satisfy their own needs that were inappropriate for children?*

18. *Was there any other family problem that might have contributed to the exploitation such as alcoholism or chronic physical illnesses?*

DEPRIVED FAMILIES

Deprived families are characterized by the neglect of their children. The parents are noted for their inadequacy and are physically and/or emotionally unable to fully provide for their children. They may leave the children on their own for extended periods of time. When the parent is home, the neglect becomes more emotional and involves ignoring the child. The primary feature of this family is an almost total lack of emotional and material resources needed to maintain a reasonable standard of living. Affection, money, and food are always in short supply. These families can be welfare families with young single mothers who never received adequate parenting themselves and had children more out of desperation than desire. Or they may be families with a chronically ill parent who dominates the family fortunes with his or her medical needs. Often the parents of deprived families were themselves neglected as children and consequently never learned how to break out of the cycle of emotional and financial poverty that has plagued past generations of their family.

Jolene

My second foster home that I moved into when I was six was probably the worst of all of them. There was nothing there for me. I was just existing and trying to survive this crazy environment. We didn't even get all of the expense money we were entitled to. It was a total rip-off. The foster mother really hated me for some reason. Plus I was the oldest girl so I had to be responsible for everybody and take care of everything around the house. The parents were always fighting. The husband was an alcoholic. I'd wake up in the middle of the night and they'd be down on the floor punching each other out. It was just madness.

The only positive thing was this other foster kid named Gene who I really liked and he was nice to me. We are still friends today. Except for him, I would stay to myself, which eventually became a problem with the mother who said I was selfish for doing this. She would play mind games on me like pretending that she was going to hit me just so I would jump—that kind of thing. I never could predict how she was going to react to something. I mean there was just a lot of yelling that seemed real inappropriate to me, and I never could understand why she was yelling at me for stuff that just didn't seem important. I remember one time Gene and I were sitting on her firescape, just talking about how nutty this family was and how basically all we had was each other. And we were talking about how mean the foster mother was. Finally I turned around and I saw her in the window. She was standing there listening to us. She asked me if I hated her and I said yes, and she said, "Well, I hate you too." From that point on, my life went from miserable to wretched. I don't know anything about this woman's pains or her problems. There had to be something going on with her. I have no idea what it was—I don't care. I just cannot imagine why anyone would treat a child in this way unless there way something seriously wrong in her own life.

◆

As with Jolene, when children are placed in foster or institutional care, they are often placed in facilities with inadequate caretakers who cannot provide the emotional sustenance that young children in placement so desperately need. The foster care system operating in this country is rife with inadequacy and Jolene's experience is shared by millions of children to this very day who simply exist under implorable conditions.

Deprivation is also a way of life for many families living on welfare or fixed incomes. These are the families who make up the permanent underclass where opportunity is scarce and hopelessness is rampant. At the worse, the parents effectively give up being in charge or taking responsibility for the care of the their children. At the best, they provide for the basic needs of their children but neglect them emotionally.

Susan

B asically I think my family experience was one of emotional neglect because my parents really had very little to give. They didn't have enough for themselves so how could they give anything to their kids? They each had very low self-esteem. Nothing ever really worked out for them and their frustrations would periodically boil over into their battering each other. In between these times, there was nothing. It was nice to have some calm, but we used to walk around on eggshells because you knew another storm was brewing. My mother was hooked on conflict and in my stepdad she had all she wanted. In a way, she devoted a large portion of her life to fighting him and whoever else he might have represented for her. The bottom line was that we got ignored because they were so caught up in their stuff.

◆

Parents who are neglectful are experienced by their children as uninterested, uninvolved, and unsupportive. They may lack the ability to be affectionate with their children or appreciative of their talents as developing people or they simply lack the energy to nurture their children's natural inquisitiveness.

Some of you may recall feeling secondary to your parents' other relationships or feeling unsafe when your mother's boyfriends were around. The feeling of deprivation was part of your concern over your mother's abilities to protect you. Some parents who fit into this category may spend their day in aimless activities such as watching soap operas, playing cards, or reading romance novels instead of being involved in parenting. A classic role reversal between the child—often the oldest or a female—and the parent—often a single mother—is common in these families.

JOURNAL QUESTIONS

19. *Was your family neglectful of your needs for medical attention, normal parenting, and participation in school situations?*

20. *Were you often left without proper parental supervision for extended periods of time?*

21. *Did your parents periodically inquire about your activities or show concern for your welfare?*

AUTHORITARIAN FAMILIES

Authoritarian families come in all varieties and ideologies. They are noted for their strict adherence to a particular ideology—religious, political, therapeutic, or personal—that dominates the purpose and function of the family. Everything comes second to the goal of supporting the purpose or "calling," including the child-rearing and the developmental needs of the children. The ideology may range from strict fundamentalist religions that promote isolation from the real world to politically inspired cults that define their identities as being in opposition to everyone else. Some groups organized as "therapeutic communities" for the treatment of addictions are really little more than personality cults based on a charismatic leader. Since the 1960s, there has been a proliferation of religious-based and personality cults that occupy the fringe of our society. The children who grew up in them are today recognizing how adversely they have been affected.

Besides their emphasis on ideology, authoritarian families often maintain a rigid hierarchical structure and total or near-total devotion to an all-powerful leader. Due to their exclusive nature, they can prevent their children from engaging in activities and having relationships with anyone outside their family or group. These families typically reject outright any behavior that is not consistent with that strict code of conduct that is promulgated by the group. When transgressions are committed, often the punishment is physically abusive. The children can be psychologically terrorized into accepting the beliefs and attitudes of the group by using the specter of God's wrath and Satan's doing to enforce compliance. A most destructive aspect any authoritarian family is the rampant invalidation and distortion of children's perceptions. They grow up doubting themselves and feel conflicted when having normal feelings and youthful desires.

Jolene

M y foster parents were part of the Seventh Day Adventists Church, which was very strict and controlling. We all went to the church school and were only allowed to socialize with other church kids. Right from the first day I got there, they were trying to convert me. Everything I did was questioned, criticized, and reviewed in terms of what God would say about it. This was a big change from my last foster home where everything was sort of chaotic and out of control. This family was organized and tight. You practically had to ask permission to sneeze. They were always worried about what other people would think about this or that. There was a lot of emphasis on show—being the good Christian, being the perfect human being, eliminating anything that would take you away from what the church said you were supposed to be. There was no life or fun to this family. They were really grim. I don't think they really enjoyed anything. Pleasure was a dirty word, except for the father who got his by coming on to me. It was so strange to attend church with this righteously religious family one minute and then have him do this to me later.

◆

As the Italian thinker Machiavelli wrote centuries ago, "Power corrupts, and absolute power corrupts absolutely." Authoritarian families essentially abuse their power and authority, believing that if you do not accept the ideology, you are a bad person. They also tend to be prohibitive, emphasizing all the things that you cannot do or else you risk being branded as a sinner or a traitor or an addict. At their essence, they are not democratic because they do not share power among family members. It is important to realize that families, just like countries, can fall into the trap of authoritarianism where children—the least powerful members of the family—are oppressed just like an outlawed political group.

Richard

When people meet my mother, they are struck by what a powerful and commanding personality she is. She comes off as incredibly urbane, sophisticated, articulate, self-possessed, and persuasive. She's very tall—over six feet—and she's really very beautiful. She's also very intense and very smart. She was too much for a young boy to handle alone. After years of being a journalist, she is now a public relations person for a tobacco company. Now everyone knows that cigarettes cause more harm to the body than anything except bottled plutonium, but leave it to my mother to make smoking sound wholesome and positive. In her mind, the Marlboro man is right up there with the Pope in terms of moral superiority. She makes people believe her and, of course, I ended up believing that I was bad for not making her happy. If I didn't agree with her, I was not only wrong but stupid, crazy, sadistic, and vengeful.

After being in therapy, I'm able to understand her better. To use psychological jargon, she is a narcissistic personality. She only has an internal reality: There is no such thing as an external world that is independent of her. Everything is an extension of her, including me.

When something contradicts this perspective you see this tremendous rage. She's like a Saturn 5 rocket blasting her way into orbit. At any moment, you know that she can go ballistic with her anger in response to the slightest provocation. By provocation, I mean just being different, having a different understanding or thought or perception. Underneath the surface image that she projects to the world, she is very insecure about herself and really has very low self-worth. In order to feel good about herself, she has to devalue everything that doesn't prop up this fabrication of a positive self-image.

You could just see her mind sorting through her experience with her kids, criticizing and rejecting what she didn't like and demanding that you give her more of what she did like. It was that way each and every day. It was like *1984*: You learned that you couldn't say what was on your mind for fear of triggering that rage. My sister and I always felt bad when she blew because we felt that we hadn't handled her well enough or given her enough understanding, support, or appreciation. That's what she told us and if you hear something enough—even when its crazy—you begin to believe it.

◆

Authoritarian families need not be affiliated with a group or religion. Families can be structured as minicults, with a parent assuming the role of the all-powerful leader and the membership being limited to family members only. Standards of behavior can easily be distorted to justify inappropriate adult behavior that results in the maltreatment of children. By virtue of their strict adherence to the authority of the leader, and compliance with a specified code of behavior and system of beliefs, these families can be extremely emotionally abusive.

JOURNAL QUESTIONS

22. *Did your family belong to any kind of religion, group, or cult espousing a particular ideology that dominated family life?*

23. *Were you subjected to harsh sanctions for expressing personal thoughts or opinions that differed from the thinking to which your parents subscribed?*

24. *Were your parents inclined to rule the family like dictators, with you, the child, being put in the role of slave or servant to their personal vision?*

ADDICTIVE FAMILIES

Addictive families share the common experience of having a parent who has some compulsive behavior such as drinking, taking drugs, gambling, being sexually promiscuous, spending money, relationship seeking, or eating. The compulsive behavior is clearly out of control and there is a tendency for the family to organize itself around the parent's addiction and the resultant behavior. The bottle or pills or other compulsive activity comes to assume lifelike proportions, almost like another family member. The result is that less of the family's resources are available for the children.

Pete

My dad's drinking was probably chronic by the time I was born and it continued until I was around seven when he quit. He was a daily maintenance drinker, a little bit at a time throughout the day. Anyway I think he was hospitalized for d.t.'s, although I was always told he had a heart attack. I don't really know the facts. Actually that was a big part of our family—protecting me from the facts about what was going on with them. During the early years, there was a lot of fighting and very little happiness. The house was always filled with resentment. My mother was always threatening to leave with me in tow because of his drinking. she would pack us up and take off for the weekend. I remember us driving away and my looking back and seeing my father sitting on the porch drunk and I'm worried about what will happen to him. After my dad stopped drinking, I gradually started to build some trust with him. I hadn't really known him sober before and even as a young boy I was afraid of him and didn't know what to expect from him. As soon as my father stopped drinking, my mother started. She gradually developed her own problem, which continues to the present.

I think I've buried a lot of feelings about him not being there for me. Feelings that could not come up because I felt so conflicted about what I saw my mom doing to him. Things were very unstable and unpredictable at this time and I couldn't really count on having a safe place. I know today that I felt abandoned. Because of their drinking, my parents couldn't take care of themselves and I feared they would be unable to take care of me.

◆

In alcoholic families, the relationship between parent and child usually involves emotional abuse. The addicted parent ignores the needs of the child while under the influence of alcohol, which the child often experiences as abandonment. The drunk parent will often become verbally abusive—blaming, criticizing, and rejecting the child. The child internalizes these angry words and grows up believing what he has heard over and over again. Depending on the personality of the parent and the degree of addiction, the parent will make inappropriate demands on the child, vacate his role as the family authority, or assume more authority than is healthy for the child's development. When the parent comes off a drug or drinking binge, he will be irritable and ill-tempered and likely to see the children's needs as demanding and bothersome.

In other types of compulsive behaviors, the parents will leave the children alone in the house to fend for themselves. Financial resources will be drained by compulsive spending and gambling, thereby limiting what is given to the children in terms of clothes, allowance, educational supplies, recreational activities, and vacations.

Leigh Anne

My mother was addicted to downers—Seconal and Demerol—anything that would make her emotionless and introverted. She slept fourteen hours a day from the time I was eight until I left home at sixteen. She was often totally out of it—asleep—but more often, she was emotionally unavailable. She had many drug overdoses, two within a few months of each other when my father was recovering from his heart attack. She had all these doctors she was getting prescriptions from, and she would make up some story to get whatever drug she wanted. She knew how to act and what to say. None of them knew the other one was prescribing the same thing. I remember there were a dozen vials on her nightstand, and even as a young kid, I associated them with her sleeping all the time. These were the years when I was in grammar school, before I developed my caretaker number. I remember being so confused at that time. Nobody was even talking to me or considering how I might have felt. Everything was done behind my back.

My mother had a mastectomy and it was a real family crisis. When she returned home with one breast, she held us all responsible for her pain and anguish. I think this contributed to her drug addiction. It never did stop. As a matter of fact, as she got older, it escalated. She never stopped smoking cigarettes; she never changed her diet. She never showed me that she even wanted to live. She always laid it on me that she wanted to die. And that's kind of the emotional relationship that we have, even to this day.

♦

JOURNAL QUESTIONS

25. *Was your family ruled by your parents' addictions? If so, which ones?*

26. *Can you trace the effects of their addictions with how they treated you?*

27. *Were their addictions directly or indirectly involved in the abusive behavior directed at you?*

By this time you may have developed some insight into what kind of abusive family you came from and the reasons for the abuse. Some clu misguided notions about your role in the abuse may die a natural death after you face the truth. Thinking about your family and parents from the perspective offered here may challenge and contradict what you have accepted as true in the past. Reclaiming the past is like weaving the threads of your new understanding together and then periodically standing back to get a good look at the overall pattern. Slowly but surely it will dawn on you what actually happened to you as a child. Out of the contradiction between your views of the past and your new views, a new perception of your family may emerge—one that begins to free you from your self-imposed guilt. Take your time to slowly, but surely reconstruct the revised pattern of your childhood existence. Write in your journal about this new perspective, allowing new questions and insights to arise. As you go forward in this process, new answers will emerge. With each step, you move farther along on your road to recovery.

Chapter Three

DISCOVERING
Your inner child

The next step on the road to recovery entails shifting your focus from your family to understanding yourself and your plight as a child growing up amid secrecy, betrayal, and fear. Think back to what it was really like for you as a child. What fears and concerns were with you on an everyday basis? What did you need to do in order to survive? How did you cope with the ever-present threat of abuse? What parts of you were really hurt and what parts came through relatively unscathed? This chapter will focus on how you survived your abuse as a child—the roles you played, the defenses you used, and the coping strategies that allowed you to face another day. It will also focus on resurrecting your inner child—that most vulnerable part of you—that was hidden inside until the threat of abuse subsided.

Now, years later, your inner child may still be locked inside, robbing you of a sense of self—your true identity that is composed of your most unique and vital attributes. You will need to wade through the layers of these defenses to reach this childlike part and integrate it with the strengths born from years of self-protection. Look for the soul of that inner child—that is, the guiding light that will carry you forward to your new beginning.

In focusing inward on yourself, I hope you will learn to appreciate your own personal story of survival. As a child, you faced incredible odds that may only now become apparent. You need to value your efforts to survive, and above all, accept them as necessary and productive. Many survivors—perhaps yourself included—feel bad about what they had to do to survive. You will need to explore these feelings and dilemmas and understand what it is that creates these misgivings. As an adult now, you may have a very different reaction to the old judgments made against yourself as a child. Nourish that compassionate, understanding part of you—however small it might be at this time—to show some consideration for what you did to survive.

During this process of self-discovery, you will come across parts of yourself that perhaps you never knew existed—personal strengths that you can rely on, talents that you can develop and, of course, the presence of soul. Mining these emotional resources entails digging into the channels of your psyche and bringing into conscious awareness the internalized pieces of your past experience. Undoubtedly, you will find things about yourself that you do not like—extreme behaviors that are no longer necessary to protect yourself, self-criticalness perhaps or the tendency to overreact. Some of these may have been learned from your parents and others are left over from how you coped as a child. Put these pieces aside for the time being until you can return to them later in recovery.

LACK OF TRUST

Children develop their sense of self by achieving a union with their primary caregiver—usually the mother—and then during the first three years of life, growing outward from this experience of oneness to forge a separate identity as a person. Out of this bonding with the mother, the psychological sense of self is born much in the way a pearl is formed in nature: The mother's love washes over this tiny entity, gradually building up, layer by layer, a separate being with a luster all its own. Over time, this process continues with the other members of the family who respond warmly to the young child, mirroring the infant's initial expressions, celebrating the baby's discovery of the world, and reinforcing his joy for life.

The child is made to feel secure and eventually grows to feel comfortable being himself. The parents encourage this self-discovery and validate the child for who he is, which becomes the blueprint for the child's own self-acceptance. Basic trust, the foundation for all healthy relationships, is learned, having been built on a series of positive and satisfying experiences with the parents that develop into expectations of more of the same. The bridge between experience and expectation is constructed with the child's perceptions of the parents' consistency, reliability, and predictability. When these perceptions are reinforced over and over again, and the child learns to anticipate the parents' consistent response to a particular situation, basic trust is established.

With abused children, this process of trust building gets derailed, perhaps even before the onset of the child abuse. When abuse occurs later in childhood, it may signal problems that have been going on for some time. The early mother-child relationship may have been inconsistent, frustrating, or possibly neglectful. As a result, you may have been thwarted in your attempts to depend emotionally on your parents. Instead of trusting them to nurture your young personality, they hurt you. Consequently you retreated from your parents, whose behavior told you in so many ways that you were not respected, appreciated, or valued. Because you were not made to feel secure, you had to develop a wall of psychological defenses to protect your inner child.

Pete

I think I've buried a lot of feelings about my parents not being there for me. Things were so unstable and unpredictable in my family during the first six or seven years of my life. I couldn't really count on having a safe place. I know today that I have this constant feeling of abandonment—like I'm about to be left. I was never able to trust that they would be able to take care of me so I tried to take care of myself. And I think I have always felt that I had to do everything on my own. I just think it fundamentally altered my life. Since being in therapy, I can see how this affects me as a human being—what I ask of people and what I feel I'm worth, what I deserve, my relationships with women, being able to be vulnerable, to receive, and to let people close to me. To let intimacy be present and not to have a confusion between intimacy and inappropriate contact. It all comes down to trusting people to be there for me and to respect me for who I am and not use me for their own needs. I struggled with that for a long time.

◆

You wanted to trust your parents and early in life you may have even acted as if you trusted them in the hope that they would be different in the future. But after experiencing and reexperiencing the pain, rejection, and disappointment, you may have gradually withdrawn your trust, feeling alone and scared. This was probably the point at which you started pulling away from people, perhaps realizing that you were on your own. After all, if you can't trust your parents, whom can you trust?

Leigh Anne

As a child, I always lived with the family secrets—the hitting, the fighting, my mother's drug addictions, and my father's job difficulties, and later, their legal problems. I never told anyone what happened in our family until recently in my late thirties. I kept it all inside because I was so ashamed that this was happening to my family. I really only had myself and it was hard to see what I really thought about these things because it was so painful to recognize them. So I didn't. I just stuffed them down and tried to forget about them. Now, in therapy, I'm going back and trying to reach them. These feelings are me and now I can let them be me.

◆

Mounting a successful defense in the battle of daily survival didn't come without some major costs. Although your inner child survived, being sentenced to your own brand of protective custody meant that you grew up with a secret. You may have felt obligated to keep the abuse a secret for any number of reasons: fear of retaliation, loyalty to your parents, or even out of a misplaced hope that your parents would somehow see the error of their ways and give you the love that you so desired. Keeping the abuse a secret means that you also had to keep your reactions to the abuse under wraps, which again left you feeling alone, helpless, and trapped. With so much of your energy being directed to your front line of defense, it is not surprising that there was less available for your inner child who may still yearn for attention, support, and validation.

JOURNAL QUESTIONS

1. *What were the buried feelings inside you as a child that expressed your true reaction to the abuse?*

2. *What does this inner child say about the abuse and what you did to survive?*

3. *What parts of your inner child are still locked inside?*

STRATEGIES OF SURVIVAL

Abused children develop a variety of behaviors, defenses, and coping strategies all dedicated to self-protection. Psychological defenses are mobilized in the same way that military defenses are constructed: All resources are poured into the front lines. In the case of child abuse, the war zone lies between you and the person in your family who abuses you. Much of the psychic energy available to an abused child is devoted to this external layer of self-protection. Like many abused children, you may also have developed an uncanny ability to perceive threats and mount an immediate counterdefense when the situation calls for it. You may undermine your emotions because they undermine your show of strength. All of these efforts have one purpose: to protect you against being psychologically overwhelmed. Although most adult survivors can point to particular situations in which they felt like they might not make it, the fact is that you did make it. Your defenses held and the vulnerable child lying inside your protective cocoon was saved. Whenever you feel in doubt about your chances for recovery, return to this thought and tell yourself that it will never be as bad as when you were a child.

Following are some of the roles and survival strategies you may have employed. The more you understand how these strategies worked *for* you as a child, the better you can recognize how they may be working *against* you as an adult.

COMMON ROLES OF ABUSED CHILDREN

There are five roles that are most commonly employed by abused children to help them cope with the abusive family environment. These categories are often overlapping in that children may use one or more roles to cope in different situations. But, more often than not, one role will represent the child's primary approach to the world. In these roles are the seeds for the adult survivor's later personality style.

The Caretaker. The caretaker or rescuer role is perhaps the most common role employed by abused children, especially female children. Designed to deflect abuse by making themselves helpful to the parents in any number of ways, caretakers are the best example of the role reversal in which abusive parents and abused children engage. By becoming pseudoparents, and making themselves indispensable to the parent, the hope is that they will be good enough to be spared from abuse. The caretaker is the role of choice for adult children of alcoholic parents and is the foundation of the codependent personality.

Susan

I think I was about eight or nine when I took over the female role of the family, and everyday my mother would write notes for all the things she wanted me to do. She would make big numbers and say, "(1) Turn on oven to 350 degrees. (2) Take casserole from icebox; stick in oven. (3) Do the white laundry. (4) Vacuum the living room." And so on. Ours was a very sexist family. I did all the female roles in the family while my brother didn't really have to do his stuff. I did the dishes, I did the setting of the table, I did the laundry, did the folding, did the ironing. I think work is a natural outlet for me and I learned that you can avoid a lot of feelings by being busy. And it was the one area where I felt effective and productive and good because I was accomplishing something.

◆

The Recluse. The recluse copes with the family situation by avoiding the involvement of the caretaker, and absenting himself, emotionally or physically, from the family. The rationale is, if you are not around, you can't get abused. The recluse may hide in closets or have some secret place to go during the crisis periods when the abuse episodes are more likely to occur. The recluse must be fairly shifty and able to be self-sustaining. He often develops his own internal world through play activities and fantasy that may give him everything his real life lacks. Boys and girls seem to share this role equally.

Richard

For most of my childhood, I played alone or with my little sister. I never had that many friends. I might have had one good friend at a time who I would play with. We would play soldiers for hours on end. Sometimes we would play in my room with the lights turned out or find a place outside under the back porch and set up our armies in the dirt. It was an escape. I also read a lot and went to a lot of movies and watched television a lot and escaped that way. I tried to stay away from my mother as much as possible. She wanted me to take care of my younger sister, which I did more as a relief to get my mother off my back. There was also a time where I was running away from home. I'd get my bag and take off for a few hours and then get scared and come back. She would be ranting and raving when I got home and threatening to throw me out for good if I didn't shape up. I look back on it now and I can see that I was always doing something to get away from her.

◆

The Scapegoat. The scapegoat or victim is the lightning rod for abuse: She attracts more than her share. She is often perceived by the family as the problem child or the black sheep. There may be something different about the victim that predisposes her to this role: She may be overly aggressive or provocative or perhaps has some special need or disability that singles her out. The victim may actually encourage this role even though she may be paying for it dearly. In essence, it is a role that gives her some identity as a person but the identity is built on her negative feelings about herself.

Leigh Anne

I was always the scapegoat—the bad girl, the one with the sassy tongue, the one that refused to bend to their will. My family didn't like females, so being the only girl, the role was cut out for me. I admit that I played it out. I would say things that would get me in trouble. Even when they were hitting me, I would get sassy back and get clobbered for it. They put me down, and put me down, and put me down, and I'd have to fight back just to function. That's how I deal with my problems: I stuff them down and they eat at me, until finally, I blow up and it will cost me in some way. I'm still real defiant and am just beginning to see that it doesn't work for me. But it worked as a child because it was the only way that I could protect myself. I knew I was going to get hit. Now, as an adult, I realize that it was a poor way of reacting under stress to authority.

◆

The Hero. The hero or heroine is the child who stands out for some particular achievement in academics, sports, or performing arts, or civic leadership. This role is less common than the others and we usually see it in children of exceptional abilities and in families where the physical or sexual abuse occurred later in childhood. These children are the quintessential overachievers who seem to succeed against all odds. The secret to their success has to do with channeling their pain and anguish *outside the house* into productive activities that bolster their self-confidence. The payoffs are obvious: attention, recognition, and adulation from people who can give these things to them. The real payoff, however, may be more emotional: Being the stellar performer temporarily relieves them from their insecurities about themselves and their family.

Pete

Sports were a very big part of my life at all times, and I got some recognition for myself because I was pretty good. I was into all the sports—football, baseball, and especially basketball. I would say that hoop was my best game. I played for school also and we had some pretty good teams. I got a lot of satisfaction from playing sports and it helped to make me feel better about myself. I also learned all sorts of skills that have helped me a lot. Playing on a team is like a family and it gets you into a whole social sphere that was real important for a guy. Sports set up a lot of things for me because it was so plugged into school and my social life. I learned to get along with people in groups and cooperate with them for a higher purpose.

◆

The Bully. The bully is the tough guy who is identified with the offending parent and follows suit by being overly aggressive or even abusive with his siblings or peers outside the family. "The best defense is a good offense" is his motto. He seeks to reverse the power imbalance that he sees causing his abuse by picking on weaker children. Underneath the aggressive bluster, however, is a scared and usually severely abused and neglected child who has few, if any, positive role models with which to identify. The bully is the next generation's offender, and his behavior as a child indicates that he has already begun his career as an abuser of children. Boys adopt this role much more often than girls.

None of the six survivors presented here adopted the role of the bully in a primary way. However, most children who are abused have some aggressive part of them that may find expression through activities where aggression can be discharged, experienced, or somehow justified. Sometimes these feelings are organized around specific situations, such as sports, dating, or hobbies, where their expression is more disguised.

Pete

I remember getting real angry over disputed calls in baseball and basketball games. I'd also get into fights and play real aggressive. Of course, we were kind of encouraged to play hardball—you know, fly into second base with your spikes up. Looking back on it now, I think I was taking my rage out on my opponents. I was actually pretty aggressive, but at home I was always feeling more guilty and passive—like my father. I guess what was happening was making me real angry and I would take it with me and dump in on someone else in another situation. Sports were perfect for that. I really love competition and winning and I always played with a lot of feeling. That's one of the reasons why I was good—because I played hard. If someone messed with me—fouled me or applied a hard tag—I'd come up fighting and my aggression would just pour out of me. I would be hot for hours, although it always made me feel better the next day.

◆

JOURNAL QUESTIONS

4. *What primary role did you adopt to survive your family ordeal?*

5. *As you grew up, did your role change, and if so, what new roles did you accept?*

6. *From your point of view today as an adult, how did these roles benefit you? What were the downsides of these roles?*

7. *What are the secondary roles that you may have adopted in certain situations?*

8. *How do you see these childhood roles being played out in your adult life?*

PSYCHOLOGICAL COPING STRATEGIES

Besides the roles that you adopted in your particular family, you also relied on a variety of psychological coping strategies to help you deal with the ever-present threat of abuse. As children, these defenses were your allies, although now during adulthood, they may greatly limit your experience of yourself and your life. Some of the seven defense strategies, such as denial and repression, are universally employed by children and adults to cope with everyday life whereas others are expressly created to protect the child from the overwhelming reality of the abuse. These latter defenses are both causes and effects of the major roles adopted by abused children and adult survivors. Identification with the aggressor, for example, is the prime defense for the child who takes on the bully role and for the adult survivor who becomes an abuser. Turning against the self is the hallmark of the scapegoat role and, to a lesser extent, the caretaker role, where the child develops an internal expectation of being taken advantage of by others. These roles and defenses seem to mutually reinforce each other as the overriding need for self-protection shapes the child's developing identity.

Denial. Refusing to accept the existence of a thought, feeling, or behavior is denial.

Susan

I think denial is in my family's blood. Especially with all the alcoholism and craziness on my stepdad's side. Nobody in the family ever talked about what was going on, how unhappy they were, or how mad we were at him. I think I just tuned it all out. If no one was home, I'd open all the windows and just let my mind go. I'd leave it all behind me— no hassles, no fighting, no disgusted looks, no shitty feelings. I learned to not see things because I had seen enough. We denied to ourselves how crappy things could be just so we could go on. My family could be very dreary and then very tense so I learned to zone things out before they could get to me.

◆

Denial is as automatic and pervasive in abusive families as it is in alcoholic families. While the children cannot deny that they get hit or molested or criticized, they can certainly deny that it affects them, or they can minimize how bad it might have been. Denial teams up with repression to make events and the meanings of particular events seemingly disappear behind a curtain of fog. By denying or minimizing the meaning of their parents' abusive actions, children can maintain the illusion that their parents are caring, loving people who are doing the best for them. This gives children hope that they will be all right.

Repression. Repression is the pushing down out of conscious awareness the memories, reflections, and thoughts that are too overwhelmingly negative for the conscious mind to handle.

Shirley

I just did not allow myself to feel the pain. That was my basic plan on dealing with the abuse—cutting off the feelings and pushing them away. They made me feel too awful. I had to get away from them, do something else that would distract me. Actually my family helped in this matter because I wasn't being believed either by my mom or my dad. They didn't think anything was wrong with what was happening. So I think their own denial made it easier for me to avoid the feelings by not validating why things felt so gloomy to me. And I had plenty of other things to deal with—the house, my younger brother, my illnesses. If I looked too hard at my situation, I would have gotten totally depressed.

◆

Repression is responsible for the lack of memories that many adult survivors complain about. If massive repression was necessary to protect yourself during episodes of severe abuse, then partial amnesia or selective memory may develop around these incidents, leaving gaps in your childhood memories. The repression of old memories will gradually lift when you feel psychologically safe enough to face them and the feelings connected to them.

Dissociation. Dissociation is a mental process that separates the mind and body, resulting in a disconnection between physical sensation and conscious experience. This usually occurs during intensely painful, stimulating, or terrifying episodes of abuse. It is an extremely effective way of protecting yourself emotionally from experiences that were too horrible to endure.

Shirley

When my stepfather would sexually abuse me, I just pretended that it wasn't happening to me. I simply disengaged from my body and the sensations that went with it. I took my consciousness elsewhere for a few minutes until it was over. There was a window behind my bed, and I would pretend I was on the outside looking in at what was going on. Or if I were facing into the room, I would look into the mirror over my dresser and pretend that what I was seeing was happening to someone else, not me. That's how I dealt with it when it would happen. I just did not allow myself to feel the feelings. It was just too much for me to consciously experience what was happening.

◆

Shirley's experience is an example of the human psyche acting to protect her inner child's vulnerable ego. Many survivors report the sensation of "spacing out" or "numbing" when situations arise that repeat the abuse scenario such as during sexual relations, during angry confrontations, or while parenting one's own children. This form of dissociation is milder than that which occurs in moderate to sever abuse episodes, such as those involving physical and sexual abuse. While protective in function, dissociation can, over time, cause one or more "splits" in the survivor's developing personality that can turn into semi-autonomous parts. In extreme cases, dissociation develops into multiple personality disorder and may not be as rare as previously believed. However, this phenomenon is not always as dramatic as the media depictions suggest.

> **Turning against the self.** Angry and painful thoughts and feelings about a parent are redirected by the child against herself in order to take responsibility for the conflict she feels toward the parent.

Jolene

E very time I was sexually abused, I thought this had to be my fault because I could have done something about it and I didn't. I think about stuff that happened in the second foster home and later on with the father in my third foster home, and I think there was no way that all of this was not my fault—it keeps happening over and over again. I remember deciding that there must be something about me that's making these people think they can just do this. I told myself it had to be my fault because it happened when I was older. I was old enough and so I should have stopped them from doing it. I was clearly this horrible person anyway because this had been happening to me for years. I felt this was a loss of innocence—like I was marked for life. Even though I didn't like it, and somewhere recognized that this was not supposed to be happening, perhaps to this very day I still think that I caused it.

◆

Turning against the self may be among the most common defenses used by an abused child and psychologically is the cause for the child, and later for the adult survivor, to be revictimized. The child has an inherent tendency to twist or distort the abuse into something that implicates him. He does this for several reasons. As mentioned earlier, it protects the image of the ideal parent. Second, it gives him a sense of control over a situation that is hopelessly out of control. Third, young children are naturally egocentric, attributing events around them as somehow related to them. For these reasons, turning against the self can trigger the strong feelings of shame that are universal in the lives of abused children and adult survivors. Shame and defense can influence the development of a personality that is characterized by masochism, which during the adult years, can trigger the self-sabotage that is so common in adult survivors.

> **Identification with the aggressor.** Acting like the abusive parent by taking on his or her characteristics and behaviors in the hope that by being like the parent you will feel powerful instead of vulnerable, thereby being spared from further abuse. This process is illustrated by the phrase, "If you can't beat them, join them."

Pete

When I was a senior I met this girl at a party. She was kind of wild and seductive. As the party was winding down, we were all pretty drunk and she invited me and some of my friends over to her house to continue the fun. When we got there and started drinking some more, one thing led to another and she let me go all the way with her, right in front of my friends. When I was done, my friends wanted sex too and she was kind of willing. Nobody forced her, but she was pretty drunk and not really capable of making any kind of a rational decision. It turned into a gangbang—three or four guys, one after the other, with the rest of us watching. Back then, nobody thought this was wrong. If sex was even halfway offered, any full-blooded, American boy took what he could get. That's the message we got growing up. Only later did I feel bad about what happened, though I kept reassuring myself that she acted willingly. I already had terrible conflicts about my sexuality and this caused more doubts about myself as a male, about being sexually aggressive. I think as a result of what was going on with my mom, I had a real conflict with my aggressiveness and passivity. I turned passive most of the time when I was sober—I'd get myself beat up and wouldn't fight back. But when I was drunk, I became very aggressive, and looking back on it now, I think I was more aggressive with this girl that night than I realized.

♦

Not surprisingly, considering the type of abuse Pete was experiencing at home, his aggression was expressed along sexual lines with another woman. Boys and men are more inclined than women to identify with the aggressor for reasons relating to social role expectations for males as well as to the biological differences. The vast majority of sexual abuse is committed by men, many of whom were sexually abused as children. Identifying with the aggressor is a defense against the passivity and humiliation, which for abused males is an intolerable position.

Prostitutes provide the best example of females in our society who identify with the aggressor. This woman in Pete's story may have been using this same defense in her willing attitude to have sex with multiple partners. However, like Pete, she also may have been replaying her own sexual victimization at home.

Pete's story raises one of the most difficult psychological challenges for an abused child to resolve: what to do with all of the anger, hostility, and aggression that is produced by the abuse. What can the child do with these feelings and behaviors if he lives in an environment where he is unable to express these feelings in a healthy way? What happens when the child is so enraged that he feels unable to control these feelings? Aggression that does not find an outlet for expression during childhood can lead to unbridled violent impulses during adulthood. By expressing these feelings through appropriate channels, you can gain some control and mastery over them instead of feeling dominated by them internally.

Sublimation. Sublimation is the psychological process of channeling thoughts, feelings, and conflicts associated with a painful life experience, such as child abuse, into some creative activity, such as writing, playing music, or playing a sport, for the purpose of expressing and discharging the energy in a socially acceptable way.

Richard

I think the main thing I did to survive was making myself president for life and commander in chief of the armed forces of the country of Middle Myria, which was this extremely powerful and enormous continental nation in an as yet undiscovered place on the planet Earth. I lived to exist in this fantasy world. I played this way from the age of six until fourteen. And my friend who played with me called his country Dinosauria because he had all these plastic dinosaurs you could buy at the Museum of Natural History. He also had all these creepy crawler citizens, which of course lent the flavor to this creepy country he had. The game always started the same way—a sneak attack by his country who pretended to be friendly but really was a sinister enemy. Being attacked would allow me to annihilate him in war and appear morally superior. I played every role there was. I was most frequently Sergeant Rock and Major Steiner. I was able to wreak havoc at my command because I had this real powerful army behind me. It was a powerful fantasy, and it kept me totally engrossed and not thinking about much else. I was the good guy, fighting for freedom and the American way.

◆

Richard's account of his fascination with playing soldiers is an excellent depiction of the sublimation of aggressive feelings through fantasy play. Play is the most powerful expression of unconscious conflicts available to a child and Richard took full advantage of his play world to express his personal vision. The anger and hostility that welled inside him was discharged through a satisfying and creative rendering of a world where he could operate in ways that were denied him in his family relationships. In his active use of sublimation, one can see how he developed into a recluse by withdrawing from external reality into his richly rewarding internal world where he was the undisputed master of his kingdom.

> **Compulsive ritual.** A compulsive ritual is the performance of some idiosyncratic behavior that offers a sense of control over the anxiety that comes from some perceived threat or challenge. Compulsive ritual is the actual name for superstitious behavior.

Richard

I was always very anxious about going to bed because in my house you never knew what you would wake up to. Was this going to be another night where my mother was going to storm into my room and wreck everything. I never knew. I'd get down on my knees and fervently pray every night. I'd say, "Please help me to be—and I would list the qualities that my mother would always rage at me that I didn't have—thoughtfulness, consideration, generosity, industriousness, and so on down the list and then I would say, "Please God, help me survive tomorrow. I love you, and I will never lose faith in you." Then I would always have to sleep on my right side because somehow I figured that the bad things would happen to me during the day would also happen at night in my sleep if I ever rolled over on my left side. So if I could train myself to always sleep on the right side, I thought I could somehow prevent anything bad from happening. I had this elaborate system that I developed to make sense of this. I felt that everything in the world was in balance and if something bad happened, then I was entitled to something good happening later on to balance it out. And it made the bad things more tolerable because I kept thinking I was storing up all these good things. Someday, I told myself, I would win a Corvette or something.

◆

Richard used the defense of compulsive ritual to control his anxiety over being assaulted by his mother while asleep. Children often feel vulnerable prior to going to bed because it sets the stage for nocturnal fantasies and fears over which they feel they have little control. In Richard's case, the vulnerability was exacerbated by the very real threat of random violence directed at him by a mother he had grown to mistrust. Children engage in what is called magical thinking to explain events and situations in ways that give them some illusion of control. Looking back on these often peculiar ideas, you may smile at the ways that your child mind worked. Some superstitious behavior may even continue into adulthood as long as you believe it still works.

JOURNAL QUESTIONS

9. *Which of the previously mentioned psychological defenses did you use as a child?*

10. *How would you evaluate their helpfulness in making your life better?*

11. *Which of these defenses are still part of who you are today?*

FINDING A SOUL MATE OUTSIDE THE FAMILY

Many of you may have understood at an early age that you would have to turn to others outside your immediate family to enrich your life. Survivors have a way of finding some good people in the world to keep them going forward. Sometimes it was an interested teacher or a caring friend or another family that unofficially adopted you as one of their own. These people became your soul mates and probably left an indelible mark on your development. Think back to your childhood to those people who left a part of themselves with you.

Leigh Anne

I actually did quite well for myself especially at school with teachers and friends. I was very outgoing and friendly and would simply make people my friends. My teachers had kind of a funny saying that whoever Leigh Anne sits next to, that's her best friend. It was wonderful. I must have drawn upon my father's social tendencies and blended them into my own personality. My high school teachers loved me—they really did. I was an overachiever in school. I got really good grades and early on I started using my creative talents in music, singing and drama to get the attention that I craved. My teachers really saved me: They were the only ones who really seemed to care about me. They encouraged me; they saw my talents. They took me out to lunch. They gave me presents. There was a lot of good love there, and it continued even when I went to college.

They knew what was going on at home—it's hard not to notice when you have a big welt across your face. It wasn't a spoken thing. They didn't say, "Hey, is your father beating you?" Instead there was a silent understanding. During my senior year, my English teacher would write little notes to my parents for the purpose of praising me so that they would appreciate me more. I knew she really cared about me and was trying to help me out. She would write "Leigh Anne is wonderful. She's a pleasure to have in class. You should really be so proud of her." Then she'd put in a real telling line like, "I know it must be a result of the love that she has from home that explains how your daughter got to be so special." These memories are as clear as can be. I'll never forget them and I will always be grateful to them.

◆

Others of you may have attempted a most unique survival strategy: getting yourself "adopted" by a friend's family. You may have felt utterly desperate for a warm, understanding mother or a family that was relaxed and interested. This is a very adaptive strategy because it shows that you have not given up on people and can see that others may have something to offer you.

Pete

When I got older and had a girlfriend I would stay at her house a lot. I felt really close to my girlfriend's mother; she was like a surrogate mother to me really. She was the good mother who was kind, relaxed, and respectful, not weird or kinky—no noticeable pathology as they say! She would just listen to us and tell us her perspective on things without really pushing it on us. She was also very caring and generous. I felt Darlene was really lucky to have her as a mother. I certainly would have liked to have her as a mother. I think she knew I was having problems at home because our families didn't live that far apart and I imagine she heard about all the drinking. She would always take time to ask me how I was in that concerned and gentle voice of hers. I think I liked Darlene in part because I liked her family so much. My relationship was as much with her family as with her, although we did get to be close. When I visit home, I still like to stop in to say hi to her mom.

◆

Still others of you turned to friends or relatives who showed an interest in your plight and reached out to you, if only for a short period of time. Their concern, care, and guidance all need to be recognized and understood for what they meant to you. Keeping them alive in your memory will help you face the past and see that you have some good things to show for it.

Susan

There were two people in my life who helped me along at critical stages. And interestingly enough, both of them took on the role of protector of me. When I was young and living in Chicago, my aunt, my stepfather's sister, played a real important role because she protected us from the fighting that was so scary to us. She stayed with us until I was in the third grade when she left to become a nun. That was real traumatic for me because she had become a good mother figure to me, being that my mom was usually working. And considering that she came from the same family as my stepfather, it was very likely that she had her own set of problems. Fortunately for us, she had a lot of kindness too. I remember just crying myself to sleep for weeks after she left and keeping her picture under my pillow. While my mother and stepdad would have their screaming fights, and so on, she would be there for us, gathering us up and moving us to a quieter place.

After she became a nun, my feelings for her changed somewhat. We didn't see her that much, and when we did, I felt she wasn't very approachable. She seemed formidable somehow, unlike the soft, caring person I remember as a young child. In retrospect, I don't believe she was very happy being a nun. She eventually quit the convent got married, and took care of her mother, who she had a lot of guilt about for some reason. I guess she was miserable there also. Then one day I called the hospital where she worked and they told me she had died. My family told me later it was suicide. She killed herself by taking pills and putting a baggy over her head. I was read sad, but I wasn't really surprised. I don't think she was ever that happy.

The other person who became a kind of protector as well as a boss was the police chief of our town. I always called him Chief. My mother used to be the radio dispatcher for the police department for years and so he came to know our family. I'm sure he knew what was going on at home because the police cruisers would make our house one of their regular stops on their nightly rounds. We were always calling the police because of my stepfather's behavior. Later on, after we finally got him committed to the VA hospital and my mom took another job, I got her old job at the police department and became friends with the chief. I became the radio operator for the department—ten-four and all that stuff. After that I became his secretary and did police reports. He really cared about me also—kind of like a daughter I think. He was real concerned about me because I was pretty young—sixteen at the time. He really like the way I worked and how I kept everything moving in the department. The chief stood for law and order and responsibility and treating people right and giving them a fair shake and telling them when they were wrong. I trusted him more than almost any man I have ever met. You could always count on him to be the same, steady person. He was a real contrast to my stepdad.

◆

Journal Questions

12. *Did you have a soul mate—a special person, adult or child—who you confided in and who accepted you?*

13. *Describe this person and how this relationship helped you.*

14. *What characteristics, knowledge, or training did this person impress upon you that have stayed with you throughout your life?*

COPING THROUGH CREATIVE OR SPIRITUAL OUTLETS

For those of you who didn't have a soul mate to rely on while growing up, you may have turned to books, movies, plays, or music to help make life more meaningful to you. A real-life or fictional character who speaks to you through some creative medium in a way that touches your personal ordeal may fill your need for a role model or spiritual guide. If you tended to be reclusive, like Richard, you may have developed your own world, one that sought to nurture some unrecognized part of you. These activities provide an important release from the limitations of your life. They helped to express some of the pain and anger as well as providing meaning, hope, and spiritual guidance.

Shirley

I was very lonely as a child. I came to a point, I suppose, of docile acceptance of the way things were. It's like I had no choice, no options, no recourse available other than what was happening at home. So I escaped into a world of books and music. I played the drums, which was probably a godsend because I could just beat the hell out of them. And my real father gave me a stereo at one point. Any extra money I had went into buying records. I had music to fit my every mood, and I found myself often feeding that mood. I had selections from classical to jazz to hard rock. Someone who has been with me all through the years is Elton John. Some of his music really spoke to me. He has a song called "I'm Still Standing" that really captured the way I felt about life. I played that song over and over again, each time feeling nourished and understood. I would especially play it when I was feeling down and crushed by life—when I needed something to give me the strength to go on. It was inspirational. I identified with what he was saying so strongly and knowing that he felt this way too was incredibly reassuring to me. For some reason, it took my loneliness and my emptiness, filled the hole, kept me going, and gave me something to work with.

I also really connected to Janis Joplin and The Holding Company. She has a song called "Ball and Chain" that also put words and music to a feeling I had for a long time. I would put that song on full blast when nobody was home and sing that at the top of my lungs. Then I knew I wasn't alone. Someone else was feeling that way. Other times when I was quite reflective, I would listen to classical music. When I'm listening to classical, I can just let my mind go, and it can explore all realms of experience, and somehow it seems to make everything better.

"Beethoven's Fifth" was one of my favorites. The "Blue Danube" and
waltzes were real inspiring. I would listen to them when I wanted to
feel light and airy. When I was feeling confused and jumbled, I could
just let myself go and try to get some clarity. With Elton and Janis, I
could get really intense, like I was experiencing the pain with them.
But the classical music would let me go. It gave me my freedom.

◆

Many children who are being abused are introduced to religion and
come to rely on their faith to help them cope with their family experience. Religion offers compassion, meaning, and guidance that many
of you found so lacking in your own families. The belief in a higher
power may have helped you tolerate the wrongs that were being done
to you and gave you hope that some day your life would be better.

Shirley

Both my music and my faith gave me hope, besides letting me know
that I was not alone. My faith gave me a sense of comfort in knowing that there was a higher power watching over me and would not let
anything happen to me. I know that seems real contradictory considering what I was experiencing, but at least I was alive. I was surviving
and I knew that God was going to give me a better life in the future. I
did go to church. I wanted to. I wasn't a holy roller or anything and I
tried not to use it as a crutch. I knew I was going to have to solve my
own problems. But it gave me something that was desperately lacking
in my family. And religion was introduced to me during a happy time
and by someone who I respected—my grandmother. When we lived
with her during our early years, we went to Sunday school and vacation
Bible school right down the street. It seemed so normal and so much a
part of a normal family existence. I think it planted a seed. It helped
keep me intact and got me to where I am now. Somehow faith gave
me faith in myself as well as hope for the future. I knew there had to
be a better life and that I deserved it. I don't know where this came
from, but there was something in my inner core that kept me going
forward and kept me battling to survive.

◆

JOURNAL QUESTIONS

15. *If you had no "living" soul mate, try thinking of a character in a
    book or a movie with whom you identified.*

16. *What kind of activities helped you survive the abuse?*

17. *How did these activities nourish you as a child and what legacy did they leave you to build on as an adult?*

HOW THE ABUSE ENDED

In generations past, child abuse usually stopped when the child either grew big enough to forcibly prevent it from happening or old enough to leave home. It is important to note that in the lives of the survivors presented here, the abuse did not end because of the intervention of the other parent or the extended family or even the child protection authorities. It ended because of actions taken by the child. In all of the six cases described, no child abuse report had ever been filed despite the fact that in three of the cases—Leigh Anne's, Richard's, and Susan's—responsible authorities had known what was occurring. Ultimately the message to you, the child, who existed in abusive family situations may have been that you had to somehow survive on your own. If the abuse was to end, you would have to take matters into your own hands.

Leigh Anne

The physical abuse ended one day when I was seventeen. My father came into my bedroom and he started at me about something or another. I mean, I'm talking something minuscule because I never really did anything bad as a child. I never defaced property, I never stole, I'm a pretty honest person. I think my one drawback was that I could be brutally honest with people, which often got me into trouble. I remember he came into my room and started building up to a violent rage again. I could see the fire in his eyes, and I thought to myself, "I am not going to let this happen." I remember I was very conscious, and I was afraid I was going to go into my "psychotic shock" because I felt my body going limp. Finally he got himself sufficiently worked up and he lifted his hand to strike me. I took all that I could muster inside of me to resist going into psychotic shock, and this one time, I was successful. And all this rage just welled out of me, and I lunged forward and grabbed his shirt, and I ripped all the buttons off the front of it, and I shouted at him, "You will never do this to me again." I was shaking with rage and a million other feelings that were just sweeping over me. And I remember the shock on his face. His mouth dropped open and he said something that kind of snapped him out of it and he just left my room. And you know what—he never did that to me again. And I realized, "Shit. I could have done that long ago. What did I wait seventeen years for?" I didn't know that I had any control over being treated like that. But he never hit me again.

◆

Sometimes the child is willing to take action to prevent the abuse because he has grown worldly enough to see that what is happening in his family is not the norm for other families, especially the families of his friends. Armed with this knowledge, the child can take a stand to protect himself whereas before he may still have been dominated by his parents' authority. Much of this change has to do with the child becoming an adolescent and shifting his focus from the family to his peers. Challenge of parental authority is a normal development of adolescence that in the case of child abuse is clearly in the child's self-interest. However, as the girl or boy moves out into the real world, the chance for exploitation increases from nonfamily members. If the child was abused in the family, the chances of being revictimized outside the home are especially great during adolescence and young adulthood.

Pete

Eventually I stopped the sexual abuse, although it wasn't something that I thought out beforehand. It stopped because other feelings rose up that created so much conflict about it that it just had to stop. One Sunday morning my mother and I were waiting for my father to pull the car out of the garage before going to church. She turned to me and asked me if we had had intercourse at a certain time because she had missed her period. And I guess it just flushed out in me the horror of what was happening. I suddenly felt terribly repulsed. I turned away from her without saying anything. I don't know what it was. Maybe it was her acknowledging that it was happening and that she was actually talking about it as though she were speaking to her husband. Maybe it had something to do with it being discussed in such a matter-of-fact way when I wasn't ready for it. It stopped then. I never went to her again. Her response to my reaction was hurt and rejection. She led me to believe that it was wrong for me to feel that what had happened between us was inappropriate or unhealthy. And my response to her reaction was more guilt and shame. I would feel pulled to her and then repulsed by her. And she continued to control me with that as I got older.

◆

JOURNAL QUESTIONS

18. *At what point did you begin to realize that your parents' treatment of you was abusive?*

19. *Did this perception result in your taking any action to protect yourself?*

20. *What were your hesitations about reporting the abuse to authorities or telling someone in a position of responsibility?*

21. *What point in time do you remember the abuse stopping?*

22. *What were the circumstances involved here and how did you feel about the abuse finally coming to an end?*

Surviving abuse as a child was a heroic accomplishment. You may have never recognized what an ordeal it was because you were so busy struggling to survive each day. Hopefully after reading this chapter you will have a greater appreciation for what you did to survive. It may be possible now to recognize what roles you adopted, the psychological defenses on which you relied, and the creative survival strategies that allowed you to develop some of your potential as a person. Perhaps the most critical question at this point is what happened to your inner child? Has your emphasis on protecting yourself over the years pulled you away from the more vulnerable parts of yourself that represent the real you?

Continue to use the journal questions at the end of each section to call up the memories of the past. Try to sketch in your conscious mind the kind of survival strategies that you employed to cope with the abuse. You may find it scary to answer these questions. Remember that you are free of your family and can discover your own understanding of what your childhood meant. Do what you can to resurrect the past and then give yourself some time to digest these important memories and feelings. In particular, make a note of the positive things you did to survive, such as establishing some healthy friendships, developing personal interests or hobbies, or escaping into books or fantasy play that relieved your distress and opened up a new world. There is a silver lining in these often desperate attempts to survive, illuminating some inherent talent and character strength that can now serve you as an adult. Look to find these strengths and talents, recognize them and nurture them as you read on. You will return to them again and again as you continue on the road to recovery. Your next step is building awareness about how the child abuse shaped your life as an adult— before you made a decision to heal.

◆

PART II

Lost Souls:
The Adult Survivor
Before Recovery

Chapter Four

COMMON
PROBLEMS OF ADULT
SURVIVORS

It is years later and your childhood ordeal is finally behind you. Released from the domination of your family, you may have felt relief and excitement over your newfound freedom. You may have gone to college or gotten a job or simply hit the road without looking back. Some of you may have entered military service while others of you turned to the clergy or joined some commune that promised a different type of family. A few of you may have felt unprepared to strike out on your own and instead moved down the street from the family home—far enough away to avoid another round of abuse but not quite outside their range of influence.

FREE AT LAST

Confident that you would now be calling the shots in your life, you might have expected that the problems of the past would be left in the wake of your family life. Optimistic but cautious about what the future might bring, you go into the world not knowing exactly what to expect, but knowing that it could hardly be any worse than what you have already lived through. You have survived and the road ahead never looked better.

Leigh Anne

I left home on my eighteenth birthday for college. I had picked the college that was furthest away from home, not because of the academic credentials—I just really wanted to get as far away from my family as I could. My mother was against it of course—I expected that. But I talked, or rather pleaded, with my father to let me go and he finally agreed. For that I will be eternally grateful to him. So on my eighteenth birthday, we got on a plane together, and he took me to the Midwest, and he stayed overnight. He got me situated in the dormitory, and met the other people on the floor, and made sure everything was OK. That night as I laid in bed I thought, "I'm free. At last, I'm free."

◆

Those first years out of the family may have been the best years of your life. The difficulties or set backs you may have initially encountered were nothing compared to what you went through as a child. Decisions had to be made about which direction in life to take, but you told yourself that you were still young and had plenty of time. It was time to sit back, enjoy whatever you found that was fun, and let the dust settle on the upheaval that was your childhood.

Leigh Anne

When I went to college I thought I could be this renewed person. I didn't talk about my family or my childhood—none of my friends knew about it. Eventually my best friend from high school ended up leaving her college and coming to live with me. She really knew where I came from. But silently we agreed to never look back. We just presented this new face to the world like two brand new people. I knew she had secrets also, but we both just didn't want to be associated with them. I started to grow as a person and discover exactly who Leigh Anne really is. It was my hippie time during my early twenties. I started wearing crystals and learned how to meditate. My friends were all healers and into meditation, and it was wonderful. I'm so glad I had this segment of my life because it was a time for refreshing and renewing myself. It was also a time of soul searching, which musically corresponded with my beginning to sing a cappella. This was one of my first efforts to heal myself—to resurrect my spirit and my self-esteem.

♦

You may have made a conscious decision not to tell anyone what had happened to you as a child, or maybe you made no decision at all. The scarlet "V" that seemed affixed to your forehead, branding you as a victim, now seemed to fade. You had genuine hope that the past would not rear its ugly head and you could become the person you were destined to be.

For many survivors, turning your back on the past was a thought-out strategy for coping with the future. In other cases, the decision to not share your past was more unconscious—a by-product of a hazy memory and a cooperative psyche. It was as though your mind had drawn a filmy curtain over your recollection of the past. It was a huge relief to let go of the awful memories and go forward with your life.

Richard

It was at boarding school during my senior year when I first started to feel like I could shake loose from my family. I told myself "Wow, there is some stability in life. There can be approval from others that's available on a consistent basis." That was very liberating. I was making choices about colleges and I think I deliberately made a decision to break away from the East coast. I had developed this abiding antipathy for New England and Switzerland because it was so connected with my mother. So I deliberately came out West because I wanted to get away. I felt like I was really getting away from something horrible. And it worked. I mean, I've never felt at home in my life, and I came here, and I suddenly felt safe for the first time in my life. I moved into a dorm, and made lots of friends. I became immensely popular, which is ironic after years of being the shy, withdrawn kid who no one wanted to play with.

♦

Everyone writes their own script for their lively twenties. For Leigh Anne and Richard, college provided a clean break from their families and an opportunity to discover who they really were. Interests, friendships, and even spirituality could flourish in an atmosphere devoid of the terror and tension of the past. Some of you may have seized the opportunity to shape your own destiny whereas others pulled back in defense. One way or the other, you set out to write the next chapter of your life.

Susan

I never went to college. For eight or nine years, I just moved around the country and worked at all sorts of jobs. I was in the fast track—have job/will travel. I've always had very interesting, unique jobs that were really challenging and appropriate for my skills. For me, working hard made me forget the past. As soon as I was eighteen, I moved out to California to live with my gay cousin who I had been pen pals with for many years. I got a job with a medical instrument company as a secretary in the personnel department. Then I went up to Oregon for a while and worked as a domestic for a friend who was having a bad pregnancy. Then I moved back to San Francisco with my cousin and started my career in computers. Then I moved to New York for a job organizing a word processing center. Later I developed an addiction to amphetamines that I took for weight control and because it made me so efficient. I needed them because the responsibility of the job I took on was enormous. I was running scared a lot—operating on the brink of disaster. I always felt that these people who had hired me were going to find out about me and I would lose my job. I didn't even know who I was at that time. But I knew I could work and for a while that's all I did.

◆

For people like Susan, life became a series of one-act plays—brief roles and many changes of scenery. Workaholism became the adult strategy to avoid the past. You may have found yourself in a winning situation only to grow uncomfortable with your success. You were unclear about who you were, more often than not defining yourself according to the situation. You may have become a chameleon—a master of all personas except your own. You found yourself going through life on autopilot, doing the same thing over and over without any sense of direction. For Susan, the pattern of moving began to feel like running scared.

JOURNAL QUESTIONS

1. *What were the circumstances surrounding your leaving home?*

2. *How did you feel about your family at that time?*

3. *What thoughts did you have about your childhood?*

4. *How did you cope with the transition into adulthood?*

5. *What hopes did you have for yourself in the future?*

NEW PROBLEMS, OLD FEELINGS

There is a predictable pattern that a survivor's life can take after leaving home and striking out on your own. After some time has elapsed, be it months or years, the glow of excitement about gaining your freedom begins to fade. The euphoria of living on your own gradually gives way to the toil of meeting adult responsibilities. Bills pile up, jobs don't work out, relationships that once seemed so promising become mired in conflict. Everyday problems take on enormous proportions. If you have children, you may find yourself losing patience or feeling trapped by the endless demands. Ever so gradually, life seems to knot up into a new set of problems. You may have started feeling some of the old feelings from your family days—depressed, hurt, angry, anxious, helpless, frustrated, and stuck. You may have noticed that people around you seem to have an easier go of it. You begin to wonder why things always seem so difficult for you. You feel like you are spinning your wheels and going nowhere.

Leigh Anne

Eventually I fell back down. I mean there were those moments when all seemed so positive but I was still in denial about the past and ultimately something would happen to bring me down. Sometime in my sophomore year, the money stopped coming and my tuition came due. My grandmother gave me enough for one more semester, and when that was over, that was it. My mother had prodded my grandmother not to help me. She was still going to sabotage me. So I was faced with having to work, but at least my mother wasn't going to be able to get me fired now. I told myself I was an adult now, which meant that I had the power to make the change. But it was much harder than I ever thought. I became angry, very angry whenever I ran into a problem. I had a whole lot of negativity. I just saw what I wanted to see and ignored everything else. When things didn't work out, I was a total downer—I put myself down, I put my friends down, I put my work down, and I put my living situation down. I would get very nervous about how things were going, half expecting some calamity. I literally had to move in order to feel OK. So I would quit my job, get up and move to some other living situation, which sometimes included living in my car or sleeping in the woods—I've done that many times in my life. If I couldn't handle something I would just run from it.

♦

At first, the tendency was to blame the situations that you got caught up in—the people who didn't treat you fairly, the jobs that asked too much of you, and the circumstances that never seemed to favor you. You felt unlucky, as though you were born under the wrong stars. Nothing that you tried seemed to work.

Pete

I graduated from the college near my home and left home for the first time. I joined VISTA, which is like a domestic version of the Peace Corps, and accepted a project out West and moved there. I got an apartment with three or four guys who were all VISTA volunteers and we moved in together. Once I got away from home, the problems immediately took center stage in my life. I wasn't able to be productive in my job. I think it was the first time in my life that my emotions were so strong that they prevented me from overachieving. The local VISTA office was a well-run organization, but I couldn't function very effectively at that time—I just couldn't deal with pressure or the feedback very well. My communication with people started breaking down and getting fuzzy. My feelings seemed to overpower me and prevent me from thinking logically and concentrating on the project at hand. I felt like I wasn't cutting the mustard there and that made me feel really horrible.

♦

Once again, you felt against the wall, but the wall was no longer in your family—the wall was in your life; the wall was in you. "Were my parents right when they said I would never amount to much? Is adult life only a different version of the childhood hell that I thought I had escaped from?" The old fight to survive the child abuse must become a new fight to save your life. For some of you reading this book, this may be the point where you are at this time. For others, it may have marked the starting point for your recovery some years ago.

Shirley

My adult life began at nineteen when I got married to my high school boyfriend. It was to be my ticket out of the family, but in a way it was only more of the same. I had a great need for love and for not being alone. I was hooked on people who needed to be taken care of. My husband came from an alcoholic family and, of course, he was a practicing alcoholic. I'd cared for my parents all my life so it was natural that I would be drawn to those kind of people as an adult. He eventually walked out on me. I was devastated. I dropped forty-one pounds—I was skin and bones. Despite his drinking, he had been a very good father, and probably a better parent to the children than I was. But he just walked away from it all, leaving me with all of the responsibilities. So here I was—I had to sell the house before I lost it, my car was repossessed, I was trying to take care of my children, trying to get my life together, and just going nonstop. Three weeks later, I found out my mom had cancer and had to have a mastectomy. My younger brother who I practically raised was going through some horrible thing. So I was back taking care of my family again. I was paying a big price for this in terms of my physical health, sick all the time, missing work, practically living in my bed. Finally this doctor said, "Hey, you're killing yourself with your own life. It's time to make some changes."

◆

JOURNAL QUESTIONS

6. *What kind of difficulties did you endure during your twenties?*

7. *How did you explain these disappointments you were having?*

8. *What feelings were triggered by people, jobs, and problems?*

9. *What attempts did you make to get your life on the right track?*

10. *What made you think your problems might have something to do with your abuse?*

THE DAWN OF AWARENESS

The dawn of awareness begins with a cold realization that your life is not working. Ironically, the problems that plague you can be the key to discovering the source of your misery. You begin to ask yourself why. Not the kind of "why" that lends itself to superficial answers or bemoaning lost opportunities. You are asking yourself what is wrong with the way you are leading your life. Why is it not working for you? How is it that the patterns of the past seem to be repeating themselves in the present? This is a necessary but risky question, because while it shifts the responsibility for your unhappiness from "out there" to "in here," it raises the specter of that old feeling of not being good enough that goes right back to your abuse as a child. The challenge today is to take responsibility for your life by asking the hard questions without the blame and guilt and bad feelings of yesterday. It may still be difficult to look at yourself and your current life without hitting yourself over the head with shame and condemnation. Reviewing your life will be a chancy and difficult next step, but it may teach you what is going wrong and how to get back on the right track.

Richard

My problems during my early twenties were caused by my unwillingness to work hard, or get good grades, or do anything for anyone else, until I got my due. I felt like I deserved two years on a tropical island with an endless supply of food and drink, and videos, and books, and games—two years of self-indulgent indolence, to make up for a life spent as a hostage of my mother. It was like what I would tell myself when I was little—all the bad stuff will balance out and eventually I'm going to win my Corvette. It finally began to dawn on me that I wasn't going to get it. I wasn't going to get the payoff for enduring all of this crap for so long. I felt rage, frustration, and sadness. It was devastating to have this lifelong illusion shattered. That was a turning point for me because it helped me stop this pattern of self-entitlement that got me absolutely nowhere.

◆

Sometimes the dawn of awareness is ushered in by hitting bottom with an addiction or growing tired of a self-defeating pattern, or in Richard's case, seeing the past for what it was—a loss that could never be replaced. The problems you face as an adult consume more and more of your energy until you come face to face with the wall of shame and desperation inside you. You cannot go on. After years of carefully constructing your denial of the past, it comes crashing down and you are forced to face the reality of your pain.

Susan

I finally hit rock bottom one weekend. I knew this woman who I've avoided like the plague because she was so bad into coke who asked me to babysit her kid and said that she would pay me with cocaine. So I was babysitting her kid, did a line of cocaine, and sat down to write a friend. All of a sudden, all these feelings just started pouring out of me. All the feelings and thoughts and fears that I'd had about the way my life was going. I was never one to cry—I've probably never cried for longer than a minute in my entire life—but that night the dam broke. I knew I needed to reach out to get help but it was the middle of the night. I guess I must have cried myself to sleep because I had a dream. I had this dream about this girlfriend who I often did coke with. In my dream, this girlfriend came over and I guess we talked, but I don't remember what else happened. When I woke up the next morning in my dream I discovered that we had had this party. There was a line of cocaine set out on the pocket mirror and a wine bottle lying on its side on my bedroom floor. In my dream I sat over the edge of my bed and just cried and cried and cried, and actually woke myself up crying. I was so relieved that it was just a dream, that it hadn't happened. I realized that the coke had made me feel like such a failure and I was so tired of trying to suppress all these feelings inside of me.

◆

You may be at this point today, saddled with a whole new set of worries, problems, and dissatisfactions. You may have tried to do something about it or avoided facing the problem altogether. You may still be confused about exactly what the problem is and look to others to explain why life is not working for you. Most survivors spend several years avoiding their problems and struggling through life. Of all the people—men and women—who I have seen in my psychotherapy practice, three quarters of them were over thirty. Most of them told me that they had been aware of their unhappiness for many years, but were never able to reach out to get help. Men, in particular, are extremely reluctant to get help because it means doing something they are culturally programmed not to do—ask for help, face their feelings, and share their experience of being vulnerable and taken advantage of. If you are thinking about entering recovery, allow yourself to just read this book and let the ideas mix with your own memories, thoughts, and feelings.

PROBLEMS FACED
BY ADULT SURVIVORS

If survivors of child abuse share many common experiences as children, it should be no surprise that they also share many of the long-term effects of child abuse as adults. These problems constitute a "survivor's syndrome" because of the pervasive impact on all areas of a survivor's life. Not everyone shares all the different types of symptoms nor do survivors share the same degree of intensity of the problems. You will have to determine which of the following problems are primary and which are secondary. Recognize what seems to apply to you, draw up an inventory of the difficulties, and write them down in your journal for future reference.

> **Relationship Problems.** Relationship problems include fighting, blaming, mistrusting, feeling misunderstood, having poor communication skills, and having difficulty with intimacy.

Adult survivors have a very difficult time initiating, maintaining, and enjoying relationships. Any kind of relationship may be problematic, ranging from collegial relationships at the workplace, to personal friendships, to parent–child relationships, to intimate, romantic relationships. Relationships for survivors may reflect the all or nothing syndrome—either too few or numerous relationships that come and go like some revolving door. In some relationships the survivor may assume a particular role that is inherently unhealthy, such as in a sadomasochistic relationship that gets played out in a remarkable duplication of the past parent–child abuse. Considering that child abuse most often occurs in the context of family relationships, the possibility of repeating old patterns in personal adult relationships cannot be underestimated.

Leigh Anne

I constantly draw people with addictive personalities in love relationships, although not necessarily in friendships. The difference between my friends and my lovers is worlds apart. My friends were always upstanding, highly intelligent, very creative, trustworthy people. On the other hand, the men that I get involved with are people who have addictive personalities—shooting up heroin, or snorting coke, or addicted to anonymous sex. I grew up watching my mother destroy herself and her family life because of that problem. I became the perfect co-addict—someone who gets her personal needs met by trying to save someone from an addiction. That's what felt comfortable to me. I've been physically abused most of my adult life by men I went out with—beaten, hit, robbed. And I kept thinking, "I can change them, I can change them." I felt like they needed me. It was validating to devote myself to fixing somebody.

◆

Relationship can be difficult because they require many personal characteristics and emotional capabilities that adult survivors have trouble with—trust, assertiveness, intimacy, self-confidence, good communication skills, the ability to give and receive affection, self-awareness, and empathy for others, and acceptance of one's own feelings and needs. The difficult relationship for adult survivors is characterized by fighting, feeling misunderstood, projecting blame on each other, and feeling overwhelmed by powerful moods. Frequently adult survivors anticipate rejection or nonacceptance and protect themselves by withdrawing into their shell or by becoming overly aggressive.

After years of not feeling the feelings or daring to express them to others, many survivors feel limited in the daily dialogue with a loved one. Making changes in your relationships begins with developing awareness about what mode of communication works and what doesn't. Try discussing with your partner when and how to best talk to each other. Other strategies for communication will be addressed in chapter 8.

JOURNAL QUESTIONS

11. *Do you find it hard to maintain close, trusting relationships?*

12. *Do you have a habit of choosing relationships that won't work?*

13. *Do you notice choosing a friend or lover because of a similarity or dissimilarity to your offender?*

14. *Do you find it difficult to give and receive affection?*

15. *Do you see a pattern of clinging or distancing yourself from someone?*

16. *Do you test a persons's commitment to you?*

17. *Do you expect to be left or rejected by your relationships?*

18. *Do you get anxious or scared when someone gets too close?*

19. *Do you often feel used or taken advantage of?*

20. *Do you often fight with little hope for resolving differences?*

> **Low-Self-Esteem.** Low self-esteem is feeling bad about yourself, expecting to be put down, feeling self-doubt, self-blame, and shame.

If there is one quality most survivors share, it is low self-esteem. Chronic feelings of being bad or unworthy or a "cut below zero" are intricately connected with all the other "self" words that may be used to describe the adult survivor—self-effacing and self-deprecating. Low self-esteem causes survivors to turn against themselves, to become their own worst enemy in a vicious redoing of what their parents did to them.

Shirley

If anyone really wanted to get close to me—genuine closeness and intimacy—I would be suspicious of their motives. I was always looking in friends for something to fill this hole within myself, instead of looking into myself for it, or having expectations of others that were just unrealistic, but, of course, I would never voice those expectations. I would never allow myself to talk about feelings before, so I had no way of asking for what I needed. If I needed to be held, it was difficult for me to admit that, let alone ask for it. I felt like I didn't have a right to have any kind of needs. I did not have a right to have any kind of love. And so I treated myself that way, which, of course, set up a pattern for how others were going to treat me. Over the years of my marriage, I increasingly felt used by the situation that I had helped to create. I was the caretaker, I was looking after my husband and kids, and when it came time for me—nothing. Of course, I'd never voiced what I'd wanted, but I secretly expected it, and when I wouldn't get it, I would feel both relieved and resentful.

◆

There are several factors that contribute to low self-esteem: the way your parents treated you, the message they conveyed about your personal value and worth, and the amount of power they granted you to make choices and control aspects of your life. While self-esteem is a fairly fixed attitude of oneself that can stay constant over the years, it is still a *learned* behavior and as such can be changed by rethinking and reworking old attitudes and perceptions about oneself. The first step in reversing low self-esteem is recognizing how you feel about your-self—the shame, the unworthiness, and the anger turned against your-self. And then you must learn to see how this shame pervades your life and causes you to make bad decisions, to give your power away to other people, and to not respect your own needs. Building self-esteem is a major concern for adult survivors and will be addressed in the recovery section of this book.

JOURNAL QUESTIONS

21. *Do you feel bad, unworthy, ashamed, or dirty?*

22. *Do you feel powerless to stand up for yourself?*

23. *Do you feel stigmatized or tainted by your childhood?*

24. *Are you endlessly critical of yourself?*

25. *Do you wish you were someone else?*

26. *Is it difficult to ever feel good about yourself?*

27. *Is it hard to feel entitled to success or good fortune?*

28. *Do you believe that others are more right than you are?*

29. *Do you compare yourself with images of perfection?*

30. *Are other people's needs more important than your needs?*

> **Self-Sabotage.** Self-sabotage includes self-destructive and self-mutilating behavior, attempted suicide, poor choices in personal and business affairs, and inability to protect oneself from harm.

Low self-esteem is the primary *feeling* of adult survivors, and self-sabotage is their primary *behavior* in the external world. Self-sabotage is any kind of conscious or unconscious behavior that undermines the survivor's successful functioning in the world. Self-sabotage may range from buying a "lemon" of a used car to losing one's checkbook to becoming involved with an alcoholic partner to engaging in life-threat-ening activities. You may allow yourself to be exploited by a boss, engage in physically harmful activities like cutting or tattooing yourself, or engage in unsafe sex. Typically the type of self-sabotage used is intricately related to the personality and issues of the survivors and their families. For survivors who grew up in addictive families, the self-sabotage may take the form of drunk driving or getting caught with illegal drugs. If their families were violent, the tendency may be to get themselves beat up or injured. In cases of survivors coming from wealthy families, losing money, getting swindled, or making bad investments may be the preferred mode of self-sabotage.

Shirley

In my adult life, I went through extreme bouts of depression and often thought of suicide, although I really only made one attempt. My husband caught me with a whole fist of pills I was about to take. I was in such bad shape but I had nowhere to go with the feelings except to use them against myself. I would physically abuse myself by biting myself in the hand and knocking my head against the wall. I took the skin off my knuckles hitting a wall. Once, I had to be taken from work to the hospital because I was too physically ill to perform my job, but I refused to admit it to myself. I could not separate anger and violence— to me they were one and the same. So I didn't know how to express anger in a constructive way, which meant that I had to keep it all bottled up inside or run the risk of becoming like my parents, which I vowed would never happen.

◆

Self-sabotage is linked with a survivor's tendency to become revictimized in a way that continues the past abuse. Studies have shown that survivors of child sexual abuse are more likely to be raped and assaulted as adults. Sometimes the self-sabotage may not be directed against the survivor but rather against someone the survivor loves. In families where sexual molestation occurred, the adult survivor who is now a mother may be surprised to find that her daughter is being molested by her husband or a friend of the family.

Reversing self-sabotage begins with building awareness of everything you do in your daily existence that sacrifices your happiness, satisfaction, and productivity. Remember, awareness first, change later.

Journal Questions

31. *Have you ever thought about suicide or attempted it?*

32. *Do you engage in life-threatening behavior?*

33. *Do you ever put yourself in dangerous situations?*

34. *Do you ever purposely harm your body?*

35. *Do you ever feel like your own worst enemy?*

36. *Do you have frequent accidents involving bodily injury?*

37. *Do you pick the wrong kind of people for friends or lovers?*

38. *Do you undermine yourself at work?*

39. *Do you often lose things like money, credit cards, and other valuables?*

40. *Do you make decisions without thinking them out?*

> **Sexual problems.** Sexual problems include sexual inhibition or promiscuity, flashbacks of abuse during sexual contact, inability to achieve orgasm or erections, low sexual self-esteem, pain or numbing during intercourse.

A variety of sexual problems and concerns have been associated with child sexual abuse, although there is much evidence to suggest that other kinds of abuse will affect the survivor's sex life as well. During young adulthood, survivors of sexual abuse tend to go in one of two directions: either avoidance of sex or compulsive sexual involvement. Either choice creates problems for adult survivors who may still be in denial about what happened to them as children. With a history of sexual abuse, adult sexuality takes on all sorts of past associations, memories, and conflicts that impair the development of a healthy sexual adjustment. Survivors' sexuality arouses far more than physical desire: It may trigger a range of painful bodily sensations and feelings of shame, guilt, and anxiety.

Pete

I think that the sexual abuse caused some terrible conflict inside of me about my sexuality and about myself as a man. For one thing, I think it really colored my sexual fantasies. I know I had a lot of fantasies about my mother and I would masturbate fantasizing about her body. When I got involved with my girlfriend, and even later with my wife, these fantasies would intrude into my mind while we were making love. Sexuality for me was filled with guilt and shame. I couldn't figure out what were appropriate sexual needs and what were inappropriate needs. I mistrusted my girlfriend and felt that satisfying her needs could somehow result in my being violated. Sexuality was all mixed up—feelings, concerns, and conflicts and I was right in the middle of it.

◆

Survivors with sexual problems often consent to sex when they really don't feel like being intimate, and then experience it as another episode of abuse. Having flashbacks during sexual contact where a sudden memory of the past abuse is triggered by some familiar touch, smell, or position is also very common. If violence or force was used in conjunction with the sexual abuse, survivors may mix up sexual and aggressive urges that may result in a preference for sadomasochistic rituals such as bondage. Sometimes sexual abuse can confuse a survivor's sexual preference. This connection, not yet fully understood by researchers, is suggested from comments made by survivors who developed a negative association to the sex of their abuser, which made it impossible for them to have intimate relations with people of that gender. Consequently they turned to people of the opposite gender to fulfill their emotional and sexual needs. Physical and emotional abuse can cause survivors to mistrust their partners, experience anxiety over the demands of intimacy, and feel uncomfortable with their body.

How can you deal with sexual problems? You can start by confiding in a trusted lover about your sexual feelings and what reactions and association you have to sex. You can suggest that he or she read chapter 8, written for spouses and partners. If you have specific symptoms or flashbacks, you may want to avoid sexual contact until you can resolve your feelings, perhaps sharing your personal reactions with a loved one who can provide understanding and support. Many sexual problems will need to be treated with professional help as explained in chapter 11.

JOURNAL QUESTIONS

41. *Do you ever have flashbacks of your abuse while having sex?*

42. *Do you ever feel numb, cold, or pain during sex?*

43. *Do you compulsively avoid sex or engage in promiscuous sex?*

44. *Do you frequently have problems with erections or orgasms?*

45. *Is it hard to say no to sex or do you use it to avoid intimacy?*

46. *Is your sexual arousal dependent on violent or abusive fantasies that are holdovers from the past?*

47. *Do you often feel dirty during or after sex?*

48. *Have you ever been sexually abusive toward another person?*

49. *Do you need to control sex in order for it to feel safe?*

50. *Do you have difficulty separating your adult sex from images of your abuse as a child?*

Symptoms of Trauma. Trauma symptoms include feelings of fear, panic, agitation and anxiety, sleep problems, numbing of bodily areas, nightmares, multiple personalities, problems concentrating, and feelings of being disconnected from your body.

Many adult survivors don't show signs of psychic trauma until years after the abuse ends. Psychic trauma is a psychological condition caused by overwhelming stress that cannot be controlled by normal coping mechanisms. Survivors often report feeling extreme anxiety, panic, general fearfulness, and feelings of disorientation. In the most extreme cases, dissociation (splitting of mind and body), numbing of the body and intrusive, repetitive thoughts and flashbacks to the abuse episode are also evident. The appearance of symptoms lets you know that your psyche is still trying to resolve conflicts associated with your past abuse. In that respect, the appearance of any of these symptoms is a helpful sign that something is wrong and immediate professional help is needed.

Pete

I reached a point where I felt like I was losing my mind. I had just turned twenty-three and my dad had just died. I felt like I reached an emotional bottom. I was still drinking a lot but had made a decision to try to stop because I knew I was out of control with it. I was so afraid all the time and it was affecting the way I functioned. I felt like I was having a nervous breakdown. I was feeling paranoid and was having anxiety attacks all the time. I had no idea what it was about. It just happened and I was totally at the mercy of it. Part of the feeling was abandonment—I felt so lost and afraid of everything. I was really tightly wound and trying not to show it because I didn't want people to think

there was something wrong with me. All of a sudden all of these feelings were erupting inside of me that I didn't understand and I couldn't
control. I was afraid that I was going to be permanently institutional-
ized. I started having self-destructive thoughts, actually thoughts about
self-mutilation—stabbing myself in the penis. I would have them
throughout the day and it started to become a compulsion. I felt so
horribly guilty about everything. I was just coming apart at the seams.

◆

Panic attacks involving hyperventilation and severe anxiety may be the
most common symptom of trauma and can be triggered by anything
your senses associate with the past abuse. Sleep disorders such as in-
somnia, sleepwalking, nightmares, and night terrors (a more extreme
type of nightmare occurring during nondreaming sleep cycles) are other
signs of unresolved trauma.

There is growing evidence that survivors of extreme and prolonged
child abuse are susceptible to developing multiple personalities as a
means of self-protection. In actuality, child abuse may be the major
cause of multiple personality disorders. In families where this develops,
the emotional environment is characterized by extreme violence where
the children are terrorized, isolated, and sadistically treated. The abuse
is often unpredictable, frequent, and extended in duration. It seems
that children who rely more on dissociating to protect themselves from
the pain and fear are more likely to develop this most extreme condition. These feelings, often never expressed during childhood, don't go
away. Instead they "bundle" together over time, to form a "subper-
sonality." These parts may temporarily take over from the survivor's
main personality and trigger a marked behavioral change. Sometimes
this second personality may be a "persecutor," which stimulates self-
abusive behavior and self-criticalness directed at the other main personality. This is the part of the survivor's personality that is identified
with the aggressor. Survivors who grew up in satanic cults, motorcycle
gangs, and extreme church families where bizarre activities and sexual
activities are commonly perpetrated on to the child are the most likely
to report multiple personalities.

When any signs of trauma are noticed, the best suggestion is to
get immediate professional help. You may need medication or hospitalization to control the anxiety if you feel totally unable to function.
The goal during this time is to make sure you are safe and protected
from hurting yourself. This crisis time will pass, but not before you see
the demons of the past that need attention in the present. Many survivors begin their treatment at this point and resolve the trauma with
good professional help.

JOURNAL QUESTIONS

51. *Do you have frequent panic attacks?*

52. *Do you have trouble sleeping or experience terrifying nightmares or sleepwalking?*

53. *Do you have sudden flashbacks of images or thoughts that are connected to the abuse?*

54. *Do you sometimes feel like another person?*

55. *Do you have partial amnesia or blackouts?*

56. *Do you fantasize a lot or feel disconnected to your body?*

57. *Do you have overwhelming anxiety that seems connected to a particular situation or stage of your life?*

58. *Do you have trouble concentrating or remembering?*

59. *Do you have periods of overwhelming grief or terror?*

60. *Do you often feel agitated and ill at ease?*

> **Physical Ailments.** Physical ailments include psychosomatic illnesses, stomachaches, headaches, asthma, eating disorders, skin disorders, and phobias.

Adult survivors of physical and sexual abuse frequently complain of a host of illnesses and psychosomatic problems during their adult lives. The most common generalized effects include stomachaches, breathing problems, muscular tension and pain, migraine headaches, incontinence, and sensitivity to illness and infection. In cases of sexual abuse, the breasts, buttocks, anus, and genitals may be the sites of discomfort, chronic pain, unexplained sensations, and feelings of fear and even phobias. Sensations of nausea, vomiting, and choking may have appeared when the survivor was forced to have oral sex. Incontinence has been found in survivors who have been brutally sodomized.

Illness can have many meanings for the adult survivor depending on her childhood experience and type of personality. Being sick can offer an opportunity for getting taken care of either by yourself or by someone else. For some survivors, the best care they ever received from their parents may have happened when they were sick. Being sick may be one of the few instances when survivors are good to their bodies. In many cases, however, illness can be the body's message that all is not well emotionally. When strong feelings are repressed, sometimes the unexpressed psychic energy crosses the mind–body threshold and establishes its presence in the form of bodily symptoms and illness.

Shirley

I didn't allow myself to feel the anger so it came out in the form of physical symptoms. These feelings were literally eating me away. I had every physical ailment in the book. Including minor surgeries, I had a total of fifteen operations in my life, not counting all the operations that I had following the car crash when I was a kid. I had a total of five operations on my stomach—it looks like a railroad map. I had chronic headaches and stomachaches all throughout my childhood and into my adult years until I started therapy. I had a complete hysterectomy after my third child was born, and a gall bladder operation, and I had my appendix out. I was having problems with my teeth. I've had torn ligaments and muscle tears as a result of playing sports. It got to where my friends would tease me that they couldn't recognize me without an Ace bandage or a cast. I was miserable. I was continually sick. It was just a vicious cycle; there was always something wrong. I noticed my children trying to take care of me the way I took care of my mother when I was a kid. I didn't want my children thinking that they had a sickly mother. Finally I had a doctor tell me I was physically killing myself. He told me that there was no explanation for all the medical problems that I was having and that it must be related to my psychological health. He recommended that I see a therapist. So I did. It was probably one of the first things I did for myself to change my life around.

◆

Sexual abuse in particular can affect gastrointestinal functioning while leftover feelings of anger may be related to migraine headaches. Eating disorders including anorexia and bulimia have been found in some studies to be more frequently found in women who have survived prolonged sexual abuse. The binging and purging behavior linked to eating disorders can offer survivors a sense of control over their bodies in a way not possible with the feelings. Phobias, such as claustrophobia, although not technically a physical symptom, are directly related to the circumstances of the abuse as in the case of a child being locked in a closet for hours as a form of punishment. Years later, closets will still evoke anxiety for the adult if the feelings of being locked up were never worked through in therapy. Skin disorders, back pain, ulcers, and asthma are other common ailments that are known to be triggered by stress. Sudden weight gain or obesity can also be related to childhood abuse, and is sometimes related to the survivor's need to feel more insulated from her body or present a more nonsexual appearance to the world, making her feel safer.

JOURNAL QUESTIONS

61. *Do you have a history of stomachaches or headaches?*

62. *Do you have any eating disorders such as anorexia or bulimia?*

63. *Do you have any loss of bodily functioning that cannot be explained by medical reasons?*

64. *Do you have any ailments that may be psychosomatic such as skin disorders, asthma, or lower back pain?*

65. *Do you have a susceptibility to infectious illnesses?*

66. *Do you have many health-related absences from work?*

67. *Do you have constant worries about your health?*

68. *Do you have significant weight fluctuations?*

69. *Do you have frequent fatigue and body aches?*

70. *Do you have negative attitudes about your body?*

> **Social Alienation.** Social alienation is not fitting in with people and groups, feeling different, not being accepted by others, and feeling stigmatized.

Most adult survivors feel stigmatized by what happened to them as children and experience people as dangerous, thereby avoiding them. Attending parties or other social gatherings can evoke anxiety, insecurities, and concerns over not being "good enough." Fear of rejection may be the most common concern for survivors who had so much of it during childhood.

Many survivors end up living in isolation because it feels safer and less threatening. The old role of the recluse employed during childhood to avoid the abuse can carry into adult life as protection against being hurt. Sometimes the threat is real; other times it is imagined. When survivors do venture into the world and attempt to establish contact with others, they may feel tremendously sensitive to how they are treated. Jokes or teasing, while intended as lighthearted banter appropriate in social situations, may be experienced by the survivor as critical or hostile and done at their expense.

Jolene

S ince I've been an adult, I've noticed that I want to be by myself all the time. During my twenties, I just started withdrawing from everybody. There were two parts of me—the outspoken politico who could lead people, and the depressed, withdrawn, and suspicious person who wanted to stay home all the time. Gradually that second part of me started taking over my life. I became a hermit, kind of like the invisible person. Part of it had to do with choosing people for friends and lovers that were just not good for me, who were controlling and critical. Eventually I resented the way I was being treated. Not knowing how to deal with it, I would get real upset and angry with them, which didn't solve the problem. So I withdrew. I got a phone machine to screen out the world. When I look back on my childhood, I really did have some good friends. They really saved me because the foster parents were so weird. But now it's different. I push myself to get out a bit and interact with people. But it's so hard for me to get close to people, to bare my soul and trust that they will have something positive to give back to me.

◆

Much of survivors' difficulties in social situations have to do with never having learned how to communicate. As children, their opinions and perceptions may have been ignored, invalidated, or judged as crazy, which left them wondering how to relate to people. Speaking with conviction, listening with interest, and telegraphing your openness to the other person through body language and nonverbal cues are hard lessons to learn if one expects rejection, criticism, and humiliation.

Overcoming the fear of social situations has to do with finding a group to belong to that gives you a positive experience relating to people. Visit some local self-help groups and just listen to what people are saying. Or you can call some of the national hotlines listed in Appendix B to speak with a volunteer.

JOURNAL QUESTIONS

71. *Do you often feel uncomfortable in groups?*

72. *Do you feel tongue-tied, nervous, or self-conscious?*

73. *Do you try to avoid social situations?*

74. *Do you feel that others may not accept you?*

75. *Do you feel different from other people?*

76. *Do you often feel misunderstood, blamed, or ignored by other people?*

77. *Do you either avoid conflict like the plague or attract it endlessly?*

78. *Do you assume a typical role in social situations that is not really you?*

79. *Do you lack trust in your judgment of social expectations?*

80. *Do you feel that other people have had a different experience of life?*

Difficulty in Handling Feelings. Such difficulties include feeling overwhelmed by anger, depression, and anxiety; having trouble recognizing, managing, and appropriately expressing feelings.

Adult survivors have all kinds of powerful feelings that are left over from the family abuse but live on in their adulthood when triggered by certain circumstances. Anxiety is caused by never knowing what to expect or how to act in social or family situations. Fear and anger are both natural responses to the threat or act of assault. Sadness is the result of recognizing that your parents could do this to you. Shame and guilt tell you that you still hold yourself responsible for what happened. Rage is the buildup of anger that could never be safely expressed within your family. Frustration is the feeling you are left with when nothing seems to go your way. Confusion is a sign that you don't know why this has happened or what to do about it. Alienation from others is the result of too many disappointments. Helplessness, hopelessness, and powerlessness are the feelings that tell you that you may have temporarily given up on life ever being better. Your feelings tell you something important about yourself, even if sometimes the message may be too scary to acknowledge.

Shirley

I'd numb myself with drugs and alcohol or push myself to the point of sheer exhaustion just to keep myself from thinking or feeling. I'm sure that's why I was sick a lot because I just wasn't letting any of these feelings get released. Instead of expressing what I was feeling, I would get bitchy and irritable—anything could set me off. But then the feelings would come out directed at my kids, which wasn't fair. I've always been unable to cry. I'd stuffed my feelings so far down and separated myself so much from them that I didn't even know what I felt. I could only recognize feelings through music: Even then it might take a few days. Nowadays, when I think something is getting stirred up inside I say to myself, "OK, I think I'm feeling anger, but is there more to it?

What else is with that? If I were to take away the anger, what else is under there?" That has been one of my biggest lessons in this recovery process.

♦

Survivors numb themselves when the feelings get too strong. Or like Susan and Shirley, who compusively worked themselves to exhaustion, you may adopt a workaholic lifestyle in order to avoid the feelings. Other may try to stuff the feelings by compulsive eating. Certain feelings like anger and rage may be so strong that they dominate a survivor's internal life, obliterating the other feelings that may also be there. At times like these, the survivor may feel very much a victim to her feelings. Learning to regulate the intensity of these feelings will be a future step in recovery.

For the time being, develop the habit of asking yourself what you are feeling at different times of the day. Some people call this a "gut check" because that is where the feelings often reside. Run through a laundry list of common feelings and notice if and when you are feeling something in particular. Write it down in your journal and describe the situation that might have triggered it.

JOURNAL QUESTIONS

81. *Do you have strong feelings of anxiety, fear, depression, and anger that threaten to overwhelm you?*

82. *Do you need to periodically withdraw from the world in order to regain control of yourself?*

83. *Do you have difficulty recognizing and expressing your feelings?*

84. *Do you tend to have an all-or-nothing experience of feelings? Intense or numb?*

85. *Do powerful feelings trigger the desire to eat, drink, take drugs, or engage in other compulsive activities?*

86. *Do strong feelings leave you feeling spacy, numb, or afraid that you've going crazy?*

87. *Have you learned to disconnect yourself from your feelings by refusing to pay attention to them?*

88. *Do you often lose control of your anger or abused someone else?*

89. *Do you often feel confused by what you feel?*

90. *Are you inclined to feel a certain feeling more often? Like anger or depression?*

Reading the information in this chapter may have stirred up many feelings and even more questions to be addressed in future chapters. Recognizing that child abuse may have had a tremendous impact on your life is a necessary step in your recovery. The pervasive tendency to sabotage yourself in any and all aspects of your life does not mean that you are a bad person; it means that you are a wounded person. Identifying the wounds and accepting the difficulties that grow out of them is an essential part of healing. Facing the anger that you have turned against yourself and possibly against others around you represents a cleansing of these wounds. As with the treatment of any wound—physical or psychic—the process will cause new pain. This may lead you to question whether the process of recovery is really good for you. You have been so used to pain in all of its myriad forms for so many years, you may wonder how this process of recovery can be positive.

When these doubts begin to mount, remember that you have survived the worst part of the abuse—your torment as a child. As an adult, you have new capabilities, new choices, and a lot more power to control your life. Try to collect momentos from your past family life and reconstruct what you felt as a child. Reflect about what your gut and your heart say about them. Use them to reclaim the past. Be open to a new understanding of what you went through. Allow yourself to draw inspiration from the positive elements in your life—your friends who support your recovery, family members who are also going through this process of change, your children who think the world of you, your spouse or lover who accepts you as a special person, or your therapist who is commited to helping you find your true self. Draw inspiration from characters in books, movies, or plays with whom you have a special connection. Do something that epitomizes the person that you want to become. Don't let the flame of compassion for your inner child expire under any circumstances.

There are many examples of people like yourself who came back from total despair and confusion to recover from the abuse and prosper in life. Leigh Anne, Richard, Shirley, Pete, Jolene, and Susan are but six people of the many millions who have converted the pain into personal strength that fuels their recovery. You too can find this inner resource of strength and use it to turn your life around.

Chapter Five

FIRST THINGS FIRST:
OVERCOMING YOUR ADDICTIONS

Addictions are the first cousins in the family tree of child abuse. Many of you grew up with an addicted parent, and now years later, find you have a similar problem yourself. You know firsthand how the drinking binges made your parent suddenly lose control with hitting or molesting, or simply losing interest. Some of you had a mother who was hooked on prescription pills, living life in a housecoat, leaving her responsibilities as a parent and homemaker to you. Or a father, addicted to alcohol and gambling, forever out of the house playing cards or playing the horses, always playing out the family paycheck. You can recall the scenes when he returned home drunk, broke, and angry and the ensuing fighting that would leave you frightened and alone.

If your parents were addicted to something—the bottle, dope, extramarital sex, any kind of compulsive activity—you probably ended up suffering for it. When you moved out, you may have been relieved to get away from someone else's problem. But, as we have seen, the past has a way of catching up to many survivors and addictions are a prime example. This chapter will identify the particular addictions afflicting adult survivors and the reasons why you may be vulnerable to them. Most important, it will describe what you will need to do to overcome your addiction so that you can get to work on your new beginning.

Pete

I began drinking when I was thirteen and then got into marijuana, which I continued using until I was twenty-four and began my recovery. As I say in AA meetings, I drank alcoholically right from the beginning—totally out of control. I was doing the same thing I saw my parents do from day one. Both of my parents were alcoholic, although they took turns being on the wagon. I was used to their ups and downs, their moods, the way the alcohol affected them so differently. My father was a passive drunk—quiet and withdrawn. My mother was another story—mean, hysterical, and I now realize, very seductive. My parents would let me drink at social functions. I guess their attitude was one of inevitability. They couldn't control it so they never attempted to control my drinking. The drinking had an immediate effect on me—from getting me thrown off the baseball team to having sex with my mom. It also allowed me to not see the parts of myself that I didn't like and the situation at home that was too ugly to face. But I had to face the problem in order to survive.

◆

It may be difficult to think of giving up an addiction that may be one of the few pleasures you experience in a life so affected by child abuse. Drinking or using drugs may fill the gaps in your personality, giving you confidence when you feel small, calming the feelings that seem so overwhelming, and offering a sense of self-control that is illusory but better than nothing. Whatever your addictions seem to offer you, it is clear that you pay a dear price. And you may still be unaware of it. Child abuse and addictions share a common trait: denial.

COMMON ADDICTIONS IN THE LIVES OF ADULT SURVIVORS

The term *addictions* is now accepted as the generic label for all kinds of compulsive behavior, whether it involves substance abuse or some out-of-control activity. Addictions are progressive, making their impact felt on everything from your decision making to choice of friends to kinds of work you feel comfortable doing. They create a personal dependency that actually reduces your control while at the same time giving you an altered sense of control. When the addictive behavior is challenged, you may feel particularly anxious, irritated, or withdrawn. You feel like you must feed the addiction or the old feeling of tension and anxiety may once again close over you. Ultimately you become a slave to your addiction, which leaves you a bystander in your own life.

ALCOHOLISM AND ALCOHOL ABUSE

A significant portion of you may be drinking alcoholically with little control over when to stop, or you may be situationally abusing it to medicate a feeling or provide an extra boost in confidence. Or you may have developed a tendency to abuse alcohol only after years of steady, social drinking. Whatever the causes, since you had already lost control of your life in childhood, losing yourself to an alcohol addiction may seem like more of the same.

Pete

From the very beginning my personality changed when I drank. From being somewhat quiet and introverted, I was transformed into a happy, glad fellow. I was a sloppy drunk—slow, stupid, and silly. When I drank, I couldn't stop and would drink myself into a blackout. Even at the age of fifteen, I knew that I had a problem. I forever tried to control my drinking so that it would do what it did for me and yet not create the problems that I associated with it—car accidents, blackouts, wetting the bed, humiliation, shame, and guilt. When I was eighteen, I tried smoking pot to help me not drink. But I couldn't control either of them and together they made things horrible. There's an old saying in AA: "When alcohol is used as a solution, it often becomes the problem."

♦

Alcohol abuse can cause blackouts during which the drinker does not remember what happened. In certain personalities, these blackouts can trigger a more ominous Jekyll-and-Hyde personality shift where a whole new personality emerges. Carl Jung, the Swiss psychoanalyst, called this the "shadow" part of our personality—the part that has been previously repressed but now takes over with the introduction of alcohol or drugs. It was during these periods when the "shadow" part ruled your parents' personality that you may have been physically, sexually, and emotionally abused. And now your drinking may threaten to do the same in a tragic repetition of the past.

DRUG ABUSE

The abuse of legal and illegal drugs is another common addiction for many adult survivors. Prescription pills such as painkillers, tranquilizers, and muscle relaxers are given by medical doctors to treat the numerous illnesses of which survivors often complain. Chronic illegal drug use including marijuana, cocaine, PCP, and heroin are also likely traps for the survivor who craves feeling good after years of being so depressed. As with alcohol, the physiological and psychological dependency fostered by chronic drug abuse can take control of you, change your personality and numb the pain lying deep inside.

Shirley

Drugs have been much more of a problem for me than alcohol, although I can't really control my drinking either. Beginning in childhood when I had that car accident that almost killed me, I was taking prescription pills for one illness or another. Later as an adult, my illnesses just got worse and I was either taking pills to treat some condition or taking pills to recover from some condition. It never stopped. You just get used to relying on them to make you feel better. I worked real hard to take care of everyone and somehow taking drugs and feeling good became my only reward for it all. When I got depressed, the doctor gave me more drugs, which I also got addicted to. Marijuana may be my favorite drug. It really relaxed me and allowed me to lose myself in music or television or reading. It's a fantasy drug and God knows I love getting lost in fantasies. When I was growing up, it was one of the best ways to forget what was happening. When I became an adult, smoking a joint put me exactly where I wanted to be—out of this world!

◆

Just which drug survivors choose to abuse often depends on their personality and how they cope with stress. For example, cocaine and other stimulant drugs such as amphetamines activate and arouse the user who may feel depressed and apathetic when straight. While the drug may "pick people up," it can also lead to extreme withdrawal reactions, impulsive acts, and aggressive behaviors. In contrast, opiate-based drugs such as heroin and barbituates typically result in a slowing down, which for parents can lead to physical or emotional neglect of their children. Hallucinogenic drugs such as marijuana, LSD, and hashish do something very different. Instead of changing their activation level, they have a "mind-expanding" effect on survivors who crave a different experience of themselves and the world.

EATING DISORDERS

Eating disorders are compulsive activities most often seen in women, although some male survivors of abuse develop them as well. These disorders are anorexia (starving yourself), bulimia (overeating followed by purging of food), and compulsive overeating. Male survivors with eating disorders tend toward compulsive overeating, with anorexia and bulimia being extremely rare. Many eating disorders are actually life threatening and can cause significant physical damage to your mouth, gums, stomach, and digestive track. Many female survivors develop the problem during the tumultuous adolescent years when they are struggling to break away from their families and discover their identity as adults. Adult survivors have many conflicts centering around sexuality, self-esteem, and self-acceptance that become entwined with food. Like other addictions, eating disorders can take over your life, something that survivors will need help in overcoming.

Leigh Anne

I was never overweight as a child. My eating would change when I was in a relationship. After years of being involved with alcoholics and drug addicts and seeing my weight fluctuate, I thought I finally found the right guy. We had been friends for nine years. We worked together as musicians and taught at a music school, and I always thought of him as the most wonderful guy—very gentle, very creative, and a wonderful musician. When we got engaged I thought my life was finally going to be different. Then one day I found out that he was an exhibitionist with a fairly lengthy criminal record for indecent exposure. Everything came apart. I immediately started binge eating and overnight I mushroomed out. Even though I've stayed this way for a while now, I know that it will come off one day. But I feel safer being larger—I'm not hassled by men anymore. I can settle into therapy and sort everything out. When I feel stronger, I'll work at taking if off.

♦

Besides insulating themselves from unwanted feelings, survivors may overeat in order to make themselves less attractive to prospective sexual partners, thereby offering a measure of self-protection. This is especially important if you have yet to resolve the feelings connected to your sexual abuse. Anorexia, on the other hand, may be connected with trying to make yourself more attractive to would-be lovers. Since many survivors typically do not regard themselves as attractive or "good enough," changing their appearance may hold the promise of finally being accepted and loved for who they are—something denied them by their family.

SELF-INJURIOUS BEHAVIORS

Many survivors develop a compulsion to actually harm their bodies by purposely cutting or mutilating themselves in some fashion. Women may "delicately" cut themselves with a knife or razor when they feel especially disappointed, pained, or loathsome. Men may engage in compulsive tattooing that on the surface seems like an attempt to billboard some macho message to the world. While all addictions are ultimately self-injurious, delicate cutting and tattoing are purposely painful and seem to be a direct outgrowth of the inner anguish that survivors carry with them every day of their lives.

Pete

After I began my recovery from alcoholism, I started having these thoughts about stabbing myself in the penis. This was really alarming to me because I knew this was screwed up but I just couldn't control it. It was the primary reason for my deciding to get professional help. It became an obsession with me but I was also terribly ashamed about it. This was before I started recognizing that what happened between my mom and me was incest. Eventually, in psychotherapy, I was able to figure out what it meant. I noticed that I started having these thoughts when I was feeling particularly bad about myself. Whenever I had sexual feelings—and I used to have a lot of them—I would feel really guilty and even loathsome as a person. Then it would start. I never actually did it to myself, although I suppose if I had never gotten help, it might have continued to get worse. It all went back to the incest with my mother and how bad I felt about my role in it. Stabbing myself in the penis was my way of punishing myself.

◆

Cutting, carving, or stabbing your body may be a most desperate effort to regulate the overwhelming internal pain by inflicting some lesser external pain that can be controlled by you instead of inflicted by another more powerful person. Because these compulsions have addictive qualities, the best way to deal with them initially is to try to substitute some new, less destructive, behavior. Sharing what you do to yourself or what you're *thinking* of doing to yourself with someone you trust is essential, despite the shame you may feel about it. As with Pete, it will probably connect back to your childhood abuse in some way. This kind of addiction is a cry for help. Getting into psychotherapy is essential to working out the underlying meaning of the self-injurious behavior.

COMPULSIVE RISK TAKING

Another addiction that is especially common for male survivors is compulsive risk taking. People can become addicted to the excitement and the threat of loss or death just as they can become addicted to substances. Sometimes the behavior may be disguised as a sport like skydiving, mountain climbing, hang gliding, or auto racing. In other cases, it may involve illegal activities like shoplifting, drag racing on highways, or part-time prostitution. Gambling may be among the most common risk-taking behaviors in that it puts one at financial risk. To understand your attraction to these activities it is essential to uncover your motivation to engage in them. It may be an unconscious suicidal or self-destructive act in which your lifesaving and life-destroying parts battle it out in socially sanctioned ways.

SEXUAL ADDICTIONS AND RELATIONSHIP ADDICTIONS

Many survivors—male as well as female—can become addicted to casual romantic relationships or particular sexual activities. Women who enter into relationship after relationship in which they get little or nothing for themselves have an addiction known as *codependency*. For men who are more inclined to separate sex from commitment the array of sexual addictions they may be vulnerable to is far more extensive.

Whereas women can become addicted to trashy romantic novels and television soap operas, men may develop an addiction to hard-core pornography. Men may fashion themselves as a modern-day Don Juan in compulsively hopping from bed to bed, never stopping long enough to discover the person within the body. Women who spend long hours in single bars may be just as addicted to anonymous sex, even while hoping to meet someone special.

Susan

I've never been one to ever track a man down, or call him, or chase him, or exhibit jealous behaviors. I'm almost excessively the other way, which is to play it cool—love'em and leave'em. During my twenties when I was moving all over the place and working like a maniac, I did a lot of sleeping around. I had an affair with my boss when I first moved out here. Then I fell into the married man syndrome and had some brief affairs with men who really weren't in a position to give much. Of course, I would sabotage it in some way. Then I would start seeing somebody else and the pattern repeated all over again. A lot of this was tied into my drinking and drug use and hanging out at bars and doing a lot of partying. I had real problems with trust and intimacy so I never wanted anyone to get too close. But on the other hand, I really liked sex and having fun and getting attention from guys. Only recently have I had "sober sex." It's real different to be physical with a man and actually feel it instead of going through it when you're loaded.

◆

Male survivors are prone to developing other types of sexual practices such as transvestitism and exhibitionism. Some men who avoid intimacy out of fear of rejection may develop an addiction to "flashing" their genitals where the rejection can be anticipated and therefore controlled. Male survivors sometimes become addicted to "cross-dressing"—using women's clothing to experience the feminine part of themselves. Cross-dressing is not considered an aberration in women because society allows women more freedom in expressing their masculine parts in the way they dress.

Other sexual addictions can involve certain types of activities such as bondage, humiliation, and sado masochism where intimacy gets contaminated by power, control, and even violent fantasies. The development of a fetish—the sexualizing of an object—may also reach addictive proportions for survivors who were inappropriately stimulated or deprived as children. Today, because of AIDS and other sexually transmitted diseases, compulsive sexual addictions can do far more than take control of your life—they can take your life away.

HOW SURVIVORS USE ADDICTIONS TO COPE WITH THE EFFECTS OF ABUSE

"Just say no" may be appropriate for children who have yet to infuse addictions into their lives. But for adult survivors, many of whom grew up in addicted families, substance abuse and compulsive activities actually perform a wide range of psychological functions of which they may be unaware. What are the long-range effects of child abuse that predispose a survivor to develop an addiction? What are these unrecognized factors that serve to maintain the addictive behavior? How do addictions complement the limitations and difficulties that survivors face on a daily basis? Following are several functions that addictions provide, which must be resolved before most of you will be able to give them up.

REPEATING THE FAMILY'S ADDICTIVE SCRIPT

When survivors are raised in addictive families, there are many reasons for continuing the pattern of addictions into their adult lives. To begin, when the family has a multigenerational history of addiction to a substance like alcohol, the possibility always exists that the survivor may have a genetic predisposition to alcohol—one that will render him or her helpless to control even a moderate intake. But even when the genetic evidence is not compelling, survivors may develop a drinking or drug problem simply because they have learned to include it in their adult lives. Carrying on the family's addictive script into your adulthood may be an unconscious way of identifying with your addicted parent, a way of feeling closer to him or her.

The national movement of Adult Children of Alcoholics (ACA) has brought family alcoholism into public awareness and has defined a syndrome that results from being emotionally abused by a parent's alcoholic behavior. A part of this syndrome is codependency, which, as I mentioned earlier, is an addiction in which the survivor dedicates herself to helping a sick partner, and in so doing, helps him avoid his own problems while getting nothing for herself.

Leigh Anne

Starting from my first romantic relationships I would attract people with addictive personalities—people who were shooting up heroin, or snorting coke, or freebasing crack, and more recently, a guy who is a sexual addict. The irony is that after watching my mother destroy herself with her various addictions, I have been so against that stuff. So how did I end up bringing people like that into my life? That's what I felt comfortable with. They needed me and it was validating for me to try to fix them—that was the one way I could feel good about myself in my family and I just kept repeating that pattern in my intimate relationships. Most of the time, I didn't even see that they were addicted. Denial was my middle name. They would hang out with their scuzzy friends or be nodding off in front of me and I would be so confused about it. I was so blind to what was going on. I didn't see the pattern until it was staring me in the face.

◆

Besides continuing the caretaker role in the form of codependent relationships, helping others can be an attempt to identify with some of the positive people in your life: teachers, relatives, and friends who were so kind to you in the past. This is a healthy part of who you are as a person and is a direct renunciation of your parents' negative influence. But codependency for the adult survivor is a double-edged sword because it can easily lead to self-sabotage and disappointment in not getting your own needs met. The core dilemma for you is not that your spouse or partner has an addiction—that is *their* problem. Your problem is that you cannot feel good about yourself unless you are saving somebody else. Learning how to put yourself first is a major step in recovery from codependency and child abuse.

MEDICATING FEELINGS LEFT OVER FROM THE ABUSE

You've all been left with a repository of intense feelings because of your abuse, the most common of which are probably anxiety, depression, fear, pain, anger, guilt, and shame. These feelings can sometimes be pushed away, but often they threaten to overwhelm you. What can you do with them and how can you make them less powerful?

For many survivors, alcohol and drugs are used to *medicate* these feelings to provide some temporary relief and offer the illusion of being in control of them. Pain can be numbed, depression can be lifted, anger can be blunted, fear can be dissolved, and anxiety can be controlled. Guilt and shame can be temporarily transformed into a sense of entitlement. Medicating the feelings does work, but only temporarily.

Shirley

During my twenties, I starting using alcohol and drugs to numb myself so I wouldn't feel all these feelings inside. I grew more concerned about my drug use because it was chronic and heavy and lasted throughout all my illnesses and all my accidents. I developed a dependence on prescription pain pills—Percodan and Tylox—and was taking two or three of them at a time. Also, I smoked marijuana chronically throughout the day. I'd start in the morning before going to work and it got to the point where I'd go out to my car on a break or during lunch for a quick smoke. And then, from the time I got off work, the minute I hit my car, to the time I went to sleep, I would be smoking dope continuously. I had drugs for every need: to get up, to work, to relax, and to go to sleep.

◆

Medicating the overpowering anxiety that so many survivors feel may seem essential in order to function in work and social situations. Self-confidence is propped up, self-consciousness is reduced, and the tendency to withdraw from others is counteracted. When the person feels inhibited in romantic or sexual relationships, the anxiety-reducing properties of alcohol and drugs can make it easier for the person to feel comfortable and enjoy her body while counteracting the old associations to the abuse. Alcohol and drugs are used sometimes to unblock the creative juices in jobs where artistic expression is necessary to produce under deadline. In our drug-dependent society, there is much support for medicating problematic everyday feelings either with caffeine to combat morning sluggishness or aspirin to knock out a tension headache. For survivors, the need to medicate their feelings may seem like a prerequisite to performing the duties of life like everyone else.

PERMITTING A
DIFFERENT EXPERIENCE OF SELF

Most survivors are tired of their lives—the frustrations, the limitations, and the worries that remind them of their childhood. Many addictions, especially those involving substances, offer you another way of experiencing yourself—one that relieves you from the inhibitions and restrictions of your everyday life. Being able to "step out of yourself" even for a short period of time can give you a glimpse of what your life could be like, if only you could be different. Parts of your personality that were hidden can now find expression. Long-held fantasies can now be played out in the real world. Relating to people becomes easier; situations and events that you once avoided now provide a thrill.

The burden of your past existence may temporarily dissolve, allowing you a sense of normalcy and even equality with others. When you typically feel insecure, a drink or a pill may allow you to feel confident, if not powerful. Many addictions like compulsive dieting and exercise, can visually transform you into a different person. Compulsive cross-dressing can seemingly transform you into a different gender. Changing your name or altering your face or body through cosmetic surgery are all attempts to remake yourself into a different person—one who has shed the past. But as understandable as it is that you want to change, the transformations fueled by addictions are short-lived.

Susan

I never really had a problem with alcohol because I never liked the taste. But cocaine was a different story. It gave me a phony sense of control and self-esteem. I can remember waiting in desperation to make a buy so I could go out and have fun in a way that I could never do when I was straight. With cocaine, I could hit the bars and play pool with the guys and really get off on beating them at their own game. It also stimulated my thinking, which was fine with me because I was more comfortable being in my head than my heart. I would get together with a friend and a gram of coke and solve all the world's problems. It gave me a sense of power that I didn't feel on a daily basis.

◆

True change must occur from the inside out, not from the outside in. Changing identities by using drugs with different physiological effects will only leave you more confused about who you are. Change begins with discovering who you are as a person and entails sorting through all the positive and negative aspects of your personality. The positive parts of you can be strengthened and nourished, while some of the less desirable parts can be minimized. However, not all parts of your personality are changeable. While self-acceptance is not part of the legacy of child abuse, learning to accept those aspects of yourself that you don't like but cannot change may be the most important step you can take.

Replaying Issues
Of Control Through Addictions

As a child growing up in an abusive family, you were routinely subjected to events beyond your control. Your parents had the power and control over your life, which when misused, left you feeling vulnerable and anxious. The child abuse often took on a predictable pattern with a build-up of tension on the part of your parent, followed by an explosion of violence directed against you or your siblings, and ending with a period of relative calm and resignation. Ironically the pattern of your addictive behavior often takes on a similar schedule, beginning with a buildup of anticipation, then with the discharge of tension when the addictive behavior is acted out, and ending in a state of satiation and withdrawal. Because of this similarity, survivors may develop an unconscious belief that they can master and control the cycle of their abuse (which left them feeling so powerless as a child) through the cycle of their addictions.

Leigh Anne

The only time I really was in control of my life—slender, healthy, and vigorous—was when I lived alone. I used to be able to eat properly and take care of myself. I was never this heavy before. But I just couldn't deal with the disappointments that relationships caused me. So I ate. It filled me up, and even though my eating got out of control, somehow it gave me a sense of control. I could eat a lot or not eat at all and it would make a difference. It was my choice and nothing that could happen out there in the world could change it.

♦

Finding new, healthier ways of gaining control of yourself, managing your moods, and meeting challenges in your environment that build up tension are also important tasks in recovering from child abuse. Recovery from addictions can actually provide the chance for you to learn new methods of taking control of your life. Facing your feelings of loss of control, understanding where these feelings originate, and talking about them with others will help you avoid the type of illusory control that addictive behavior provides. You can learn to anticipate situations that reduce your sense of control and implement new behaviors that will give you real power and control in healthy ways.

DEPENDENCY ON
ADDICTIONS INSTEAD OF PEOPLE

Everyone has a need to be nurtured and feel secure. Most adults turn to their loved ones to get these needs met in an exchange of give and take. For obvious reasons, survivors have a lot of anxiety, fear, and inhibitions about relying on others to have these dependency needs met. Certainly as a child you couldn't control your parents abusing you. As a result, the idea of turning to people as a resource is fraught with ambivalence and contaminated feelings. Many survivors adopt an approach–avoid style when it comes to relying on people to satisfy their dependency needs. The hope for getting something brings you closer to people while the fear of being rejected or disappointed pushes you away. These feelings are not easily dismissed.

Shirley

It was real easy for me to isolate myself and use my drugs. I didn't go out and party too much. I didn't drink a lot with my friends because I couldn't control it once I started. I'd have one drink, and then I'd want more. And I would drink to the point where I'd black out and not remember the next day. I felt that it was just safer for me to stay home and do the drugs rather than risk embarrassing myself or possibly getting hurt in a car accident. I guess that deep down it was more important to me to get the feelings I got from the drugs than what I got from my friends. At that time, it was still hard for me to get close to people. They were still somewhat of a risky proposition to me. I was still inclined to take care of them, but after a long week of work and taking care of my kids, I had had enough of that. I didn't really know how to get what I needed from people without giving to the point of exhaustion. So I started staying home a lot just like when I was a kid. I'm so used to taking care of myself, being alone, entertaining myself with music, reading, or watching TV. I had my kingdom on the couch—that was my heaven and I was the queen.

◆

Addictions can complement a survivor's tendency to withdraw from people by offering her a sense of reality that she can control and not risk being disappointed. They can fill you up, temporarily eliminating that empty feeling inside. Some addictions, especially involving compulsive activities, may have an unconscious connection to some unfulfilled primary need such as love or security. Objects and activities can take on particular unconscious meanings and representations for people, which are a direct link back to their childhood and what they never got as children. The blanket dragged around by Linus in the "Peanuts" comic strip is one example of how an object comes to represent some unsatisfied emotional need—in his case, security.

Like the security blanket used by Linus, survivors who have been abandoned or mistreated by their parents at an early age sometimes become attached to certain objects or develop a fetish—an adult version of a security blanket—that makes them feel more secure and less anxious. The compulsive activity concerning the fetish also adopts a schedule whereby the person feels the need to periodically engage in the behavior or else the old feelings of abandonment or insecurity will return. When the compulsive activity temporarily resolves these feelings, an addiction is born because there will be a need to return to the behavior again and again.

A major change that you as a survivor with an addiction must eventually achieve is to find ways you can get your needs met through healthy relationships by picking people with the capacity to give you what you want and who expect you to be able to give back to them. This means working through the leftover feelings of fear and disappointment that relationships stir up in you. Substance abuse addictions will have to be dealt with first before you will be able to get at these deeper feelings.

THE FIRST STEPS IN
DEALING WITH YOUR ADDICTION

I can't stress enough that if you have an addiction involving substance abuse it is important that you deal with that first, before you attempt to recover from the effects of being abused, because substance abuse will make it much harder for you to reclaim memories and buried feelings that are so essential to your recovery. Other addictions involving compulsive behaviors may not be as inhibiting to the child abuse recovery process and therefore can be treated simultaneously with your work on the past abuse, unless the accompanying legal or financial problems prevent you from making the necessary commitment to your recovery. The following list of questions can help you determine if you have a problem with some kind of addictive behavior.

SELF-TEST FOR ADDICTIONS

1. Do you typically engage in addictive behavior following periods of stress or emotional distress?
2. Do you notice that you engage in the addictive behavior more frequently and for longer periods of duration now than in the past?
3. Are you not always aware of when you initiate the addictive behavior? Is the addiction sometimes outside of your conscious awareness?
4. Do you hide the addictive behavior or feel ashamed or guilty about it?
5. Do you often feel agitated and restless if you have not engaged in the addictive behavior for some time?
6. Do you feel uncomfortable or secretly resentful when family members or friends discuss your addictive behavior?
7. Do you persist in engaging in the addictive behavior even when your health, personal safety, or financial status may be negatively affected by it?
8. Do you find yourself regretting some aspect of the addictive behavior but rationalize to yourself why you keep doing it?
9. Have you made attempts to limit the addictive behavior in some way in an effort to gain some control over it?
10. Do you notice that your priority for the addictive behavior keeps rising, often affecting commitments made to others?
11. Do you notice that the addictive behavior has severely compromised certain aspects of your life?
12. Do you look for ways to alter your lifestyle or living arrangements to allow for more time to engage in the addictive behavior?

13. Do you increasingly feel despondent about the direction that your life has taken and question whether your addiction has something to do with it?
14. Has your addictive behavior resulted in your making decisions or engaging in other behaviors or actions that you deeply regret?
15. Are you now limited in engaging in your addictive behavior due to some negative consequence of the addiction such as deteriorated health, medical problems, legal sanctions, or financial restrictions?

If you have answered "yes" to more than three of these questions, it is likely that your behavior is taking on an addictive or compulsive quality. If you have answered "yes" to three of the first five questions, it may indicate that you are in the early or developing stage of an addiction. Answering "yes" to at least three questions in numbers 6 to 10, would suggest you are entering the middle stage of addiction. Three or more "yes" answers to questions 11 to 15 indicates that you are in the final stage of addiction.

FOUR STEPS TO OVERCOMING YOUR ADDICTIONS

After determining if you register on the addictive scale and where, you may need to consider what steps to take next. If you are addicted to a substance, all of the following treatment components may apply to you. However, if your addiction is to a compulsive activity, all the but fourth component—residential detoxification program—will be relevant to your needs. Eating disorders that combine elements of substance abuse (although most foods are not addictive) and compulsive activity (the addiction here is more to the activity of binging or starving) are the lone exception to this dichotomy. Although detoxing from food is not necessary, many survivors with eating disorders may need a brief hospitalization if their medical condition becomes risky due to prolonged anorexia.

    If you are in the first stage of addiction, you may need only the first few components of the recovery program. The latter stages will probably require that you enter a residential detox program to deal with the more long-term effects of drinking or drug use. The key components of a comprehensive program of recovery include the following:

1. 12-Step self-help support group specializing in the addiction you have

2. Educational program about addictions
3. Medical evaluation for physical or neurological ailments
4. Residential detoxification program
5. Comprehensive aftercare program
6. Professional psychotherapy

STEP ONE:
ADMITTING THE PROBLEM

After reading this chapter, you should have a clearer idea of whether or not you have an addiction, and if so, what kind of addiction. Remember that with substance abuse addictions, denial is part of the problem. Review your responses to the Self-Test for Addictions to figure at which stage of addiction you may be. If you are still confused about whether you have an addiction, you can read one of the books referred to in Appendix B, visit a self-help group, or schedule a consultation with a therapist.

There are many organizations that focus exclusively on addictions, such as the 12-Step groups, and you can get additional information by contacting them. You can always ask your family or friends if they have any feelings or reactions to your drinking or drug use or compulsive activities. Put all of this information together and try to be honest and objective about whether an addiction is part of your life. Facing a problem is always the first step in doing something about it. Considering these suggestions and reading this book can be the first steps in determining if child abuse is a reason for your unhappiness as an adult today.

STEP TWO:
JOINING A SELF HELP GROUP

After accepting that you may have an addiction, the best next step is to enroll in a self-help group that specializes in your particular addiction. Self-help groups will be discussed at length in chapter 10. For now, let me say that they can be an invaluable aid in your recovery from addictions as well as from child abuse. Not only are they a source of information but they are a source of emotional support that you will need to wean yourself from an addictive substance or from a compulsive activity. You need to develop new ways of relating to people and there is no better place than in a supportive, accepting group united in trying to overcome their addictions.

STEP THREE:
DETERMINING THE NEED FOR RESIDENTIAL
OR INPATIENT DETOX

If you have an addiction to a substance, in some cases self-help groups and/or professional therapy will not be sufficient to help you gain sobriety. Many alcoholics or drug abusers who have a long history of addiction may require a brief stay at a residential or inpatient detoxification center in order to break the pattern of addiction. Most drugs, alcohol included, are so addictive that simple willpower is not enough. Your body may have developed a tolerance to the substance that will put your immediate physical health in jeopardy if you suddenly try to stop taking it. Many detox programs are now available and are covered by insurance plans. They are either part of a hospital or are freestanding institutions in the country. Typically the average length of a stay ranges from seven to twenty-eight days, although the time can be extended if your particular needs so dictate.

For many long-standing substance abuse problems, starting your recovery in one of these programs makes a lot of sense. First, it immediately interrupts your pattern of addiction. You do not have to rely on your own willpower to stop the addiction. The program staff do it for you by maintaining a controlled, consistent environment. But the value of these recovery centers goes beyond that. They inundate you with information about your addiction, educating you on aspects of the problem that you might have never considered. They will introduce you to the various 12-Step programs modeled after Alcoholics Anonymous and show you how to use them to gain control of your life. They will provide medical services for you if your body reacts to the sudden loss of a drug and they can prescribe medication that will ease your withdrawal period. It will be easier for you to succeed in quickly turning your addiction around. Many of these programs will make available to you an aftercare program located in your community that can support your newfound sobriety while you resume your job and personal life.

How do you know if you need a residential detox program? If you have had more than three relapses in your efforts to gain sobriety, you may need a more powerful treatment program. When the addiction has been established for more than five years, you should consider entering such a program. Talk to friends who have stayed at recovery centers for ther ideas. See a professional therapist who is trained in substance abuse treatment for a consultation. This therapist may be able to recommend a particular program. Visit one of the local recovery centers and speak with the staff about the program and how it might benefit you.

The bottom line is that these programs cannot hurt your recovery process. In other words, you have everything to gain from them and nothing to lose. Many people will argue that these programs are expensive and time consuming. My argument is that you will finally be spending time and money on yourself instead of your addiction.

STEP FOUR:
DESIGNING A STRONG AFTERCARE
PROGRAM

After gaining sobriety or breaking the pattern of addiction, care must be taken to avoid relapses. As mentioned before, recovery programs usually will have community-based aftercare programs that will reinforce the key components of your initial detox program. It makes sense to use an aftercare program for at least a year and often longer following sobriety. An aftercare program usually involves all of the components of your comprehensive program with an emphasis on the 12-Step groups and professional therapy. Many people who have years of clean and sober living will go through periods where they are at risk for relapse. Checking into a recovery center for a brief period can provide the external support to make sure that you don't relapse.

You will need a clean and sober mind to recover from child abuse. To break through the mask of denial and permit the process of recovery to begin, you will need information, support, and practical solutions. Total abstinence from the addictive substance or compulsive behavior may be the safest and quickest way to move beyond the addictions to your process of recovery
 People do recover from their addictions. Pete, Shirley, Susan, and Leigh Anne are among the millions of survivors who took the first step in recovering. Overcoming your addictions will increase your sense of control over your life and give you confidence to face the past, to look at your childhood through sober eyes, and see once and for all what happened, how it affected you, and what you must do to resolve the pain.

Chapter Six

SURVIVING ON THE JOB

We all know that being able to function well on the job is an essential ingredient for success in our work-oriented society. Money, status, respect, power, and material consumption are all yours if you can solve the job challenge. Choosing a career and finding the right job has much to do with your identity as a person and your ability to negotiate in your own best interests. If you are confused about who you are, what you like doing, and how you derive meaning from life, you may feel lost when it comes to setting a career direction. Likewise, if you lack self-confidence and expect to be treated unfairly or to lose out to others, landing the job of your choice may seem forever out of reach. When you are still emotionally tied to your parents and their attitudes and values about how you should operate in the world, you may end up pursuing careers or making job decisions that seem right only because they say so.

Richard

I always used to look at myself in the mirror when I was little and ask "Who am I?" "God, what are other people going to see when they look at me?" At the airport while waiting in the customs line across from a bank of mirrors I'd see myself standing there and think to myself, "Oh, that's what I look like." I mean I had no vision of myself at all. "Am I talented, or am I a failure, or what am I?" Choosing a career tapped into all of these questions because my family had such high career expectations for everyone. If you weren't something really special—like a best-selling author or an academic or a scientist—you were nothing, a total failure. I remember my mom saying that my father "could have done this or done that, but no, he dropped out of graduate school and went back to his family business and now look at him." She had such contempt for him. As a child, I remember I didn't want to end up with that summation of my life, so I tried to figure out what kind of career would bring me recognition and respect—everything that I never got as a child. The problem was that I was viewing my options through my mother's values.

◆

The world of work often goes one of two ways for the adult survivor. Many of you who have continued the caretaker role into adult life may have found that applying the same high-control, problem-solving acumen you used to survive your family ordeal has made you a manager's dream. You are used to hardship, so no task is too difficult. There is less fear of being abused, although the possibility for exploitation may exist in not being fairly compensated for all that you do. But, in your mind, the equation may be comfortingly simple: Do better than anyone else and you might get more than you ever got in your family.

Susan

I've always gotten a lot of validation through my jobs. Work for me has been a godsend. It allowed me to put into practice my natural talents for organization and problem solving. I was incredibly dedicated and I would work outrageous hours to make sure the job got done. I made a connection with computers just at the right time and have been able to get all sorts of jobs that are interesting and pay well. Computers are a natural occupation for me because I learned as a child to turn off my feelings and to just think things out like a computer. I'm a great troubleshooter. Give me a problem, I'll cut through it, we'll get the solution, I don't let the emotions get in the way. My bosses loved me.

◆

For the majority of survivors, however, the story may be vastly different. To your horror, the job can become a new arena for abuse where the old feelings of self-sabotage, dissappointment, and resignation find new outlets for expression. If you have yet to work through the feelings surrounding your childhood abuse, your experience with co-workers may end up reinforcing your worst impressions about yourself. What messages do you send to yourself when you suffer a setback in the job world? What feelings get stirred up when you are turned down for a job, passed over for promotion, or fired?

Leigh Anne

My early years in the music industry were a struggle just to keep money in my pocket and some hope in my heart. I was booking bands, trying to set up gigs for myself, promoting concerts for others. I did a lot of free work with the community as a volunteer. I also started teaching music. I had a lot of jobs and there were a lot of changes. I started seeing a pattern develop. I couldn't make the jobs last. I would get real bored with a job after about a year. I get very restless, just like when I was a kid when my parents would move every two or three years. I would feel the same kind of feeling welling up inside of me. It's like a bubble on your car tire—it gets bigger and bigger and you know it's going to pop at any moment. It would create tremendous anxiety in me. I felt like I was going to crash unless I made a change. So, I did, except I would always go out in flames. I would start being rude to people. I would think in terms of wanting a raise and what I'd have to do to get it. Maybe that'll make a change, if I get a raise. More than once, the raise strategy has produced the complete opposite of what I wanted: no raise and no job.

◆

For the survivor who did not receive many rewards for taking on the caretaker role, the legacy of the recluse, scapegoat, or bully may assert themselves in the job situation. These more problematic roles can wreak havoc in your job adjustment. Avoiding co-workers, getting blamed for things you may or may not have done, and letting your aggression get the best of you may be the underlying causes of your job problems. Once you land a job, your performance may be affected by personality conflicts with co-workers, authority problems with bosses, evaluations that cite inconsistency, absenteeism, low productivity, poor judgment, and even insubordination.

Certain aspects of your job may be especially difficult for you due to the latent effects of your abuse. For example, making public presentations, working as part of a team, or trusting your boss or co-worker to follow through on an assignment may bring up many of the old issues. However, work is a bottom-line business and the reasons for your job dilemmas do not usually count for much as far as your boss is concerned. Consequently when things are not going well at work you may begin to feel discriminated against—once again. While the reasons may have more to do with you and the problems associated with the past, please remember that this doesn't mean you are bad—only that you will need to make changes to get ahead.

Most survivors often feel trapped in work situations that may parallel the group dynamics of their families. Your boss becomes your parent; your co-workers become your siblings; your job position becomes your family role. Even the constant reorganizing and restructuring that plagues many businesses can remind you of the unpredictability of your family. In such an environment, many of the old feelings of anger, resentment, devaluation, and exploitation may resurface.

You may want to ask yourself what style you employ in the work setting. Try to be objective in looking at how you function at your job. What role do you adopt at work and how does it differ or repeat the role you assumed in your family? What are your specific problem areas and how do your individual reactions and the corporate culture mix to create these dilemmas? Use the following checklist to gauge your job conflicts.

JOB CHECKLIST

1. Are you happy and satisfied in your current job?
2. Is it difficult for you to land a quality job that is equal to your experience and abilities?
3. Do you recognize any repeating patterns in your job history like getting fired, missing out on promotions, or abruptly resigning for personal reasons?
4. Is it hard to present yourself in the best light during job interviews?
5. Do you have difficulty fitting in with co-workers?

6. Do you initiate job responsibilities or try to avoid them?
7. Do you have a problem with absenteeism? If so, what keeps you out of work?
8. Are you prone to personality conflicts with co-workers or authority problems with bosses?
9. Do you have difficulties with achievement or feeling deserving of promotions?
10. Are you worried about making faulty judgments or acting impulsively?

COMMON JOB DILEMMAS FOR ADULT SURVIVORS

Following are nine common work-related conflicts in which adult survivors typically find themselves. Not all of these will necessarily apply to you because as a worker you will have a unique blend of strengths and weaknesses that will attract some types of conflicts while eliminating others. Read them over and answer the journal questions at the end of each section. If they apply to you, try to develop more awareness and understanding about them by writing your thoughts in your journal.

CONFUSION OVER CAREER CHOICES

Because many of you are still confused about what kind of job or career you want, you may either be pursuing high-profile careers that are products of long-held childhood fantasies or settling for any kind of job that will pay you enough to put food on your table and a roof over your head. Careers in professional athletics, entertainment, academia, or creative writing may have been appealing during childhood because of the recognition, acceptance, and money involved, but the reality is that they are extremely competitive and demanding, with success being achieved by only a small minority. In many cases, the fantasy may be more enjoyable than the hard reality that calls for years of personal sacrifice, endless preparation, and more than a few strokes of luck. Survivors need to realistically evaluate their chances for success in these careers and determine if the struggle will ultimately pay off.

For those of you who grew up buying into what your family

wanted you to become, you may be totally confused about the type of job that would actually make you happy. There was little consideration given to your preferences as a child, and now as an adult, you are not used to registering what you like and don't like. You wanted to believe that others knew what was best for you because you were used to giving up your power to others. But what may have been the safest strategy as a child is a prescription for disappointment as an adult. After years of struggling with indecision, you may have gotten to a point in life where a choice must be made. Moving away from some misguided career plan may feel for some like abandoning a close friend in a time of need. You may feel a great sense of loss and still have little direction to guide your future plans. You need to be the one behind the wheel of your life, not the passenger in the back seat.

Richard

For years I denied wanting to write because my mother was a writer, and she was miserable. So I told myself I wanted to be a scientist. I didn't know anyone who was a scientist, but I was interested in zoology from some of the books I had read as a child and so I decided that being a scientist would make me happy. I decided that I would have to go to graduate school, which means being a student for another ten years. I told myself that if I could just get into Harvard I'd be happy, because if you're a graduate student at Harvard, you are supposed to be happy by definition. The only way to find self-acceptance is by getting some kind of degree and being an academic. Even after I got this job working for my friend who did environmental reports I still held out the plan that I would go back to school and become a zoologist, or later on, a documentary filmmaker. Everyone I talked to about filmmaking described it as this incredibly depriving experience. I don't want to be deprived. I don't want to lead a circus life, constantly be running around like a lunatic, begging for money, and working crazy hours to finish a film that will be shown once on PBS at three o'clock in the morning. But it was so hard for me to accept that maybe I wasn't going to be something approved of by my family.

◆

Besides unrealistic job goals, the survivors' tendency to settle for less when it comes to jobs may be the biggest obstacle to obtaining what they really want. Growing up, you may never have been encouraged to set your sights high enough or to think purposefully about what would satisfy your needs and interests. Remember, though, that it is never too late to make a change. In this day and age, many people are going back to school and making career changes in the middle of their adult lives. Admittedly, this presents some formidable risks, to say nothing of the impact on your lifestyle. But if you develop a realistic plan and get whatever training or schooling might be necessary, it can be done. The first step may be to complete your recovery, discover who you are as a person, and find out what interests and talents you have.

JOURNAL QUESTIONS

1. *Are you still confused about your life's work?*

2. *What needs and interests does your current job satisfy or not satisfy?*

3. *What personal or family influences steered you toward the job you have today?*

4. *Did you give yourself adequate time to discover what your life's work would be or did you settle for less when you accepted this job?*

5. *Do you fantasize about some other career that may draw on more of your talents and interests? If so, what?*

LACK OF CONFIDENCE IN GETTING A GOOD JOB

The process of searching for a good job can be extremely threatening because it requires personal characteristics that many survivors feel are difficult for them such as having initiative in the face of strong competition, overcoming fear of the inevitable rejections, and believing that they have something to offer. You may be confused about how to find the jobs that do appeal to you. And you may be inclined to settle for jobs that are below your level of experience and ability. Low self-esteem—the all-too-familiar albatross around the neck of the adult survivor—can once again invisibly shape the choices you make. Many of the survivors I see in my practice are placed in jobs that fit their fears but not their talents. Their intelligence and capabilities far exceed the demands of their jobs, which are more suited to their emotional vulnerabilities. Safety and acceptance have overriden all of their other concerns in their choice of jobs.

Richard

I went through several jobs while I tried to decide what I wanted to do with my life. Most of the jobs were in the service industry like being a busboy in a restaurant and a clerk in a video rental shop. At the time, I was willing to settle for anything because the rent was due, I owed money to my girlfriend, and I was terrified of the real world. Any employer that would accept me was good enough for me. I remember the horrible scenes that my mother would paint about what life would be like without money: You starve, you move to a tenement apartment, and everyone beats you to the few good available jobs. I didn't really expect much from the real world because I was made to feel so biased against it. Some of these jobs worked out and some didn't. I didn't really matter that much because I never had much investment in them. I was a failure in the restaurant business because I kept forgetting to put the zucchini on the salad. Then I got a job working for a video store where I was more successful because I was valued there. They gave me all the hysterical people to talk to on the phone. I was real good at calming them down and soothing their anger when they couldn't get the tape that they wanted. I knew all about that, of course, from years of dealing with my mother. I stayed there for about a year but eventually left for some stupid reason. I just floated around really, more lost in fantasy about what I could be doing than dealing with the harsh reality of actually getting a good job.

◆

For many survivors, the job interview brings up their worst fears and anxieties. Job interviews are stressful by nature because they are designed to evaluate you: your person, your skills, and your ability to get along with other people. The situation can easily revive the old feeling of not being good enough. Depending on how you are able to control your anxiety and perform under stress, the interview can be experienced as anywhere from outright torture to mild discomfort. No one likes to have to sell themselves, but for the most part that is what it takes to get the job. Because job interviews can be formal, sometimes little effort is made to help you feel comfortable or reassured that you are performing as expected. You must rely on your perceptions, judgments, and personality to read the situation accurately and quickly and know how to respond in a way that will create a favorable impression. For most survivors, this is very difficult to do.

JOURNAL QUESTIONS

6. *Do you hate looking for a job? If so, why?*

7. *Are you confused about what kinds of jobs are right for you?*

8. *What feelings get stirred up when you're applying for a job?*

9. *What aspects of a job search are the most difficult for you? What attempts have you made to resolve them?*

10. *How do you react to job interviews? Are you able to present yourself in the best possible light or do you freeze?*

DIFFICULTIES FITTING INTO THE CORPORATE CULTURE

Once gaining employment, many survivors who were victims of abnormal interpersonal relationships in their families have trouble fitting in with the various work groups and office relationships that comprise the social environment in most companies. Most jobs make significant interpersonal demands on employees, requiring them to communicate effectively, share power and responsibility, resolve differences, and place company goals ahead of personal motives, all of which may be challenging for the adult survivor.

As noted before, the company can also become a second family, with some of the positives and many of the negatives. Starting a new job as an outsider is an uncomfortable position for anyone, but especially anxiety provoking for someone who has worries about being accepted and treated with respect. Functioning in a group may never feel totally safe for some survivors, but breaking into an already established group may be even more challenging because it may bring up the old feeling of being "one down." In companies where office politics are unusually thick, it can seem like you are entering another dysfunctional family. And some companies do operate like a dysfunctional family!

The formation of alliances, a natural occurrence in any organization, can feel threatening to you if you once felt pushed aside in your own family. Fitting into a hierarchical structure where everyone has different levels of power and authority can be alarming to someone who has experienced the abuse of authority. Respecting personal and organizational boundaries that are essential to the smooth, consistent functioning of a work group may be a new lesson for the survivor, who grew up in a family completely lacking boundaries.

Pete

My first job with a local VISTA office was a real challenge, because emotionally speaking, I wasn't ready for all that was required in terms of relating to people and working as part of a team. It was a very structured environment with shifting deadlines, multiple projects, and constant pressure. I just couldn't deal with the pressure or the feedback very well. When I got any kind of negative feedback, I just wilted. Criticism became a moral issue and I took it to mean that I was a bad person for having deficiencies, for not being everything I needed to be or should have been. Dealing with people became painful and something to be avoided or plodded through. I looked around at the other people and they seemed to thrive on the give and take, the rush of beating a deadline, and the sense of satisfaction that comes with a job well done. Job frustrations or criticisms would roll off their back. I have always taken things personally, even back in Little League baseball. When things went badly, I inevitably expected to be judged harshly by everyone else. Even at this job, I imagined they thought I was a liability to work with, and I may have been. But my fears only made things worse and I dealt with them by withdrawing even more. My confidence was on the floor and I felt helpless. When I had a chance to move on, I did.

◆

The biggest challenge for the survivor when work conflicts start to mount is to resist the tendency to assume the dysfunctional roles of the past. Although the caretaker role may be the most functional when applied to the workplace, the accompanying need to control and the expectation for perfection may cause resentments and competition with co-workers that could lead to destructive power struggles. More often than not, the role of the recluse seems to be the common strategy employed by survivors who are intimidated by the interpersonal demands being made on them. Withdrawing from others may make you feel safer, but it may also affect your job performance and limit your chances for promotion. More than anything, it means that you are putting yourself on hold, refusing to overcome the past and to learn more effective ways of relating to others, which could lead to a more satisfying work life.

The most dangerous role to assume is the scapegoat because you then become the target for every frustration, resentment, and hostile motive swirling through the office environment. Co-workers may notice your defensiveness and withdrawal. They may talk about it and sometimes the group will ostracize you instead of trying to understand what may be causing the rift. Considering that many survivors do not feel comfortable in groups, you may misinterpret what is going on. If you feel like you are being scapegoated again, your job will feel intolerable. Resignation, dismissal, or self-sabotage may become imminent. In many instances, the best recourse may be to change departments or jobs if it doesn't seem like the problems can be worked out.

JOURNAL QUESTIONS

11. *What is it about the company culture that is most difficult for you?*

12. *How would you describe the role you employ in interacting with your co-workers?*

13. *How do you feel working as part of a team?*

14. *What aspects of your company remind you of your dysfunctional family?*

15. *How do you respond to the different levels of authority found in work stations?*

PERSONALITY CONFLICTS

Personality conflicts are among the most common dilemmas faced by adult survivors in the workplace and may be the underlying cause of job stress, firings, and resignations. Adult survivors are prone to interpersonal conflicts for many reasons such as poor communication and conflict resolution skills, difficulties with trust, and tendencies to expect the worst from people. These tendencies are amplified in the work environment due to stress, competition between employees, and because work relationships do not have the same level of emotional investment that personal relationships do.

Personality conflicts often start when survivors feel offended by something said or done by a co-worker. These feelings fester and grow in magnitude, often resulting in survivors changing the way they relate to that person. It is often difficult for survivors to confront the co-worker in a constructive way. More often than not, survivors withdraw from the person, allowing the situation to affect their job performance, ultimately feeling oppressed by the whole situation. Sometimes these feelings and reactions begin to carry over to other work relationships to the point where survivors feel discriminated against.

Shirley

I gave up a position within a bank department because of a conflict with another manager. I was promoted to an officer in her department and it was a mess. This woman was a very domineering woman, who also had a lot of problems. I know she had a drinking problem and she may have been a survivor herself. And she had it in for me and we locked horns. At first, I bought into her image of me as stubborn, that I didn't know what I was doing, that I couldn't handle the job. But after a while, I realized I could make things work better than her and in fact my co-workers saw me as more competent than she was. Then out of desperation, she gave me a thirty-day notice to improve, which I knew was really unfair. This was a turning point, because in the past, I would have felt defeated and not able to speak up for myself. But this time was different. I responded to her charges in writing, pointing out where she was wrong. Also, I recruited some help from an old boss who respected me and who knew of my abilities. That was a big step for me also because I usually fight my battles alone. I had my old boss help me write it because I knew it would be read by others and I didn't want to personally attack her, but it needed to be firmly worded in order to challenge her false statements. As a solution, I requested that I leave that position and go unassigned in the bank, allowing me to float around as a problem solver. This option was approved and it worked out very well for me.

◆

Personality conflicts with authority figures that never get resolved are a shortcut to the unemployment line. Even when the conflicts do not totally get out of hand, it can hurt a person's chance for promotion and disrupt job satisfaction. Many survivors have difficulties with authority figures because they grew up with parents who misused their authority. You may feel sensitive to how your boss uses power over you in the work setting. If you are offended by the way you're being treated, you often have little recourse but to accept it as an unfortunate aspect of your job or leave. One thing is for sure: it is not healthy for you to stay in an abusive job situation, since it would be a clear repetition of the family abuse that you are dedicated to changing.

When problems with co-workers do occur, it is essential that you try to resolve the differences before a full-blown personality conflict develops. This requires that you pinpoint the source of the conflict and are willing to recognize that you may be reacting personally to a co-worker's comments or deeds, which were not really personal attacks but simply business strategy. That is why it is often best to focus on the *issues*, not your *feelings*, which tend to get in the way of resolving these situations. If your attempts at coming to a resolution flounder, and you find yourself growing increasingly unhappy, it may be best to transfer to another department or look for another job. Beware of your tendency to label this move as a failure. Remind yourself that your decision was based on an objective analysis of what was best for you.

JOURNAL QUESTIONS

16. *Is there someone at work with whom you have ongoing conflicts?*

17. *Does this person have a position of authority over you?*

18. *Do you feel suspicious of your co-workers' motives and question whether they can be trusted?*

19. *Is it difficult for you to resolve personality conflicts, thus allowing you to continue working with the person?*

20. *Do you tend to personalize your interactions with others, causing you to feel defensive and sensitive to feedback?*

DIFFICULTIES WITH ACHIEVEMENT

Jobs require you to produce, to be effective, and to contribute to the overall goals of the organization. These expectations can cause trouble because achieving and being successful works against the self-sabotage with which so many survivors struggle. As you read in chapter 4, self-sabotage is a powerful destructive force in the lives of survivors before recovery. Nowhere is this tendency more of a dilemma for a survivor than in the workplace. Self-sabotage will undermine your best intentions to achieve, succeed, and prosper within the job environment. It can surface in the most innocent guises, from forgetting to complete a key operation to misunderstanding some information in a contract or memorandum. It can take the form of a conscious self-destructive act such as offending your boss or knowingly violating some company policy. Or you may adopt more passive forms of self-sabotage such as anticipating failure or not standing up for yourself. Self-sabotage may often present itself at the moment you are about to succeed, for example, communicating some uncertainty while a customer is about to sign a contract or doing something at the last minute to take yourself out of the running for a promotion.

Many survivors experience new job challenges not with excitement and enthusiasm but with fear of failure and the anxiety that comes with having to perform. Telling yourself that you will never get anything as good as what you have is one way to discourage yourself from climbing the career ladder. You may still remember past disappointments at previous jobs or even years ago at school when you failed a test or lost a game. These memories may still haunt you and reinforce the notion that you will always be unsuccessful.

Pete

W hen I was a retail clerk, I did my job very well and eventually I was offered management jobs. But I don't know what exactly happened. The promotion was the next step, but I was not able to accept it for some reason. It just caused a lot of internal conflict because at some level I felt like I never deserved it, despite my bosses thinking that it would be best for everyone. Promotions meant that I was doing something well and success was something that went against this feeling I had of being bad and dirty because of what happened to me with my mom. I guess it was a form of self-punishment to deny myself the rewards of working well. Promotions also meant that someone else was losing out, which would make me feel even more guilty. All in all, the safest thing to do at the time was to stay where I was and not do anything that would make my life more complicated.

◆

Changing this tendency to self-sabotage will make an enormous difference in your job life. By overcoming the negative judgments of the past, you can creatively and confidently approach any opportunities that may arise. Promotions, more money, appreciation, and validation are the riches that job prosperity can bring you. Why shouldn't you get your fair share if you demonstrate your value as an employee? Admittedly, there is some risk involved. For many survivors, holding onto the status quo is the safest bet, even though your situation involves the same old disappointments. Try choosing another path and get some help in making the necessary changes. You may not have as much to lose as you think.

JOURNAL QUESTIONS

21. *Are you sometimes your own worst enemy by making mistakes at crucial times?*

22. *Do you sometimes hold yourself back just because it seems safer than risking an all-out quest for success?*

23. *Do you feel that nothing you ever accomplish is good enough?*

24. *Are you reluctant to promote yourself within the company or push for better compensation?*

25. *Are you afraid that success will somehow make you vulnerable or the target of resentments?*

WORKAHOLISM

Workaholism is common among survivors who were once caretakers as children and now, as adults, overperform in the service of their jobs, often to the detriment of their personal health and relationships. The compulsive need to work often stems from your enormous need for appreciation and control over others. Having a demanding boss with high expectations only increases your compulsion to meet whatever demands are placed on you even when they are unreasonable or impossible. In many ways, this scenario replicates the old dynamics of the family where, as a child, you were also subjected to unreasonable demands without any rewards. However, since you are used to extreme situations, you may actually feel comfortable working in this type of environment, although the emphasis is now on production, not destruction.

Shirley

I've always had pretty good jobs. I started working at sixteen and have never stopped. Work for me was a way to avoid what was going on in my life. At its best, it was a gratifying experience because I found that people needed me—plus it paid me money. At its worst, it was no better than being at home—only I didn't have to be abused to be accepted. There was a lot of acceptance for me at my job. I wasn't always fairly compensated for all that I did, but compared to where I came from, I got a hell of a lot more. There is a lot of the caretaker in my work style. For one thing, I have no boundaries. I assume I must take care of any and all problems that exist. I will go to any length to solve some conflict and I'm actually a pretty good problem solver. In a way, this strength is also one of my greatest weaknesses, because in trying to do it all, inevitably I neglect myself and even my own job. I would work myself to the bone. I would never take any time off, but come the weekend, I would be crashed out on the couch for forty-eight hours. One time I came into work so sick that they had to call an ambulance to take me to the hospital. I think this style is typical of an adult child of alcoholic parents—all that responsibility and not enough credit.

◆

You may see other workers able to put their jobs in perspective, leaving their work behind when they resume their private lives. Unlike you, they do not feel the compulsion to overachieve in order to feel good about themselves. For the caretaker hooked on measuring her self-esteem by her job success, the psychic payoff will never be fully realized. Yet you continue the pattern because it may feel like the only thing you have going for you. So you hold onto it for dear life, often at the expense of your physical health and personal relationships.

JOURNAL QUESTIONS

26. *Do you consistently work more hours per week than is realistically expected?*

27. *Is it hard for you to delegate tasks, preferring to keep your hands on several tasks at once?*

28. *Are you a perfectionist and inclined to drive yourself?*

29. *Do you tend to take more responsibility for the way things turn out than is reasonable?*

30. *Do you suffer from stress-related illnesses and burn-out?*

ABSENTEEISM, JOB INCONSISTENCY, AND LOW PRODUCTIVITY

Absenteeism is often a problem for the workaholic whose personal needs are being ignored to satisfy job demands. When feelings are denied over an extended period of time, eventually they cross over the mind-body nexus to find expression in physical symptoms such as headaches, ulcers, chronic viruses, colds, and flu. It's as though your conscious mind refuses to recognize your need for physical and emotional replenishment so your physical body, in effect, goes on strike to make the demands heard. Getting sick functions like a safety valve for many people, because if they do not periodically get time off to renew themselves, they may have a more serious setback such as a heart attack or psychosomatic ailments. Workaholics adopt the all-or-nothing approach to life, whereby they steadily overwork until they drop from exhaustion, retreating to bed until a new cycle is initiated.

Susan

My absenteeism has always been a problem at my job, but I'm a real hard worker, so they tolerate it. But I have always had at least two or three days a month where I would shut down. Emotionally and physically shut down. Sometimes it would come on the weekends, but other times I'd have to skip work. I would stay at home behind closed doors, lying in my bed and just becoming catatonic. I'd sleep a lot and watch TV and read trashy novels—just vegetate. I wouldn't do anything. Perhaps it would be more accurate to say that I couldn't do anything. My son who was only six would have to scramble for himself. These would be my dark days when I'd usually be depressed and feel horrible. It was like all the feelings I had stuffed down in the previous month would just take over and overwhelm me. All I could do was ride it out. It was like I needed this time out in order to produce at the level that I—and the company—had come to expect.

◆

Absenteeism also plays a role in the work life of survivors who grew up assuming the roles of the recluse, the scapegoat, or the bully and who are often linked to job inconsistency and low productivity. Sometimes the missed work is related to weekend drinking or drug use, which leaves the survivor in no shape to assume job responsibilities on Monday morning. Other times the mounting pressures of work or the presence of an unresolved personality conflict can push the survivor to call in sick, more out of a sense of not being able to cope with the situation than due to a blatant avoidance of responsibility.

Underlying these more broadly focused problems are feelings of anxiety, depression, aggression, and passivity that the survivor has a hard time managing in the ever-changing work environment. To your employer or supervisor, however, the reasons for your regular absences or periodic slowdowns may not matter. In the work world, the bottom line is getting things done, and if you are not meeting that basic expectation, you risk losing your job.

JOURNAL QUESTIONS

31. *Do you typically take more than two sick days per month? If so, what are the usual reasons?*

32. *If the reasons have to do with medical problems, are the illnesses considered stress-related or psychosomatic?*

33. *Do you periodically need time off just to get a handle on your emotions?*

34. *Do you go through periods where your mood disrupts your job performance or affects work relationships?*

35. *Are you inclined to avoid aspects of your job that involve collaborating with a co-worker or boss who has offended you?*

PRONE TO EXPLOITATION

For many survivors, past abuse may have left you with a tendency to be taken advantage of by life, people, and events. Issues of self-protection are enormously difficult for survivors, and the job situation can capitalize on your low self-esteem, difficulties with achievement, and workaholism.

Leigh Anne

For twenty years, I allowed myself to be used—hard work for low pay—which only reinforced my low self-esteem. I just kept working against myself, beating my head against the wall with jobs that exploited me and people who ripped me off. Finally, this is the first year of all of my adult life where I'm taking care of myself. I just realized that one of the biggest changes I'd have to make is to be able to say no to people when I need to. I need to start acting in my own best interests. I had to learn to stop booby trapping myself. My mother made a career of booby trapping me and then I took on the role myself. Well, I realized that nothing was going to get better in my life if I kept doing that. It took me twenty years to learn this lesson but I finally learned it. And now I'm facing what I need to do to really change it once and for all.

◆

Learning how to stand up for yourself in the job world is a real must. People who cannot assert their needs at work will end up being exploited, which is only a more subtle form of emotional abuse. Bosses and supervisors can make mistakes, but you shouldn't have to be the one who takes the fall for them. If you want to avoid being exploited or treated unfairly, then you will need to start challenging authority. You may need help to protect yourself. Sometimes that means seeing a therapist or seeing an attorney.

JOURNAL QUESTIONS

36. *What job situations ended up being exploitative of you?*

37. *What feelings and reactions did you have in response to these situations?*

38. *What aspects of yourself and your abuse do you think contributed to the exploitation?*

39. *What aspects of your boss or the company contributed to the exploitation?*

40. *What did you learn from these situations that you can apply in future jobs?*

PROBLEMS WITH DECISION MAKING

Most jobs require countless decisions to be made, large and small, every day. This can be a real challenge to the adult survivor who grew up in a family where thinking and action were ruled by impulse rather than logic, and where you were rarely encouraged to think out problems or allowed to test your decision making within the safe confines of your family. The ability to accurately perceive interpersonal situations, to gather and organize information, to use one's judgment to assess what is happening and then to act in a prudent and rational manner is a process that takes time and practice—something that survivors usually must learn later in adulthood.

Many survivors have a hard time trusting their own judgment when it comes to making decisions. Part of this difficulty is based on your track record, which isn't always good due to past incidences of self-sabotage. But even when your perceptions are accurate, when your thinking is logical, and when your decision-making process is objective, you may still doubt yourself.

The tendency to act impulsively, out of anxiety or desperation, is common for survivors who witnessed flash reactions in their families. Considering that people often perform their work under stress, it is even less likely that survivors will know how to calmly analyze a situation or decision before acting.

The possibility of making another wrong choice takes on enormous implications ranging from "I'm no good at this job" to "I'm a bad person because I can't figure out what to do." The part of you that somehow feels "defective" ends up being reinforced by this attitude. For many, the solution is to make no decision, avoid the controversy by withdrawing authority and power in the hopes that someone else will step in and make the call. But to do so is to shirk your job responsibilities, which can mean losing your job.

Richard

I had some turbulence at work where my boss—a woman with the same name as my mother—blamed me irrationally for something that wasn't my fault. I just got really mad, although I have learned from my mother to never show it. Instead I went into my therapy session and let it all out. Had I gone in and used my anger on her, I would have been canned. But as it was, I was able to get a grip on myself until I could decide what to do. The problem was that I was so flushed with emotion that I was having a hard time conceptualizing the problem. I knew there were organizational problems in our department that explained what happened, but I couldn't get beyond my sense of outrage at being betrayed. I was planning to logically diagram it out for her and then propose a change that would make things better for everyone, including me. But it was like I had molasses on the brain—I couldn't put it together. Plus I was real nervous about approaching her after she unloaded on me. I knew I would have to have something really good worked out or she would think that I was blaming her for the problem. While all of this was going on, she decided that it was her fault after all because the office wasn't organized properly. I was shocked, because based on my history, I never expected a woman in an authority position to take responsibility for a mistake that was rightfully hers. You kind of expect that everyone will repeat the same old patterns.

◆

Because of past abuse, many survivors feel hopeless about climbing out of the hole that they have dug for themselves at work. When you make one mistake, you may often feel that you have cast your lot in life. Change seems very hard and you may not be sure that you will get a second chance at doing things better. Much of this thinking can be traced directly to your family. You were probably not given much room for making mistakes. One false move and you were branded stupid or lazy or a failure.

So much of learning is related to the process of trial and error: trying something out, making a mistake, learning from the experience and applying your wisdom when you have a second chance. Most supervisors and jobs will give you more than a second chance to get something right. The question is whether you will give yourself a second chance or if you will again apply your family's misguided attitude against yourself. Retreating into ambivalence when it comes to making a decision is only a ticket to vocational limbo. Allowing yourself to learn from your mistakes and make it right the second time around is the survivor's best strategy for growth.

JOURNAL QUESTIONS

41. *Is it hard for you to make decisions? If so, why?*

42. *Are you worried about making a mistake; do you feel ambivalent and confused?*

43. *Do you find that you need more reassurance and validation for actions taken than other employees do?*

44. *Are you prone to misundertandings, misperceptions, faulty judgments and impulsive actions?*

45. *Do your feelings get in the way of solving a problem?*

Many of the survivors I've seen in my practice have made major career leaps once they were able to overcome some of the difficulties they recognized in their jobs. One of the best ways to challenge the old, destructive messages is to have them contradicted on a daily basis by

people who know your work and are objective in evaluating your performance. When a boss or a co-worker acknowledges your talents and
efforts on the job, you can use this recognition to challenge the negative
attitudes and judgments of the past that you so blindly adopt in the
present. In essence, success in your job life can lead to a happier and
more fulfilling life.

Chapter Seven

THE
*C*ALLENGE OF
PARENTING

Parenting can be the most joyful, satisfying, and renewing experience a survivor can have. It can offer a supreme opportunity to resolve the wounds of the past through a healthy parent-child bond, one that is filled with love and appreciation instead of rejection and disappointment. Becoming a parent also allows you a second chance to experience some of the wonderment and innocence that your childhood never had. It can be a time to discover and nurture your own inner child, which will become the heart of your emerging identity as a healthy parent.

Considering the enormous social changes taking place these days, you may be parenting under some novel circumstances. You could be one of two working parents or a single parent, or you could be a stepparent, adoptive parent, foster parent, or gay parent.

Trying to overcome the poor parental role models of your past is challenge enough without the difficulty of raising your child alone. But many survivors are forced to do just that. Dealing with the strains of blending two families into one, or helping your children accept a new lover in your life requires understanding, negotiation, and maturity.

For you to try to find a healthy alternative to your own abusive parenting, doing it all differently may not be as easy as you expected. The endless demands your children make, the power of old parenting messages, and the intense emotional reactions that children provoke are especially taxing for the adult survivor who may have limited re-sources on which to rely. However, with recovery, you *can* become the parent you never had.

Pete

I see both of my parents in me. I can see my mother's part in me to fly off in a rage when I get frustrated or tired. As of yet, I haven't done it but I have certainly come real close a couple times. It scared the hell out of me because when my wife and I decided to have kids, I vowed that I would never be that way with my own children. But these promises I've made to myself get challenged in the heat of the moment. In these situations, I can also see my dad's indecisiveness and passivity in me, the part that ends up taking second place to my tendency to react strongly, which I got from my mother. These pieces of my parents seem to float around inside me, and if I'm not careful, they can influence the way I am with my kids. I always have to keep an eye on those characteristics in me, because I don't want to be like my parents.

◆

Parenting for the survivor before or during recovery is like facing a fork in the road: at major junctures you will need to take a different road from your parents in the manner you raise your child.

> Being conscious about the choices you are making in raising your children and learning alternative behaviors to reduce the stress on yourself and protect your child are your major weapons in defeat-ing the tendency to repeat the past abuse.

This chapter will not attempt to teach you how to parent your child. No book can teach such a complicated and personal endeavor. How-ever, there are some suggestions that can guide your development as a parent and identify some of the inevitable pitfalls lying in your path. Remember that you have strengths and weaknesses and finding your soul as a parent requires you to identify those parts of yourself you want to draw from as well as those parts that need to be contained.

Start by answering the following journal questions to discover the barriers that can work against your becoming the parent you want to be.

JOURNAL QUESTIONS

1. *How would you like to be different from your parents?*
2. *What are you afraid of repeating in your own parenting?*
3. *Which of your "buttons" get pushed by your children?*
4. *How hard is it for you to be a quality parent?*
5. *How do you know when you need help, support, or even a respite from parenting?*

GHOSTS IN THE NURSERY

It is inevitable that having a child and assuming the role of parent will put you face to face with your past—only now the roles are switched. You are no longer the dependent, vulnerable child who must roll with the punches. You are the parent who has the authority to shape your child's formative years. With any sanctioned power comes a moral responsibility to do what's right. The choice is now up to you to break the chains of intergenerational abuse. Becoming a healthy and loving parent will not only benefit your child but also yourself as the gains you make in parenting become the cornerstone of your foundation of recovery.

Selma Fraiberg, a noted child psychologist, wrote about the adult survivor who becomes a parent and encounters the "ghosts in the nursery." As you care for your children, you too may be aware of the ghosts of your parents, urging you to react the same way to your children as your parents did to you. These ghosts die hard. Your parents may be long gone from your everyday life but their ways of doing things—especially childrearing—can still maintain a dark influence over your parenting. Paradoxically, these ghosts grow more powerful when they are ignored and tend to disappear when consciously confronted and challenged for what they are. This gives you a choice as a parent—the fork in the road. You have the power and opportunity to be a different kind of parent. Or you can let these ghosts rule your parenting and repeat your painful past with your own children.

CONSCIOUS VERSUS
UNCONSCIOUS PARENTING

Some survivors are fully aware of what issues will be raised when they have a child whereas for others bringing a child into the world is simply the next step in becoming an adult. When parenting is unconscious, it is almost impossible to see how the ghosts of your parents are influencing you to repeat the past. It is important to ask yourself why you decided to have children and what you hope to get from the experience.

Susan

I had Sam for all the wrong reasons—selfish reasons. When you do that, your parenting becomes motivated by sheer guilt and you start off on the wrong foot. I wanted a child to give me the unconditional love that I never got. I did not see him as an individual. I did not acknowledge that I was bringing a person into the world who would have all the needs that I had as a child. I was very naive. I remember being six months pregnant and feeling, "Oh, what am I doing?" Even today I just cringe when I let myself feel the disappointment in myself and the sadness for him. I was really out of my element—I was just grasping for straws. I had that sinking feeling in my stomach that I'd gone beyond what I was ready and able to handle.

◆

CAN YOU BE
THE PARENT YOU NEVER HAD?

When it comes to parenting, many survivors assume that they are starting at zero. However, even the most abusive parents and families have moments that are positive and healthy. The trick is to remember these good times, nourish them, and build on them. You have most likely had some positive experiences in childhood with people who showed you a healthy type of caring. These are the "good" ghosts of the past. Recalling these positive influences in your life can also nurture your growth as a parent. Memories of teachers, relatives, and parents of friends who related to you in a way that modeled empathy, respect, consideration, and support are available to you. Your task in becoming the parent of your choice is to assemble these positive pieces of parenting into a more unified identity: one that will safely anchor you during the inevitable stormy times.

Pete

My mother taught me to be disciplined. Some of her methods may have been unhealthy but the net result is that once I started dealing with my addictions and my feelings about the abuse I was able to gradually take control of my life. I use this discipline everywhere in my life, from my business to my recovery. There is no doubt that I never would have been as successful in either area if I hadn't had this discipline to fall back on. Nowhere does it help more than in my parenting. I have a clear idea of the behaviors and the attitudes that were destructive to me and I use my discipline to control these tendencies to fly off the handle. My dad gave me something different: He was sensitive, he liked to be with people, he was understanding, he liked nature and sports and taught me how to play hard but fair. All of these things have helped me in my business where I must relate well to people and be fair in the way I'm pitching my sale. But it took me a long time to separate the good stuff from the bad. During recovery, the contaminated parts I got from my parents were always the focus. It wasn't until later that I could see the more positive aspects of my parents in myself.

◆

REDISCOVERING YOUR INNER CHILD

Seeing your children smile at you, observing their joy in discovering their new world, watching them roll over and eventually stand up for the first time can rekindle that long lost sense of what it is like to be a child. Sensing their vulnerability and dependence on you can touch the innocent child still alive within you. What feelings does that inner child have? How do those feelings get expressed? Do you ever listen to them, allow yourself to be guided by them? Your child will connect with these buried feelings inside you. But you must pay attention to them and give them acceptance and validation in order for them to develop.

Susan

The most difficult aspect of parenting is to be a child myself. I have a terrible time with that. I never used to play with my son. Anytime I involved myself with him as a parent, it was always on adult terms and very intellectual. You can see that in him, too. He's pretty serious and has very good verbal skills. It's very difficult for me to be childlike. But I'm getting better at it. I'm getting to the point where I can really enjoy playing with him and the other kids in the park. I have to push through some real comfort zones to get there though. As a kid, I was always used to holding myself in, being serious and not allowing more spontaneity to come out for fear of getting my parents riled up. When I play with Sam, he sometimes wants me to do the gooniest things. I get uncomfortable. I'm afraid of looking silly.

♦

Many survivors did not have much fun during childhood. You didn't have many opportunities to play because you were too busy assuming adult responsibilities. You never felt secure enough to take a risk in discovering something new because life was already filled with enough risks. As a child, you were looking for safety, consistency, and relia-bility—all grown-up values that worked against the natural self-discov-ery that children should experience.

SUGGESTIONS FOR PARENTS

1. Educate yourself about parenting and child development by reading, takin g classes, and getting involved in support groups and school-based volunteer programs. Find a good pediatrician who can be a partner in your child's physical development and your development as a parent.
2. If the stress of parenting reaches the danger level, there are options you can consider to keep your child safe. Call a tele-phone hotline to talk out your frustrations with an understand-ing volunteer who is also a parent. If you fear that you will abuse your child, call a social worker at the local child abuse agency or social services agency to temporarily place your child at a respite program for children. If you have relatives whom you trust, ask them to take care of your child while you get some help.

3. If your child is having difficulty at school or home, consult a psychologist or counselor who specializes in working with children. The professional will also work with you to help your child resolve whatever problems he may be having.

THE PARENT TRAPS

Despite your best efforts, you will inevitably make mistakes because parenting is demanding, complicated, and challenging for *everyone*. For the adult survivor, there are aspects of parenting that are bound to amplify the stresses, concerns, and conflicts that may be left over from past abuse. I call these the "parent traps" because these situations are the most likely to trigger unhealthy parenting responses. Children, as any parent will testify, have a way of "pushing our buttons," especially the ones that stick out the most. And adult survivors have many of these buttons. Think of the following parent traps as those buttons that are tied directly to your abuse. When your children push them, your choice is like approaching a fork in the road. You can repeat the past by unconsciously doing what your parents did or you can make the right turn that leads to your ultimate destination: realizing your potential as a healthy, loving parent.

POWER, CONTROL, AND AUTHORITY

Child abuse, on one level, can be seen as a parent's abuse of power over her child. If you've never worked through the feelings and conflicts over this imbalance, the chances are that your suppressed reactions may surface in your relationships with your own child whose power is less than yours. Parents, by definition, should possess more power than their child because the child is ill-equipped emotionally and intellectually to make good choices in most major issues. But the child needs to possess some control, appropriate to his or her age, in order to develop initiative to practice problem solving and to learn how to be effective in the world. By testing their ideas and actions against the world, children learn self-confidence, which eventually leads to self-esteem.

Typically many survivors deal with the task of sharing reasonable power with their children by going toward one of two extremes: either by taking too much power or too little power. If you came from a neglectful, chaotic family and assumed the caretaker role as a child, you may assume more power than is healthy for your child. You will readily recall what an out-of-control family feels like and vow not to let the past repeat itself with your child.

Susan

I now know myself well enough to see what a control freak I am. Of course, it has worked for me in some parts of my life—growing up in my family and at work. I think I channel a lot of my anxiety about things into the need to control things. And my parenting brings up a lot of anxiety about being good enough and feeling guilty for decisions I've made in the past. When he was real young, I probably gave up control for Sam's care in inappropriate ways. Always dropping him off to babysitters may not have been the best for him. Now, as he has grown up, I can see where I try to control him in various ways. I wanted him to do things my way. I wanted to share time together doing what I wanted. I would see him do things that were really an individual expression of who he is as a person, but would judge it to be wrong and then try to get him to change it. As a result, he can be kind of sneaky at times because he anticipates that I'm not going to approve of certain things. I've learned to be more accepting now and not to judge everything he does.

◆

More commonly, survivors are so afraid of becoming like their abusive parent that they will abdicate their rightful authority, giving up this aspect of responsible parenting because it is too conflict-laden for them. This is a major trap for the well-meaning parent, because while you are avoiding the abuse of power, you are also denying your children the wisdom and experience necessary to guide their development, especially when their safety is in question. Parents like this often turn to other people for advice, in effect recognizing the need for parental intervention while avoiding the personal responsibility that comes with making a decision.

Journal Questions

6. *Do you find yourself telling your child what to think and how to feel?*

7. *Do you often expect your child to act and behave like you?*

8. *Is it hard for you to allow your child to make choices?*

9. *Do you back off from being the family decision maker because you are afraid of being too controlling?*

10. *Do you rely on other adults to decide what is best for your child?*

CONTROLLING YOUR ANGER

As a parent, controlling your anger may be the most important and difficult task you have. Although anger is a natural response to being abused as a child, in most cases, you were probably prevented from expressing anger in your family for fear of being abused again. What happened to all your anger? Have you learned how to express it constructively or is it something to be avoided like so many other feelings associated with the past?

Pete

Anger has been present very, very little in my parenting because I've forced myself to be so acutely aware of it. My mom would get so rageful, especially when she was drinking, that I knew that I had to really control this tendency in myself. There has been really only two times when my anger crossed the line. One time I came home from work pissed about something and I slapped Alicia's hand when she started grabbing things off the dinner table. And I slapped it hard. It felt abusive because of what I felt inside when I did it—rage. And then a couple of weeks ago, she hit the baby and I grabbed her too hard. I grabbed her and jerked her a little bit before taking her to her room. Again, it felt inappropriate because I wasn't comfortable with it. It reminded me of my mother treating me with a lot of harshness. I realize that I have that in me. But I try to be aware of it and watch out for situations when I know I'm on edge. I've talked to my wife about it so that I'm not alone in trying to control it. Actually, one little plan that has worked is for me to turn the situation over to my wife and I just leave the scene for a few minutes until I calm down.

◆

Most survivors get angry when their children do things that they were not allowed to do as children. The feeling of unfairness and perhaps rage associated with certain situations when you got abused suddenly reappears when your child does the same thing. After years of feeling powerless to do anything about this unfairness, you now have the power to do something. In this moment, the rage can overwhelm your reasonable response, and you may end up directing it at your child instead of at your parent.

There is nothing wrong with feeling anger, especially when the situation provokes it. The problem is how you deal with it. Your own parents probably lost control of their anger prior to emotionally or physically abusing you. Anger that fuels behavior in the form of hostile words or corporal punishment can easily lead to abuse according to the definitions provided in Chapter One. The important distinction to be made concerning handling anger has to do with separating the *feeling* from the *action*. This represents another fork in the road: directing the expression of your anger *away* from your children, not at them.

There are constructive ways of handling and expressing anger that will protect your child from being abused. Below are a few suggestions.

1. Become aware of the body signals that tell you when you are starting to feel angry.

2. When you feel these signals, take a "time-out" for yourself. Put your child in a safe place and take a few minutes to calm down. If your spouse is there, turn the responsibilities over to him or her.

3. Try to figure out why you are getting so angry at what your child is doing. What messages are running through your head about the meaning of your child's actions?

4. Call a friend or a parenting hotline and tell them what you are feeling. Discuss with them what your child may be triggering inside you.

5. Write in your journal about the connections between your child's behavior and the buttons that are being pushed. Reaffirm that you have a place to express your feelings (friends, hotline, journal, spouse) and that you *can* be a different parent.

6. Engage in a different type of behavior that will discharge the feelings through constructive actions. Some people scrub walls. Others go for a jog or do some exercises. Do whatever reduces your stress.

JOURNAL QUESTIONS

11. *Does your anger tend to come out more with your children than with other people?*

12. *Does your anger trigger certain behaviors before you have a chance to make a better choice?*

13. *Do you ever feel more like your parent than yourself when dealing with your child?*

14. *Are you aware of the situations where your children push your "anger button"?*

15. *What methods have you found to control your anger?*

RESPECTING PERSONAL BOUNDARIES

As described in Part I, abusive families are characterized by parents who act like children, children who function like parents, and the tendency for individual personalities to either merge together or grow rigidly distant. Emotional needs and reactions of one parent often dominate the family atmosphere. Personal needs to control situations interfere with individual expression. Sexual urges of parents are satisfied without consideration for their effects on the children. Maintaining boundaries, in essence, is the awareness of separateness between family members and the recognition that everyone—children included—is an individual and as such deserves respect and equality.

In families where the parents' needs dominate the day-to-day functioning, children can be seen as mere extensions of their parents. Richard's relationship with his mother is a good example of a parent using her child for her own emotional needs. Children in these families are not respected as individual people with their own ideas, preferences, and rights. Children need to have their rights as people affirmed: their right to privacy, their right to disagree, their right to say no to certain types of affection, their right to be different.

Pete

One thing that I was uncomfortable with as a parent was the whole issue of household nudity and changing my baby daughter's diapers. I still have a lot of confusion and worry that something that I do might be considered abusive. I need to check out a lot of my reactions with my wife. Our little girls would run around the house naked and come into the bathroom when I was taking a shower or jump on my lap without any clothes on. At first, I'd get real nervous. All sorts of alarms would go off inside my head. When I first had to change our baby's diaper, I was afraid to clean her very well down there because I always associated the touching of a child's genitals with abuse. I had to separate my motives for touching her. My mother crossed that line and I guess I have some worry that maybe I would also.

◆

For adult survivors who grew up in "boundary-less" families, physical and emotional closeness can be scary and confusing. The line between you and your child can become murky. How strong of a presence can parents tolerate before dominating their children's development as people? How close can you get before some invisible line is crossed that says you have departed from your proper role as parent? When does physical affection become sexual arousal? At what point does taking your child into your confidence become making him your confidante? When survivors themselves are victims of blurry boundaries in childhood, there is added uncertainty about how to act, what is appropriate to disclose to their child, and when their concerns should supercede their child's desires.

Journal Questions

16. *Do you feel confused about how physically or emotionally close to get with your child?*

17. *Is it hard to let your children express their personal opinions and preferences if they differ with yours?*

18. *Do you ever use your child as a personal confidante?*

19. *Is it difficult for you to distinguish between sensual feelings and sexual arousal?*

20. *Do you often feel like you are the child and your children are your parents?*

Parenting versus Recovery

At times, during the course of recovery from child abuse, the investment of time, energy, and money in becoming your true self can conflict with the demands of being a parent. On the one hand, you feel dedicated to being an available and attentive parent, while on the other hand, you feel the need to discover who you are as a person. Going back to school, changing careers, and attending therapy sessions are three commitments to your self-discovery that will take you out of the house, often at night when your children may be needing you most. Your children will be affected: There is no sense in denying the obvious. With any change comes a period of stress and transition before the changes get integrated and a new type of normalcy takes over.

Survivors often have mixed feelings about this stage of their lives, sometimes feeling guilty for addressing their own needs and putting themselves first for once. The old role of the caretaker will clash with that reawakening part of you that wants to respect your personal needs for growth. This conflict may escalate if your children react with anger and hurt to all the changes.

Shirley

I also had to experience some distance from my family when I was going through my recovery. I had to take that time for myself. I'd never given Shirley that time before. There is no doubt that it did take time away from my children. But it was necessary for my own process, and it has made me a better parent today. To be what I think is a quality, effective parent requires time, consistency, and love. Before recovery, I would come home emotionally zapped. My kids would say, "Mom, I told you this and now you've forgotten it." And I was so good at tuning things out, I wouldn't remember what they had said. I felt so emotionally distant and I knew it was causing problems for them: They were acting out and they were unhappy. But I also knew that before I could give any more to them, I had to give something to myself, and that took time away from them. You have to focus on the end result and just try to make the best of it while going through the struggles of recovery. In the long run, it pays off because you become a more fulfilled person and they get a more complete parent.

◆

As Shirley's story illustrates, the process of self-discovery begins with an awareness of your needs as a person. Only then, can you reach your potential as a parent. It is essential to acknowledge the changes that taking time for yourself will bring. Your children will need reassurance that things will ultimately work out for the best for yourself as well as for the family. Discuss with your spouse ways that he or she can take over for you at key times when you need to spend time on your recovery. Indicate your willingness to compromise with your children and spouse, by taking their special needs into account without unduly sacrificing yours. By sharing power and responsibility with them, they will feel included and respected, and not abandoned and ignored.

For example, if your schedule will necessitate several nights out of the house, have a family meeting to discuss how your children and spouse feel about your being gone more and suggest what they can do to pick up the slack. Offer to set aside some other family time during the weekend perhaps. Or trade some household responsibilities that can more easily be accomplished with everyone's new schedule. Be creative and understanding and your children will surprise you with their consideration.

Although your children are entitled to know something about your recovery and the reasons why you are directly changing your life and indirectly changing theirs, they should be spared the troubling details of what happened to you in the past or the magnitude of your struggle to overcome the abuse. They will always want to see you as their strong, effective parent, not the hurt and vulnerable little child who was once abused. Remember that respecting boundaries will preclude your sharing more than they might be able to emotionally handle. As they grow older, more information may be appropriate, providing they indicate some interest. The best guide in determining what to tell them about the abuse is to keep your answer within the scope of their questions. Children rarely ask for more than they can emotionally handle. If they ask about something that makes you uncomfortable, tell them that you're not ready to talk about it right now or you will say more about it when they are older.

JOURNAL QUESTIONS

21. *Do you feel guilty spending time on your recovery if it takes time from your children?*

22. *Is it difficult to balance your personal needs with family responsibilities?*

23. *Do you have difficulty negotiating solutions to conflicting schedules with your children?*

24. *Have you tried to resolve these conflicts with your children? If so, what has worked and what hasn't?*

25. *How have you talked with your children about the past? What have you learned from their responses?*

DISCIPLINE AND PUNISHMENT

Children need discipline almost as much as they need love, respect, appreciation, and support. But the idea of providing discipline brings up anxiety and uncertainty for many survivors because it was often so mishandled by their own parents. Discipline was the guise under which corporal punishment was administered. And corporal punishment triggered the abuse. But discipline and punishment are two different items. Discipline is defined as "training to act in accordance with rules" whereas punishment is described as "the infliction of a penalty as a consequence of some transgression." Corporal punishment, with its emphasis on spanking and other physical acts, is only one type of punishment. Increasingly, child development experts are questioning the overall value of using corporal punishment. They reason that instead of encouraging the development of a child's internal controls over her unacceptable behavior, it may actually work against this goal because it relies on violent solutions to deter a similarly unacceptable behavior.

For you, using corporal punishment unleashes all of your unresolved feelings about the past abuse; fear of losing control over your anger and anxiety over becoming an offender. Eliminating corporal punishment as an option for punishment is a big step in reducing the likelihood of repeating your parents' mistakes.

Pete

Setting limits and discipline are the most complicated issues that my wife and I had to sort out. At first, we disagreed on what form of discipline we were going to use. My wife thought that we should spank the kids because she thought it had worked on her. But she was never beaten the way I was and I was real adamant that I did not want to spank. Spanking and beating were just too close together for me. I guess I still didn't quite trust that I could spank in a healthy way. So we started reading about discipline in some of the parenting books. We wanted to be as informed as possible. What we discovered is that kids need reasonable expectations about what is OK and what is not OK to do. They need to know that there will be consequences for their actions if they misbehave. But it doesn't have to involve hitting them. We started using "time-out"—putting our daughter in her room for five minutes when she wouldn't behave.

◆

Just as with issues of power and control, survivors who are parents fall victim to the familiar "too much to too little" syndrome when it comes to discipline. On the one hand, many parents will be fearful of repeating the past abuse, and lacking knowledge about how to provide effective discipline, they simply avoid the issue by withdrawing their authority and control over their child's behavior. Children run wild, never learning to be accountable for their behavior, because no one has made the connection between their actions and consequences. These children often have school problems because they have never been socialized. On the other hand, parents who do not perceive that the way they were treated as children was abusive are more inclined to rely on the same mode of punishment.

The task for parents when it comes to handling discipline is to emphasize communication with your children. Let them know what is acceptable and unacceptable behavior. Put words to the choices available to them so that they will begin to think before they act. Use positive reinforcement to reward the appropriate choices of behavior instead of waiting until some transgression occurs to intervene with some negative consequence. You don't want to become a "no-no" parent—one who bases his attempts to teach discipline on all the negatives: bad behavior, bad consequences, and bad feelings. Children invariably add "bad me" to the list of judgments, which is the beginning of low self-esteem.

If the strategy of building on the positives is consistent, reliably rewarded and reinforced with words, there will be less need for it over time as your children gain the ability to socialize well with others. However, punishment will be necessary at times to enforce some necessary limit on the child's behavior. When children test the limits of acceptable behavior—and eventually they will—a different type of punishment can be used that avoids the traps of spanking or hitting. Like Pete, try a "time-out" method where your child is put in her room for a few minutes (depending on her age). After the time is up, make sure to talk with her about why it happened and what she needs to do differently in the future. Finish with some positive ending to the situation that helps your child feel accepted. You can tell her how much you love her, but that you don't like that behavior.

Journal Questions

26. *What feelings have you had when you've used corporal punishment on your child?*

27. *Are you fearful of becoming abusive with your children?*

28. *Do you feel confused about how to discipline your children without becoming an abuser?*

29. *Where are you on the "too much/too little" spectrum of discipline and punishment?*

30. *What other methods of discipline have you witnessed from friends and other parents?*

PROTECTING YOUR CHILD FROM ABUSE INSIDE AND OUTSIDE THE FAMILY

If adult survivors have difficulty protecting themselves from further victimization, it is not surprising that their children are also vulnerable to abuse. Many studies have demonstrated that the children of abused parents are several times more likely to be abused within the family as well as within the community. What really happens to make survivors' children more at risk for abuse? For one thing, survivors who have not addressed or worked through their own abuse are the most likely to miss the signs that their children are being abused. This can be a startling discovery for the adult survivor and may lead to a sense of despondency and personal failure.

Shirley

I've learned that you're not any good to yourself or anyone else until you go back and take a look at your past, because whether you realize it or not, it is affecting who you are today. For me, it affected all my different roles in life—as a lover, as a friend, as a student, but most important, as a parent: how I interact with my children, how I listen or don't listen to them, whether I pay attention to something that isn't quite right with them and get them what they need to make it better. My childhood taught me not to block things out. If, as a parent, I do the same thing with my children, I am putting them in jeopardy because I may be blocking out the same type of thing that I blocked out when I was being abused as a child. Children can be an accident waiting to happen if the parent is not providing close supervision.

♦

Protecting your children goes beyond protecting them from physical, sexual, and emotional abuse. Parents need to be on the lookout for any situation that is inherently unhealthy for their children. Look at the normal situations in which your child may find himself and check to see whether you are seeing the whole picture. Does your child play at a friend's house where the parents' drinking problem prevents them from providing adequate supervision or subjects the children to bizarre behavior? Does your child attend a day-care center where the staff is so overwhelmed that an atmosphere of uncontrollable chaos prevails? Does your child complain about a teacher who demonstrates attitudes toward him that are negative, demeaning, lacking in encouragement, or downright destructive?

USING YOUR INTUITION

You want the best for your child, so allow your intuition—your inner voice—to guide you when something doesn't seem right. Ask your child if something is upsetting him, make a visit to the day-care center or school, call the teacher or the friend's parent. Put the facts together in a way that explains what your intuition is about. Allow yourself to err on the side of being too conservative or overprotective, especially if your child is under ten. If you find that you are avoiding a potential problem area, ask yourself why. Talk to someone about it: a friend, another parent, your pediatrician, a volunteer at a parent hotline, a therapist.

Susan

The biggest lesson that I've learned about being a parent is to listen to my instincts concerning what is safe and what is not. I made a mistake once in not listening to myself and it almost cost my son his life. It was Martin Luther King Day and school was out. I'd taken Sam and some other kids to the beach, including a teenage girl who I hoped would be a second in charge of babysitting. Anyway, I decided I didn't want to go down onto the beach with the others because it was too difficult to get to. But my instincts told me, "If it's too difficult for you, you're not going to be able to get to them quickly." I think a lot of parents get into this dilemma of "should I or shouldn't I do something?" But I told myself that this older girl was there and I just delegated everything to her, but without verbally telling her so. So I sat up on the cliff while they went down onto the beach to play.

They were playing with the ball in a circle and Sam's back was to the surf. I was reading my book and I'd look down on them from time to time. All of a sudden, I looked up and Sam was gone. I started yelling at the girl in a frenzied panic and then I saw Sam's head bob up in the water. A wave had hit him from behind and had taken him out. I screamed, "Get him out." But I couldn't move. I just stood there paralyzed in fear, knowing how long it would take me to get down there and knowing that whatever had to be done had to be done quickly. Finally some surfers started running out to Sam. When I saw them running, it somehow released me. I just slid down the cliff like it was a slide, shredding my clothes. By the time I hit the beach, the one surfer was carrying Sam out. The waves had stripped him totally naked. He was in shock but he was still breathing.

This really brought up a lot of stuff for me. For several weeks, I would replay this scene in my head before I would go to sleep. I thought I had lost him. My instincts told me, "Don't do this," and then I heard this other little voice saying "You mother him too much, give him some space." What I've learned is that when something doesn't feel right, especially when it concerns the safety of your child, you have to act. You have to play it safe. I felt like I got a second chance and I'm never going to forget it.

DEALING WITH YOUR OWN ABUSIVE FAMILY

The desire to share your children with your parents and their grandparents is natural and compelling. A healthy relationship between your child and her grandparents can be a wonderful experience for everyone involved. But, as only you can testify, your parents and your family may have real shortcomings when it comes to dealing with children. The same issues of protection exist for your children and their grandparents that existed with you as a child. Nobody was able to protect you, but you can protect your child now.

Pete

There's a part of me that wants my mom to see her grandchildren but I don't think I'm ready for it yet. My concerns are that it would have to be safe for me and my family to do that and I'm still not sure of that. She is still too contaminated a presence for me and I wouldn't want to put my children through such an experience, especially with me being so conflicted about it. I have come to accept that she's not going to change, and if I were to introduce my children to her, I'm going to have to be ready myself for whatever feelings or reactions may come of it. I know she is still an alcoholic and I just don't trust that she would be entirely appropriate with me or my kids. But I truly hope that someday before she dies we will all be ready for it. The desire to have her see my children runs very deep inside me. To see three generations of my family together would be very gratifying indeed.

♦

When the issues of the past abuse have never been identified, confronted, and resolved, common sense dictates that great caution should be exercised in determining whether your child should have contact with your extended family. In cases where you are estranged from your family and know that the offender or offenders have yet to receive treatment for what they did to you, you may need to make a difficult decision about denying your family and your child access to each other.

If you decide to prevent contact with your family, you will need to explain it to your children in a way that they can understand. Be aware that such a decision may represent a loss for your children and they may have feelings or questions about it. Rely on some of the suggestions mentioned earlier in the chapter regarding talking to your children about your abuse. Avoid going into the disturbing details of what your parent may have done to you. Emphasize how you and your family have different opinions about children and what is best for them. Talk about how you want people to treat your children the right way and that your parents have not always been able to do that. Ask them how they feel about not seeing their grandparents and tell them that you might reconsider when they are older. If you have other relatives who can be trusted, see if you can develop those relationships so that your children can have a positive experience with some part of their extended family. If you do not have other relatives, try elevating close family friends to the status of "aunt" or "uncle" so that your children will have some experience of an extented family relationship.

In many cases, it may not be necessary to cut off all contact between your children and your family. When the past abuse has been brought into the open and some resolution has been reached indicating that the abuser or abusers accept responsibility for what they have done, some other options may be preferred. In many situations, supervised visits will *always* be required to ensure the protection of your children. However, in those cases where you and your family have worked through the abuse, you may give them a second chance to be the parent—or grandparent—that they never were for you. Let your family know what your expectations are for them and what you will do if they revert back to their behavior of the past. Monitor the situation closely and be careful not to slip back into the old denial should some danger signal appear.

TEACHING YOUR CHILD ABOUT PERSONAL SAFETY AND BODY RIGHTS

When parents must increasingly rely on outside services for the care of their children, it is essential that children are given appropriate information about how and when to protect themselves. There is some controversy about whether such training is effective or if in some cases it simply scares the child. Obviously there is a right way and a wrong way to teach your child about safety. What is clear is that children do need help in knowing how to protect themselves, especially considering how much time they may spend away from you.

Many of today's parents may recall their own parents' early efforts at teaching about personal safety. Not answering the telephone or door bell when the parents are not home were the first and most obvious steps for self-protection. The old admonition to "never accept candy from a stranger" was in recognition that children have always been vulnerable to kidnapping and molestation. Whereas in the past my mother would warn us to stay away from the gypsies who would occasionally visit our town, today there is more recognition that abuse is perpetrated by people who are known to the child. Today a more complete approach to training is recommended in light of the apparent increase in kidnapping and child sexual abuse. We now know that most child molesters try to build a relationship with children before any attempt to molest them is made. Children need to know that in some situations they need not obey an adult if the request being made conflicts with what they have been taught. Below is a list of some of the points that can be made with children to give them some rights in protecting themselves.

PERSONAL SAFETY RIGHTS

1. Children have the right to say no to being hurt or treated in a way that they don't like.
2. Children have the right to run away from someone who they think is trying to hurt them.
3. Children have the right to ask for help from a person they trust: a parent, friend, teacher, or policeman.

4. Children have the right to tell their parents if something is bothering them.
5. Children have the right to privacy when they are using the bathroom, changing their clothes, or sleeping.

BODY RIGHTS

1. Children have the right to control what is done to their bodies, except in situations involving legitimate medical treatment.
2. Children have the right to say no to touches that don't feel good to them.
3. Children should have a say in how they dress and look.
4. Children have the right to do or say anything in order to protect themselves from physical harm.
5. Children may need permission to ask questions about their bodies.

These personal safety and body rights can be introduced to your children around the age of five or when they are about to enter school or day care. Although this is a serious subject, try to be natural and relaxed when introducing the topic. Explain to your children that they are getting older and are learning how to take care of themselves more. Try to use words that they will understand and give them permission to ask questions. Observe how they might be reacting to the discussion. If it seems counterproductive to their general well-being, drop it until they are older.

HOW TO CHOOSE
A SAFE DAY-CARE CENTER

Picking a good day-care center can be a frustrating and time-consuming endeavor requiring preparation and research into what your community offers. Currently there are about 229,000 day-care facilities across the country serving approximately 7 million children. But it is clear that the supply of quality, licensed programs falls far short of the ever-increasing demand.

Inevitably, many parents are finding that they have no choice but to turn to small, unlicensed, family day-care programs that operate out of a family home. These services vary greatly in quality and are not required to adopt state-mandated standards designed to provide safe-guards for the children. Children may be more vulnerable to physical, sexual, and emotional abuse in these types of programs.

Contrary to the sensational media reports about abuse at day-care centers, licensed day-care centers are actually safer for children than their own homes based on the number of reports filed during the last few years. However, these figures might change dramatically if rates of abuse in unlicensed family day-care programs were considered. The lesson for parents is as follows:

1. The parent has the ultimate responsibility for choosing a safe day-care program.
2. While licensed programs are preferable over unlicensed programs, this factor alone does not ensure they are safe and enriching programs.
3. By researching programs carefully and using the screening interview described in Appendix C, parents can locate quality programs.

WHAT TO DO IF YOUR
CHILD REPORTS BEING ABUSED

Survivors' worst fear is that what happened to them during childhood may happen to their children. Familiarize yourself with the signs of abuse described in chapter 2. Remember to use your intuition if something doesn't feel right concerning your child and take action. In most reported cases, the abuse is discovered when the child tells somebody about it.

Believe your children. It is essential that you take what they say seriously and deal with the situation in a responsible manner.

By not taking your child seriously or dismissing his claim of abuse, you may be unwittingly repeating the secrecy and denial of your own abuse. By believing your child, you are showing that you are on his side and will help him through this troubled time.

DO CHILDREN
EVER LIE ABOUT ABUSE?

Quite frequently, parents who are confronted by their child's allegations of abuse will question whether the abuse really happened. The types of abuse being disclosed may be so horrific that parents may find it too difficult to believe that such an incident occurred, especially if it involves someone they know or care for. In the vast majority of cases, children do tell the truth about something as serious as child abuse. But there are some limitations in their ability to remember specific details. While you can generally trust children to tell the truth concerning whether someone did something to them, the details of what actually happened or when it might have occurred may be subject to distortion.

Depending on their age, children may confuse or distort the facts surrounding the circumstances of the abuse. Young children have not developed the mental functions necessary to determine the time or sequence of events. The typical questions about when it happened, what happened first, and how it ended will be beyond the developmental capabilities of many children. Many children up to age three or four are able to distinguish the gross elements of reality, like whether something happened today or not. But they have trouble accurately reporting the fine details of the abuse, such as the who, what, when where, and how of the situation.

WHEN FALSE ALLEGATIONS ARE MOST LIKELY TO OCCUR

We now know that certain circumstances are likely to trigger false allegations of abuse. If the family is going through a divorce or custody battle, the child may be subject to pressures from a parent to perceive some incident as abusive when it is not. In these cases, the child may feel obligated to go along with the parent's charges out of a sense of duty to that parent, often a mother who was left by the father. In situations where a child, especially a teenager, feels angry, rejected, or abandoned by a parent, the motive for the accusation may be to get revenge or signal deep emotional pain. When these special circumstances are not present, the chances that your child is telling the truth about being abused are very great.

MAKING A CHILD ABUSE REPORT

Reporting child abuse over the telephone to the police or the Child Protection Service authorities is the next step in doing what is best for your child. Remember that child abuse is a crime and should be reported not only to protect your child but to protect other children who may also be abused by the offender. If you or your child tells a teacher, child-care worker, or any health-care professional, he or she will most likely report the incident because he is legally mandated to do so and may be committing a misdemeanor if he does not. Do not try to contact the alleged offender yourself for whatever reason. The police or child protection team investigating the charges should take care of that. Your job is to support your child through this crisis.

Many parents have misgivings about making such a report because it involves the authorities and raises concerns for their child. In recent years, many police and child protection personnel have received special training that allows them to handle the delicate interviewing of a traumatized child. Talking to a stranger about something as painful and embarrassing as child abuse will be upsetting to most children. Some officials are better at interviewing than others, however, and I would be remiss if I didn't acknowledge that the situation can be mishandled by the police, social workers, and court personnel.

Many child abuse cases drag on seemingly forever especially if the case goes to court. Some agencies will want to interview and reinterview your child over a period of weeks, which is not helpful to your child. Try to be an advocate for your child and negotiate reasonable expectations involving only one interviewer. If the first interviewer videotapes the session, it may eliminate the need for several interviews. If you feel that the process becomes destructive to your child, you will need to weigh your civic responsibility in light of doing what is best for your child. If the investigation phase becomes too demanding, let the authorities know that you may pull out unless changes favoring your child are made. Many parents have opted to drop the case at the court stage because it was too emotionally upsetting for their child to testify in front of their alleged offender. Unfortunately the legal system still does not favor the needs and limitations of child witnesses.

Many states have victim protection services available, which can pay for the medical and psychological treatment that your child will most likely need. And many cities have special child abuse treatment services that will provide crisis counseling and short-term therapy for you and your child, but only if there is an official child abuse report made.

Susan

I had a situation where I should have made a child abuse report but I didn't. I had a neighbor who lived across from my apartment complex who abused her eight-year-old daughter. The girl was friends with my son and the mother and I would share babysitting. I wasn't that crazy about the mother personally, but it was convenient to share child care. She was into partying and as a result tended to be neglectful and verbally hostile to her daughter. On several occasions, we used to hear her hit her daughter who would then cry for the remainder of the night.

Once when I was babysitting her, I gave her a bath and noticed some bruises on her behind that I thought were made with a hair brush. I didn't do anything about it. I felt like it wasn't my business, and besides, I saw the mother doing some things that I had done in the past, so who was I to challenge her?

My son was really upset about it. I had a self-help book about child abuse in the house and he wanted me to give it to the mother. That should have clued me in that something was wrong. But it was easier for me to look the other way—I had done that my whole life. Finally I was having a meeting with my son's therapist and was mentioning what was going on. All of a sudden, he tells me that he will have to report it. I was shocked and scared. I felt like I did something wrong to mention it. The therapist made the report and a few days later the police paid her a visit. She was real upset and found out that it had come from me. We had this angry confrontation outside my apartment. She felt betrayed that I didn't come to her first—maybe I should have. But I don't think she would have listened. Anyway, it didn't turn out that well because the people doing the investigation didn't find sufficient evidence to prosecute. The mother turned down their offers for counseling and then prevented her daughter from playing with my son. He was upset about it and it was difficult to convince him that we did the right thing. In retrospect, it's hard to see what it all accomplished except that the mother now has some idea that what she's doing isn't cool. I should have handled this situation a long time ago. But I still had so much denial about my own abuse that I couldn't see it happening when it was right under my nose.

◆

ACTING IN THE
BEST INTERESTS OF YOUR CHILD

If your child reports being abused, the following guidelines should be helpful in responding appropriately. Be aware that handling such a situation will be very difficult for you, especially if you know the offender. Don't go through it alone. Get support for youself, and if it rekindles the old feelings of being abused yourself, consider seeing a therapist. The better shape you are in as a parent, the more you will have to give to your child.

1. After comforting your child, calmly ask her to tell you the whole story as best she can.
2. If any part of his story is unclear (and it may be), calmly ask the questions necessary to clarify the confusion. Be aware that your

questions may raise doubts in your child about whether you believe him or not. Provide as much reassurance as necessary for your child. It is more important for you to give your child emotional support at this time than to gather information.

3. Tell your child that what happened was wrong and not her fault. Tell your child that both of you may need to meet with some people to tell them what happened. Also, in the case of sexual abuse, the child needs to know that she will visit a doctor for a checkup.

4. Look up the phone number for the county or city agency that is responsible for investigating child abuse reports, or call the police and ask for the right number. Call immediately and make the report. You will be asked several questions about what happened. If you are not sure of some answers, say so. Ask what the process of investigating the allegation will involve and what will be expected of you and your child.

5. Immediately make arrangements for your child's contact with the alleged offender to be severed. If your child was abused at a school or day-care center, call the principal or director and ask that the alleged offender be suspended pending the outcome of the case. If this cannot be arranged, then you should keep your child safely home until other arrangements can be made. It usually is best for your child to resume her normal life, although guaranteeing her safety is even more important. Under no circumstances should your child be allowed contact with the alleged offender. Explain to your child whatever changes in her life may be temporarily necessary. Again, provide as much reassurance as she needs.

6. All children need help in dealing with the experience of being abused. Arrange for your child to receive counseling by a trained professional experienced in child abuse treatment. Explain to your child that this is necessary so that he can feel better about what happened. Individual and/or group therapy is the best type of therapy for your child to receive during the early stage. If the abuse has gone on for an extended time, therapy of longer duration may be necessary to work through all of the feelings and trauma experienced by your child.

WHAT TO DO IF YOU
OR YOUR SPOUSE IS THE ABUSER

The most difficult situation is when you, your spouse, or someone connected to your family is abusing your child. Remember that the principle of doing what is best for your child still applies, only now a significant change is necessary in your family life.

The first step in dealing with this situation is to act immediately so that the abuse stops and will not resume in the future. Recognize that physical, sexual, and emotional abuse are learned behaviors that are deeply ingrained in the personality of the abusive adult. Abusive behavior usually continues unless someone steps in to provide the abuser with necessary controls over his behavior. Making a child abuse report on your spouse or partner may seem extreme, but it may be the only way to guarantee that the abuse stops and the abuser gets the help necessary to change.

Ask your partner to move out of the house until he can get help in acting more responsibly with your child. Don't send your child to friends or relatives because the child may feel as if she is the problem. Be clear to everyone involved that the problem is the abuser's behavior. You may feel as if you're being forced to choose between your child's needs and your spouse's indignant reaction. By acting decisively you are really choosing to protect your child while setting the stage for your spouse to get help. It is in everyone's interests that this situation be handled the right way. Make the right choice in doing what is necessary to protect your child. If your relationship with your spouse cannot survive your effort to do the right thing, then maybe this is not the right relationship for you. And it certainly is not a safe relationship for your child.

Susan

In the earlier years, a lot of my abusive behavior took the form of emotional abuse, mostly verbal stuff like being harsh, mean, ignoring Sam, letting my anger get the best of me, taking it out on him. The words that came out of my mouth were the same that my mother used on me. When I would say these things something would click inside of me and I would know it wasn't right. It was like a split screen operating inside of me where half of me would be my mother and half the child in me. Nothing Sam did was that bad to deserve what he got from me verbally. I can remember when he was about four years old and just learning how to get me angry—I used to grab his arms and shake him, and then grab him by the neck, and march him like a puppet to his room and just shove him in and slam the door. It was like I was saying, "You better get away from me, kid." When he was older, I actually started to do the sessions in the bathroom just like what my mother did to me. I feel real bad about this now. It was always following a situation where he'd get me angry or I was in a panic that something happened to him. I'd take him into the bathroom, close the door, and start to wallop him with a paddle. I would click into some kind of trance almost, the same way that I used to sense my mother would change when she was in there with me. I would lose control of my anger in the bathroom and hit him a lot harder and longer than I really needed to. I'd feel like a machine—hot feelings coursing through a cold exterior. I would disconnect from the reality of the situation, like I had no sympathy for whom I was doing this to. Then when it was over, I'd walk out of the bathroom and I'd click back into my old self. Immediately I would start feeling guilty about it.

♦

The second step *requires* that you or whoever was abusive, get immediate help in the form of professional therapy, involvement in a support group for parents, and use of crisis services on an as-needed basis. The same advice would apply if you or your spouse is on the *verge* of acting abusively toward your child. Don't give into these impulses to repeat the past. Do whatever is necessary to prevent yourself from hurting your child. Reach out for help and admit that you have a problem. End the shame and guilt associated with your own abuse by acting differently for you and your child. You will feel pride and a sense of mastery over the past.

Susan

Well, the awareness of what I was doing didn't come to me until I started therapy, when I finally started to acknowledge that I was abused as a child. I had a breakthrough when it finally dawned on me that I was repeating the bathroom scene with my mother when I took my son into the bathroom for his paddling. It all started to fit together like a puzzle. The way she and I would click off into a kind of rageful trance, the way she and I would be ignoring one minute and then so angry the next. I was horrified to discover all of this. My denial had protected me for years; now it was preventing me from seeing how I was replaying the past with my own child. Only with therapy could I have seen this. It took a few months of sessions before I was ready to put my awareness into changing my behavior. Sam and I started to talk these things out. I started to tell him when I had overreacted and would acknowledge that my behavior was not fair to him. I let him know that it was sometimes hard for me to control myself when I got so mad. He could hear it and understand it and work with me on it. Nowadays, when I get really lit up, he knows to pull away for the time being. I go into my room for a few minutes until I can compose myself. Then I come out and talk to him calmly about how I'm feeling. He is always relieved. We are a lot closer now and I know this has helped him trust me more. I'm really proud of him. He has learned how to speak up and tell me when he doesn't think I'm treating him fairly. I wish I could have done that when I was a child, but at least I was able to do it with my son.

◆

JOURNAL QUESTIONS

31. *Have you ever suspected that your child may have been hurt or abused? If so, how did you deal with it?*

32. *Have you carefully screened your child's day-care center, baby sitters, and any other person who assumes temporary care for her?*

33. *Can you be completely assured that your own family is safe for your child?*

34. *Have you ever suspected that another child was being abused? If so, what did you do about it?*

35. *Have you ever felt close to hurting your child? Do you suspect that you might be abusing your child now?*

JUDICIAL ABUSE: WHEN THE LEGAL SYSTEM FAILS

Unfortunately, reporting the abuse of your child to the authorities does not always turn out the way it should. Investigating and resolving child abuse cases requires enormous resources that quickly overwhelm many county social service and child protection agencies. The procedures that these agencies employ to investigate the abuse sometimes leaves the child feeling revictimized. Even if formal charges of abuse are made, the legal system has its own limitations that are quickly exposed by cases that rely on the young victim's testimony. The result is sometimes a miscarriage of justice that may leave a parent questioning why he or she bothered to make a report in the first place.

The adversarial nature of our court system can be ill-suited to handling child witnesses and the more delicate issues of psychological evidence around which these cases usually turn. Often, the child's word is the only real evidence that can convict an abuser and resolve the case in a way that protects the child. While medical psychological experts can testify on the child's behalf, similar experts testifying for the alleged abuser often negate the value of expert testimony, leaving the burden of proof on the child witness. As indicated previously in this chapter, children are often not able to give the type of detailed, consistent testimony deemed necessary to convict an adult, especially considering how many of them are still traumatized by the events they are being asked to describe. Even in cases where the child is a believable witness, opposing counsel can usually find ways to exploit the child's cognitive immaturity or vulnerability to anxiety to discredit his testimony.

The shortcomings of the legal system are most evident in cases involving allegations of sexual abuse in young children from divorced or separated families where child custody and visitation rights are also an issue. These are the cases where the only witnesses to the abuse are the child and the alleged abuser, where there is often no physical evidence of the alleged abuse and where, in the emotional turmoil following marital discord and divorce, both parents are often suspected of having a motive for the charges. The child's interests often get lost in these cases in the fervor to protect the civil rights of the parents. For example, even when the alleged abuser has had a previous conviction for sexual molestation in a prior marriage, this information cannot be considered by the court despite the fact that withholding such information could be said to violate the rights of the child. If a guilty parent is acquitted of abuse, in most cases, the court will reinstitute this parent's visitation rights which, in effect, can sentence the child to more abuse.

In response to this failure of the legal system to protect the interests of their child, hundreds of parents of child abuse victims have opted to take the law into their own hands in order to protect them from additional abuse. Instead of complying with a court order forcing them to either share custody with the ex-spouse who is the alleged abuser or permit the other parent to have unsupervised visitation with the child, some parents are taking their children on the run, relocating to new areas of the country and adopting new identities to avoid detection. Currently, there is a clandestine network of some 1000 safehouses nationwide—a new "underground railroad"—set up to provide sanctuary to these parents and children who have been orphaned from their past lives by unfavorable court decisions.

The parents who choose such desparate measures and the volunteers who support the underground railroad appear committed to helping protect the child from further abuse. While their purpose is laudable, there is a negative impact on the child which may go unnoticed in their efforts to protect children from sexual abuse. Living on the run can be physically, emotionally and developmentally damaging—travelling long distances under cover, often without adequate financial or material resources, adopting aliases and disguises, staying places with strange people and never knowing what will come next. The FBI or private investigators are often involved in locating their whereabouts and bringing them into custody. The child is forced to live with a different kind of fear, apprehension, and anxiety than that associated with ongoing sexual abuse. In many cases, the child is deprived of a stable, consistent life with adequate schooling and opportunities to make longstanding relationships. In essence, the parent—in most cases, the mother—accompanying the child becomes a criminal, in violation of a court order. And psychologically, the child is cast in the role of the accomplice.

Clearly, adopting a fugitive's existence to protect the child from abuse is not the answer, although considering the circumstances surrounding many of these cases, it is an understandable alternative. Any loving parent facing the same dilemma would likely consider such extreme measures to protect her child from abuse. As in the last century when the underground railroad offered protection to slaves when the law failed to grant them civil rights, the existence of this new underground railroad is another sign that our laws are failing another group of citizens—our children.

The solution is to direct our efforts at the source of the problem: the laws that prevent the alleged abuser's past history of child abuse offenses from being entered into the court testimony; the police and court procedures that put the child through a bewildering array of interviews, depositions, and examinations over the course of months or years, and the futile practice of pitting one mental health expert against another that often cancels out the desparately needed expertise of quality psychological testimony. There is a way out of this legal quagmire, but it will take a combined effort from mental health specialists, children's rights advocates, legal scholars, juvenile court judges, and most importantly, the legislative and judicial branches of government to make it happen. Children, by virtue of their lack of power in our society, must be granted additional legal safeguards in order to protect them in the face of reasonable doubt about their safety. Anything short of this is a violation of *their* civil rights.

For an adult survivor of child abuse, raising a child can be an exhilarating affirmation of your growth as a person. It can also be tremendously challenging, demanding, and stressful, especially if you have yet to acknowledge the effect of your own child abuse. Learning to be a good parent takes a desire to look at parts of yourself that you may prefer to keep under wraps. It also takes a commitment to learning healthy ways of relating to your child that may be dramatically different from the way your parents treated you. Finally it takes a willingness to ask for help when feeling stressed or out of control. Remember that you can be a healthy parent. It will take work, but as Shirley, Susan, and Pete have described, they are doing it differently and so can you.

Chapter Eight

SOUL MATES:
FOR FRIENDS, LOVERS,
AND SPOUSES

This chapter is for the significant people in the lives of adult survivors—friends, lovers, spouses, and co-workers—virtually anyone who has a relationship with someone who was physically, sexually, or emotionally abused. Being close to an adult survivor before or during recovery presents many questions and challenges that may evoke a wide spectrum of feelings in you ranging from confusion to anger, concern to despair.

Not surprisingly, the difficulties and reactions that survivors face prior to recovery may be hard for you to understand if you have not had an abusive childhood yourself. If you were abused or grew up in a dysfunctional family, the problems stirred up by their recovery may either compound your own struggles to heal or stir your compassion, support, and understanding. This chapter addresses the myriad issues that come between the survivors and their "significant others" and shows you how to help your loved one through the course of recovery, without sacrificing your own needs.

Regulating the amount of help and support you can provide the survivor without draining or overextending yourself is the prime challenge you will face. Clearly, playing a role that in the long run will deplete you is not the answer. While many of you will be reading this chapter to understand how you can help, perhaps the most important lessons will be presented later when self-help suggestions are offered to you on how to protect your interests in the relationship as well. Common dilemmas faced by partners of adult survivors will be discussed and information will be given on how to handle these delicate issues without setting back their recovery *or* sacrificing your own personal needs.

Although many survivors tend to withdraw from social situations and social relationships out of fear and anxiety, most desparately hope to establish a caring bond with another person. Their hope, of course, is that the relationship with someone like you will be different from the destructive experiences they've had with their parents and perhaps other adults in their recent past. Although they may see you as a safe person, getting close to someone raises the old feelings that may push them away, despite their best intentions. This approach-avoid tendency may be confusing to you if you don't understand how difficult it is for them to reach out. The ability to establish and maintain a caring, mutually satisfying relationship is a significant milestone in their recovery process. And you—the friend, the lover or the spouse—can play an important role in their healing.

Richard's Wife

We have been together for seven years now and I'm still learning how his relationship with his mother intrudes in our marriage. It changes all the time. My first memory of it is when Richard and I were first getting involved, and we were at a bar having a glass of wine and talking. And I asked him about his mother, and he told me that his mother was a saint—perfect and wonderful, and on and on, and I'm sitting there thinking this can't really be true. So, I said, "You gotta be kidding. No one's mother is this perfect." Then he goes on to talk about how she actually treated him and how she would shriek at him and then beat him up physically. I wasn't completely shocked by the news, although I was saddened by it. I thought about my views of child abuse and I guess I thought that everyone, to some degree, gets abused by their parents. What he was telling me seemed similar to what everybody talks about. But over the years, it has become clearer to me how his mother, Daphne—or the ghost of Daphne—plays a subtle and sometimes not so subtle, role in our relationship.

◆

Having established a relationship with a survivor, you have probably seen many of your loved one's difficulties "played out" within the relationship. He may have expressed strong feelings that seemed way out of place under the circumstances, or misunderstandings and misperceptions may frequently crop up, and his passivity, aggression, or withdrawal may have made it impossible to communicate.

Depending on where they are in recovery, survivors' lives are often full of conflicts over work issues, parenting responsibilities, intimacy, trust, and sexuality, that are bound to show themselves in some way. If their abuse was severe, survivors may exhibit symptoms of trauma such as bodily ailments, sleep disorders, and numbing of feelings during sexual contact. All of these problems end up affecting you.

Richard's Wife

It can be so terrifying to wake up in the middle of the night when Richard is having a sleep terror and playing out this scene in our apartment involving some attacker who has broken in. I've been thrown to the floor because he is running somewhere to get away. And I can never get him to wake up or calm down. I used to just try and say, "If you're having a nightmare, that's OK," but he just wouldn't wake up. Then I would get involved in the drama, but that would only make him worse. I've had the best luck just saying whatever seems to be a solution to the problem. Like he'll say, "There's a man in the doorway and he's got a gun." And I'll wake up and instead of saying, "You're having a nightmare," I'll say, "No, I think he left." Gradually he starts to calm down and I talk him back into bed. The next morning he will have no memory of it whatsoever.

◆

Survivors may turn to you for things they never received from their family: support, understanding, reassurance, validation, and advice. Their needs may seem enormous and are not always well articulated. Instead of asking directly for something, they may hint around or say nothing at all. Only later will their true intentions be expressed, often after a buildup of disappointment. You may tell them that you are no mind reader, but their confidence in having their needs met by others is not very great. They may have learned that it is safer to remain quiet rather than to ask for something that will likely be denied. Or the opposite may be true. They may have learned that you only get heard when you are out of control. This is yet another piece of the child abuse legacy. You must convince them that this can be different with you, that they can trust that you will take them seriously.

Pete's Wife

I knew before we got married that there were some problems between Pete and his mother, but I thought it was just because she was an alcoholic and was not a good mother. At the time, I was dealing with my own drinking problems, so I had my own denial about my family. Having adopted AA as my philosophy of recovery, I encouraged him to forgive her and move on with his life. I thought if he just followed the 12 Steps, he would work it out for himself. But I was wrong about that. I remember after we were married, we were sitting at the kitchen table one night and he just flat out told me that there had been incest between him and his mother. And I had never known anybody that it had happened to, so I was surprised in a way, but the funny thing was that I wasn't really shocked by it. I immediately felt hatred toward his mother and felt really sad for him. Then he told me that he was thirteen when it happened, and my first thought was, "That's kind of old for it to happen. He should have been able to stop it." And as I have learned more about incest, I have grown to understand without a doubt that it was not his fault. His mother is a very sick woman and the incest was an outgrowth of their very sick relationship. What I didn't know at the time was how this would come to affect our relationship. Surprisingly, it didn't seem to affect our sex life. What it really did was make it hard for him to be intimate in an emotional way.

◆

HOW DOES THEIR
ABUSE MAKE YOU FEEL?

When you are close to someone who is recovering from child abuse, inevitably it will raise many questions for you. You may feel outraged by what happened to this person as a child and murderous rage toward the parents or other abuser. Or you may feel shame or embarrassment and try to avoid the topic altogether. You may wonder about your own childhood and feel relief or guilt that you were never abused. Initially it may be impossible to fathom what it was really like for this person, and as a result, you may not know what to say or how to comfort her. After hearing about her childhood over and over again, you may want her to hurry and deal with the situation once and for all, allowing your relationship to go forward unencumbered by the emotional baggage of the past. When this doesn't immediately happen, frustration, resentment, and impatience may set in, leaving you feeling helpless and confused.

In some cases, it may raise new questions about incidents in your past that you had long forgotten. Hearing someone else's experience may cast a different light on how you understand episodes in your past that you were once content to label as only "weird." What the survivor goes through in recovery will definitely challenge your own denial about your past, how you feel about the survivor, and perhaps, how you feel about yourself.

How you deal with these feelings and reactions may influence how you are able—or not able—to respond to the needs of the survivor in your life. Accepting that you will have these strong feelings and not reacting to them as threats will enable you to listen and be open to the experiences being shared with you.

Shirley's Lover

I would say that my initial reaction to hearing about her abuse was dismay. I wasn't shocked because I know it's something that goes on in the world. But to have someone that I knew and am close with actually go through an experience like that brought my feelings out for her. I felt really sorry for her. It sounds to me like she never really had a childhood. I found myself feeling anger toward her father for doing what he did but perhaps even more anger toward her mother for allowing it to happen. That may sound strange, but I just think her mother was a real accomplice in the whole thing—what with dragging Shirley into her marital problems and expecting her child to handle him for her. That was wrong and the sexual abuse was part of all that. She just wasn't around enough for the kids. I think I developed these attitudes by listening to Shirley and finding out what really happened. I asked a lot of questions about it and was really interested. That's the type of person I am—a lot of natural curiosity. I wanted to know her feelings and reactions, and what went on, and how it happened, and that sort of thing. Out of all this, we became better friends. I was able to tell her how I felt and that was good for me back then. That was when we were friends. After we got involved as lovers, it brought up a whole other set of feelings and reactions because everything became more intensified. We had to talk through all of those feelings as well.

◆

How strongly the survivor's struggle to recover affects you depends on how close the two of you are. As friends or co-workers, you may not see the full range of feelings and difficulties that survivors are struggling with because they will usually not trust people enough to be open with them. They may avoid you out of shame or anticipate being judged or rejected. You may know about their troubled past and want to reach out to them, only to be frustrated by their unresponsiveness.

If you are in an intimate relationship with a survivor, the experience may be quite different. Generally, the closer survivors are to another person, the more their true feelings, conflicts, and apprehensions will surface. Life with a survivor can be a roller coaster ride of constantly shifting moods and feelings; arguments and fighting can escalate in the blink of an eye and hurt feelings and bruised egos may seem like an everyday event. You may feel totally confused about why this relationship is so difficult and about what you are doing to make it seem so conflictual. You care deeply for you friend or spouse, but find yourself wondering what the relationship is offering you. Although what happened to him was awful, his childhood abuse is affecting you, and this seems unfair.

It may be difficult to understand the situation if you were raised in a normal family, but the survivor is simply not used to healthy give-and-take relationships. When he was a child he tolerated not getting anything, but as an adult he may expect to have it all. When this happens, you may feel the relationship is unbalanced. You may feel like you're being used by the survivor. This is probably the most common reaction reported by close friends, lovers, and spouses of survivors. Resolving this conflict in a way that works for both of you is the central challenge of your relationship.

HOW LONG BEFORE RECOVERY?

How long will it take before the problems of the past stop interfering in your relationship? While this is a common question, there is no simple answer. Much of it depends on how severely abused the survivor was during her childhood and where she is in her recovery. In cases where the child abuse was moderate or severe, recovery can take several years, certainly more than two years and sometimes as long as ten years. However, you may see some positive changes in your relationship much sooner. Certainly the first year or two of recovery is the most critical, when the survivor is reclaiming old memories and dealing with feelings and attitudes that have been pushed away for so long. This period is when she may experience the breakthrough crisis, when these old feelings and memories come quickly to the surface and threaten to overwhelm her.

It is important to realize that you don't have to put yourself on ice for the years that it may take for your friend or spouse to recover from the abuse. You can actually be an active participant, by showing interest, support, and understanding, but also by expressing your tolerance limit. No matter how rocky things seem, you can take comfort in knowing that things are evolving in a positive direction.

BASIC RELATIONSHIP ISSUES

Certain issues and problems faced by adult survivors will affect all types of relationships—intimate ones as well as friendships. Below is a review of some of the most common dilemmas that are discussed in terms of the effects on you. Again, not all survivors' relationships will reflect every area. Try to understand when and how these issues come up in your relationship.

IS THE SURVIVOR MISTRUSTFUL OF YOU?

Trust is the major issue that undermines the sanctity of your relationship with a survivor. Because survivors grew up in families where their trust was betrayed on an everyday basis, it's no surprise that trust also becomes an issue in their adult lives. Trust is not something that can be turned on and off. It is something that must be developed over time. Rebuilding trust will take energy, consistency, and self-awareness on your part.

You may find that lack of trust is a constant issue between you and the survivor. She may feel like you're not trustworthy and may question you about where you have been or ascribe peculiar motives for your actions. You may notice that she acts in ways that undermine your trust in her, such as being secretive or inconsiderate of your feelings.

Survivors want you to be perfect, and when you fall short, the brittle-
ness of their trust can easily shatter.

Shirley's Lover

S hirley had trouble accepting trust in someone else and being able
to understand that someone else could care about her and want to
make it better for her. It took a long time for her to mostly trust me. I
don't think she's even reached that point yet where she can trust me
100 percent. Even though she knows that she doesn't have to worry
about that with me, there's something inside of her on an unconscious
level that stops her from completely trusting me. She's never been able
to rely on anyone for anything and thinks she will have to do everything
for herself. But it definitely has gotten better over the years because I
am very trustworthy and I have in a sense proved myself to her. I try
to show her that I'm someone that she can lean on and that she can
come to me and talk to me and rely on me for whatever it is, whether
it's emotional, or physical, or monetary. It's made a difference in how
she feels. Eventually it sank in that "this is someone you can trust."

◆

Expect trust issues to get stirred up if you are inconsistent or unpredictable, if you quickly change your mind, or if the survivor is not able
to predict your mood or your reaction to a particular situation. Trust is
built on a series of transactions or negotiations. If you say you're going
to do something, it's really essential that you follow through. If for
some reason you can't, it's important that you get to the survivor first
and tell her that you're not going to be able to follow through and
explain the reasons why. It may also be important for you to come up
with an alternate solution.

Building trust takes communication, negotiation, execution, and
accountability. *Communication* has to do with the wording of an agreement between you and the survivor. The survivor asks you to do something, you respond with a different idea, and what follows is basically
a *negotiation* between these two points of view leading to a decision
with which both of you can live. The agreement is then carried out or
executed. Then there must be some kind of *accountability*, a recognition
that the agreement was carried out and the results are duly acknowledged by both partners. As this process happens over and over again,
the survivor begins to feel more trusting, expecting that this process
will get repeated again and again. And as time goes on, and as the

number of repetitions increase, he'll feel more confident that what happened with you will also happen in the future.

WHAT ARE THE BARRIERS
TO INTIMACY IN YOUR RELATIONSHIP?

Intimacy, or the ability to get close in a personal relationship, is also founded on trust. Intimacy and trust go hand in hand. When trust is low, there's very little chance for intimacy, because the closer you get, the more the survivor will feel threatened by you. (If you're a friend of a survivor, intimacy will not be as much of an issue as it is in romantic relationships.) Intimacy means sharing parts of yourself with another person and expecting to be treated with respect, consideration, and understanding. Survivors feel a lot of anxiety about getting too close. When a child learns that parents can hurt as well as provide love, ambivalence develops as to the safety of close relationships. Abused children learn that intimate relationships can cause tremendous pain and adult survivors carry this ambivalence with them into their later intimate relationships, undermining the belief that they will be accepted for who they are. In their mind, the closer they get, the more likely it is that they'll be abused. Approaching you may bring up many of these same feelings. Survivors will go very delicately and cautiously, looking for every sign that they may be about to get hurt.

Pete's Wife

When Pete and I were in the early stages of our dating, intimacy didn't seem to be an issue. He would hold my hand. He would kiss me. We would talk. He was very physical. As we began to get closer and more committed to each other, he began to pull away. I would hug him and he would pull away. I would expect to kiss him good-bye when we left, or when I would come home, to kiss him hello. And he would never do that. He was afraid to let me get close to him. I remember that he couldn't tell me he loved me until right before we got engaged. We had been going out a year and a half and seeing each other every night and he would sign his cards, "Your friend, Pete." At times, he would turn into this little puppy dog and ask "Am I really worth having a good family, home, and wonderful job with? Do you really think I'm worth it?" And I wanted to cry when he said that because I couldn't believe that he felt he wasn't worth loving.

But at other times I didn't feel so understanding of his difficulty to being close. He made me angry. I couldn't understand why he couldn't just hug me when I needed a hug, be there for me when I needed it, be more understanding and sympathetic of how I felt. I know he has been a caretaker in his family, but he has never been a caretaker of me. He's not that good at giving. I know it brings up a lot of issues for him, but after a while I just get tired of it all.

♦

Creating a more intimate relationship starts with doing what you can to make it safe for the survivor. That means finding out what makes him feel secure and what makes him feel scared. Often his fears will not seem logical or grounded in reality. You want to convince him that you are someone good and safe, but somehow your words are never enough.

Survivors have learned that actions speak louder than words. Remember the reality that shapes their mode of relating to you is based on the past, not necessarily on what happens in the present with you. You can demonstrate that you are safe to get close to by being sensitive and understanding and considerate. You need to listen carefully and take what they say respectfully. It is essential that you not force yourself on them by pushing your point of view or plan of action because this is the one "button" that will trigger their anxieties about loss of power and control. By demonstrating over time in all sorts of ways, large and small, that you will treat the survivor with respect, honesty, and consideration, the barriers to intimacy will gradually melt.

DO YOU STRUGGLE
OVER POWER AND CONTROL?

Power and control issues are likely to intrude on virtually all aspects of your relationship: dividing household responsibilities, sharing parenting duties, making decisions, even making love. Survivors tend to either be control freaks, seeking to make the call on most every topic imaginable, or they exercise control in a more passive, covert manner.

For survivors, these issues are both scary and essential to their feeling safe. Although authority was misused by their parents, survivors probably had to find ways to take some control as children in order to protect themselves from further abuse. And since survivors' first order of business is self-protection, you can understand why control is so important to them.

On the other hand, taking control means being active and decisive, as well as feeling somewhat entitled. If this is difficult for the survivor (as it often will be), the ways that she takes power and control may be more indirect. She may try to get her way by using her moods to influence people or by acting helpless in order to get her partner to do things for her.

Shirley's Lover

S hirley has always been very stubborn and very independent. Her defense mechanism is to take control of situations. The problem is that control is also an issue with me. I didn't have the type of childhood she did, but I didn't have an ideal childhood either. I've also learned to deal with life by putting myself in control of all situations. And so when you have both of us wanting to be in control, it causes problems. The control situation is compounded because we work together and I am her boss. She tries to get control by being real good at what she does. She's very task-oriented, hard working, and can manage others. In most organizations, she moves right to the top. But in our situation, I'm always above her. There have been times when we haven't agreed on how to handle a situation, and because I do have the final word, she has to go along with what I say, and so that's very difficult for both of us. She ends up feeling resentful and I feel somewhat guilty for having all the power. It can get really uncomfortable when we come home from work after having had some conflict, because once we walk through the door, we are supposed to be equal. Sometimes this doesn't work that well and what happens at the office spills over into our private lives.

◆

Begin to discuss the need to share control and power more evenly. It's important that you raise this issue in a way that will increase the chances of the survivor hearing you and not feeling threatened. It's best to talk about what you need rather than what she shouldn't do. If you phrase your question in a way that will make the survivor feel as if she's being forced, chances are she will react by attempting to take more power and more control.

HOW ARE DEPENDENCY AND CODEPENDENCY PLAYED OUT?

Dependency and codependency struggles go hand in hand for survivors and their relationships. Dependency refers to your capacity to rely on someone for emotional support whereas codependency occurs when you are the provider of the support. Both are healthy and natural aspects of intimate relationships when they are mutually shared by both partners. But in many survivor relationships, dependency and code-pendency evolve toward the extremes—too much or too little—with one person exclusively taking on the dependent role and the other taking on the codependent role. Because past abuse thwarted their natural tendency to become dependent on their parents, adult survi-vors have a hard time managing the degree of dependency in their personal lives. Sometimes survivors cannot let themselves become de-pendent to any degree, lest they risk a second betrayal. Sometimes their solution is to continue the caretaker role they perfected during child-hood and adopt the codependent role in a relationship with a friend or partner who is overly dependent. Other times they may become overly dependent, expecting their partner to take care of them as if they were children who needed reparenting.

Richard's Wife

Three years into the relationship, I realized there was something wrong with the domestic arrangements between us. I felt as if I was involved with someone who had just gone through a divorce—a man who had been living with a wife for ten years and was used to their household being run in a certain way. I would have to remind myself that Richard had never been married before, although it seemed that he and his mother had been husband and wife. Where that came out in our relationship was that Richard couldn't be an equal domestic partner. We fell into this real mother-son arrangement where I was really the caretaker, in both an emotional sense and domestic sense. I felt like I was being cast in the role of the good mother who was going to make it all better. While Daphne had made Richard like a slave around the house, I now was going to offer this serene home where he got waited on, and nothing was ever asked of him, and he never had to take on any responsibility. This went on for about a year before it started occurring to me how we hooked together as a couple. I am a very strong and dominant woman like his mother is, except the differ-ence between Daphne and me is that I'm also very self-sufficient and independent. I feel safe emotionally when I have a lot of control, and one way I could feel like I have control in this kind of volatile relation-ship with him is to play the caretaker. So my tendency to control and not need much for myself fit very nicely into his fantasy of never being bothered or expected to do much. That was until I got furious about it.

◆

You will need to look at how codependency enters into your relationship. Do you tend to focus on the survivor's needs to the exclusion of your own? Do you enmesh yourself in his problems and define the relationship in terms of how he is doing? Is your self-esteem tied up in how well you are helping him to cope with problems? Do you feel anxious when he makes overtures toward independence, autonomy, and self-sufficiency?

DO THE SURVIVOR'S FEELINGS THREATEN TO OVERWHELM YOUR RELATIONSHIP?

By now you probably understand that adult survivors have many feelings about their abuse that they were unable to express during their childhood. And there is no more likely place for them to be expressed than in a close relationship such as yours, which promises some degree of safety. But the way that they express their feelings may cause a real problem for you. You may notice something is bothering them and ask what's wrong, only to have them say, "Nothing." Or they may react with feelings so intense that they seem inappropriate to the situation.

Richard's Wife

I feel like both of us are pretty moody, but naturally Richard takes the cake in that area. His specialty is reacting to minor situations in an overblown, melodramatic fashion. Some of his scenes are almost violent in terms of his histrionics. When something happens to upset him, it evokes this catastrophic mentality in him, and his emotions reach a fever pitch for the smallest of reasons. Things will happen that are really just everyday frustrations for most people and he'll just lose it. It will take hours for him to calm down. I used to get all caught up in it also— ride the roller coaster with him up and down and back and forth until he gradually calmed down and settled into a more reasonable point of view. But this took time and it was exhausting because he was directing his feelings at me. Now when he gets charged up about something ridiculous, I stay more neutral and tell him, "I'm not going to go on the ride this time." It's hard to always be working on catching yourself when this stuff comes up and to know how not to get engaged with it. I bet that's a very common position to be in as a spouse of a survivor.

♦

Anger may be causing the most problems in your relationship. Part of the problem is that the anger usually gets directed at you and does not necessarily abate after a few moments of shouting. Some survivors have explosive tempers that can be triggered by the smallest event. The anger may actually seem to feed on itself and escalate rapidly to the point where you fear it may become violent, whereas others have perfected the "slow-burn technique" where their anger simmers just below the boiling point for days at a time as you struggle to find some logical explanation.

It is important to discuss your reactions to the anger during quieter moments, explaining how you feel. See if you can't negotiate how and when the survivor can express his anger and how you will need to respond to it. Next time the anger erupts, react in the way you had agreed upon. After the anger has abated and a relative calm has returned, review how the experience worked or didn't work. Try making improvements and let the survivor know how important it is that he cooperate. Ultimately if his anger consistently reaches the point of becoming abusive, you will need to make a decision as to whether this relationship is healthy for you to continue.

DOES CONSTANT FIGHTING THREATEN TO DESTROY YOUR RELATIONSHIP?

If handling anger is a problem in your relationship, then fighting may be the next level of aggression. All friends and spouses will occasionally fight, but in survivor relationships the fights may be more frequent and destructive. Fighting can mean many things to the survivor: a normal expression of disagreement, a way to feel separate from you and in control of the relationship, a way of expressing outrage at what the survivor sees as another betrayal, or a way of releasing what she perceives to be anger in you. Fighting may be the only way the survivor has learned to resolve conflict. Whatever the reasons, the reality for you is that the relationship becomes volatile, and after many bouts, you may feel exhausted and frustrated by the lack of alternatives.

Richard's Wife

We had a whole lot of conflicts the first few years of our marriage. We would fight about how much time we'd spend together or whether or not our relationship had a future. But what I noticed about our fights was that they would quickly escalate and rage on for hours and put our relationship on the brink of dissolution. He was always thinking that he had to break up, whereas I was used to a process of fighting, calming down, talking it out, and resolving it. But with Richard, it just would escalate instantly. There was like this catastrophic imagination that he had about our relationship, and if things were not a certain way, well it just wasn't safe enough for him to be with me. In his eyes, conflict always meant disaster. Always. Conflict always meant violence—not necessarily physical violence, but some violent act, like breaking dishes or acting out in some dramatic fashion. After one of our fights, he told me that he had gone up to the roof of the apartment building and threw books off the roof because he was so upset. It seemed to me an overreaction. I remember thinking to myself that this stuff isn't about me or our relationship. This comes from someplace else.

♦

There are a number of fair fighting techniques that can help change destructive fighting into resolvable disagreements. It's important to speak for yourself, to talk about how you feel, instead of focusing on what the survivor does or how he feels. Sometimes it's helpful not to bring up old business, but to keep the discussion focused on the matter at hand.

Compromise is an essential ingredient of conflict resolution, even though the survivor runs the risk of feeling like he's losing power and control. Make it absolutely clear that compromise is basically a fifty-fifty proposition. You'll both win some and lose some, and you'll both be equally compromised. But when the conflicts seem to escalate beyond your control, therapy as a couple is an option. By providing a forum for each person to be heard and understood, it offers the safety and objectivity that only the presence of a trained referee can offer. Entering therapy is no guarantee that all your problems can be worked out. However, you and your partner will learn some tools to resolve the most difficult impasses that might otherwise end your relationship.

DOES THE SURVIVOR MAKE YOU INTO THE ABUSER?

Survivors have a tendency to project their own feelings or the feelings of their parents onto the people in their personal lives, possibly causing you to feel misunderstood, blamed, or criticized. It is important to realize that virtually everybody tends to replay certain situations from their childhood in their personal relationships. The adult survivor is no different, although the situations, issues, and conflicts that they're playing out may be more unsettling if you end up being cast in the role of the villain, or worse, the abuser. You may even notice yourself responding to the survivor in ways that sound remarkably similar to what you've heard about the survivor's family. Through the processes of projection, transference, and reenactment, you and the survivor may unconsciously be recreating the dynamics of his family relationships in the hope of resolving them.

Richard's Wife

B eing involved with Richard, I often had this uncanny sense that I was in a play and reading someone else's lines. There is an unconscious pull to be a certain person for your spouse so that both you and he can work something out. It's confusing because when you're doing that you know there's something inside of you that is willing to be in this play, to play this role and try to resolve something. Of course, you never admit it, although it's tempting to just sit there and point the finger and go, "Well, you're making me do this. You're making me act this way." I think couples start to play unconscious roles for each other by taking on parts of their parents and behaving like them. I felt some kind of identification with his mother, even though it was horrifying to me to be like her. And sometimes I really couldn't tell the difference. It's like, "Well, when am I acting like his mother and when am I acting like myself?" I guess I have sort of internalized her somehow just by being around Richard. And I think that one reason I stayed in the struggle with Richard so long is that it was a way for me to work out issues about my own parents who don't have the drama and distinctiveness that Daphne has. It was really uncanny. After a while I got tired of it and learned to say "Hey, that's not me, that's your mother. That's some expectation that you carry from your childhood that has nothing to do with our relationship."

◆

It is important to remember that when the survivor in your life says hurtful things or acts in selfish ways it is only the past making an appearance and nothing you can do or say will make much difference at that moment. Recognizing that you don't deserve all of the venom that is being showered on you will help to put your relationship conflicts in their proper perspective; some of their problems have to do with you and some don't. Not getting defensive or taking personally the charges that are directed at you will go a long way toward helping to construct a safe, less volatile relationship.

Is Decision Making and Planning a Stumbling Block?

Decision making and planning are also issues that frequently cause conflict between survivors and their friends or spouses. Decision making, just like control, is sometimes very difficult for survivors because they're afraid to make a mistake, even while doing something that might be in their best interests. Ambivalence tends to rule supreme here. Sometimes they will shift the decision making to you and you may be inclined to take on that responsibility. But watch out: This may be a trap. If you make the decisions and they aren't right, survivors are in a position to criticize you and blame you. Therefore, decision making and planning should be shared, and if there's a reason why that can't be done, the reason should be discussed in a compassionate and understanding way. You can take on the role of being the reality check for the survivor's suggestions and he can do the same for you. Coming up with your own ideas and then running them by him for his input will begin a healthier process of shared decision making.

Richard's Wife

Richard and I used to have a lot of conflicts about taking vacations together because vacations were a source of great trauma for him and his mother. She would scoop him up and force him to take charge of vacations, and so it became impossible for us to travel together without memories of those horrible trips with his mother. So we would make reservations and he would agree and then, at the last minute, he would say, "We can't go," or "This is a terrible idea," and there would be all this back and forth stuff on the night before a major trip to Europe. And I would get real nervous about what kind of trip this would be. Could this be a different trip than what he experienced with his mother, or is it going to be the same nightmare repeated with his wife? Over the years, what developed was that he would let me make the decisions because it was safer for him. He didn't have to risk expressing his opinions, preferences, or needs. He would just go along with me, and because I'm real assertive, it would seem like it would work. But then if he didn't do his pre-bon-voyage number, later he would let me know that it wasn't what he really wanted after all. I would then be responsible for how everything turned out and he was the one who would sit back in silent reproach if things didn't go well. Now I avoid this by telling him, "OK, think about this for a while. I've expressed my opinion very strongly, but that's an opinion; it's not the law. We will not decide until you make some decision that you're willing to live by."

◆

DOES THE ABUSE AFFECT YOUR SEX LIFE?

If your lover or spouse was sexually abused as a child, chances are it will affect your sex life in some way. Some survivors avoid sex because it brings up too many unresolved memories and feelings whereas others engage in promiscuous sex, which gives them a sense of control over their past victimization. Quite frequently the type of sexual problem is intricately related to the type of sexual abuse survivors experienced as children. If they were genitally fondled, they may feel overwhelmingly anxious if their adult sex partner stimulates them during foreplay. They may have flashbacks to the abuse, physical sensations that accompanied the abuse, or they may engage in their old defenses to psychologically separate themselves from the present experience.

You may feel concerned about having sex out of fear of hurting or upsetting your partner. If, at first, you were not aware of her past sexual abuse, you probably did not understand if and when she had a reaction to the abuse while making love to you. She may not have told you because she felt shameful or because she expected a negative reaction.

Pete's Wife

When we first became intimate, I didn't notice any sexual hang-ups in Pete. When I found out about the incest, I remember being surprised about this. But, over time, more subtle things emerged to indicate that sex may not have been as smooth for him as I had thought. For one thing, Pete has a lot of sexual energy: He would make love constantly every day if time permitted. This took some getting used to because I didn't feel the same urgency to always be sexual. He also feels guilty when he masturbates and will sometimes come to me and ask me if it's OK that he did it. And I would have to give him permission in a way because he felt so conflictual about it. When, for some time, he had thoughts about stabbing himself in the genitals, we would talk about that and try to understand why it was happening. I'm really glad he can talk to me and not feel like it's something that he has to endure by himself. I know that he is still aroused by older women and sometimes has trouble separating his attraction for me from the old attraction to her. Basically I just try to remind him that he's a good person and that it is OK to still have the feelings he has about sex and that he's getting well.

◆

Partners of survivors can play a special role in helping them work through feelings about sexual abuse that plays havoc with their sexual pleasure. Encourage your partner to share his feelings about sex and sexual abuse. Let him tell you what would make sex more enjoyable and less anxiety provoking for him. Try to accommodate his needs and limitations while remaining understanding and supportive. Remember that sex was forced on him and to pressure him to have sex now will ultimately be counterproductive. Some survivors feel the need to abstain from sex for periods of time while undergoing therapy. This may be hard for you to accept, but listen to why your partner feels this is necessary. Try to discover other ways of being physically affectionate with him. Sometimes certain sexual acts may be more repugnant to him than others, and a candid discussion about acceptable alternatives may reveal a compromise. Try reading some of the books on abuse and sexuality listed in Appendix B to gain a more complete understanding of the issues. If the sexual problems are severe, or if the survivor is unable to have sex, consider getting sex therapy. Most sex therapy teaches you, the partner, to assume the role of a coach in helping the survivor discover ways of enjoying sex. Usually sex therapy is most productive in the latter stages of recovery after the survivor has worked through many of the feelings associated with the sexual abuse in his individual and group therapy.

How Do You Deal with the Survivor's Self-Destructive Behavior?

Many of you may be most concerned about what to do when the survivor becomes self-destructive, that is, suicidal, addicted to alcohol or drugs, or engaged in behaviors that are clearly acts of self-sabotage. If you are the only one close enough to the survivor to notice what's happening and to be in a position to do something about it, this may raise many concerns for you because, not being a professional therapist, you may not know how to proceed in a way that assures the survivor's protection without risking her feeling betrayed.

You can talk to the survivor about how concerned you are when she does things to jeopardize her well-being. Ask her how she is feeling when she acts this way. Try to get underneath the suicidal or self-destructive act to the feeling that might be triggering it. Tell the survivor that you care about what happens to her and that it hurts you when she's doing things that are self-destructive. Tell her that you want to support her and encourage her to get help.

There are many concrete actions that you can take when the survivor cannot help herself. You can call a local Suicide Prevention Hotline. You can get information about the services they offer that might be of help to you or your friend or lover. If the survivor is actively talking about suicide, try to develop a contract with her that she will get into therapy or talk with you first before making any attempts on her life. It's important for you to have the telephone numbers of the police, firemen, and emergency rescue services as well as the survivor's therapist if she has one. Don't be afraid to call these numbers if you believe that the survivor's life is in jeopardy. When it comes to suicide it's best to play it safe and ask for help if you have any doubt about the survivor's safety. If the survivor has a therapist, you may want to inform him about what's going on and put the emergency operations into the therapist's hands. The therapist will know who to call and how to temporarily hospitalize the person so that the survivor is prevented from hurting herself. If the survivor is extremely isolated, and on the verge of hurting herself, you can call the police yourself and have them do a "home and safety check," which will determine if involuntary hospitalization is necessary. If the survivor has taken some pills or is in a physical condition that might deteriorate, you can take her to the emergency room of any local hospital. Once there, provide the doctors with background information to help them treat the survivor.

When the survivor is abusing drugs or alcohol, many of the same considerations for suicide apply. You can begin by speaking with him about his drinking or drug use, what it's doing to the relationship, and what ultimately it could do to his life. If the survivor has a long-established history of alcohol or drug abuse, you may consider talking with him about going into a residential detox program to begin that first step on a road to recovery from addictions (see chapter 5). Many detox programs and residential treatment programs have a service called *community intervention*, which involves planning a meeting between the survivor and all of his friends to speak to him about their concerns over his substance abuse and to help him make a commitment on the spot to entering a residential detox program.

For many survivors with a long history of addictions, an intervention may be the only recourse. And it does work. Research shows that many people stop drinking or using drugs when they are prompted by family and friends, or in some cases mandated to enter treatment by a court. This direct strategy is based on the understanding that many people who have a drinking or drug problem will not independently refer themselves for treatment. Denial is part of the addictive process, and for the survivor to suddenly realize that he's got a problem is extremely unlikely. To organize a drug intervention, contact the local residential detox program. Ask if there is a service for community interventions. Make sure that you plan this very carefully, calling all of the person's friends together, talking with them well before the intervention and getting a sense of how they view the problem. Ask them if they can contribute some time to help the survivor face his problem.

WHAT SURVIVORS NEED FROM YOU

1. **Believe what they tell you about the abuse.** When survivors disclose to you that they were abused as children, believe them. You may have your doubts about how it happened or if it happened, but keep them to yourself for now. It's important to realize that abuse often gets obscured by survivors' psychological defenses, making it difficult for them to fully reclaim the memory. If survivors are in a process of reclaiming those memories, it doesn't help to have their beginning glimpses questioned and challenged by a supposedly non-biased third party. Understand that they're at the beginning of a long process involving remembering, reclaiming, and ultimately, disclosing what happened. Supporting their efforts to reclaim the memories is the proper role for you at this point

2. **Accept what they say about the consequences of abuse.** Many survivors will have notions about how the abuse affected them and will link past events with current problems. These ideas may not always sound logical to you or may sound completely farfetched. It's important once again that you not challenge them. Simply accept what you are told and let the survivors continue to refine the connection over time.

3. **Reinforce that the abuse was their parents' responsibility.** It's important for you to accept and to reinforce that child abuse is the responsibility of the parents. Children, by virtue of age, and lack of maturity and social development, are not in a position to either stop the abuse or be responsible for the abuse. This is a critical point because survivors will need you to be on their side. It will be helpful if you can understand and empathize with the dilemma they faced as vulnerable children. Spend time discussing and understanding from their point of view what it was like for them growing up under the constant threat of assault.

4. **Educate yourself about the long-range impact of child abuse.** It will be really important that you understand the issues, the

consequences, and the long-term effects of child abuse. The more you understand, the easier it will be for you to empathize with what your partner is going through. Many of the ideas about child abuse may be hard to believe. Certainly child abuse affects psychological development in ways that are complex and confusing. By knowing something about these issues, you'll be in a better position to be supportive and to share in some aspects of the healing.

5. **Accept survivors' feelings about the abusers and their families.** Recognize that survivors are basically in a process of reclaiming their feelings and their true identity in terms of what they went through as children. Many of their feelings and reactions may seem extreme, but understand that child abuse is a very extreme phenomenon. They grew up in families that constantly took away their feelings and negated them, distorted them, or invalidated them. It's important that you don't do the same thing.

6. **Give empathy, support, validation, compassion, encouragement, and hope.** Survivors need many types of emotional support that they never got from their own families. This may place a very large burden on you to give them things that you may not ordinarily be so comfortable giving. Because many of their perceptions were never validated by their parents, it's important that you do so now. Encouragement and hope are also essential because the road to recovering from the effects of child abuse is long and arduous. If they feel encouragement and hope coming from you, they will be able to take it in and use it for themselves.

7. **Confront them with their self-sabotaging behaviors and intervene to protect them if and when necessary.** If survivors are engaged in any kind of self-abusive or self-destructive act, it's important that you intervene and make an attempt to protect them. Although they may object to this at first, ultimately they will trust you more because you are showing them that you really care.

8. **Encourage them to get the help they need to recover.** Recovering from child abuse requires the proper help from many different resources: therapists, self-help groups, AA sponsors and other 12-Step groups, friends, family, and partners. Some survivors may try to do it on their own, which can be a great mistake. Remember that child abuse affects everybody connected with the survivors and it will be in everyone's interest for survivors to get enough support for themselves. You can play a significant role in encouraging them to seek professional help and in supporting their ongoing commitment to it. In

many cases, psychotherapy can immediately benefit survivors' relationship because it provides time in which to develop some needed perspective on how they create conflict with their partners and friends. Therapy can also be a situation for strong feelings to be expressed that might otherwise have been directed at you. Ultimately when survivors have a good support system and therapeutic program, there will be less demand put on you to be everything for them. Over the long haul, you will grow increasingly appreciative of this other support.

9. **Respect the time, energy, and resources that it takes to recover from child abuse.** Remember that recovering from child abuse may take several years, although things may begin to get better much earlier in the recovery process. It is impossible to say exactly what individual people will need in terms of time, effort, and financial and emotional resources, because everyone is different and the types of abuse vary greatly. It will be of tremendous support if you are able to accept whatever it may take for the survivors to get better without pressuring them to resolve the many issues according to *your* timetable. They never had things tailored to their needs as children and it is essential that they get that opportunity now. If they say that they need something in particular (time, space, a different type of relationship) in order to resolve an issue or move ahead with their recovery, try to accept it as a legitimate need, even if the need conflicts with your feelings. You can, however, tell them how you feel and hopefully resolve the situation in a way that works for both of you.

10. **Be allies with them in their struggle for a renewed emotional life.** Survivors truly need a soul mate—someone who can listen to how they feel and be a sounding board for their confused perceptions; someone who can tolerate the expression of strong feelings of pain and anger; someone who can become a true ally in their efforts to overcome the past. In order to be accepted as an ally, you may need to go through the survivor's test of confidence, which may mean putting up with a range of reactions, feelings, and attitudes as we discussed.

WHAT SURVIVORS DON'T NEED FROM YOU

1. **Survivors don't need you to question whether the abuse happened.** Determining whether the abuse happened and the

circumstances under which it occurred is the responsibility of the survivors. They will need to do that on their own and hopefully will continue to clarify what happened during the course of their therapy. Here you need to play a supportive role rather than taking over and processing the information.

2. **Survivors don't need you to tell them how to feel.** Their feelings may seem extreme to you at times. But these feelings come out of a very extreme situation. As they continue to express their extreme feelings and work them through, their feelings will become less extreme.

3. **Survivors don't need you to express the abuser's point of view.** It's very important that survivors feel you're on their side, that you can see their point of view, and that you're not on the fence between their point of view and the point of view of the offender. Trust, or rather their lack of trust, is why you need to appear so completely on their side. Later during the process of recovery, this changes as the survivors are more ready to see other points of view. Sometimes it's easy to take on an opposite point of view from survivors, especially if conflicts continue to develop. Eventually the survivors will begin to experience you as the abuser, a role in which you clearly do not want to be placed.

5. **Survivors don't need you to force your own ideas about the abuse.** Recovering from child abuse involves a process of reclaiming buried memories, feeling the buried feelings attached to them, and understanding the meaning of past events and the long-range impact of them. This is a long process that seems to aid in survivors' clarification of their new identity as a person. This may also be the most productive part of long-term psychotherapy. Because it is so essential to recovery, it is best if you do not impose your own ideas and point of view too strongly on this process when survivors are essentially trying to catch up and put the pieces of the past together in a way that's meaningful to them.

6. **Survivors don't need you to develop a codependent relationship with them.** Survivors don't need someone who will take over for them and treat them like a victim. They need to take the responsibility to get well and to make their own mistakes. Eventually the survivor will change, and if the relationship is based on you being the helper and the survivor being the sick one, it will become a barrier to growth. If you are taking a codependent stance with the survivor, get help for yourself. You can do more for the survivor if you are giving out of concern rather than out of a need to avoid your own problems.

7. **Don't judge survivors for the way they are responding to the aftereffects of abuse or the pain involved in healing.** Everyone heals from abuse differently, depending on personality, strengths, and vulnerabilities. This process is hard enough without someone the survivor trusts making it more difficult by judging the response to the challenge of recovery. If the survivor's reactions are destructive to the relationship, say so directly without being punitive or harsh.

8. **Don't coddle survivors or collude with their denial of what is happening to them.** Survivors don't need to be treated like babies. They do need support and understanding, but they also need to know the score when it comes to your feelings and the relationship. They need to be able to correctly perceive reality.

SELF-HELP FOR FRIENDS, LOVERS, AND SPOUSES OF ADULT SURVIVORS

Despite the hardships and challenges involved in a relationship with survivors, there are things you can do that will help you cope with the pressures while keeping your own life on track and meeting your own needs. Perhaps the most important message to be conveyed to you is to understand that you cannot change survivors or make them recover from the effects of child abuse. What you can provide will be of significant help to them, but the responsibility for changing and dealing with the past rests squarely on their shoulders. When that responsibility shifts to someone else, they are definitely off course. While we have been focusing on what you can do to help the survivor in your life, the following suggestions focus on you and what you can do for yourself to cope with the relationship.

UNDERSTANDING CONFLICT AND TENSION

Periodically try to remind yourself that this relationship will have its stresses and strains due to the long-range impact of child abuse. Accept these limitations on a temporary basis (the problems should gradually remit as recovery proceeds), and don't try to evaluate or judge the relationship according to other relationships you've had in the past. This acceptance is very important to the survivor and may be just as important to your own successful coping.

GIVING WITHIN YOUR LIMITS

Know what your capabilities are for giving. If you try to give beyond what you're capable of giving, resentment, withdrawal from the survivor, and possibly the end of the relationship follow. No one person is able to give everything that a survivor needs. Some needs will always go unsatisfied, and this is one tragedy of child abuse that survivors ultimately need to accept. What's very important for both survivors and their partners is that survivors obtain their emotional supplies from multiple sources: from you, friends, partners or spouses, therapists, support groups, and possibly family members.

You need to be able to say when you cannot give anymore, and to say it in a way that doesn't make the survivor feel rejected. Often this means speaking before you are utterly drained. Let the survivor know that you have your limits and that you want him to know so that he won't be surprised when you are not able to give him what he needs when he expects it. Saying no without rejection may be one of the most important things you can learn. Try to point out that you have some needs too and ask if there's a way the survivor can meet your needs.

GETTING SUPPORT FOR YOURSELF

It is essential that you develop your own support network of friends, outside activities, and in some cases, therapists to augment what you are getting—or not getting—from your relationship with the survivor. Recognize that it may be some time before the survivor can give back to you what you have been giving to him. While he goes through recovery, there will be times when your needs will go unmet if you depend on him.

One of the best ways of getting support and understanding for what you are going through with your partner is to meet with other partners of survivors, either individually or in a group. Some communities and mental health agencies offer groups for partners of survivors, although in many areas, such services are not yet available. You can contact agencies to see if they would be interested in sponsoring such a group or talk with some local therapists who provide psychotherapy services to survivors to see if they would be interested in leading such a group. Many partners of survivors may find what they need at Al-Anon meetings or groups for adult children of alcoholic parents. In some cases, it may be best to start your own support and education group as Susan desc.¨es in chapter 10. Such a group will offer a place to talk about the difficulties involved in survivor relationships and the strategies that can be employed for maintaining a healthy presence in your relationships. Remember there is strength in numbers and you do not need to rely solely on your own internal resources to cope with the pressures.

SEPARATING YOURSELF FROM THE IMAGE OF THE ABUSER

As described earlier, there's a natural tendency for survivors to unconsciously and subtly nudge their partners into the role of the abusive parent. They do this by projecting some of their own feelings and expected behaviors onto you, which are linked in their mind with the behavior of their abusive parent. This is called *transference*. Transference is basically the experience of relating to somebody as though that person were some other significant person. Everyone *transfers* to some extent, but the process can become destructive when it occurs in a survivor relationship with a partner who is unaware of the potential traps. Ideally this process should eventually occur with a therapist who is trained to use it therapeutically.

With adult survivors, the natural tendency to transfer characteristics of the abusive parent onto their loved ones becomes part of a process that can be schematically described as a "Y." There are four components to this process: projection, transference, reenactment, and resolution. *Projection* is the starting point for the process and can be located at the base of the stem of the "Y." The survivor projects onto you her fears, feelings, and expectations of the way others have treated her and will treat her. If the projection continues, it develops over time into *transference*, which is located at the fork in the "Y." At this point, the transference relationship begins to lock into a relationship similar to the one that occurred in the past between the survivor and the abuser. Within this transference relationship, conflicts get reenacted around particular circumstances in the life of the survivor. This is a critical point in the psychological health of the relationship because the process can go in one of two directions: *reenactment* of the abusive relationship (located on one wing of the "Y") or *resolution* leading toward a healthier relationship (located on the other wing).

This reenactment is important because it is the survivor's way of resolving the abuse by trying to discharge some of the old feelings surrounding it. The problem is that the power to repeat the past is so strong that chances are the reenactment will not result in a new resolution or a new type of relationship, but will tend to repeat the old abusive pattern. Thus, relationships get mired down and can become destructive.

Distinguishing yourself from the abuser is accomplished when you tell the survivor that you feel he is making expectations and judgments about you that are not consistent with how you see yourself or what your intentions are. Point out ways in which you are being different and that your intentions are being misunderstood by him. If there's a part of you that is aggressive or defensive, and is being triggered by the survivor, it is crucial for you to admit it and look for ways to bring it under control.

When you and the survivor develop enough awareness to see the negative reenactment going on and then highlight the differences between you and the abuser, you will be heading toward the resolution. This is a major turning point and the point at which your relationship can begin to offer the promise of something truly exciting.

HELP TO
ESTABLISH HEALTHY BOUNDARIES

You may have noticed that the boundaries between survivors and you frequently become unclear, leaving you confused as to where you end and they begin. It's important that you define who you are and accept that the survivor is a separate person with a separate set of thoughts, feelings, behaviors, and concerns. You can speed that process along by being clear about how you feel, how you think, what choices are right for you, and to state them clearly and concisely in a manner not experienced as rejecting or hostile by the survivor.

SEEKING PROFESSIONAL HELP

Getting stuck is something that happens in every relationship. In survivor relationships, there may be several low points where you wonder if things will ever change or how long you can continue without getting more of your needs met. Your efforts to support the survivor and work through the never-ending conflicts can tire even the most committed soul. You may find yourself questioning your feelings for the survivor and the very nature of your relationship. Ever so slowly, the thought about taking a break in terms of a trial separation or even something more permanent may enter your mind. Everyone has these moments. If you find yourself having these thoughts once in a blue moon, or after a particularly troubling event, there is no cause for alarm.

But when these moments of despair occur more and more frequently, it may be time to take an inventory of your emotional investment in the relationship. Are you getting *anything* positive from being involved with the survivor? Are you feeling discouraged because your efforts to resolve conflicts seem to go nowhere? Is the person changing into someone for whom you have fewer and fewer feelings? Are you beginning to doubt the reason for your involvement with the survivor? Ask yourself these and other questions to help you clarify whether the relationship is offering enough. Share your concerns and questions with the survivor, with your friends, and with your support network and try to focus on doing what's right for you.

And again, most important, consider getting some professional couple's therapy to resolve the stuck feelings. Let your partner know that the relationship is not working for you and that your confidence in being able to sort out the conflicts is waning. If you select an experienced couple's therapist, who is savvy in the issues that survivor relationships present, it may be well worth the time and expense.

ENDING THE RELATIONSHIP

Sometimes you reach a point where you feel like you have given everything you have and nothing is working. You have tried couple's therapy and have worked with your lover or spouse to untangle the knots of communication only to find that nothing changes. You may even have tried or want to try a trial separation to give yourself some needed perspective on what you want and what you're not getting. When this is the case, you have a responsibility to do what's right for you. If you decide to leave a relationship with a survivor, it doesn't make you bad or inconsiderate. You are entitled to make a change in your life so that you can get what you want.

If you are leaving, it will naturally cause grief and distress. There is a right way and a wrong way to leave a personal relationship. It is important that you be honest with yourself and the survivor about what you want to do and why. The best way to leave is through mutual agreement, or if that is not possible, through mutual understanding and acceptance of each other's position. There is also a right time to leave and a wrong time. Leaving on impulse or during the course of a heated argument is destructive and irresponsible. To leave a survivor in the middle of some vulnerable period will be hurtful to him or her and arouse guilt in you. You want to leave in a way that leaves you feeling proud of yourself and respectful of the other person. This means talking about your plans and compromising with the survivor to accommodate both of your needs. This phase of the relationship will also take time. Time spent doing it right will make the ensuing period of adjustment much easier and increase the likelihood that the change will be productive for both of you.

WORKING TO
BUILD ON THE POSITIVES

Without denying the difficulties and complexities of relating to a survivor in recovery, it is important to promote the positives about your partner and the relationship that makes it all worthwhile. Seeing the positives and affirming the reasons why you are willing to go through the tough times is a necessary part of the process. Not doing this or endlessly focusing on the problems is a sure way of dooming the relationship. You are involved with the survivor as either a lover or a friend because you care about him as a person. You were able to sense his essence as a person without getting blinded by the surface turmoil. Hard-won changes and successful solutions to some thorny relationship conflicts should be applauded regularly and referred back to when the going gets rough. With each layer of appreciation and encouragement, you will build a reservoir of trust and commitment that will see you through the most challenging moments. One day in the not-too-distant future, you will sense it was all worth it: You both worked for something that will give you joy for the rest of your lives.

Pete's Wife

Our lives have really worked out since Pete started his business. We were able to buy a house and to have two children. Since I work only two days a week, it allows me to be home with my kids. I feel like we are finally reaping the fruits of our labors. We've developed into a team that covers for each other when either of us is down. The biggest thing that I had to do was be patient while he worked through all of this. I admit that there were times when I wasn't sure whether we would make it. I remember Pete several years ago as a scared, anxious, and insecure man taking the bus to work at a job he hated. Despite all the hardship, he never seemed to lose sight of his desire to heal himself from the incest. I really admire him for that. I saw this part of him early when it was only a glimmer. I decided that I would take my chances and sign on with him even when the future looked bleak because I believed in his spirit. I was right about that. It carried him through and I have grown in the process with him. And the prosperity that we have gotten is like nothing I thought we would have.

◆

The biggest challenge facing friends, partners, and spouses may be knowing how to balance your own emotional needs with those of the survivor without undermining the relationship's basic principle of mutual sharing. Being aware of your limitations and knowing how to take care of yourself when the survivor is caught up in the demands of recovery will make your adjustment much easier. Communicating and negotiating with the survivor during the give and take of the relationship may be a necessary lesson for the relationship to prosper. While accepting that it may be stressful at times, try focusing in on the part of the survivor's personality that you so cherish while working toward the kind of relationship that you both desire. Remember that with recovery, survivors *do* overcome many of the barriers to trust and intimacy that have plagued their relationships in the past. If you accompany them on their healing journey, the chances are great that you will someday arrive at a happier, more satisfying life together.

·

A Program
of Recovery

Chapter Nine

SOUL SEARCHING:
*P*REPARING FOR RECOVERY

Now is the time to put your new understanding of the past and your awareness of current problems into action. After reading the first two sections of this book, you know something about what you went through as a child and the long-term effects it has had on your life as an adult. As Part III will illustrate, recovery is about healing the wounds and changing the maladaptive parts of yourself left over from the abuse. This chapter will explore what some survivors may need before embarking on their road to recovery. Chapters 10 and 11 will provide information on the tools of change. Chapters 12, 13, and 14 will outline the three stages of recovery spanning twenty-one steps.

Before you can begin the road to recovery, you will need to make a decision to act. This is the point that stumps many adult survivors. The challenge here has to do with your willingness to take a risk in promise of a future payoff. Recovery can sound like a risky proposition, especially when you have been let down before. There may be conflicting parts inside you that either call you to action or warn you of potential disappointment. As you encounter these thoughts, you may pass many layers of defenses and attitudes left over from the past. Parts of you may tell you to give up the idea of ever feeling better or maintaining hope for a different type of life. Better to play it safe, this chorus of doom sayers sing, and muddle through life where shame and disappointment are your constant companions.

But there is another part of you that may be heard as a voice or felt in the heart, which represents hope and the possibility for something better. It is that part of you, revitalized by the knowledge you have gained about your family and the abuse, that has left a sense of empowerment and anger along with the hurt and fear. Use that part to fortify your determination to enter recovery. That part, which will become the core of your new sense of self, is emotionally, psychologically, and spiritually linked to your soul and will fuel your motivation to act.

Your soul was never vanquished by the abuse, although it may have gotten temporarily lost. It still believes in your essential goodness and your right to rejoice in the spirit of human existence. It still believes in you as a person and your burning desire for a better life. Your soul can be one of your greatest sources of strength, if you are able to draw from it. Think of your soul as your cosmic parent pulling for you to heal the wounds and to change yourself so that you can be reunited with it in your new beginning, when your life becomes an expression of your true essence as a person. You must reach for that spark and then hold on to it for dear life, for recovery is a long and difficult journey. With each step of recovery, this spark will burn brighter, eventually forging your new sense of self.

CHALLENGING THE MYTH
OF DOING IT ON YOUR OWN

Where are you now in deciding to make a commitment to recovery? For many of you, you may resist admitting the need for outside help. After reading the previous chapters, you may agree that the past has deeply affected you but you are still holding onto the idea of making the changes on your own. Be advised that changing on your own—to the degree that is necessary to truly recover from the effects of child abuse—is just another form of denial. Survivors who try to change on their own procrastinate, rationalize, and avoid. They make feeble efforts to do something different in their lives, only to lose steam when the going gets tough. Ultimately they give up out of frustration and confusion without necessarily admitting this to themselves. Consequently they are never really happy and the abuse continues to take its emotional toll. Some survivors go through several attempts to change on their own before realizing that they do indeed need help. Others are not so fortunate. The bottom line, however, is that the resistance to getting the help you need is really resistance to change.

WHAT SURVIVORS
MAY NEED TO MAKE A COMMITMENT
TO RECOVERY

There are specific reasons why it takes survivors of child abuse a long time to get the help that they need. What has to happen for you to get to that critical point? What will it take for you to make that fateful commitment to change? Following are four of the most useful and necessary types of support that survivors may need to obtain before making a genuine commitment to recovery.

VALIDATION AND
ENCOURAGEMENT FROM OTHERS

Many survivors need to connect either personally or indirectly with someone who has had similar problems and has successfully overcome them. Through this important identification with another person, survivors receive validation for their problems and a sense of hope and entitlement that they too can change and recover.

Leigh Anne

Intuitively I knew that I needed to do something to get healthy, although for a long time I didn't know what. I read *Out of the Shadows* by Patrick Carnes, which is about sexual addictions, because I was involved with someone who turned out to be an exhibitionist. And then I read a book by Elizabeth Taylor called *Elizabeth Takes Off*, which somehow spoke to me in a way that the other books didn't. She uses the term "click" to describe when you really understand what you need to do in order to change. I think it's a perfect terminology. Reading that book for me was like clicking on a light switch. I've been in the dark for so long and I was searching for the light—something to either help me or lead me to the help. I strongly believe that it all stems from inside.

You have to really want to make that change. So I read that book and thought, "That is me." This is what really motivated me to get my butt into therapy.

◆

The idea of first identifying or connecting with someone who has traveled the road to recovery is not new. Alcoholics Anonymous and other 12-Step groups encourage new members to take a sponsor—someone who has successfully recovered and is considered wise to the ways of the program and capable of leading another person in the same direction. Many businesses recognize the power of this concept when they set up mentor programs that pair a new employee with an older, more experienced manager who guides the younger protégé's development. A loving and healthy family in which parents guide and nurture the child to maturity is the best mentorship program around. But adult survivors may need to look elsewhere for this type of personal, caring encouragement that recognizes their unique dilemma. When they find it in a self-help group, a mentorship program, or a church organization, or as in Leigh Anne's case, in a book by a celebrity who had the courage to reveal her personal hardships and triumph of change, it may provide the extra impetus needed to act.

An Ultimatum
to Get Help or Else!

Some survivors would have forever postponed getting the help they needed were it not for the pressure applied by a spouse, friend, or family member. As described in chapter 8, having a relationship with a survivor who has yet to go through recovery can be a frustrating and conflict-laden experience. Clearly it is in the interests of both people as well as the relationship itself for the survivor to make the decision to act.

Richard

I guess it was my wife who really forced me to deal with my mother and the effects of the abuse. After we got married, we were having a lot of conflicts about sharing—the give and take of a relationship. She and I came from similar families in that neither of us got our needs met by our parents. As an adult, she continued denying her needs and I helped her by being demanding and hostile because I was so fed up with living with needy women. So, in a sense we were a perfect match for each other: She did all of the giving and received very little back and I finally got taken care of by a woman I could get mad at. It really was very unbalanced. After a few years of this, the shit started hitting the fan. She started getting sick to death of having to battle me for everything and then getting only crumbs in return. So she started confronting me, which invariably would lead to this mean, rageful fighting. When we got into a fight, I became this vicious animal and would start to smash things and she'd get real spooked. She'd say, "I worry that you're really violent like your mother," and frankly, so did I. I forget exactly how it came up, but eventually she said, "I don't think we can go on unless you get into therapy." She meant it. It was an ultimatum on our relationship and I believed her. I hated being pushed into it, but I guess at some level I knew it was the best for me.

◆

Unfortunately, some survivors, like alcoholics, will not be able to make the decision to act until they hit bottom in the sense of losing everything. This is a truly sad outcome because it would be better for everyone if the survivor could see what he needs to do before learning the lesson the hard way. Many survivors, like Richard, do get the message earlier, but not without some consistent pushing by someone who cares.

AN UNDERSTANDING
OF THE TOTAL PICTURE

Many survivors are faced with the dilemma of having so many other problems in life—medical problems, family problems, job problems, financial problems, and addictions—that it can be difficult to see the real source of their difficulties. Because you are always putting out one fire after another, you never develop the needed perspective to see the overall patterns in your life, or what you need to do to make it better.

Shirley

It is difficult to pinpoint when I really began my recovery because I had so many other problems in my life that I was trying to deal with that were either directly or indirectly related to the abuse. My life was a mess at the time. Physical problems, confusion about my life, and nothing really working that well. Even my kids were having problems.

I eventually became addicted to all the medications prescribed for my illnesses. Finally this one doctor got so frustrated with me for not getting better that he told me my medical problems were psychologically based and recommended that I get into therapy. The problem was that my first therapist was a real quack and I almost lost faith in therapy as a result. But I continued with some support groups, writing in my journal and taking classes in psychology, which I got a lot out of. I was doing a lot of good things, but was running into a wall—not really resolving anything. I decided to give it one more shot—that time with a female therapist. She was great because she could see what was happening underneath the surface and helped me to see what my real problem was.

◆

Chronic medical problems that seem (and are diagnosed by medical doctors) to be physiologically rather than psychologically based can set survivors on the wrong treatment plan that often results in a reliance on an increasing variety of medications to bring about relief. When physical symptoms do not abate, as they often will not when the root cause of the symptoms is not addressed, survivors feel helpless and frustrated, often reverting to the old notion that "something is wrong with me because I can't get well." As in Shirley's case, eventually the medications become yet another problem—a new addiction that must be dealt with first before "talking" therapy can be effective.

Shirley was able to get on the right track with the help of a professional therapist who understood that the medical problems and addictions were one of many manifestations of the child abuse. Many survivors initially flounder among the various conceptualizations of their problems and begin a pattern of treatment hopping that reflects their decision to act, but in a way that prevents a true commitment to the proper program of recovery. If you are not able to organize such a plan yourself, it is essential to get professional help to aid you in sorting out the many needs and problems into a multifaceted treatment plan.

DEALING WITH AN
ADDICTION BEFORE THE ABUSE

For some survivors who have an addiction, the decision to act involves attending one of the many self-help groups that are so effective in helping survivors gain control over their addiction or compulsive activity. Most addictions, especially substance abuse, need to be addressed before work on the abuse can begin in psychotherapy.

Pete

By the time I graduated from high school, I knew that something was wrong, but I really didn't want to face it. My solution was always to run away. So I did a couple of geographicals—that's AA terminology for moving around to avoid your problems—but it didn't work and I was still real confused about why other people were getting good jobs and getting married and I was being left behind. Actually the first time I was "twelfth-stepped" was by two guys who knew my dad. They belonged to the AA fellowship in our home town. They talked to me about AA, gave me some literature, and then I attended a talk they gave. I was initially turned off by the almost religious fervor of it all, but it planted a seed in my head, because when I moved out here and was still having problems, I finally just reached a point where I had to make a choice for myself. I felt like it was either "do or die." That was really the beginning for me.

◆

Pete's resistence to AA was long-standing, and like so many people who dismiss this proven alternative, he cited the religious content of the program as the reason for not giving it a try. But Pete's resistance operated on two levels. He avoided attending the meetings for years until he "hit bottom" in an emotional sense. Pete reached a point with his drinking where he was losing control of his life. Many survivors get to this do-or-die point with their addictions. Some, like Pete and Jolene, use the crisis to motivate their decision to act whereas others take an often fatal plunge into hopelessness and self-destructiveness.

But Pete, like many other survivors, ran into a second level of resistance after initially deciding to get help. Pete avoided really making a commitment to the program for eighteen months until he could more fully trust the people and the process. This type of resistence to real involvement is experienced by many survivors who enter therapy. Your difficulties with trust and the fear of being judged or blamed can prevent you from letting the treatment really help you. What I have seen many survivors do is enter therapy and then unconsciously work to defeat its potential effectiveness. Then the survivor feels entitled to say "Oh, I tried therapy or AA and it didn't work for me so I gave up on it." This is a most unfortunate development because the combination of self-help and professional help is really the only way to truly recover from the effects of the abuse. Ultimately you may be giving up on yourself. Be careful not to fool yourself into thinking you are making a commitment to change when you are really only making a half-hearted investment. Stick with your plan long enough to give it a fair chance to work.

MAKE A
CHANGE IN YOUR LIFESTYLE

As you go through recovery, you will be experiencing all sorts of mental, emotional, and quite possibly physical changes that will create a certain amount of stress on your body. If you are vulnerable to illness because of other factors, the pressure of facing a painful past may further exacerbate or precipitate stress-related ailments that can undermine your recovery. Thus it is often helpful to make changes in your life-style that will compliment the changes you are making in yourself, your feelings, and your attitudes. Look at your eating habits. Are you eating loads of junk food with too much salt, caffeine, and sugar? An unhealthy diet will only sap your energy, trigger mood swings, and increase your blood pressure, leaving you vulnerable to stress-related illnesses. Watch for any increase in the amount of alcohol and prescription or nonprescription drugs you use. What about exercise? Are you out of shape and run down? Think about enrolling in a fitness program or joining a hiking club.

Recovery is very hard work and you will need to build into your busy schedule some time for recreation and relaxation. Consider taking up a sport that you loved as a child that can be both fun and can offer you the chance to meet some new people. Racquet sports are especially satisfying for those who are looking to discharge some of the excess anger and aggression that is stirred up during recovery. Hobbies and activities with your children can reduce stress. Try to develop some activities that are rejuvenating and relaxing and arrange your schedule to permit the time. You will probably make these types of changes eventually when it gets easier to act in your own best interests. Why not consider making them now when they can really benefit you?

INTRODUCTION TO
THE THREE-STAGE, 21-STEP
RECOVERY PROGRAM

Recovery from child abuse is a demanding process that will take approximately several years to fully accomplish depending on the severity and duration of your abuse. Each of the three stages and twenty-one steps of recovery that will be presented later in chapters 12 through 14 will help you to resolve the conflicts and issues in an orderly and timely way, preparing you for subsequent changes, much like the developmental process of childhood. In essence, recovery is a form of re-parenting, although the parents in this case will be your therapist, members of your support group, and last but not least, yourself.

Steps 1 to 7 involve building the foundation of your new self by reclaiming the past and working through the trauma of abuse. The second stage, Steps 8 to 14, challenges you to build the structure of your new self by eliminating self-sabotaging behaviors and enhancing your personal capabilities. The third stage, Steps 15 to 21, involves refining and strengthening your new personality so that you can thrive in the world. Each step starts with "I" in affirmation of *your new self*—inside and out—and the healing and change that shape your resolve every step of the way.

Those of you who have attended 12-Step groups aimed at overcoming your addictions should be comfortable with the 21-Step program offered in chapters 12 through 14. Don't be put off by the additional nine steps. Recovery from child abuse requires some extra resolutions compared to recovery from substance abuse or compulsive behavior.

Think of the steps as a road map designed to prevent you from getting lost. However, not everyone follows this road map in exactly the same way. People are too complex and different to expect that degree of conformity. To be honest, many of you are willful, stubborn drivers who need to explore the side streets of life before deciding to take the main road. This is fine—as long as you eventually get there. The steps may then be regarded more as general markers along the road. You may change the order of the steps somewhat if that seems to work better for you or you may repeat old steps as new memories and insights resurface. You may even create some of your own steps that are more relevant to you and your childhood experience. My advice is to make the steps work for you. Recovery is truly an individual process, the limits of which are bound only by your belief in yourself.

The purpose of this chapter has been to help prepare you to make the kind of commitment to your program of recovery that will bring about true healing. I fully recognize that for most survivors thinking about the road ahead can be truly terrifying. As the stories of the survivors suggest, you are not alone in this feeling. But the bottom line is that eventually you must reach out to a friend or an acquaintance who is a survivor or to a self-help group or a therapist who is experienced in working with adult survivors. Nothing will change unless you make the decision to act. Other survivors have done so, despite their trepidations, and so can you. There may be other strategies to prepare you to act that are not included here. You may know in your heart what you will need to do to initiate your program. Take control right from the beginning. Everything written here is designed to support your efforts to act, not to impose a rigid system. Anything that helps you to act in the interest of recovery is good. Just do it—for yourself.

Chapter Ten

Self-Help

The self-help movement is sweeping the country and its message is simple but powerful: You can get help for many of your problems by sharing them in a group with people facing the same dilemma and you can help them in return. Currently more than 12 million people participate in some 500,000 self-help groups focusing on problems ranging from addictions to alcohol, drugs, and food to compulsive activities to physical and mental illnesses to the stress associated with living with a person confronting these concerns.

Alcoholics Anonymous (AA), the respected elder of the self-help movement and model for the new generation of self-help progeny, is now more than fifty years old and boasts a worldwide membership estimated to be 1.5 million people. What is the allure of these groups that are springing up overnight in corner storefronts, church basements, and community centers? This chapter will identify how and why self-help groups are so effective in helping people to take control of their lives and will describe what different groups may have to offer you, the adult survivor, who is ready to make a commitment to recovery.

A closer look at what these groups have to offer will explain their current popularity and why survivors can benefit from them. To begin, most self-help groups cost nothing to join. They are available almost everywhere and anytime. They accept everyone who has an interest in the topic or a willingness to change. They offer valuable information and tips on current resources, functioning as ad hoc clearinghouses tailored to the concerns of the members. They offer twenty-four hour support during times of crisis as well as an antidote to the universal plague of isolation, stigmatization, and shame that people face today. They can be inspirational, energizing, and empowering. In short, self-help groups can offer a tremendous lift of spirit if you are struggling with giving up an addiction or overcoming abuse. But self-help groups can provide something even more special for adult survivors—a sense of family that you never had.

As yet, there is no one self-help group addressing the specific concerns of survivors of all types of child abuse. However, considering how quickly these groups are proliferating, it may be only a matter of time before such a group develops. In the meantime, adult survivors can attend one of the many self-help groups available in most communities: Alcoholics Anonymous (AA), Adult Children of Alcoholics (ACA), Parents United (PU), Parents Anonymous (PA), Overeaters Anonymous (OA); and the newcomers to the field: Incest Survivors Anonymous (ISA), Fundamentalists Anonymous (FA), and Sex and Love Addicts Anonymous (SLA).

HOW SELF-HELP GROUPS
BREAK THE ADDICTION CYCLE

Most self-help groups rely on the structure and philosophy of the 12 Steps and 12 Traditions as defined by AA. These 12 Steps, which are adapted by each self-help group with AA's permission, offer a fairly rigid code of tenets, expectations, and suggestions designed to bring about a spiritual recovery that will result in sobriety. The steps are designed to be worked individually and in progression until resolution is achieved. When recovery is complete, the person is able to work all 12 Steps each day of his or her life in a program that continues well after sobriety is attained. Ultimately a spiritual awakening is what the AA philosophy calls for to create a different type of lifestyle necessary to sustain sobriety.

THE 12 STEPS OF
ALCOHOLICS ANONYMOUS

1. We admitted we were powerless over alcohol—that our lives had become unmanageable.
2. Came to believe that a power greater than ourselves could restore us to sanity.
3. Made a decision to turn our will and our lives over to the care of God *as we understood Him*.
4. Made a searching and fearless moral inventory of ourselves.
5. Admitted to God, to ourselves, and to another human being the exact nature of our wrongs.
6. Were entirely ready to have God remove all these defects of character.
7. Humbly asked Him to remove our shortcomings.
8. Made a list of all persons we harmed, and became willing to make amends to them all.
9. Made direct amends to such people wherever possible, except when to do so would injure them or others.
10. Continued to take personal inventory, and when we were wrong, promptly admitted it.
11. Sought through prayer and meditation to improve our conscious contact with God *as we understood Him*, praying only for knowledge of His will for us and the power to carry that out.
12. Having had a spiritual awakening as the result of these steps, we tried to carry this message to alcoholics, and to practice these principles in all our affairs.

Pete

A A has meant a lot to me. I know I couldn't have stopped drinking without it. It has offered more than that though. It has saved my life and given me small practical tools as well. I met my wife at AA and we worked the program together. For the first time in my adult life I was able to have some fun without being drunk. It offered me a place to go to hear people who I could relate to on a lot of levels, to air my feelings and to be able to tell the truth, basically. The 12 Steps outline three ideas for a "spiritual design for living" that I try to live with every day of my life: to trust in my Higher Power whom I call God, to clean my spiritual house, and then to share it with others. So what it offered me was a kind of tool kit for taking care of some of my living problems. Perhaps as important, it gave me a community of friends, who, in turn, gave me love, friendship, and acceptance. Even if you're not an alcoholic, these are pretty special gifts. If you are a survivor of child abuse, they can mean the difference between hope and despair.

♦

On a practical level, if you have an addiction, 12-Step groups may be the best strategy for gaining sobriety and control over your life. In most cases, intensive psychotherapy alone is simply not powerful enough to stop the physiological and psychological urges to drink or engage in compulsive activities. Self-help groups patterned after the 12 Steps create a single-minded focus on stopping the behavior that is crucial to breaking the cycle of addiction. The strategy of focusing on achieving this one goal, day by day, or hour by hour, if necessary, and providing the human resources necessary to reach this goal are the main reasons why AA and other 12-Step groups are successful.

Once people have some initial success in controlling their addiction, an amazing thing happens. They are flooded with a sense of well-being and elation and hope, which in turn can bring about a self-confidence that can stimulate other, more deep-seated changes. Alcoholics are encouraged to "work the steps" because their initial experience tells them that "the steps work." While this may sound like circular reasoning to the uninitiated, the bottom line is that the addictive behavior has been halted, at least for the time being.

This identification with the program sets in motion a whole new way of thinking about yourself and your identity in the world. The process of attaining sobriety begins to snowball into wholesale recovery, and over time, a different lifestyle. Hanging out at the corner bar is replaced by attending meetings. Friendships with old drinking buddies dissolve as new relationships with group members develop. The simple act of holding on to the bottle of beer or shot glass is also replaced with something new—holding on to the Big Book, the Bible of AA that describes the 12 Steps and Traditions. Recovery brings about a new way of living.

OTHER BENEFITS
OF SELF-HELP GROUPS

There are other rewards for adult survivors who choose to participate in self-help groups that address their particular needs as survivors and offer a level of support necessary for recovery. Even when you are not

afflicted with an addiction, these groups can be a tremendous source
of care, concern for your struggles, and motivation for you to change
your life.

Leigh Anne

A ttending a self-help group meeting is like participating in a group
commiseration: A bunch of people sit in a room, share personal
stories, receive feedback, and learn new ways of coping with life. While
you're there, you don't always know what benefits you're getting. But
you leave thinking about something that you heard that clicks inside:
"God, at least I got a way out," or "At least I heard somebody who
had the same story," or "At least I'm not alone." That is the most
terrifying experience as a child and as an adult, to feel that sense of
aloneness that you are in this thing by yourself. Being in a self-help
group teaches you that this is not the case at all. For every crazy problem
that I've ever had to deal with, there are two hundred thousand other
people in Western civilization going through the same thing. And also,
there's the feedback, which I eat up like a bowl of ice cream. I love
feedback. My favorite flavor is "Tell me what you think!" And you
don't have to use your real name: They let you have your anonymity
and still give you the opportunity to speak from the heart. Even if you
don't say a word, there's so much to be gained by listening to the
sponsors and the speakers. Sometimes, I just think, "God, that's way
beyond anything I've every suffered. Maybe my life wasn't so bad after
all."

◆

Self-help groups offer a sense of belonging that was probably not available in your family. The experience of "fellowship" so often referred
to in AA is a powerful remedy to the loneliness and isolation experienced by many adult survivors. If you come from a family that is still
in denial or unwilling to change their abusive attitudes toward you,
these groups can become your surrogate family.

Self-help groups can offer more than information, support, understanding, and acceptance. As Leigh Anne described, you can be as
active or reserved as you want. The choice is up to you. No one will
push you to do or say anything before you are ready. Thus a needed
feeling of safety is created for survivors who commonly feel like outsiders, intimidated by strangers and authority figures. Safety and acceptance may be the most important criteria of self-help groups because
you can be yourself without fear of being judged, rejected, or criticized.

Because you will come in contact with group members who have faced and overcome similar problems, you can learn about your own maladaptive behaviors of which you were previously unaware and try out alternative behaviors that are modeled by more experienced group members. This can be done just by watching and listening to the stories being told by the speakers. When you are ready to speak directly about your own experience, you can ask for feedback or simply sit down, comforted by the notion that no one will criticize you or invalidate your point of view.

GUIDE TO
SELF-HELP GROUPS

Listed below are descriptions of five self-help groups that specifically address the issues faced by adult survivors of child abuse. AA is not included in this list because I have referred to it previously and because it does not directly address physical, sexual, or emotional abuse. Unfortunately there is no one national self-help organization that sponsors groups for survivors of all three types of abuse. Each group has its particular focus and you can decide which may be best for you based on the type of abuse you suffered as a child. Parents United, Parents Anonymous, and Fundamentalists Anonymous do not use AA's 12 Steps, but are organized around a steplike program similar in structure. In general, the proliferation we see of new self-help groups reflects the need to adapt the addiction concept, as represented by the 12 Steps, to something more comprehensive and specific to the impact of child abuse.

ADULT CHILDREN OF ALCOHOLICS (ACA)

Al-Anon, the group for the family and friends of alcoholics, began a new type of group in 1976 for the adult children of alcoholic parents. With more than a thousand groups nationwide, these groups have created an awareness of the long-range effects of growing up in an alcoholic family. Although ACA groups are still heavily focused on alcoholism, the discussions in these meetings address all the ways that parents' drinking can affect their relationship with their child and the long-range effects of alcoholism on intimacy and caretaking tendencies. In effect, ACA groups address many of the issues of emotional abuse, and as such, have much to offer survivors who were themselves emotionally abused as children, whether or not their parents were alcoholics.

Pete

AA groups and ACA groups are very different. I participate in both so I can see the differences pretty clearly. ACA groups are not as rigid in their focus as AA groups are. While AA members limit themselves to talking about alcohol and the Steps, people in ACA tend to bring in all sorts of related material including what they have learned from their therapy. A lot of people don't like it for that reason. Personally I have found it very helpful because it offers a much more unique perspective: The "shares" are very individualized, and by listening to them, you can learn something really new and apply it to your own situation. People in AA tend to share the same stories over and over again. Most of the people in ACA are also in therapy in contrast to the AA people who are often dead set against it. Primarily the first and most fundamental thing about ACA is that the emphasis is on what it was like to grow up in an alcoholic family. It allows you to identify with other people's experience, which cuts through the sense of isolation— the isolation that said, "I'm different. My situation was unique and terrible." And, as well, you hear what people are doing about it today. It was at an ACA meeting that I first heard a woman talk about being an incest survivor and that was very important to me. You would never hear that at an AA meeting.

◆

The popularity of the ACA movement has spawned "derivative" ACA groups that are unaffiliated with Al-Anon. These newer ACA groups do not follow the 12 Steps and 12 Traditions of AA and have developed their own meeting formats that reflect a greater variability in subject matter. Many people describe these groups as less structured and focused than the Al-Anon-sponsored groups and as more likely to address general psychological topics in addition to the more typical addiction issues. These groups may actually border on being more like psychotherapy groups than self-help groups, which in some cases may be a liability considering that the members usually have no professional training. To determine which type of ACA group you're joining, just ask whether it is affiliated with Al-Anon.

PARENTS UNITED (PU)/DAUGHTERS AND SONS UNITED/ADULTS MOLESTED AS CHILDREN

Parents United, a self-help group for families affected by child sexual abuse, was established in 1975 by Dr. Henry Giarretto, a psychologist who had previously started a court-mandated treatment program for child sexual abuse offenders in Santa Clara County, California. Out of recognition that everyone in these families needed help, not just the offenders and the victims, Parents United started special small group meetings for the "nonoffending" mothers, as well as for the daughters and sons who were molested.

Parents United has grown rapidly and now boasts over a hundred chapters throughout the United States and Canada and has served more than twelve thousand people. The organization provides services for adults molested as children (AMAC groups) who are no longer living with their families or no longer dependent on them. This component may have the most to offer for adult survivors of sexual abuse who have not developed offender behaviors. Because PU has a group for every person, adult or child, who was or is affected by sexual abuse, it is the largest community resource for this type of family problem available in the United States today.

Parents United is unique for several reasons. It was the first program of its kind to focus on the issue of child sexual abuse. Besides providing more services to incest survivors, offenders, and families than any other national organization, PU works with law enforcement authorities on the complex criminal-legal-psychological issues that are raised by these cases. Often the family is referred for help when the father (most commonly) is given probation following the charge of sexual abuse and is mandated to attend the Parents United program. Unlike most other self-help groups, Parents United has affiliations with mental health professionals who may act as the facilitators of groups. In contrast to the spiritual base of AA, Parents United draws from the work of psychologists Abraham Maslow and Carl Rogers. The basic philosophy of PU is that people who molest children do so not because they are evil but rather due to their violent reaction to their frustrations over not getting their needs met. The focus of the self-help groups is to help all family members develop a "high self-concept . . . that will enhance the processes of self-awareness and self-management, as well as feelings of family unity and growth."

Instead of the 12 Steps, Parents United has its own creed developed by three mothers who are charter members:

> To extend the hand of friendship, understanding and compassion, *not* to judge or condemn.
> To better our understanding of ourselves and our children through the aid of the other members and professional guidance.
> To reconstruct and channel our anger and frustrations in other directions, *not* on or at our children.
> To realize that we *are* human and do have angers and frustrations; they are normal.

To recognize that we do need help, we are all in the same boat, we have all been there many times.

To remember that there is no miracle answer or rapid change; it has taken years for us to get this way.

To have patience with ourselves, again and again and again, taking each day as it comes.

To start each day with a feeling of promise, for we take only one day at a time.

To remember that we *are* human, we will backslide at times.

To remember that there is always someone willing to listen and help.

To become the *loving, constructive and giving parents or persons* that we wish to be.

When you join Parents United, you go through a series of brief, eight-week groups. There are different Preorientation Groups for offenders and nonoffending parents and children and then a larger Orientation Group where adult victims and offenders are enrolled together. From this "base" group, members move to more specialized "open" groups when the group members and the professionals involved think they are ready. Other groups include the Adults Molested As Children's Groups, Women's Groups, Men's Groups, Couple's Groups, Alcoholic Problem Groups and Recontact Groups. Recontact groups are composed of offenders and adult survivors who use psychodramatic techniques to confront their parents, who are played by surrogate offenders in the group. These techniques help them recontact repressed rage and vulnerability that they can vent in a safe, therapeutic way. Groups usually have eight to ten people (with the exception of the Orientation Groups, which can have more than thirty) and are run by a trained professional who is recruited from the local community and may have an affiliation with a community mental health program. The facilitators provide minimal direction and structure, preferring the group process to be more defined by the individual members. Classes and individual counseling are also provided as needed and as requested by members.

There have been two criticisms of the Parents United program that come mostly from the professional community. The first has to do with the capacity of PU to identify and screen those sex offenders who are true pedophiles—men who have a more serious personality disorder—that are not effectively treated by the PU program. Because they were not initially screened, there was a question as to whether offenders were getting the proper treatment to gain control of their sex and power urges so they could reunite with their families. In recent years, PU has instituted a ninety-day assessment period whereby professional staff may observe all offenders and recommend them for outside treatment if their behavior indicates a more serious disorder.

The second concern has to do with reservations about PU's commitment to family reunification when it is in the best interests of everyone, including the children. But some professionals have concerns that this philosophy may be applied when it is really not in the best interests of the child. Much of this concern goes back to the question of whether the offender has been sufficiently treated so he can be with the child. In this sense, the strategy of family reunification is only as good as the treatment of the offender. As PU continues to refine its ability to identify and refer those offenders who require more specialized treatment, this concern should disappear.

PARENTS ANONYMOUS (PA)

Parents Anonymous is the oldest and most recognized self-help group dealing specifically with physical abuse. The group was started in 1970 when Jolly K., a parent on the verge of physically abusing her child, walked into a mental health center in southern California and demanded immediate help, only to be given an appointment three months later with social worker, Leonard Lieber. Desperate to get help for herself before turning her rage on her child, she and Lieber began organizing a self-help group for parents who abused or were about to abuse their children. The group, first known as Mothers Anonymous, eventually became Parents Anonymous, and now has a total of twelve hundred weekly meetings nationwide and in five foreign countries.

PA is not based on AA's 12 Steps and instead defines itself as a modified self-help group run by a facilitator-therapist and sometimes with a chairperson, a concerned parent who volunteers to support the group. The facilitator organizes speakers and discussion topics on parenting issues, child development, and the building of the parent's self-esteem. Parents learn alternatives to abusive parenting behaviors, problem-solving techniques, and ways to reduce stress. PA meetings are not supposed to be psychotherapy, but will help with your coping skills and will bring you together with people who are struggling to be better parents. Generally eight to sixteen people meet once per week in community agencies that employ the facilitators. Discussion, sharing, reaching out to others, and supporting personal growth through education and therapy is the philosophy underlying the program. PA is not for people who have been sexually abused. The prevention of physical and emotional abuse is its most basic purpose. PA will provide a specified number of group sessions for the parent who has been charged with felony child abuse as part of a jail diversion program and will cooperate with the probation department to provide follow-up supervision.

PA has recently started another group called SPEAKS (Survivors of Physical and Emotional Abuse As Kids), which is the brainchild of social worker Linda Levinson. As of 1988, there were five groups operating in the Los Angeles area. Other groups are planned for Albuquerque and the San Francisco Bay area. There groups are very similar to the PA groups, although the focus is more generally on adult survivors of physical and emotional abuse and not as much on parenting and child abuse prevention, as with PA. They are free, open to both men and women of all ages, with or without children. They actively encourage interested people to start groups in their own areas and will send information about selecting a professional and the program format used. Feeling left out of incest and addiction groups, survivors of physical and emotional abuse now have their own forum in which to reach out to others and gain support for their childhood experiences, united in their efforts to heal and change.

INCEST SURVIVORS ANONYMOUS (ISA)

Incest Survivors Anonymous is about eight years old and now has 160 chapters worldwide including meetings in the Netherlands, Canada, and England. Adhering to the 12 Steps and 12 Traditions of AA, and adapted to incest with the permission of AA's Board of Directors, the program simply substitutes the word *incest* (meaning all sexual abuse) for *alcohol* in the AA approach and supports members seeking their Higher Power to recover from the effects of the abuse. Like the other self-help groups, ISA is also a voluntary, nonprofit organization that charges no fees to participate. Hats are passed at the meetings to cover the costs of coffee and printed literature. The founding of new groups is encouraged and a "starter package" is offered that can be obtained by mailing a stamped, self-addressed envelope to the national office listed in the Resource Directory in Appendix B.

The meetings generally follow the AA meeting format and include enough time for everyone to speak about their experiences as a child and an adult in recovery. Some communities offer more than the standard participation meeting, scheduling men's groups on one night, women's groups on the next, and groups referred to in their vernacular as "Nothing Too Heavy to Share in Recovery." Much of the focus is on healing the wounded child inside and supporting each other's efforts in recovery.

ISA is also different from all other groups in that meetings are closed to anyone who is not a survivor of some kind of child sexual abuse. Therefore, no visitors are allowed. The definition of incest is very broad: any sexual behavior directed at children that involves "touching and nontouching, overt and covert, verbal and nonverbal." Significantly, ISA does not welcome sex offenders or "initiators" as they refer to them. They reserve the right to prohibit anyone from the meeting who they feel acts like an initiator. The organizers of ISA recognize that survivors need to deal with their addictions before working on the abuse issues and suggest coinvolvement with AA if alcoholism is also a problem.

Some members of ISA were victims of satanic ritual sexual abuse and other extremely traumatizing experiences involving cults and parents who were pedophiles. Information, support, understanding, and recovery for these most extreme childhood experiences are available and will be gladly shared. Despite the severity of the childhood experiences shared in the meetings, the atmosphere is decidedly upbeat and committed to realizing the goodness available in life. Two favorite slogans are "Don't Quit Before Your Miracles" and "You've Got to Feel It to Heal It."

FUNDAMENTALISTS ANONYMOUS (FA)

Fundamentalists Anonymous (FA) is the newest of the self-help groups, providing meetings for adults who grew up in families reflecting extreme religious values as found in fundamentalist religions and charismatic and pentecostal movements. Only three years old, the organization was founded by an ex–Wall Street lawyer (and Yale Divinity School student) Richard Yao and banker James Luce who themselves grew up in fundamentalist families and have recovered from the effects that they now conceptualize as the "fundamentalist mindset." They now have almost fifty chapters nationwide and almost forty thousand members.

Meetings are begun by reading the Statement of Purpose of FA that describes the organization as a support group for those who have been hurt by their fundamentalist experience. Members include ex-fundamentalists, adult children of fundamentalists, concerned parents, spouses, relatives, and close friends who have been part of the movement. The group is secular and does not recruit members. Religion is not discussed in the meetings and no churches are endorsed. FA is not antireligious or atheistic but objects to the fundamentalist mindset. FA defines fundamentalist mindset as a "dysfunctional way of processing reality characterized by massive denial and psychological dependency." The major problem of the fundamentalist mindset is cited as an "inability to tolerate ambiguity and uncertainty in life and an inclination to paint everything in black and white, right and wrong, and good and evil." FA's goals are to provide a supportive environment to free each other from the fundamentalist mindset and educate the public on the dangers of fundamentalism as a mental health hazard and threat to basic civil liberties.

The focus in the meetings is on FA's 5-Step Program called TOAST: (1) Taking responsibility; (2) One step at a time; (3) Association; (4) Self-esteem; and (5) To be brave, act brave. This simple program seems to be a compilation of some of the favorite sayings and prescriptions found in various self-help ideologies. In essence, it supports recognizing the problem; taking the first step; reaching out to like-minded people to help each other, to provide support, and to build self-esteem; and finally, changing by trying to live differently until it becomes your nature. With the strengthening of the so-called "New Right" religious movement, many more people may be asking for help to challenge emotional oppression caused by religious fanatacism.

SELF-HELP GROUPS
UNAFFILIATED WITH NATIONAL ORGANIZATIONS

In many communities, there are self-help or support groups for adult survivors sponsored by local community organizations such as rape crisis centers, child abuse prevention agencies, community mental health centers, county victim assistance programs, and women's centers. Usually these groups are started when the community expresses a need and staffs organize meeting times, space, administrative support, and professional consultation. How the groups are set up varies depending on the orientation of the founding members and consulting professionals.

STARTING YOUR OWN SUPPORT GROUP

Some survivors prefer to start their own support groups either because they want a smaller, more personal group with a particular focus or because of the lack of organized self-help groups in their area. You also have the choice of starting a new chapter of one of the organized self help groups or you can do what Susan did and organize a group loosely based on principles borrowed from 12-Step groups and self-improvement workshops.

Susan

I had been in several groups beginning with AA, but found myself constantly calling my friends to discuss this and that and they did the same with me. Some of them were in various groups—weight loss, AA, and some of the Women, Sex, and Power workshops—but a few were complaining about problems that were bogging the groups down. So I had this idea to pull everyone together to see if we could start our own group. I decided to have it at my house so I wouldn't need to get a baby sitter for Sam.

My friends were real enthusiastic so we planned a meeting. Really the hardest part of it was getting ten women to agree on a date. I ended up being the facilitator basically because I was the common denominator—the one everyone knew and trusted. I was a caretaker from way back, and I guess they expected me to lead the way because I had the idea.

We had the first meeting and decided several things. First, we would not just focus on one topic or issue. We all had all sorts of things going on—dieting, career, parenting, recovery from alcohol, drugs, men—you name it, we talked about it. We also decided to ask everyone to make a three-month commitment. Absences were not to be tolerated lightly. We all felt everyone had to be up to date on everyone in order to be helpful when needed. Confidentiality was discussed and we agreed that nothing should leave the room. Our philosophy was we were there either to get support or give support. So every Tuesday evening for some three years we met from 7:00 to 10:00 P.M.

Over time, it became a very successful group. We had our struggles, that's for sure, but we relied on each other—helping with resumes, covering for child care, providing moving services, book exchange, and tons of emotional support. Every three months or so we would have evening potlucks and take people out on their birthdays.

Each meeting would start with a few minutes of social time; then each person would go into whatever was happening in her life. It was agreed that no one would interrupt and no "cross-talk"—no dialogue with any one person while sharing. After each person went, there would be some comments and discussion before the next person would go. A lot of material came up. In retrospect, I believe it was a successful group because everyone was very committed. The chemistry was very good, although there were times when some members would really battle things out with each other. But we also got what we wanted: some social and personal contact with people, a sense of community, a helping hand in a crisis for some and a healthy dose of reality for others. When the group suffered, the reasons had to do mostly with gossiping about members, which caused hard feelings and some people being judgmental about what was happening to someone else. And, sometimes, it would turn into therapy, which never seemed to work because we didn't really know what to say to people in certain situations: We weren't professionals and I believe we got in over our heads at times.

If I had to do it again, I would suggest we bring in a facilitator— some professional trained in groups—once a month to help sort out the snags between people that tended to linger on too long. We had some people who would get bogged down in storytelling and dominate the time unnecessarily. We tried to deal with it tactfully but what I learned is that people's issues just come right out when you provide a safe place for them to talk. Some people use it constructively while others need much more.

Eventually I got burned out being the facilitator and decided to leave. The group is still going on but they had a hard time figuring out who was going to take over my old role. I think it was too much my group for their sake and mine.

◆

If you decide that you want to start your own group, unaffiliated with any national self-help program, recognize that there are particular organizational and structural questions that will have to be resolved in order to create a workable meeting format. This will take time, patience, and a good deal of compromise. It may be best to formulate some general ideas at first and then refine your meeting format with the other group members so that everyone has a sense of "ownership" of the group process and structure. The most pressing issues in starting a group have to do with (1) who will be involved; (2) what will be discussed; (3) how the meeting time will be structured; (4) what the goals or desired outcomes will be; (5) schedule, location, and duration of the group; (6) financial matters involving cost of coffee or refreshments if provided; (7) how members will leave and join the group; (8) who, if anyone, will act as the facilitator; (9) what the rules will be for making decisions, resolving disagreements, and issues of confidentiality; (10) whether the group will be a "drop-in" or "high commitment" group, the latter being better at preserving group cohesiveness.

USING SELF-HELP
GROUPS IN YOUR RECOVERY PROGRAM

WHERE TO LOOK FOR SELF-HELP GROUPS

The best place to start looking for groups is in your local telephone directory. If there is no listing, consult the Resource Directory in Appendix B for the telephone numbers of the central offices of various self-help organizations. Call and ask for a location nearest to you. Another idea is to call some of the toll-free numbers of the national self-help clearinghouses also listed in Appendix B. They will have the latest information on the nearest groups to you. If there is no group available, they can send you additional information to help you start your own group. Most towns, even in the remotest rural regions, have at least one AA meeting. Even if alcohol does not figure into the concern you are facing, think about visiting a meeting. Often you will learn of other types of self-help groups.

CHOOSING THE RIGHT
GROUP AND MEETING FOR YOU

Besides choosing the right type of group, there are also choices to be made concerning which group meeting to attend. Although all 12-Step groups are similar in format and structure, they may have very different "atmospherics" depending on the type of person for whom the meeting is "pulling." For example, there may be twenty or more different AA meetings scattered around major metropolitan areas, each attracting a particular type of person depending on location, time, and individual characteristics of the core regulars. There are groups that advertise themselves as sensitive to special populations such as gay people, management types, single mothers, minorities, and foreign language speakers. In short, the group is as much defined by the members who attend it as it is by the 12 Steps. Consequently you may like one group more than another. Therefore, when checking out a self-help group, it is important to visit several meetings before deciding on one in particular. If you find that you are not comfortable in one meeting, don't let that sour you on the idea of self-help groups in general. Keep looking until you find the one that is right for you.

HOW MEETINGS ARE ORGANIZED

Most self-help groups will have different types of meetings depending on the purpose and needs of the membership. Some groups may be limited to men or women or newcomers or those wishing to focus on particular steps. Groups patterned after AA may offer "speaker" meetings where one, two, or possibly three people will speak with no time for discussion provided. In "discussion" meetings, only one person will speak with the remaining time devoted to a general discussion open to all. In addition, 12-Step groups may have "open" and "closed" meetings, the distinguishing feature being whether visitors are invited.

Most meetings of each self-help group will follow a relatively consistent format that may adapt somewhat to the shifting needs of the group. Usually the meetings will begin with a brief social time when coffee is served before the secretary calls the meeting to order. The secretary is someone, usually well along in recovery, who has volunteered to "manage" the meeting, making sure there are enough speakers, refreshments, chairs, and so forth. AA's Serenity Prayer may be read followed by the recitation of the 12 Steps leading into a "share": a personal story told by one of the speakers in which he describes his problem with alcohol, the effect it has had on his life, and some lessons derived from his recovery. If discussion is part of the meeting, the group members will comment on what the story may have meant to them. Criticism, judgmentalness, or airs of superiority are surprisingly absent in the group members' comments as care is taken to ensure the respect for and consideration of the speaker's possible vulnerability. At the end, new business or announcements may be voiced, followed by a prayer, before the meeting is adjourned. Spirituality and prayers are treated as a ritual as well as a religious matter, allowing members to participate in a way that is comfortable to their own beliefs. Following the closing prayer is the main social time of the meeting where personal contact can be established between group members, comments exchanged, and statements of appreciation and validation extended to the speakers.

ATTENDING THE FIRST MEETING

Attending your first meeting may be the most difficult one of all because you are not completely sure of what to expect. Depending on what makes you more comfortable, you can consider going with a friend, or better yet, someone who has attended the meeting previously who can act as your unofficial sponsor. Allow yourself to just get a feel for what it is like: Sitting and listening is always acceptable and you are not expected to say anything if you don't want to. Some of the smaller groups will make a point of giving each person a chance to speak, but if you don't want to, simply tell them you "pass" and they will move on to the next person.

Pete

I had tremendous problems about joining AA with all that religious stuff, but finally, I went to a meeting and sat in the back and just listened. Fortunately, nobody bothered me, although everyone was real friendly. It took me almost eighteen months to really join AA in the sense of participating in the meeting. I just didn't trust anyone. I didn't want them to find out who I was. I just sat in the back meeting after meeting, just feeling scared and uncomfortable. One thing that I really like about AA is that nobody pushes you to talk. That was real important for me because I was really scared. I slowly grew more comfortable and eventually it got to the point where I started confiding in people at the end of the meeting. I also got a sponsor and gradually started working the steps.

◆

How to Get the Most Out of the Meetings

Most of you will develop an idea of what you like about the meetings and may even arrange your schedule so that you can attend a particular meeting that offers what you want. There is an old saying in 12-Step meetings: "Take what you want and leave the rest." For survivors who do not have a spiritual sense or who may feel uncomfortable with the idea of "giving yourself up to a Higher Power," this advice may allow you to still get something from the meetings without feeling obligated to believe in anything that doesn't fit for you. Remember that it is your right to get what you want, not what other people think you should get. The bottom line is making the meetings work for you.

Susan

I have gone to all kinds of self-help groups. I started out with AA. I didn't discover ACA until a little later and then also tried OA (Overeaters Anonymous) and CA (Cocaine Anonymous) because coke was my real weakness. But I'm not hard-core about the dogma. I don't work the steps. I go to the meetings for my own stuff, but I don't embrace the whole thing completely. I do maintain total abstinence from coke, however. I believe that most of the 12-Step groups tap into the same stuff—the underlying core stuff inside all of us who grew up in dysfunctional families. Only everyone chooses a different drug to cover it up. That's my personal belief, but it seems to fit a lot. I don't think there's ever been a meeting that I've ever gone to, no matter what the size, where there isn't one person who makes a statement that you really connect with. But I go for other reasons besides the information. I go for that energy and the support and a sense of belonging and total acceptance.

◆

LIMITATIONS OF SELF-HELP GROUPS

Despite the enthusiastic tone of this chapter, there are some limitations and shortcomings of self-help groups that need to be mentioned. Although any healing process demands trust in the caregiver or caregiving organization, the responsibility for your recovery starts and ends with you. This means that you will need to be prepared to go against the advice of real or would-be "experts" if what they are proposing does not feel right to you. Ultimately this responsibility to choose what you think is best for you relates to the empowerment issue that you may be struggling with during the course of your recovery. Admittedly, you may make mistakes in choosing what to believe, who to trust, and how to change, but they will be your mistakes, not someone else's.

The above word of advice is especially applicable to getting the most out of self-help groups. To begin, recognize that most self-help groups are run by people without professional training. Thus, the members, even those "veterans" in positions of authority, are doing the best they can based on their personality, their level of conscious awareness, and their interpretation of the particular group's recovery model. But they are not usually professionally trained. Consequently, people running a meeting or operating as a sponsor or even sitting in the audience responding to someone's story will not always know the right thing to say at a delicate moment or will be able to censor a hurtful word or a destructive suggestion.

While most groups follow the 12 Steps and 12 Traditions, remember that, like the U.S. Constitution, everyone seems to have their own interpretation of what is helpful and good. Sometimes groups as a whole can get stuck on a particular ideological slant that restricts more accommodating interpretations. Quality control varies greatly from chapter to chapter and meeting to meeting within the self-help field. With the exception of Parents United (which only recently instituted regional oversight committees), the various national organizations do not provide any supervision or review of what actually transpires in each group. Therefore, don't take everything you hear as gospel. If you hear something that doesn't feel right, pay attention to that feeling and try to explore its merits and demerits objectively. You may be the one who is right.

Because the groups are free and open to anyone who is interested in the subject matter, they can attract people with more serious emotional problems who may rely on the group for therapy instead of support and information. Self-help groups are not a cure-all. When meetings are dominated by a person who is trying to use the group for the wrong reasons, it may be upsetting for survivors who grew up tolerating their parents' inappropriate needs.

In some groups, members who have yet to resolve their personality problems may gravitate toward leadership positions such as chairpersons of subcommittees, sponsors to new members, and even group cofacilitators. Groups that provide services for both abusers and survivors are especially prone to this kind of problem. People who abuse children have abused their authority, which if never completely treated, makes it more likely that they will do the same in other situations. These organizations recognize this risk and have developed safeguards to protect against inappropriate expressions of power by members within the meeting. However, these safeguards are not always adequate.

I have heard of situations where people who supposedly "recovered" have aspired to positions of power and authority within a meeting or organization where they, in effect, continued their role as the "offender" in their behavior and attitudes toward others. Cleverly, they may cloak this now more subtle behavior in the ideology of the organization, which makes it more difficult to detect. This can be a very dangerous situation for adult survivors because, after much work, you may have grown to feel safe in your meeting and trusting of those members recognized as leaders by the group. If you have not gotten to the point in recovery where you can assert your opinion and stand your ground, it may be difficult to deal with these leaders, especially if they are overly assertive and manipulative.

Remember that people who act authoritatively are often the ones who can become authoritarian. Prior to recovery, survivors who were once victims can easily become "subjects" of someone else's power needs without knowing it may be unhealthy for them. The best suggestion I can make in this regard is to ask yourself how these people make you feel. Be aware of anyone who regularly brings out your own passive victim part. If in doubt as to what may be happening in a group or with a sponsor, sound out other people whose judgement you trust. You don't have to give your power away anymore.

Some of the limitations of self-help groups for adult survivors have more to do with the 12-Step ideology and the rigid focus on addictions and sobriety. Some of the issues addressed by the steps are not helpful to the survivor who is dealing with much more than just sobriety. The idea of "giving yourself up to a Higher Power" may work against the idea of personal empowerment that is so important for a survivor who had little control or power as a child. The idea of forgiveness, which is promoted as a step in recovery, may be premature for survivors who have yet to work through their feelings of betrayal and loss of innocence. In the end, the personal experience of being physically or sexually abused or emotionally tormented and the issues that it raises are very different than being addicted to alcohol or growing up with alcoholic parents. Where it is similar, the 12 Steps have much to offer. Where it is not, it is best to look somewhere else.

Pete

The 12 Steps certainly offer me a foundation not only for sobriety but for the kind of spiritual healing that recovery from alcoholism demands. But quite frankly, from my experience, working the steps does not fully address the reality of being abused and growing up with abusive parents. I tried it. I feel like I tried it damn hard. I was just stacking the deck against myself by pretending to feel forgiveness before I had ever worked through the pain and rage and disappointment. It's not meant for it. Step work is not encompassing enough to take into account the enormous impact that incest has on a person. And I think that we in AA try to make AA be a cure-all and it's not. I see other people being confused by it because there are a lot of alcoholics who were also abused as children who get their minds screwed up by it. As an ACA, I feel frustrated that step work can't fix these problems also but we are taught to let something go that we can't change. So now I don't use AA to fix my abuse issues. I recognize that its the wrong wrench for the problem. That was when I started going to ACA groups more and then got into my own therapy.

◆

One final concern about self-help groups, AA in particular, has to do with the prevailing bias against professional therapy expressed by some of the more devout members. Much of this negative attitude is a carryover from the past when medical professionals, unschooled in the addiction process, attempted to treat alcoholics with medications and "talk" therapy while diminishing the value of AA. Clearly some damage was done in the past in not fully recognizing that addictions require special treatments. But now many health professionals do have training in treating addictions and have grown to respect the value of AA in helping people achieve and maintain their sobriety. Nevertheless, the bias continues, in part because of the many old-school AA people who insist that there is only one way—the AA way. This kind of rigid thinking does a disservice to those recovering people who are also survivors and who need to deal with both concerns to make the kind of wholesale changes that total recovery requires.

CAN YOU RECOVER
WITHOUT SELF-HELP GROUPS?

You probably can tell that I am a firm believer in the value and effectiveness of self-help groups, especially when it comes to dealing with addictive behavior. For the survivor facing many of the issues referred to here and in previous chapters, self-help groups offer you so much of what was not available in your family: love, support, acceptance, understanding. Who knows, like Pete, you may meet your future spouse there! Why would you not want to consider something that would make your recovery process easier? Examine your resistance to participating in self-help groups and try to understand if your reasons are part of what you are trying to change in yourself. Are you avoiding a meeting out of fear of being rejected? Are you afraid you won't fit in? Perhaps it is still too hard to reach out to others for help. I am not going to say that you cannot truly recover without being involved in a group because I know from my work with my clients that anything is possible. But will your participation in a group make it easier for you to cope and possibly break down some of your fears and the tendency to isolate yourself? In most cases, I would say yes. Consider everything you read, listen to what others say, and listen to your soul about what feels like the healthiest choice for you as a person. As always, the choice is yours.

Shirley

I tried going to AA meetings for a while and it was helpful to some degree—to know that I wasn't alone and that other people were also struggling with their issues. But I did not go to them for long. I wanted to be in groups with women only and that was not available in the AA meetings in my area. Also I found that what a lot of the people were talking about in the meetings, I'd already faced and resolved in my own program. So I found them to be very depressing and not really beneficial. I found that I got more of my needs met through my therapist, through my classes, through my journaling, through talking with friends one on one, than the AA meetings. So I opted out of AA and I admit that I beat myself up for this because so many people tell you that AA is the only way to recover from your addiction from alcohol. But it just wasn't so for me. I needed help to get off the drugs and alcohol, but I did it through professional therapy and my own program. Everyone's different. Obviously some people are going to need that type of program.

USING SELF-HELP
GROUPS AS A ADJUNCT TO THERAPY

There are some cases where "more is better," and for adult survivors who are facing painful memories and struggling to make enormous changes inside themselves and outside in the world, the combination of self-help and professional help may be the most powerful therapeutic strategy available in recovering from child abuse.

Pete

Personally I think that AA, ACA, and therapy have been a wonderful complement for me. Actually I've felt that I've gotten some real good second-hand therapy in ACA meetings, which I have brought back into my own therapy. But I think that any survivor of abuse needs first and foremost a safe place to be extremely vulnerable, which is what talking about the abuse brings up. At the beginning of this process, I think you need individualized care. You can't get it in a group meeting with forty or fifty people sitting around. I mean it's very difficult to tell even your closest confidante about the intricacies of incest or abuse and to get the right guidance and support back is a tall order for a nonprofessional. For me, the process of one-on-one therapy, week after week, uncovering and discovering what happened and taking apart the complexities involved was essential. Having a trustworthy professional gave me my safe place. That's why, to me, self help and therapy are such a great complement because there's the sharing and the support that comes from peer-type help that isn't available in therapy once or twice a week. On the other hand, I never would have uncovered what was going on with my mother and my reactions to the abuse without good professional help. Taken together, they both worked for me.

◆

Self-help and professional help can together provide a program of recovery that is more than the sum of its parts. Therapy, especially individual therapy, may be the safest place to explore the vulnerable feelings and memories that need to be shared with another person. Out of this protective relationship, you can decide to share your experiences in a group with others and bask in the recognition, support, and validation on a larger level. As you have read, this can be incredibly powerful and give you the inspiration to continue working on the road to recovery. Think of the combination of professional help and self-help as an alternative to the ideal relationship you would have wanted with each of your parents and your family as a whole. Both are important, and in the case of adult survivors, both can be powerful therapeutic mediums in which to recover from the past disappointments.

Chapter Eleven

PROFESSIONAL HELP

Psychotherapy has come a long way in the first hundred years of its existence. No longer confined to the treatment of the seriously emotionally ill, psychotherapy has broken out of the back wards and into the lives of tens of millions of people who today are using it to enhance their personal happiness, resolve conflictual relationships, and cope with the increasingly complex demands of modern living. The National Institute of Mental Health has reported that in 1988 approximately 20 percent of the adult population—one out of every five people have some type of emotional distress requiring therapy.

Many survivors are still confused about what psychotherapy is and how it can relieve emotional suffering. Basically the process entails you, the client, meeting on a regular basis with a professionally trained person who establishes a "therapeutic relationship" to help you resolve your emotional concerns. Unlike the treatment of physical ailments where the doctor is expected to provide a "cure," which the patient passively accepts, the therapist-client relationship is both collaborative and "reparative" in the sense that the interaction is used to establish a comfortable, consistent, and safe place for you to share your inner conflicts and self-doubts unhampered by the demands that exist in other relationships. The work of therapy then is to identify, explore, and understand these inner conflicts—conscious and unconscious—that hold you back from being who you want to be. In doing so, you are helped to reclaim the old memories, gaining insight into the causes of your abuse as you become able to express those long-repressed feelings associated with the wounds.

The idea of a reparative relationship makes sense in the case of the adult survivor because your abuse occurred in a relationship with another person, most likely your parent. By developing a different type of relationship that is safe, respectful, sensitive to your needs, and dedicated to healing your wounds and facilitating change in the world, you can "re-do," in a sense, the destructiveness you internalized from your parents and you can replace it with something very different: a healthier sense of self, gained from your active collaboration with another person, in this case, a caring, professional therapist. This process unfolds over time, gradually deepening as your understanding of yourself and the dilemmas you faced as a child begins to shift. As the wounds heal from within, you are free to make healthy changes in your behavior, your relationships, and your attitudes toward the world.

Therapy cannot make the effects of the abuse fully disappear. You will always remember what happened and will probably always feel some residue of your childhood pain. The psychological scars may be with you forever, but if they have really healed, they will not hurt as much. With true recovery, you will not be limited in the way you were in the past. Human beings have tremendous resilience and capacity for change, owing to our capacity for self-awareness. Our ability to intellectually and emotionally understand ourselves and consciously change our behavior based on this understanding is what makes us so unusual—and so capable for using the psychotherapy process.

CONFRONTING YOUR RESISTANCE TO GETTING PROFESSIONAL HELP

There are many reasons why most people—survivors or others—are reluctant to enter psychotherapy. All of the reasons are legitimate and all of them will have to be addressed and resolved before you will pick up the phone to make the first appointment with a therapist. To begin, there are vestiges of shame associated with seeing a "shrink" that have to do with fears of being seen as "crazy" or incapable of managing your own life. This thinking derives from the earliest use of psychiatry to treat the severely mentally ill in insane asylums. In the last thirty years, however, the mental health field has begun to improve its image dramatically. But old attitudes die hard. If you live in a rural area, you may still be subjected to other people's prejudices about seeing a therapist.

Many survivors avoid seeing therapists out of a fear of dealing with the past and facing the damage associated with the abuse. This fear is understandable since no one wants to experience hurt. People avoid going to doctors and dentists for the same reason. However, as adult survivors, you need to face the past and assess the damage in order to know how to embark on your recovery. Doing it with a trained professional who is also a caring and committed person may not be nearly as hard as you think. Remember that the right therapist for you is one who will let you establish a comfortable pace. In other words, you must have a high degree of control in your therapy: That is your right and that is what works best for survivors.

Some survivors believe that they can use good friends, spouses, or fellow members of their self-help group to provide what a therapist would provide. This is typically a mistake since no friend, spouse, or group member can provide professional psychotherapy or consistently handle the enormous emotional demands that a therapeutic relationship must entail. If you try to rely on someone close to you for therapy, even the most caring person is likely to burn out, leaving you once again feeling guilty, rejected, and abandoned. You will want the same person with whom you started therapy to be there for you as long as you require help. Only a professional therapist has the structure, expectations, and training to provide that for you. Don't shortchange yourself by setting up a process that may ultimately disappoint you.

Some men have an even greater difficulty than women in admitting that they need help. In a society that worships the "strong, silent types," boys and men can learn very quickly to be fiercely independent, to handle feelings by themselves, and to resist admitting weakness. To expose their hurt, vulnerable part is to undercut their masculinity. And there is an additional concern for males. If you were sexually abused by a male—and over 90 percent of sex offenders are male—the concern about homosexuality may force you to keep the shame inside, away from the judgments you have come to expect. Fortunately the women's liberation movement has spawned a men's liberation movement that is challenging many of the most destructive attitudes that imprison men. Men such as Pete and Richard are increasingly reaching out to others and getting professional help when they need it. Hopefully, just as women have defined a more realistic role for themselves, so will men. And the time is now.

Many people resist going into therapy because it can be very costly. Psychotherapy can be expensive, especially if you select a therapist in private practice who has years of experience and training. Considering that therapy may take several years, paying the cost of one or two sessions per week can turn into a major financial burden very quickly. Fortunately most insurance programs are willing to pick up at least part of the cost of mental health services, although the amount of the reimbursement varies greatly. Look carefully at your insurance policy and be clear about what it covers. If your insurance does not cover "outpatient mental health services," it may be wise to change insurance policies, if possible, to acquire mental health benefits. My advice is to do this *before* you enter therapy. Insurance companies have a clause called a "preexisting condition," which they use to avoid reimbursing for mental health services if you were already in treatment by the time you started the policy.

It is also possible to receive therapy from a variety of other sources that will not be as costly. Many therapists in private practice offer some low-fee services for those on limited incomes, provided you can attend during off hours (mornings and afternoons). Local hospitals; colleges; graduate programs in medicine, psychology, and social work; public community mental health programs; and private, nonprofit, community counseling centers offer mental health services at a reduced fee, although the experience and training of these therapists may not be as advanced. Counseling interns and psychology assistants who are not yet licensed, but who work under their supervisor's license, are another low-cost therapy alternative. Since these therapists are not yet licensed, be careful to pick someone who is supervised by a fully licensed professional experienced in treating adult survivors. Although you may not have much choice if you cannot afford to pay "full fee," remember that quality control of professional services is reduced when the therapist is not licensed.

Without insurance benefits, your monthly therapy bill may be roughly the equivalent to your monthly car loan payment. But, unlike your car payments where the loan expires at about the time you start looking for a new car, the investment you make in your therapy will bring you benefits for the rest of your life. And not just in terms of your emotional happiness. My colleagues and I agree that one important gain made by many clients we treat is that they find better-paying work. As self-esteem and self-confidence grow, clients are able to widen their expectations and discover richer economic rewards. In other words, the money you invest in your therapy will pay dividends in the form of bigger paychecks for many years to come.

Finally the biggest impediment to going to therapy may have to do with a very personal reason, something that is significant only to you. I can't predict what that may be, but many survivors usually report a unique reason for not wanting to get professional help.

Jolene

I don't feel at all resistant to therapy now, but I certainly did in the beginning. It always takes a while for you to start to tell somebody all this stuff about yourself—stuff that you're not really clear about or know where it will lead. Part of this resistance was that I have been very pissed off about even having to go through this stuff again. I feel like all this stuff's been done to me, but now I have to be the one to do something about it. I mean, give me a break! Once is enough. It wasn't my fault. It's unfair to have to go through it again. It's taken me a while to say to myself, "Yes, you do have to do something about this if you want to change." Even now, there's always a twinge of resentment that goes along with it.

◆

CHOOSING THE RIGHT THERAPY FOR THE RIGHT STAGE OF RECOVERY

The next three chapters will outline the steps to be taken in each of the three stages of recovery. While professional help is an integral part of the recovery process, survivors may be confused or unclear about what kind of professional help is best for each stage. Psychotherapy is provided in a variety of formats, or modalities, as they are refered to in the field. Each of these therapy modalities has something to offer the adult survivor at particular stages of recovery. Besides more fully describing the different types of modalities available, the listing below will suggest what stage may be the best time to use them and the reasons why.

INDIVIDUAL THERAPY

Individual therapy is the prime therapy modality because in most cases it will be the backbone of your recovery program from the beginning stage to the final stage. Your individual therapist will become your "anchor": the one person who will go through all of the feelings, memories, and changes with you and provide the reparative relationship that can challenge the abusive relationship you had with your parents.

Individual therapy is the safe place where you can first disclose the abuse and face the feelings at a pace that is right for you. Because it is between you and your therapist alone, it will be easier to discover what you want and how you would like to proceed. This gives you maximum control, which will help immeasurably in being able to talk about the most personal and difficult aspects of the abuse. From there, you can add other treatment modalities as you and your therapist see fit.

There may be a question about seeing your therapist more than once per week. Although costs need to be considered, it is often extremely beneficial to increase the frequency of therapy to twice or even three times a week during the early stage of recovery. This is the critical time when memories are breaking through and you want to maximize the opportunities that this crisis period often creates. Seeing your therapist more often allows you to more quickly work through some of your most overpowering feelings and fears. You don't want to re-experience the abuse alone anymore. Your therapist is the one to see you through this especially difficult time.

GROUP THERAPY

Group therapy for adult survivors is especially powerful because it challenges their isolation, stigmatization, and sense of not fitting in. Unlike self-help groups where the stated purpose is mostly educational, supportive, and inspirational, group therapy is led by one or more therapists who will help you identify current problems, expand your understanding of personal dilemmas as a child, and when necessary, challenge distorted perceptions and self-sabotaging. The other group members will also help you to change, as you will be doing for them. Support, validation, and acceptance are also in abundant supply as group members learn to share their most personal secrets and gradually develop trust and a sense of belonging in a way perhaps never experienced before.

It is best to enter group therapy in the latter part of Stage One or the early part of Stage Two recovery. Refer to the beginning parts of the next three chapters for an introduction to the goals of these stages. Part of the reason for delaying the group therapy is that you will be hearing other people talk about what happened to them as children. This can stir up a lot of feelings about your own abuse. To get the most from group therapy, you will first need to have some experience in dealing with your own powerful feelings before it can become emotionally safe to hear others' stories. Once you are no longer overwhelmed by your feelings, the group therapy can give you so much:

Listening to how others face and deal with the effects of the abuse can be both illuminating and inspiring. You will learn ways to cope that have never occurred to you. Also, being in a group will provide feedback on how you relate to people—something that might be scary to hear but that you need to know before you can make any changes.

You may meet people who will become your close friends—people you do not need to deceive. Acceptance of you and your feelings are legitimate expectations and benefits. Some survivors prefer to start with an introductory group that is very structured and is limited to people of the same sex. Mixed group therapy can be helpful in Stage Three to address the feelings that survivors have toward members of the opposite sex.

COUPLE'S THERAPY

Couple's therapy, as described in chapter 8, involves the survivor and his or her partner or spouse meeting with a therapist to resolve conflicts in their relationship that are directly or indirectly caused by the effects of the abuse. For many survivors in recovery, couple's therapy can be helpful in a crisis situation when the relationship is threatened by divorce or separation. In other cases, couple's therapy may be called for during Stage Two or Stage Three when the survivors have made significant changes in their personality and thus require a restructuring of their relationship. Couple's therapy is usually of shorter duration than individual or group therapy and more focused on particular problems or concerns. Typically many couples will be in and out of couple's therapy as new issues emerge and help is required. If you are already in individual therapy, and couple's or family therapy is advised, I recommend that you and your partner see a different therapist than the one already working with you or your partner. This way the couple's therapy is separate from your individual therapy, reducing the chance of the therapist favoring one partner over the other.

FAMILY THERAPY

Somewhat similar to couples therapy in purpose, scope, and duration, family therapy calls for everyone in the survivor's immediate family to meet with a therapist to increase communication, resolve conflicts, and help the family accept the changes being made by the parent who is in recovery. Often family therapy is recommended when one of the children presents problems either at school, home, or as a result of some disciplinary action. Many times these problems are a cry for help.

Family therapy is typically based on systems theory, which holds that when anyone in the family changes, such as a parent who is a survivor undergoing recovery, it affects everyone else and in extreme situations calls for a major adjustment in the roles, expectations, and relationships between each of the family members.

What often happens in families where a parent is recovering from child abuse is that the children resist the healthy changes that they see their parent making because they may have become used to taking on pseudoparenting and household duties to help their once dysfunctional parent. Now with the parent making positive changes, the children feel lost, confused, and possibly unneeded when their parent wants to re-assume his or her rightful responsibilities. It may be hard for a child whose identity rests on being a caretaker to go back to being a child again. As the parent gets stronger and the family becomes more stable, the children will feel safer in voicing resentments they may have had during the past when the parent was unable to pull his weight. Children will often go through a payback period when they seek to punish a parent for inappropriate demands they experienced prior to the parent's recovery.

Family therapy is often useful when survivors are in Stage Three, when their parents and siblings have responded favorably to the survivor's disclosure and confrontation regarding the abuse. Referred to as family reconstruction therapy, this type of work can be remarkably rewarding for survivors because it offers them a chance to put into practice their personal changes with family members who were responsible for the abuse. And it can establish a new foundation upon which survivors can relate to their family in a healthy way without the exploitation and betrayal of the past. Not all survivors get to this point, but when it happens it represents the highest level of resolution possible. Read on to chapter 15 for more about this.

SEX THERAPY

Sex therapy is often recommended in the third stage of recovery for survivors who may still have sexual problems that have their root in their childhood sexual abuse. It is best to delay sex therapy until most of the broader emotional issues surrounding the sexual abuse have been resolved. Sex therapy is conducted by health professionals who have had special training in treating sexual dysfunction and have completed a certificate program accredited by the American Association of Sex Educators, Counselors and Therapists. Their methods are more educational and behavioral than insight-oriented and they often rely on exercises done at home either alone or with a partner. The purpose of the exercises is to desensitize or decondition the survivor's old feelings and behaviors about sex and to replace them with those that permit healthy sexual enjoyment. These techniques can generally be described as building self-awareness of one's body and erogenous zones, learning progressive relaxation techniques to calm anxieties about sexual contact, and acquiring assertiveness and communication skills to discuss sexual likes and dislikes with a partner. By gradually teaching the survivors new skills and ways of taking control of their bodies, plus reducing the unpleasant associations between sex and the sexual abuse, survivors can overcome their paralyzing inhibitions and can enjoy sex with a trusted partner. Sex therapy is usually short-term, not exceeding six months of weekly sessions.

Many sex therapists prefer to work in a couple's format with the survivor's partner or spouse, thereby enlisting him as a collaborator, in helping the survivor overcome her fears of being intimate with another person while teaching her new techniques for managing the intense sensations and feelings that can become aroused. If the survivor is not in a relationship, techniques are offered that can be performed alone. The use of sex surrogates, a controversial strategy involving professionally trained sex partners who work with the client to desensitize him to sexual relations, is not recommended with survivors because of the anxiety that being intimate with a stranger typically evokes.

BEHAVIOR MODIFICATION
TREATMENT FOR PEDOPHILES

Special therapy programs are necessary to treat sex offenders who correspond to the fixated type of sexual disorder referred to previously as pedophilia. Parents United, a self-help program referred to in chapter 10, is not recognized as effective in treating these types of abusers who have a more serious type of disorder. Although much research still needs to be done in this area, it seems that the best type of treatment for pedophiles is a combination of intensive group therapy in conjunction with a behavior modification program that attempts to "decondition" the abuser's sexual arousal from stimuli depicting children as sex partners. This is achieved by using aversive conditioning techniques that pair a sexual arousal stimulus such as a picture of a naked child with some negative consequence, either real or imagined. Treatment consists of disrupting an abuser's physiological arousal to children, which is a learned response, by applying a mild electric shock or some imagined punishment like jail when the erotic stimulus is presented. Over time, a new learned response gradually replaces the old one as the treatment substitutes a more appropriate stimulus (such as a picture of an attractive adult partner) and then positively reinforces the arousal triggered by the new stimulus by allowing the abuser to achieve some sexual gratification. Some programs have also used a drug called Depo-Provera to physiologically reduce sex drive, thereby reducing the likelihood of the abusers acting on his sexual urges.

Unfortunately there are few programs that provide this type of needed treatment. More often than not, when sex offenders are diagnosed as pedophiles, their treatment options are greatly reduced. Ultimately society pays a price for this void because pedophiles often surround themselves with children just as alcoholics are always around liquor. The implications are obvious.

GUIDE TO
SELECTING A PSYCHOTHERAPIST

Selecting the right psychotherapist may be the most important decision you will make in your recovery. Relying on one person to help you reclaim the past, understand what happened, share your most personal feelings and reactions, and help you toward health and healing calls for a special person with special qualities and special training. For this reason, having knowledge about the different types of therapists and therapy options is essential before you begin interviewing therapists and narrowing down your choices.

CONFIDENTIALITY

You should know that what you discuss in therapy is confidential and protected by the law. This concern is one my clients reveal, having so often felt betrayed by parents, authorities, and the legal system. Like any doctor-patient or attorney-client relationship, the information you disclose in therapy is kept private. You control the privilege of disclosing this information. This means that your therapist does not talk about you or in any way reveal your identity. By law and by ethic, therapists may not disclose whom they see in therapy. Confidentiality is the backbone of a trusting therapeutic relationship. You have a right to your privacy and your therapist is expected to ensure that right. A breech of confidentiality by a therapist is subject to sanctions from professional organizations that establish standards of practice.

There are a few instances when the confidentiality must be broken by your therapist. One such instance is when you make a serious threat to the welfare of some individual. According to the 1976 Tarasoff decision, your therapist is legally obligated to report to authorities such threats as to protect from harm an innocent third party. Therapists who fail to do so commit a crime and can be punished by law or through civil litigation. Also therapists may break confidentiality if you disclose serious intent to harm yourself and require hospitalization to protect you from committing suicide. Your therapist will inform the police, hospital, therapists, and members of your support network to make sure that you get the help you need to stay alive. You may not always agree with this, but therapists are committed by law to value human life and to protect you from harm, even when threatened by your own temporary despair.

One other situation challenges the sanctity of the confidential therapist-client relationship. When professional records are subpoenaed by criminal or civil court to provide evidence in a legal proceeding, you lose the right to confidentiality. This may be a factor to take into account if you choose to seek legal redress for the abuse. If this concerns you, discuss it with your therapist.

QUALIFICATIONS

Below are my ideas of some of the basic qualifications that therapists must have to be considered appropriate for treating adult survivors of child abuse. Some of these ideas are endorsed by professional associations whereas others are based on my own clinical experience in working with survivors. These are minimal qualifications and you may have other qualifications that are important to you. Add them to this list. Keep this list with you when you speak to therapists and after the meeting write down your impressions of how they rated.

TYPES OF PSYCHOTHERAPY PROFESSIONALS

There are four categories of mental health professionals who have received clinical training and supervision that qualify them to provide therapy for adult survivors: psychiatrists (M.D.), clinical psychologists (Ph.D., Psy.D., Ed.D., D.M.H.), clinical social workers (M.S.W.), and marriage and family child counselors (M.A.). All of these disciplines require at least a masters degree, and psychiatrists and psychologists possess doctoral degrees. Roughly speaking, the masters-level disciplines reflect two years of classroom training and two years of practicum training in psychotherapy, and the doctoral-level professions reflect four or more years of classroom training and two or more years of practicum training.

Many people who consider entering psychotherapy are confused about the differences between the various mental health professions and wonder if and how the type of therapy offered is influenced by the degree that the particular therapist has. Briefly the differences have mostly to do with the type of training and theoretical orientation provided during the therapist's degree program. For example, psychiatrists are first trained as medical doctors and then receive extra training in psychiatry that permits them to prescribe medications, unlike the other disciplines. Because of this emphasis on medical training and the use of medications to address emotional problems, psychiatrists tend to be grounded in more traditional Freudian theory and biological approaches to behavior, and practice the so-called "medical model." In contrast, psychologists are trained to emphasize theories of child development, human motivation, perception, sensation, and mental functioning, all of which explain how psychic processes determine behavior. Social workers are trained in traditional casework methods that emphasize a bio-psycho-social perspective in helping clients to function better in their social environment. Marriage and family child counselors, the newest of the mental health disciplines, are trained in counseling the various members of the family and draw from family systems theory to strengthen the functioning of the total family unit. These distinctions are gradually beginning to blur as each discipline borrows from the other's orientation and focus to broaden their understanding of human behavior and treating emotional problems.

Which one is best for providing psychotherapy for adult survivors? While some research indicates that the more training and experience a therapist has in providing psychotherapy, the better the service usually is, other research suggests that the human qualities of the therapist— the caring, intuition, compassion, and geniuneness—may be just as important. My advice? Naturally, I am somewhat biased because I am a psychologist and I respect the scope and philosophy of a psychologist's training. However, I have also received training from psychiatrists, social workers, and family counselors who were all excellent in their own right. In the end, who the person is and how he or she conducts therapy may be more important than the particular profession to which she belongs.

LICENSED PROFESSIONALS ONLY

While it is difficult to recommend a particular mental health discipline, I strongly suggest that you consider only therapists who are fully licensed in one of the four disciplines. All licenses require the candidate to fulfill a specified number of clinical hours under the supervision of a senior, licensed therapist as well as to pass a written and oral examination. Some states may have other professional licenses that I am not familiar with or no professional licensing structure at all. Many people in rural areas that do not have many mental health practitioners rely on priests, ministers, and other clergy who are not licensed in their counseling duties. In those states where there is no licensing body, your task of sifting out the helpful therapists from those insufficiently trained or who lack experience will be more difficult and even greater care should be exercised in getting quality referrals, interviewing potential therapists, and in states where licenses are not available, asking for professional references. It is important to choose a licensed professional in order to ensure a certain level of quality control in the services they provide.

THEORETICAL ORIENTATION

As described previously, each of the four disciplines reflects an underlying philosophy or school of thought that shapes the particular therapist's concept of human behavior and behavior change. Clearly some approaches are better than others when it comes to treating adult survivors. Psychiatrists and other therapists who fully embrace the classical Freudian notion that sexual abuse is more likely to be a fantasy or wish fulfillment on the part of the female child is not an appropriate orientation for helping an adult survivor overcome the very real trauma of abuse. Likewise the technique of psychoanalysis where the therapist remains extremely reserved and doesn't interact with the client as much as the other types of treatment is not recommended for survivors who may end up feeling neglected. Some therapists who believe that emotional suffering is relieved by manipulating and applying pressure to the body—the bioenergetic approach—will not be effective with adult survivors who may experience the therapy as a reenactment of the abuse or an intrusion on one's physical privacy, inducing a loss of control over powerful feelings. Other more "fringe" therapies like Primal Scream, which encourages a rapid ventilation of feelings, may actually be harmful with certain people at certain times of recovery who may already feel overwhelmed by their feelings.

I believe the preferred theoretical orientation for adult survivors is one that helps you to understand and change the effects of the abuse on your sense of self and personality style. Always remember that there are layers of effects, ranging from current difficulties to underlying causes of those difficulties, that will take you back to your childhood and the type of relationship you had with your parent before, during, and after the abuse. It is therefore essential that your therapist have a developmental approach to be able to conceptualize how all of these influences, positive and negative, are incorporated into your personality, your pain left over from the past, and your strengths as a person. Understanding how your experience affected you will suggest specific ways that therapy can help you. These orientations are sometimes reffered to as *self-psychology* or *ego psychology*. They help you to strengthen your sense of self, gain control over your behavior, and learn healthy ways of expressing your feelings connected to the abuse. I would suggest that this approach is the most beneficial to adult survivors because it is broad-based and can take you from the beginning of the first stage to the end of the third stage, from reclaiming the past to integrating a new sense of self.

EXPERIENCE IN TREATING ADULT SURVIVORS

Another important qualification to look for in choosing a therapist is his or her experience in working specifically with adult survivors of child abuse. This is an important criteria because a particular type of treatment is required, which is then modified to address your special needs as a client.

Since the end of the Vietnam War, there has been a growing body of research on the diagnosis of Post-Traumatic Stress Disorder (PTSD), which defines the psychological impact of war or vitually any catastrophic experience on the human psyche. Research is showing that the effects of war trauma are similar to those experienced by survivors of child abuse. Out of this research new ideas about the treatment of trauma have evolved requiring new therapeutic skills and techniques that your therapist should possess. These approaches include strategies that help you to reinterpret the abuse situation and use this new understanding to challenge the old self-destructive tendencies that are as much habit as personality trait. Assertiveness training, stress reduction, and anger management may be helpful early in recovery. Other approaches that encourage the resolution of trauma are more appropriate for the second stage, such as guided visualization, creative expression, dream analysis, and in select situations, hypnotherapy. As always, the particular techniques should be employed as part of an overall plan of treatment that is tailored to where you are in recovery.

OTHER IMPORTANT CONSIDERATIONS

Beyond the basic qualifications for an experienced therapist, survivors may have other considerations to take into account in selecting a therapist that relate directly to their abuse. Recognize that you do have special therapy needs and give extra thought to some of the following issues, which may result in a better therapeutic relationship.

SEX OF THE THERAPIST

For many survivors, choosing a male or female therapist is a big consideration. Female survivors who were sexually abused by their fathers may not be comfortable with a male therapist and they may prefer a female therapist who they feel can be more understanding of their position and experience. The same may be true for males survivors. Some survivors who were severely abused may base their decision on which parent helped them the most. Even when the father was the offender, some women may prefer to see a male therapist because they had the classic incest mother—withdrawn, in denial, and inadequate—who not only failed to protect them but offered very little to them in any way. Other women may have too much rage toward men to feel safe and positive working with a male therapist. Likewise men who were abused by their mothers may not trust a female therapist to act in their best interests.

You should choose whoever will be the better helper. There are instances in which you may deliberately select a therapist of one gender early, and later in your recovery you may elect to see a therapist of the opposite gender in order to more thoroughly integrate your conflicting feelings about the abuser.

PERSONAL STYLE OF YOUR THERAPIST

Many survivors have a common desire when it comes to imagining the kind of personal style they would like in their therapist. Warm, caring, skillful, perceptive, supportive, practical, engaging, and intelligent are just some of the adjectives I've heard from clients in response to my question about what kind of therapist they were seeking. Much depends on your personality style and what makes you comfortable yet you may also need someone who can motivate you to share what you need to reclaim and work through. Think about what kind of style may be best for you by imagining what kind of therapist would make you feel the most comfortable.

Leigh Anne

I like to have feedback: That's my own personal style. And that's why my therapist works great with me because he gives me a lot of feedback. If I'm in a bind with something, we'll explore it together and he will help me come up with ideas on what options I have. Then we talk about whether I'm ready for those kinds of actions. He doesn't push me, although if I am doing something that he doesn't think is completely healthy for me, he will ask questions about it. We've gotten to the point where we can disagree about things, but he is often right! He tells me though that he thinks my judgment has gotten better.

◆

NO EVIDENCE OF UNETHICAL BEHAVIOR

It needs to be stated that there are therapists who are unethical, unprofessional, or outright incompetent. Adult survivors who have trouble protecting their interests and saying no to authority figures may be especially vulnerable to exploitation in the therapy situation. Recent research indicates that sexual contact between therapist and clients is at an all-time high despite growing evidence that therapist-client sex is extremely destructive to the adult survivor and can seriously derail your recovery.

If your therapist has ever talked of initiating or has engaged in sexual contact with you, you should know that such behavior is unethical, unprofessional, damaging, and is now illegal in many states. If you are unsure about your therapist's intent, please consult another therapist, doctor, sponsor, or friend to help you determine what would be in your best interests. Adult survivors may be among the most vulnerable to sexual contact with a therapist, especially if you were sexually abused as a child.

Short of this abusive danger sign, there are other indications that the therapist you are considering may not be up to professional standards. Taking phone calls during the session is a practice that some hospital-based therapists must do, but if it becomes repetitive and intrusive practice, you may need to address them. In a private practice situation, this should not be tolerated. Your needs should come first in the session and the therapist should not be conducting other business during your time.

Jolene

One therapist I saw met clients in her house, which was kind of weird to begin with. The first session she told me, "I'm going to be answering the phone and I'll be cooking and sort of running around and that's kind of the way that I am. So if you don't think that will work, we should probably not work together." So when she said that to me, I thought, "Well I don't know how I'll feel about that." Inside I didn't like this idea much, but I just wasn't able to really voice my opinion at the time. But later on I began to resent it quite a bit. We would be talking and she would get up to put something in the oven, and if I wanted to be heard, I'd have to get up and go into the kitchen. At the time, I thought, "Well, this woman told you exactly what she was going to do, and you said that it would be fine, so you can't say anything now." That's how I saw it then. And she was sort of an abrasive personality which kind of intimidated me. It just didn't work out. I could never get comfortable with her. The six months I met with her were really a waste of time.

◆

Another worrisome sign is a therapist who shares personal information too often or refers to himself or his own point of view to an extent that impedes your discovery of how you feel. Therapists have to have a good sense of their own boundaries and a high degree of security to allow you to use the time as you see fit. When this essential quality of the therapeutic relationship is violated, you may no longer have an environment conducive to developing trust and working on issues of identity, power, and control.

Survivors do have some recourse should their therapist violate some ethical or professional standard. Clients can contact the state board that oversees medical or mental health licensing. If you are unclear as to whether your therapist is doing something unethical or illegal, you can consult with the state board, anonymously or not, to determine what actions, if any, you may want to take. Often, unscrupulous therapists will show their hand during the initial sessions in a way that foreshadows future problems. Go with your instincts if you don't feel right about somebody.

RECOMMENDATIONS

Now that you know what kind of therapist you are looking for, you can begin the process of locating one who will fit your expectations. Many of the strategies used in selecting any professional service can be a good start in looking for a therapist. Getting references from friends or members of your support group who have used therapists may be the best plan, especially if they have knowledge about specific therapists who have training and experience in working with adult survivors. If this strategy is not productive, try contacting your local child abuse prevention organization, mental health association, or professional referral services for references. Make sure you mention your criteria for the type of therapist that you want.

Leigh Anne

I began looking by getting out the good old phone book and looking up any agency that was involved in the issues that I was working on. I even wrote a letter to Dr. Ruth because at the time I was living with a sex addict. I called therapists who if they weren't appropriate for me would give me referrals to other therapists who they thought might help. Well, after a while I started getting frustrated because I really couldn't afford the high costs of therapy, so I decided to try the county mental health program because you can pay on a sliding scale basis. I met with several therapists before I found someone who felt right. Dealing with the system was also difficult but you can't give up on yourself—this is your life! If he hadn't worked, I would have continued ranting and raving until I found somebody that I could work with.

♦

GROUND RULES
FOR SHOPPING AROUND

Even if it may not be easy for you to do so, I strongly recommend that you talk and meet with several therapists before making any decisions. Some therapists may resent this strategy and will encourage you to begin to work with them before you feel ready to make a commitment. Therapists are subject to the pressures of self-interest like anyone else. Stick to your plan to survey the available options before making your decision.

When you contact a therapist on the telephone, state right away that you are looking for a therapist and ask if she will respond to some brief questions. The most important questions to be asked on the phone are the ones that may eliminate her immediately from consideration: Is she licensed, how long has she been in practice, does she have experience working with adult survivors of child abuse, and what is her fee structure? If she quotes a fee that is beyond your means, ask if she sees some people on a sliding scale basis.

If therapists are not willing to answer these questions, this may indicate an unwillingness to accommodate what you think is important. Considering how essential it is for you to feel empowered in your own therapy, it may be best to continue your search should you get such a response. If she responds in a way that feels right to you, consider making an initial appointment. Let her know that the purpose of the session would be to further discuss what you are looking for and to see if you and she might make a good match. Sometimes it will take more than one session to get a sense of her as a person and her style as a therapist. Expect to be charged for any face-to-face meeting whether you are shopping around or not. Therapists make their living by charging for their time—usually fifty minutes for a session—and initial sessions are no different. Therefore, it is unreasonable to expect them to speak with you on the telephone prior to making an appointment for more than ten to fifteen minutes without charging you. At the end of one of these sessions, don't feel obligated to make a decision on the spot. But you do need to let the therapist know how you want to proceed from this point. If you are still unclear as to what you want to do, simply tell her that you want to think about the meeting, consult with other therapists, and make your decision in whatever time frame you have set. Shopping for a therapist can be an expensive and confusing endeavor. Sometimes too much information can be as bad as too little. Figure out how much time and money you can devote to this process and plan your appointments accordingly.

If you have never been in therapy before, it makes even more sense to see several therapists before making a decision. It will take a few sessions before you will grow comfortable with the therapy situation itself, let alone decide what therapist or what therapeutic style you like best. In other words, there is a learning curve operating here and you won't be really proficient in determining your preferences until you have some experience with this type of professional interaction.

EVALUATING THE INITIAL SESSION

There are many considerations—both objective and subjective—in evaluating the first session with a prospective therapist. The objective considerations are easier. Are you certain you can afford his fee? Does he have an opening in his schedule that matches your schedule? Does he accept direct insurance reimbursement? And does he expect to remain in practice in the area for several years? If any of these questions cannot be resolved, then your decision is made for you.

The subjective considerations may take far more reflection and soul searching, and may ultimately determine your choice. Ask yourself the following journal questions to organize your impressions.

JOURNAL QUESTIONS

1. *Did the therapist help you feel comfortable talking about your problems and reasons for entering therapy?*

2. *Did she show some understanding of your dilemma and indicate some willingness to be of help?*

3. *What aspects of the therapist's personality and therapeutic style did you like or dislike?*

4. *Did she listen carefully and show interest in your comments? Did you feel understood but not intruded upon?*

5. *Was there anything she said or did that raised questions about her therapeutic skills, professional standards, or knowledge of therapy with survivors?*

6. *Do her professional qualifications check out?*

7. *Did you agree on fees, schedules, policy on missed sessions, and emergency consultations?*

8. *Was the therapist's style of interacting with you conducive to your being able to share your painful feelings about the abuse?*

9. *Did you feel the necessary personal connection and match with this therapist so that you could begin to trust her?*

10. *Is this the therapist you want to see once or twice a week for perhaps as long as several years?*

The Therapeutic Contract

After a few sessions with the therapist with whom you have begun treatment, it is often a good idea to try to summarize again what therapy can accomplish. Both the therapist and you can once again see what you are aiming to achieve so that you both acknowledge the purpose of your work. This process will culminate in a therapeutic contract that can serve as your common agreement about what you are working toward. This contract will, at the outset, necessarily be a broad outline, to be clarified, altered, and perhaps even suspended as you and your therapist become more familiar and informed about your needs as a client.

You might begin with fairly vague questions such as, "Why do I feel so depressed?" or more specifically, "I want to look at what happened to me as a kid so I can make changes in my adult life." What to work on and in what way will be largely determined by where you are in your understanding of yourself and your past. A skilled therapist will help you determine what needs to be addressed first, such as relationships, jobs, or particular symptoms that have somehow disrupted your adult life, and what can wait until later. Start there and work backward to the past.

MEDICATION OR HOSPITALIZATION

There may be times when you or your therapist think that medication or hospitalization might be in your best interest. This is a delicate subject because you may have any number of reactions to this idea, most of which will be negative. But sometimes in the first stage of recovery, survivors may go through a breakthrough crisis and need immediate relief that medications and hospitalization can provide. Anxiety and depression can sometimes become overwhelming and threaten to set you back in recovery, or worse, bring you to the point of suicide. There are new medications on the market that will help in managing your most intense feelings without the addictive potential of other drugs. Some survivors have more biologically based anxiety and depressive states that resist conscious control and can only be managed with the aid of specific medications. If your therapist is not an M.D., you will have to meet with a psychiatrist for a medication evaluation so the proper drug can be prescribed. Your therapist should be able to refer you to one for this purpose. As always, you need to discuss the purpose and plans for using medication with your therapist and make a decision based on what would be best for you. If you do not want medication, you have the power to say no and expect your therapist to accept it. However, in some instances where your therapist feels that medication is crucial to your well-being, he may not want to continue treating you without it.

Hospitalization is recommended in several situations to ensure that you are safe while reclaiming memories and feelings associated with your painful experiences. Some survivors may even feel suicidal when they remember what happened to them and face the feelings attached to the memories. When the survivor is exhausted and overwhelmed by daily responsibilities, it may be helpful to enter a hospital briefly. During these times, much work can be done in resolving the traumatic reactions left from the past. Therapy should increase to three or four times a week during such crisis periods. Remember, there are great opportunities for change to be realized during a crisis.

SIGNS OF PROGRESS

You will know when therapy is working by taking note of any number of positive developments. You may find it easier to talk about the past and your feelings about the abuse. Or you may find yourself emotionally connecting with your therapist as she learns more about you and comes to understand more deeply how you were affected by the abuse as a child. In some cases, you may feel like you are opening up to yourself, reaching a new level of awareness that you never knew you could have. You may feel like you are making progress by cleansing the old wounds. Although you may still feel pain and anguish, now you may notice some relief and hope. You may find yourself making better choices in life and gradually eliminating self-sabotaging behaviors. There may be other concrete changes you notice based on your stage of recovery. Your relationships may be less conflictual. You may be better able to manage your money. You may have more patience with your children. And some of the changes may be more emotional. You don't feel quite as depressed as you used to. You notice little bright spots in your everyday outlook that spur you on to do more work. You may feel hope where only despair once existed. If the signs are good, you and your therapist must be doing something right. Stay with it and ride the wave of recovery all the way in.

Leigh Anne

I think that my therapy really took off when I started seeing results in my life. I wasn't so scared anymore. I had more resolve. I felt like I could have an impact on myself. I look forward to my therapy once a week. At the risk of sounding egotistical, I really think he likes me. I can tell that he takes pleasure in seeing me come into the room. I save up things that I wanted to talk about and I know that I will walk in there and be able to say anything that's on my mind. He never starts the conversation. I always initiate the topic which I like very much. We can sit there quietly for a few moments, but knowing me and how verbal I am, we always move toward a useful topic. He has a great sense of humor, which is great because I love to laugh. He'll just say something at the right time and make me realize that I'm being too serious, or I'm not being serious enough. We will talk about other stuff like politics or finances or morality or whatever. But we always settle on deeper stuff before long. I can go as deep as I want or stay on the surface. He has helped me to look at obstacles as opportunities. And he has helped me look into the mirror of my soul. I enjoy it, and I embrace it, and I love it.

◆

SIGNS OF RESISTANCE

As you continue on in therapy, you will notice that you go through cycles of productivity as the effectiveness of the therapy seems to ebb and flow. Certainly the type of therapy you are undergoing is very hard work. It is exhausting to face these powerfully painful feelings week after week without wanting to put them aside for a while. When the wish occurs to put issues temporarily aside, or to rest rather than face troubles or problems, you should know that this desire is natural and probably short-lived. Therapists refer to such moments that interfere with moving forward in therapy as resistance. People do not heal and change in a straight line. They go two steps forward, one step back. Plateaus are reached and time is often needed for consolidation of the changes being made before going forward again. When you go backward in therapy, the form that your resistance takes can give your therapist important clues on how to help you understand your internal barriers to change.

Resistance happens on the inside—slowing the healing of old wounds—and on the outside—creating obstacles to making needed changes in your life. Sometimes you'll be aware of your own resistance and other times it must be pointed out by your therapist. If and when this happens, try not to take offense. Your therapist is simply doing his job in pointing out the barriers you are unconsciously erecting.

Determing the causes for these fallow periods can be very confusing. It is best to discuss your concerns directly with your therapist who may have noticed the same thing. Talk about where the therapy started to go off track for you. Do you notice any connection between what you and your therapist have been working on and your reluctance to press ahead? What, if any, misgivings do you have about your therapist or how he has been conducting the sessions lately? Are your feelings about what is transpiring in the sessions similar to past stretches when you felt like avoiding therapy? Are you suddenly more concerned about the cost or time you are investing? Have you started missing sessions without really taking a look at what you are avoiding? Are you thinking about terminating therapy prematurely or seeing another therapist who offers a different or more promising approach? All of these questions are important, but there may also be reasons for your misgivings. Explore the meaning behind the feelings and actions with your therapist and try to understand what is really going on before making any big decisions about ending the therapy.

SIGNS OF INCOMPATIBILITY

Just as there are signs of resistance, which have more to do with your internal reactions to the therapy, there are signs of incompatibility with your therapist, which may have more to do with who your therapist is as a person and how he conducts the therapy with you. Consider first whether you have hit a resistant phase to be sure this phase is not confused with incompatibility.

For instance, you may never have developed the type of close rapport that you had initially hoped for and can identify specific reasons why, most of which have to do with the therapist. It may have something to do with her style; you want her to talk more or be more engaging or warmer in her interactions with you. Maybe you feel that the therapist's own issues, beliefs, and values get in the way of exploring your thoughts. Perhaps the therapist thinks that different material should be focused on or has ideas about why you think or feel or behave in a certain way with which you don't agree. He may be easily frustrated, possessive, heavy handed in giving advice or critical of decisions you have made that seem to make good sense to you. This type of interaction can sometimes develop into a pattern of fighting and power struggles that never get resolved. When you try to discuss some of your concerns, your therapist dismisses them and offers an easy explanation that doesn't satisfy you or implies that you're imagining things. You may be tempted to trust your therapist's impressions rather than your own. But if you are unable to work out your differences, it may be in your best interest to consult another therapist or to discuss your feelings with a friend who has been in therapy. Remember therapists are not always right. If you feel like you are not getting what you need to recover, make a change. Your responsibility is to yourself, not to your therapist.

Shirley

I first went into therapy in 1978 and I was seeing a psychiatrist who told me I was showing signs of homosexuality. He brought that up every time I brought up the incest issue. He didn't want to talk about incest; he wanted to focus on my being gay and that I was only now going through adolescence and was questioning myself about my sexuality, as most people do during adolescence. I didn't want to deal with it. I started hitting drugs harder. Of course, he was prescribing all of these tranquilizers. He kept upping the dosage and in a way it worked because I could get out of bed and take care of the kids but I was still having all of these physical ailments. Then he decided he wanted to start a group and he wanted me to be a member. So I went twice. I was just shocked. There were women there who were totally incapacitated. Some of them had just gotten out of mental institutions. I questioned him. "Why am I there?" And he said, "I want them to see your strength." That did not seem right. I felt good that he was giving me a compliment, but it finally dawned on me that I was being used again. I left shortly after that.

◆

TAKING A BREAK FROM THERAPY

At times it may seem like you and your therapist are hashing over the same material again and again with little observable gain. You may ask yourself who ever gets completely "cured"? If you reach this plateau and consider temporarily stopping therapy, this may be the time to do it—not permanently stopping but just a temporary breather before resuming at some future date. Discuss your reasons for taking a break with your therapist and listen to his reactions to this idea. Ask him if you could return at a certain point and negotiate some sessions to prepare for stopping. Of course, it is important to determine whether your desire to stop for the time being is not just another form of resistance. Many survivors will prematurely leave therapy once the major changes are made. This is truly unfortunate because what often happens is that old habits and patterns may reappear if you haven't given yourself enough time to fully assimilate the healing and changes you have made. If you find it difficult to hold your gains after stopping therapy, you may have left too soon.

For many survivors, being on your own can be a fresh experience in sorting through everything that you have accomplished. You deserve some time to relax and reflect on what you have resolved and where you might like to direct your energies in the future. In contrast, many survivors develop enormous pride in what they have accomplished and see no reason to stop a process that gives them so much guidance and promise. Therapy becomes a natural ally in their thirst for continued growth and self-improvement. In short, you can resolve the issues of the past to whatever level feels right to you. The important consideration is to continue working in therapy until you have made the changes necessary to lead a happy and productive life.

KNOWING WHEN
TO TERMINATE THERAPY

When you reach a point where you have resolved most or all of the steps outlined in the three stages of recovery, you will probably recognize that it's time to terminate your therapy. You eventually reach a point where you can be your own therapist. You have the perspective to understand your feelings and reactions to life events and the capacity to make additional changes when the need presents itself. You may notice that your relationship with your therapist has changed, as you rely more and more on what you think as opposed to what she thinks. Finally you feel strong and stable and prepared to meet life's challenges.

Discuss your thoughts with your therapist and listen to what she has to say. Give it some time to see if nothing new comes up to resolve. On occasion, the thought of termination may stimulate a particular issue or topic you have left unaddressed. Work this through before setting a date for a final session. Terminating therapy can bring up unexpected anxiety and worry over whether it's the right thing to do, and you may find yourself temporarily regressing to old behaviors. Allow you and your therapist plenty of time to fully air all of the reactions, fears, hopes, and misgivings. Terminating means saying good-bye to someone who has worked along with you through your most personal experiences and painful feelings. It may even bring up once again the old feelings of being alone or losing your parents. Rest assured that these feelings are a natural part of saying good-bye to your therapist. Once you go out the door, you will be carrying much more with you than you had when you first entered. The memories and experiences of your therapy and your relationship with your therapist will stick with you for the rest of your life.

USING THERAPY IN THE FUTURE

Who says you can't go home again? One of the nice things about psychotherapy for adult survivors is that you can leave and return if new work is needed. Many survivors benefit from going back in therapy to resolve special challenges. Getting married, giving birth, raising children, changing careers, working through conflicts with spouses, having your children move out on their own are a natural span of events. The turns in life may stir up old feelings and you may again consider entering therapy. Many survivors have lifelong relationships with their therapists as new needs arise. Knowing that you can return probably offers some comfort when terminating therapy.

Chapter Twelve

STAGE ONE
*R*ECOVERY:
STEPS 1 TO 7

As I explained when I introduced the three stages of recovery in chapter 9, the twenty-one steps you are about to embark upon are meant to be adapted to your particular situation and needs. In Stage One recovery, your main task will be to acknowledge the reason for your out-of-control life—the abuse—and then begin to regain some self-control and stability by working through the symptoms of trauma left over from the past. Out of a new awareness of the long-term impact of abuse, commitment to recovery is born. As you begin to reclaim your childhood, it will also be necessary to identify and then slow down the self-destructive and maladaptive patterns that may currently plague your adult life. It will be very hard to work the steps if your life consists of one calamity after another, as is often the case for adult survivors. Therefore, some degree of calm must be restored before you can begin to face your abuse. The steps in Stage One will help you begin to heal the wounds inside, paving the way for changes to be made later in Stage Two and Stage Three.

Stage One, like the other two stages, can take anywhere from one to three years to complete, depending on how severely you were abused as a child and the extent of emotional damage you suffered. Sometimes the first stage takes the longest and the remaining two stages take less time because of the momentum you will create as you resolve the most challenging early steps. Remember that recovery is an individual process, the pace of which only you can determine. It is essential that you not try to race through the steps. Find a rhythm that feels right to you. You want your healing and the changes that grow out of it to last a lifetime, providing a stable foundation for your new sense of self and your new beginning.

How do you know when you are finished with one step and are ready to move on to the next? Listen to the voice of your newly developing self—that fair, honest and objective sense inside you—that is growing stronger day by day. This voice will signal when you feel resolved, when you are no longer denying or struggling with the task of the particular step. The step is accomplished if you can demonstrate the task in action with another person: your therapist, partner, or members of your self-help group. If you move forward to another step prematurely, simply admit it to yourself and return for a second chance at resolution. You don't have to be perfect in recovery. Do it your way but hold it to the new standards and values that you desire to have for yourself. Listen to this voice and cultivate its developing wisdom. It will lead you forward to your new beginning.

STEP 1

I have resolved the breakthrough crisis, regaining some control of my life.

This first step represents the first sign for many survivors that their past has caught up with them. Survivors often experience what I call a breakthrough crisis—when something happens to release a flood of old memories, feelings, and even physical sensations of the abuse. Although not all survivors experience the crisis to the extent that it temporarily destabilizes their lives, for many it can be the most harrowing time in recovery and the impetus to finally face the past. For those of you who experienced less severe abuse, the breakthrough crisis may manifest itself not as a new crisis but rather as a low-grade, perpetual state of disorganization in which everything that can go wrong does, day after day, in a never-ending spiral that only reinforces your worst feelings: anxiety, depression, and shame.

The more dramatic breakthrough crisis experienced by survivors of extreme and prolonged physical and sexual abuse where terror or violence typically occurred is usually triggered by some event—seeing a movie or having a relationship that unexpectedly turns abusive or a sexual experience that somehow parallels the sexual abuse during childhood. In my psycotherapy practice, I have had clients call me who had a flashback to their abuse simply from reading a flyer announcing the formation of my group for "men abused as children." You feel like the sacred, little child again with none of the control that you have developed as an adult. You may even think you are going crazy and may come up with all sorts of possible explanations for what is going on.

As a child, you developed formidable psychological defenses to protect yourself against this massive assault and probably continued relying on these rigid defenses into adulthood until they no longer worked. This is where you may be now. A breakthrough crisis means that your psyche is going through a massive realignment designed to bring the past into sync with the present. Like an earthquake, this realignment results in powerful feelings and energy being released and can create periods of disorganization, helplessness, and incredible fear. Survivors of severe abuse often have mini-breakthrough crises with each new set of abusive memories that surface, although they are usually never as tumultuous as the first.

The breakthrough crisis is actually quite normal, although it certainly does not feel normal to you. Crises are scary. You have been used to screening out stimuli that might trigger these feelings only to now feel like you have lost control of your mind. Although it is scary, it is best in the long run to let these feelings out. Rest assured that this is a temporary experience that will gradually subside as you express the feelings and learn new techniques for regaining a more flexible type of control. Although this crisis is normal, special precautions must be taken to help keep you safe and to promote the healthy integration of these memories and feelings. Anyone is vulnerable in a crisis and there have been reports of survivors making suicide attempts or engaging in other self-destructive acts in response to the crisis. Remember that the Chinese definition of crisis translates to "danger and opportunity." Your task during the breakthrough crisis is actually quite simple: Minimize the danger to yourself by reaching out for help while riding this tidal wave of feelings safely into shore.

Jolene

When I got into my early twenties, I was actually pretty depressed, although I really had no idea why. Not a clue. What made me finally call a therapist was that I'd seen that movie on television called *Sybil*—the woman with twenty-three separate personalities. As I was

watching it, I thought, "My life is being flashed before my very eyes."
It was pretty wrenching for me to watch this. I remember feeling so
scared and powerless and despairing and I couldn't really figure out
why. All I knew was that there seemed to be this storm of feelings
suddenly brewing inside me. I felt like I was ready to explode. I started
to physically shake and I couldn't control it. I tried to reassure myself
that nothing that bad had happened to me as a kid. But that didn't
work—these feelings wouldn't go away—they stayed with me and actually started to take on a life of their own. I felt like I was coming
unglued. A week later I just couldn't handle it anymore. I decided that
I needed help. So I called this therapist who had seen me when I was
a kid.

◆

SELF-HELP

1. Give yourself permission to get whatever you need to face this
   crisis. Reaching out to a therapist and support group as well as
   family and friends means that you will not have to be alone
   anymore.
2. Write in your journal some positive affirmations about the
   breakthrough crisis. "I survived the abuse, I can survive this
   also." Or "Out of crisis, there can be opportunity." Write whatever sentiments or beliefs that come to you about positively
   managing this crisis even if you don't feel that positive right
   now. Do whatever is necessary to give yourself the hope and
   strength you so desperately need.
3. Learn a simple 7-Step relaxation technique. (1) Sit comfortably;
   close your eyes; (2) imagine lying down on an ocean beach; (3)
   listen to the waves build, crest, and wash over the sand; (4) feel
   your breathing; (5) focus on your breathing—inhale, hold three
   seconds, and release. (6) repeat the cycle of breathing and
   washing away tension over and over again until the relaxation
   gradually washes over your entire body from lungs to toes;
   (7) continue the cycle again and again, permitting you to attain
   ever-deeper levels of relaxation.
4. Relieve unnecessary pressures on yourself during your work in
   this step. If possible, you may need to give yourself a temporary
   sabbatical from work, school, and normal domestic duties while
   you struggle with the breakthrough memories. Of course, some
   may actually prefer to work as a way of coping. Judge for yourself how much time you will need for taking care of yourself
   during this period.

5. Don't make any big decisions during this time—including whether to kill yourself! It may be hard to think straight right now and you don't want to make your predicament any more complicated by acting on impulse. If you are suicidal, immediately call your therapist and schedule an emergency appointment. Call a suicide hotline if you are desperate and no one is available. Reach out to friends and sympathetic family for help. One day in the future when your life is better, you will be glad you did.

PROFESSIONAL HELP

1. The breakthrough crisis can be a remarkably productive time in therapy because the memories and feelings are so accessible. However, you will also need help in expressing and managing the feelings, without stifling them. Ask your therapist for help in modulating your experience of these feelings so that you can deal with them piece by piece. You have a right to go at your own pace so let your therapist know when it feels too overwhelming to continue focusing on the memories.

2. It may help to see your therapist more frequently than once per week during this time. Discuss with your therapist whether this would be advisable. Also make sure to check that you have an emergency phone number to reach your therapist during evening hours. You and your therapist may want to develop a crisis management plan involving actions that you can take to help calm yourself and gauge when you will need emergency help.

3. If you feel like you cannot cope, tell your therapist and explore ways to slow this powerful process down. You may need to put some distance between yourself and these memories until you can regain sufficient control to feel safe again. In some cases, taking medication to help you cope or entering the hospital for a brief stay will be helpful. Not everyone will need this, but many survivors who are recovering horrific memories may benefit from this level of support.

STEP 2

I have determined, intuitively or objectively, that I was physically, sexually, or emotionally abused as a child.

Step 2 asks you to determine and then acknowledge to yourself that you were abused as a child and that the effects of the abuse may be causing your difficulties as an adult. Many of you who are still recovering memories about your past may not yet have objective evidence of child abuse. Your evidence may be more intuitive—a feeling that something was done to you that eludes memory awareness. Despite the absence of hard evidence generated from yourself or others, these intuitive feelings are significant and should not be dismissed. Many survivors of abuse were either too traumatized or not psychologically capable of organizing memories into words and images that can be recollected years later. If this is where you are in your recovery, continue to work this step to reclaim the memories and clarify the kind of abuse you suffered. If you and your therapist are patient and persistent, it will come to you eventually.

An important subgoal in this step is learning to accept your feelings about the abuse, whatever they may be at this time. They may not make complete sense to you, but the feelings are there for a reason. In the same way that the pain from a bruise tells you of a physical injury, the feelings associated with the abuse signals what kind of emotional bruise exists inside. You will need to figure out what those feelings are telling you instead of tossing them aside. Remember, survivors usually had their feelings invalidated by their parents, so not seeing your feelings as valid now may be more of the same thing. Give yourself the benefit of the doubt when it comes to verifying your feelings. You will need time and help in sorting out what happened without the denial and distortion of the past.

At this point, associating the abuse with your current problems as an adult may be the most tenuous of connections. It will take more work on the forthcoming steps in Stage One before this link can be firmly established. In the meantime, keep an open mind as you explore the reality of your abuse, letting the ramifications emerge with the new information and understanding that you develop.

Jolene

I think the most important thing was for me to realize that what happened to me was sexual abuse. I couldn't minimize it anymore—pretend that it was something else. Once I recognized that, a lot of anger came out and I told myself that it is all right to be pissed off about it. In fact, I think it's probably a pretty healthy reaction to it. Just calling it what it was allowed me to see how so many of these problems that I had were related to it. I used to think it was because I was crazy. Calling it abuse allowed me to have a reason for all of these feelings. I don't know if I could have faced them if it meant that I was crazy or I deserved to be treated that way. I realized that I had always lived life at arm's length from my feelings: My autobiography is just an outline with no color or detail filled in. But now there's a lot of hope and strength that grew out of that realization and it allowed me to go forward.

◆

SELF-HELP

1. Write down the date that you first acknowledge the abuse to yourself. This date will become the birthday of your recovery. Remember it well because you will need to honor this date in subsequent years when you are enjoying the fruits of your labor.
2. Pull out the old family album and photographs or home movies and look at them several times for a week or two. Just leave them around the house so that you can ponder them at your leisure. If you have no photographic records of the past, you can do some visualization exercises such as imagining taking a walk through your old house, your relatives' house, or your old school.
3. For those of you who enjoy art, draw a picture of your parents and family members. Draw a picture of yourself as a child. Add as much detail as you can recall. If the words describing the abuse episodes are still escaping you, try drawing pictures of whatever memory fragments you have of the abuse. More details of the visual images will probably come to you as you continue to sketch what happened.
4. You might consider writing your autobiography, starting with your first memory and working to the present. Some of you may be able to make a trip back to your hometown to research your autobiography. Interview the people who knew you as a child and ask them about their memories and perceptions of you back then. Just let the impressions, memories, and feelings wash over you. Write them down in your journal for future reference.
5. Start recording your dreams and nightmares in your journal and then reread the dreams a week later and write down whatever impressions, specific feelings, or images that come to you. Don't worry if everything seems disconnected. As you add the details to the picture of your childhood, the pieces will begin to fall into place.

PROFESSIONAL HELP

1. Talk over with your therapist fears and apprehensions about remembering the abuse. What are you afraid might happen if you remember it all? What reason might there be for wanting to keep these memories at bay?
2. Talk to your therapist about what, if anything, you might need to be able to reclaim these memories—more time, specific assurances, information from your therapist, or alterations in how you and your therapist structure the sessions that might help you feel safer and in control. Whatever it might be, you have the right to tailor your therapy to your individual needs.
3. If you have not been able to remember the specific episodes of abuse after a year or so of therapy, ask your therapist if he or she thinks it would be beneficial to undergo hypnotic or age-regression techniques to reclaim these memories. Not all therapists are trained in or comfortable with these techniques because there may still be good reasons for your not remembering and your therapist may want to respect them. However, these techniques have been shown to be effective with certain people at certain times in recovery.

STEP 3

I have made a commitment to recovery from my abuse.

All survivors who have recovered from child abuse can point to one moment in time when the thoughts about change and the hopes for a better life overcame their wall of denial and resistance. After acknowledging that you were abused and the effects that are undermining your life as an adult, the next step is to do something about it. This is a critical step for many survivors because moving from *thinking* about the abuse to actually *doing* something about it in the form of a commitment to a program of recovery is a large leap indeed. In many instances, survivors can flounder at this point for many of the reasons identified in chapters 9 and 11. Because this step is more like a leap, it may mean more to you than many of the other steps when you finally achieve it. Taking this giant step means you are no longer a passive victim of the past. You are now truly a survivor in the sense that you are motivated to overcome the effects of your abuse and are initiating change in the present in the hope of a better future. You are building on your acknowledgment of the abuse and recognizing that although you have been deeply hurt by it, you have not been vanquished.

What does it mean to make a commitment to recovery? Basically it means action—reaching out for help by joining a self-help group and entering therapy with an experienced professional who will work with you from this step all the way to Step 21. This step will not be achieved until you undertake both of these tasks. If you are still not ready, there is still something you can do to bridge these first two steps in a way that may help you to eventually join a group or therapy. Consider disclosing to a spouse, trusted friend, or clergy what you are struggling with. Disclosing your abuse to someone else can be extremely powerful because it can shatter the silence and secrecy of the past as well as your expectation of a negative response. Choose who you first tell very carefully. You want this to help you and encourage you to go forward, not set you back.

Some survivors, like Susan, have gone through the motions of making a commitment to recovery without necessarily putting their heart into it. Like her, you may have attended self-help groups or started therapy without really intending to face the reality of your childhood or the feelings associated with it. During the initial stages of recovery, you too may discover that you are avoiding some crucial aspect of yourself or your problem that may only hinder your progress.

Susan

I had been in groups and workshops and even therapy for a few years before I really started my recovery from the abuse. A lot of the help I had gotten before was for my head—intellectual understandings that didn't really capture what was going on inside of me. I would say the real turning point was this one night when I did some coke and I sat down to write a friend, and all of a sudden, all this stuff just started pouring out—feelings and thoughts and fears about the coke, my life, my situation, how I felt about myself. I had never cried for more than a minute my entire life, but that night the dam broke. One of the things I learned in my support groups was to follow through on goals, which for me had been to get back into therapy. I remember just laying there thinking how I needed help and I knew I had to reach out, and that there was one person—my ex-therapist—who if I called and told her this would hold me to it and make me face it. It was four or five o'clock in the morning when I made that call. This is when my recovery really began.

◆

SELF-HELP

1. Write in your journal about the circumstances or insights that caused you to make a commitment to recovery at this point in time.
2. Who, if anyone, has inspired you to get help?
3. Describe that part of you that is motivated to get help and make changes.
4. How does the voice of your internal "naysayers"—the part of you who opposes making such a commitment—justify not going forward with recovery? What are these reasons and how do you counter them?
5. Write an affirmation in your journal about your commitment to recover from child abuse. It can be a poem, a letter to yourself, a statement of your goals, or an unsent letter to your parents declaring your intentions. This can become your personal manifesto that you can return to during the most difficult times of recovery for strength, inspiration, and encouragement.
6. Use the information presented in chapter 10 to find and join a self-help group of your choice.

PROFFESIONAL HELP

1. Use the information presented in chapter 11 to select a warm, caring, and experienced therapist, someone who can be there for you when you go through the ups and downs of recovery.
2. Once in therapy, share with him or her your thoughts on what you want to accomplish and the work you've done to date. Remember that your therapist will likely be intuitive, but not a mind reader. By sharing your memories of the abuse as soon as you feel comfortable, you will help your therapist devise a plan for healing that acknowledges your past work, and at the same time, focuses on your present needs.

STEP 4

I shall reexperience each set of memories of the abuse as they surface in my mind.

This step represents the major task of the first stage of recovery and may require the most time to accomplish. Often survivors of extreme and prolonged abuse will need to return to this step again and again as new memories of the same or other episodes of abuse surface. This step essentially involves going through the memories of the abuse and expressing them in as much detail as you can remember with your therapist.

Reexperiencing the abuse means many things. First, you will need to reexperience the various feelings, express them as you feel them, and be able to eventually label them so they don't seem confusing and overwhelming. Second, see if you can describe any of the sensory impressions connected to the abuse: visual images, sounds, smells, tastes, and tactile sensations. Third, recall what you thought about the abuse during and after each episode—the words you spoke to yourself. Notice if you have any *body memories* of the abuse while you are re-experiencing it: aches, pains, numbing, or other physical sensations that suddenly appear in key locations of your body such as your arms (hurt while trying to ward off the blows), genital areas (physically injured during episodes of sexual abuse), and face and mouth (pains around your neck and cheeks due to being slapped, gagged, or forced to orally copulate the abuser). These sensations mean something, and by allowing yourself to reexperience them, you will help discharge them, allowing them to gradually fade away. Finally, try to remember what behaviors you engaged in during and after the abuse. Did you try to run away and hide, roll up into a ball to protect yourself, or fight back and scream? Or could you do nothing but stand there or lie there in a state of paralysis while the abuse occurred? What about later? Did you run out of the house, crawl under the bed, hide in a closet, or wash in the bathroom?

I know this step will be very difficult to achieve because it means returning in your mind to the scene of the crime. But this time you can have all of the control you need. It will not be as painful or scary as when you were a child. Remember you are dealing with memories, not your current life. Go slowly, step by step, memory by memory, so that you can manage the feelings and share your reactions with your therapist. Please don't try to do this step without professional help.

Shirley

I went to an Elton John concert about three or four years ago, and it was the first time I got to see him in person after listening to his music for years when I was growing up. I credit him for saving me because I was filled with such loneliness and emptiness and he helped me fill the holes inside which kept me going. And at that time I was doing a lot of work in my therapy about the abuse and really facing it in a way that I had never done before. So he starts playing my favorite song called "I'm Still Standing" and it brought me right back to those days again. This is the song that I would play after getting molested or beaten. It was the song to make those feelings go away or to take me away from those feelings. But now with Elton right in front of me, playing this song, it brought everything right back. The feelings just started pouring out of me and I was having these flashbacks to the abuse and my body was totally charged up. It was scary and exhilarating at the same time. I remember I was playing the drums with my hands on my thighs and really crying. I was not even aware I was crying because I was in some kind of trance. When I got home, I had these big bruises on my thighs. I was totally exhausted and kind of at peace with myself. Even though I was literally beating myself up, it was a real cathartic experience.

◆

Self-Help

1. Record in your journal each episode of abuse that you recount in your therapy, describing your story in the way that other survivors have told their stories in this book. Draw pictures to accompany the words and to clarify the surroundings. Give as much detail and emotional expression as you feel comfortable doing. Drawing and writing in story form is helpful in organizing and integrating the past experience for you in a different way, one that takes into account your adult perspective and knowledge. Try to sort out exactly what happened and your reactions then as well as now. Work toward a more complete understanding of the abuse episodes that incorporates the roles played by your parents, your family, and the forces at large.

2. This is the step during which you really need to take good care of yourself because this work can be so exhausting. Exercise, plenty of sleep, stress management, maybe even some vitamin therapy are highly recommended. All of these things can help your body stay healthy and vigorous while you work on your psyche.

3. If you are tired of writing, try audio recording your memories and listening to them a few weeks later, choosing or not to add new segments at the end of the tape. Relistening to these tapes several months later may be especially eye-opening because it may confirm your progress in remembering as well as triggering new memories.

4. What about that group you were going to join? By Step 4, it is highly recommended that you be involved in a self-help group for the support and encouragement that you will need in making this step. Remember you cannot recover alone.

PROFESSIONAL HELP

1. In your work with your therapist, explore your reactions to talking about the abuse. How do you find yourself expecting your therapist to react? How do you feel after disclosing especially personal segments of your story? Do you feel less ashamed of what happened now that you have shared it with someone else? Are you able to talk more easily with other people about your abuse and your work in recovery?
2. Remember that you have the right to control the pace of your therapy. At times, you and your therapist may disagree on what pace is best for the particular stages of recovery. At times, you may want to go faster, while he thinks you should slow down. Other times, he may want to push you to deal with something if he thinks it would benefit you.

STEP 5

I accept that I was powerless over my parents' actions, which makes them, not me, responsible for the abuse.

You know by now that survivors grow up believing the classic myth of child abuse—that they were somehow responsible for the abuse, not their parents. The reasons supporting this myth are as varied as your imagination is fertile. "I let him do it to me." "I should have been able to protect myself." "I liked certain aspects of the abuse—the attention, the gifts, the pleasurable sensations, or the sense of being special." Besides what the child may say about the issue of responsibility, the parents often accompany the abuse with indictments like "I'm beating you because you are a bad boy." "I am showing you how much I love you." "I wouldn't be calling you stupid if you showed me you have more than half a brain in that head of yours." "You have the devil inside you and I'm going to beat it out of you." These words are truly toxic because they do more than just unfairly place the blame for the abuse on your shoulders; they eat away at your positive sense of self and have continued to do so in your adult life.

You can challenge the words of your parents that are still ringing in your ears by understanding your dysfunctional family and recognizing the real reasons you were abused. This is an essential step in recovery, because without seeing that your parents were at fault, it will be very difficult to face the remaining tasks of recovery: turning the anger at yourself around at them, uncovering your shame, and understanding how the abuse affects your life today as an adult. Understand first of all that you were the child and you had neither the power nor the authority to make your parents do anything. The abuse was their responsibility because, quite simply, they were the adults, they had the power, and they did it to you. And nothing you could have done would have changed this because parents, families, and society are set up to give the power and authority to the adults—often males—and children are given little or no power.

Besides accepting the hard facts in determining who was responsible, consider this. As a child, you were in no psychological condition to say and believe that what your parents were doing was wrong. You were dependent on them, so you couldn't risk alienating them by pointing out the truth, even if your child mind was precocious enough to sort out the complexity of issues and loyalties that are stirred up by child abuse. And no child can do this effectively because her intellectual capacities are not sufficiently developed to do so. You desperately wanted to love them and be loved by them. Think back to what it would have been like for you, the child, to accept that the people who were supposed to love you were actually hurting you. Most children can't face this horrible reality because they would emotionally orphan themselves in the process and nothing could be worse than that.

Pete

It was really important for me to have my therapist do a reality check in laying the responsibility for the abuse on my mother, and to a lesser extent, my father. I grew up believing what was in her eyes— that I was the evil one and she was the poor, unfortunate one. The continual reinforcement that I got in my therapy helped me finally believe that I wasn't the perpetrator and that I wasn't evil. It took a long time to distinguish who really had the responsibility and to begin to see myself as a boy who wasn't supposed to be in charge. Once I understood that and began to believe in my heart that I wasn't responsible, I started to have some legitimate anger about what happened instead of guilt and shame. Being able to see the truth has been so helpful in all areas of my life. To get a handle on reality where my mother is concerned has helped me to deal with other people who want to take advantage of me.

♦

SELF-HELP

1. Write in your journal the words you recall your parents using to place the burden of responsibility for the abuse on you. What

was the tone in their voice, the look in their eyes when they said those words? What reasons did you use to hold yourself responsible for the abuse?
2. Imagine what you would say to your parents or abuser today about who was responsible. What feelings do you notice within yourself as you say this to them?
3. Sharing your story in a self-help group that explodes the myth of child abuse can bring some needed validation for seeing things the way they really were. Groups are so powerful in challenging these long-held ideas because so many people shared the oppression caused by this one myth.

PROFESSIONAL HELP

1. What is your therapist's response to the question of responsibility for the abuse? How do you feel about this response? Is it helpful or not? Tell him what you feel and discuss what you need from him in this regard.
2. As I mentioned in Chapter 11, some therapists encourage their clients to use the "empty chair" technique to talk back to their parents or abuser. This can be extremely empowering after years of keeping your thoughts and feelings about them to yourself. This technique can also stir up old feelings of being disobedient and fearful of being abused again. Explore what your resistance is to addressing your parents in this safe, controlled way.

STEP 6

I respect my anger as a natural reaction to the abuse and I am learning to turn it against neither myself nor others.

Anger is a logical reaction to child abuse. Yet survivors have such a hard time with anger, lashing out or repressing it, not knowing when it is and is not appropriate. You were angry as a child but probably were not able to safely express anger in your family. You may still be afraid of your anger because it may have been intricately connected with many of the bad things that happened to hurt you. But bottling up your anger will also block your recovery, because without ventilating this anger, it may turn into aggressive behavior.

Where did that anger from the past go? Most survivors, especially the caretakers, scapegoats, and recluses, turn the anger against themselves, which is probably the major reason for their difficulties as adults. Fighting, criticizing, or withdrawing from your lover, spouse, or children are also likely problems, especially if your childhood family was ever violent. If you are a parent now, you need to recognize how your anger is triggered by your children pushing the wrong buttons at the wrong time. As was true with your own parents, it is now your responsibility to control your behavior and your anger and to protect your child.

If you have to express your anger to better manage it, the best strategy is to externalize it, that is, to get rid of it by discharging it outward. But do it safely, with maximum control, and direct it where it belongs—at your abusers. Of course, it is not always possible to do this, nor is it always advisable. Chapter 15 will explore confronting your family directly. In your therapy, there are many ways to access this anger, turn it away from yourself, and express it indirectly at your abusers. Practicing how to express your anger and learning how to turn it on and off will not only be therapeutic but will give you the skills to use your anger in appropriate situations in the real world.

Leigh Anne

Believe me, it took me many, many sessions before I could even admit to how angry I was at my mother. My hatred for my own mother really was the force that, literally, drove me nuts. This anger was brewing inside me and getting stronger and stronger. And so one session my therapist pulled an empty chair right in front of me and asked me if I wanted to say something to her right now. He handed me the box of tissues, so I could cry if I wanted to, and said, "There's your mom, right there. This is your opportunity. What are you going to say to your mom? What are you going to tell her?" I'd go back and forth through days of therapy and never be able to resolve saying what I felt about her. I would just cry. I'd just hold it in and think how the most powerful thing a young girl could say is "I hate you." That's like blasphemy! That's a horrible thing to admit and I just couldn't bring myself to say it, although all those years I felt it so strongly. So I talked to the chair finally this one session. I shouted, "I hate you." "Why," she said, "Why do you hate me?" And I said loud and clear, "I hate you because you did this and this and this and this and on and on." And I said, "One of the worst things you ever did was kill my dog— you killed my dog and then lied to my face. You hate everything about me and everything that you thought I would like you opposed for no reason. And, of course, you never remembered my birthday." This took the whole session and it was a tremendous, cleansing, catharsis— so resolving and resounding. I just felt so much better after that one day. It was so hard to get to that point. Later on we did it with my father and we did it with my brother. My therapist made me face the things that I would not face, and those were the most important sessions we had.

◆

SELF-HELP

1. Review the anger management techniques that were described in chapter 7.
2. There are many ways that you can safely express your anger on your own without hurting yourself or anyone else. One of the best ways is to engage in active sports where you can bash the ball: tennis, racquetball, baseball. Virtually any kind of activity such as aerobics or dancing will reduce your feeling of anger just from the physical exertion. Other more direct expressions of anger are breaking glass, hitting pillows, screaming in your house or car (though not when driving), and learning martial arts or self-defense skills. Other more intellectual avenues include getting involved in public speaking and protest marches.
3. Write drafts of letters to your abusers about how angry you are with them. You can really get a lot of the anger sorted out by writing long letters that detail every aspect of on your anger you can imagine. Whether you send them or not is up to you. Sending these types of letters is considered a family confrontation, so you may want to discuss it with your therapist to see if you are ready to deal with this whole separate issue.

PROFESSIONAL HELP

1. Explore using some techniques for expressing anger at your abusers in your therapy sessions. Besides the "empty chair," psychodrama and other Gestalt therapy techniques that use role playing and reenactment of family situations are especially powerful for survivors who want to practice expressing anger toward their parents.
2. The major work of therapy during this stage is to practice a more flexible control over your anger in various situations. Identify situations where you lose control of your anger as well as situations where you need to use your anger more constructively

to stand up for yourself and avoid being taken advantage of. Work out new routines to handle your anger and then practice these routines in your sessions before trying them out in your everyday life.

STEP 7

I have reconnected with my inner child whose efforts to survive can now be appreciated.

This step involves turning inward away from the violence and pain of your abuse to reach inside to your inner child and begin learning how to nurture and develop this vulnerable part. This is both a grieving and healing step because what you now give to this child will be restorative and fulfilling, a foundation upon which you can build other changes later as you work the future steps. This is also a step that will teach some needed self-acceptance of what you as a child did to survive the abuse. By now, you know pretty much what happened, who did what, and how you felt about it. It is now time to continue the work begun in Step 5 to forgive yourself for any of the millions of reasons that survivors have to blame themselves as children for the abuse. Working this step means further identifying and challenging these outdated notions and making corrections in the distortions based on what you now understand was happening. Along the way, you need to appreciate and validate yourself for surviving this ordeal. As you accept what happened, invariably you will open yourself to accepting more and more of you and that child within.

As self-acceptance develops, you may notice your relationships beginning to improve. Accepting yourself may make it easier for others to accept you. You will be pleasantly surprised, if you haven't yet had the experience. Allow yourself to share these new feelings about yourself to people you care for and trust. Look for acceptance and understanding, and if you don't get it, ask for it. Let this vulnerable part explore being dependent and intimate with someone and see if you can feel the trust starting to build. If you feel afraid, try to figure out why and share your thoughts with this person.

Richard

What came out in my therapy is that the way I survived my childhood was to constantly be a mess and miserable and constantly forgetting things and breaking things and losing things. That way, I was able to keep this "howling void of need"—my mother—away from me. She was always wanting something from me; there was always some demand being made of me. It's like, "Oh, God here we go again." And of course she picked up on this message of my being incompetent. God knows she helped cause it! On the other hand, she kept wanting to set me up as her super male who could handle everything that she couldn't handle, which was a lot. To counteract this, I expended tremendous energy over becoming totally hapless. And, you know, it worked pretty well and I could actually take some comfort from it. It's still comforting now to be hapless and helpless because you sort of feel relieved of everything. It can still be very soothing to this day to not have responsibility, much to my wife's chagrin.

◆

Self-Help

1. Pick one photograph of yourself as a child that you especially like, frame it, and put it where you can readily see it. If you don't have a picture and cannot get one from family or relatives, try drawing a picture of yourself as a child. Don't worry about being a good artist. It may be better to let your inner child draw a child's drawing. If it fits, put it on your refrigerator.

2. This is a good time to renew your relationship with your children and plan new activities with them that allow you to be a child also. If you have time, consider volunteering at a day-care center or school and let yourself enjoy childhood from your new vantage point. Use your time with children to let your inner child come out and express itself through the activities of a healthy childhood: drawing, telling and listening to stories, playing games, and singing songs. Enjoy this inner child and reclaim it as an important part of who you are today.

Professional Help

1. Many survivors describe a particular feeling or sensation in their bodies that over time comes to represent this wounded inner child. Explore that feeling with your therapist and see if you can't bring this part of you into sharper focus. What does this wounded child feel like to you? Are there any metaphors— images that capture the bodily sensations—that could explain what this child is experiencing? Many survivors report feeling empty inside or cut off below the neck or having a hole in the stomach. Exploring the inner child through your own personal metaphor may help you and your therapist figure out how to heal the wounds.

Chapter Thirteen

STAGE TWO

RECOVERY:

STEPS 8 TO 14

Stage Two shifts the focus away from the details of your past abuse to the impact of the abuse on your adult life. This stage represents the intermediate point in your recovery where the healing and change occur more in tandem, one reinforcing and complementing the other. The cornerstone of Stage Two is taking an honest inventory of your current problems and then dedicating yourself to identifying and changing the behaviors that underlie your troubles—much like Step 4 in AA. For adult survivors, this means going beyond an awareness of self-sabotage to taking direct action against it.

Stage Two also requires you to delve deeper into your psyche to face your shame, the core feeling experienced by so many adults from dysfunctional families. Shame must be challenged and ultimately turned into self-acceptance. You are now able to accept and express your grief over the disappointments in your childhood and mourn the loss of the fantasy for the ideal parents. By letting go of childhood hopes for the parents who failed you and feeding your budding self-acceptance, you can give birth to a new sense of entitlement. You can be your own person and decide how to live your new life. Altering distorted perceptions and beliefs and learning how to control your aggressive behavior will fuel the changes in your personality, ending forever the possibility of repeating the abuse with the next generation.

Rarely does recovery proceed in a neat progression, especially during this middle stage. There will be sessions in your therapy when you depart from the focus on your abuse, heading in new directions that seem either too pressing to ignore or especially promising for needed insights. Stage Two may also find you examining your relationship with your therapist as you develop confidence in asserting your opinions and perhaps disagreeing with his point of view. This is a very necessary and healthy development because your therapist is the best person to use for practicing your new autonomy.

STEP 8

I have made an inventory of the problem areas in my life.

Taking a full and honest inventory of the problem areas in your life is the initial step of Stage Two recovery because you first have to target what you want to change before you can begin to change it. By now, it should be fairly clear to you how the abuse has affected your life as an adult. If you are still unclear about this, review chapters 4 through 7. You may have other problems that impede your enjoyment of life that are not even mentioned in this book. You can add them to your inventory. This inventory is more than just an account of your problems; it will become a blueprint for the changes that you need to make to create your new beginning.

Leigh Anne

Well, right now I'm struggling. The ray of hope for me is to just deal with the everyday problems that I have. I feel like I live life on a teeter-totter—up and down, up and down. Nothing is too consistent in my life. I'm still moving around a lot and changing jobs all the time. I need to change that. I need to integrate my experiences in the past with what I'm learning in therapy. I have made some changes, but I realize I have more work to do. I need to decide about this relationship I am in and then deal with my weight. I have more conscious expectations of myself now. I do have the power to take control of my life, to give it some connectedness and stability. Fortunately I have very strong values. I have integrity and I'm gritty and I'm damn stubborn! I've been blessed with these things and they're going to help me go forward to the next level. And as far as the future, that's another area that I need to figure out—my career. I really don't know what I want to do.

◆

SELF-HELP

1. Go back and review your journal entries that you made while reading chapters 4 through 8 and list the concerns and problems as you go along. Which of these problem areas is the most disruptive to your life? Which needs to be resolved or lessened before you will be able to resolve others? Which needs to be resolved before you lose something important like a personal relationship, a job, or your life. For example, if you can't afford the cost of your therapy, and have lost your health insurance because of unemployment, job problems may be the biggest barrier to moving forward with recovery. If you are so depressed that you are immobilized in your life, and are contemplating suicide, getting help with managing your feelings would be the best place to start. If you feel like you might strike your child (thereby risking possible legal charges as well as triggering another round of self-hatred), focusing on parenting issues may be at the top of your list. Put a priority rating (1 is low and 5 is high) next to each of these desired changes and review the sections of this book that address these areas.

PROFESSIONAL HELP

1. Review your inventory of concerns with your therapist and discuss how to best work on these life problems as you continue to heal the wounds within. This will give you a sense of control over your recovery and help you to learn to speak up for what you want and develop a consensus with another person about how to proceed. While your therapist may have reasons for wanting you to address certain things first, it is your decision that counts the most.

2. Many of the problems you will identify that are common among survivors, such as physical ailments, sexual problems, severe mood disorders, parenting problems, and work-related concerns, will require the services of a specialist in the particular problem area. For example, if you have body memories that

manifest themselves in muscular aches and pains, soreness in certain areas of your body, or decreased flexibility of joints, consider seeing an acupuncturist who may be able to provide either topical, or depending on their treatment orientation, systemic relief for these symptoms. Acupuncture treatments can also release specific feelings, especially fear and anxiety, that can become localized in the specific areas of the body directly affected by the abuse. However, unless your acupuncturist is also a trained psychotherapist, you will need to resolve and work through whatever feelings arise in your own individual or group therapy.

Sexual problems can be more directly addressed using specific behavioral techniques that may be outside the area of competence of your therapist. Severe mood disorders, reported by some survivors whose parents were so afflicted, may be more physiologically based than simply a delayed reaction to the abuse, thereby making some of the new psychotropic medications more effective than psychotherapy alone. In such cases, a referral to a psychiatrist for a medication evaluation would be a good idea. Likewise, parenting problems may require either a consultation from your pediatrician or a referral to a child or family therapist. In general, this is the time during recovery when you can develop a more detailed strategy for treating the various symptoms of the abuse that do not readily remit through your weekly therapy sessions. This view reflects a more holistic approach to recovery that seeks to take the best that each therapeutic school has to offer and apply it strategically in a comprehensive treatment plan that is an adjunct to your "base" therapy.

STEP 9

I have identified the parts of myself connected to self sabotage.

This step involves identifying and sorting out all the various parts of yourself so that you can understand which parts are helpful and which are connected to the many faces of self-sabotage. Self-sabotage will probably be a major source of the life problems you identified in Step 8. By now you know where the self-sabotage comes from and how it affected you as a child. As an adult you need to see how it is expressed on an everyday basis and to acknowledge the part of you that seems to govern this behavior.

As you identify the parts of you responsible for the self-sabotage, you will probably discover adult versions of many of the childhood roles you played. Many of the most commonly adopted roles that adult survivors used as children are often still employed but are labeled differently now: codependent for caretaker, masochist for scapegoat, offender for bully, leader for hero, and eccentric for recluse. When taken to the extreme, these roles will create problems for you in your real life, although aspects of some of them may actually be helpful in daily functioning. For example, caretaking is an essential part of parenting, although dominating or overcontrolling your child is also common with codependent mothers. Try to identify what roles you adopt as an adult—the helpful ones as well as the problematic ones. Learning to strengthen those healthy, unique, and talented aspects of yourself while controlling the others will be a major task of Stage Two and Stage Three recovery.

Pete

Through my therapy, I have learned that I was driven by an unconscious guilt and shame about my father and his ineffectiveness as a person and my guilt over supplanting him as my mother's favorite. So I defeated myself by denying my success. I set myself up to fail because it was the moral thing for me to do and I felt so immoral with the incest and power that I had at home. On some level, I think that I could not come into my own as a person because to be strong and healthy and productive meant success which meant immorality. So I unconsciously chose the harder, rockier road with little reward, out of a sense of duty and loyalty to my father. Prosperity and success and leadership, which are all tied into my job and career, were taboo. It also had a lot to do with the lack of a postive role model on the part of my dad. I saw a castrated man and so I carried out my own castration really by defeating myself and having those thoughts of mutilating myself. It really messed up my masculinity because I thought I had to castrate myself if I got anything good—power, pleasure, success, or money.

◆

SELF-HELP

1. Write about these adult parts of yourself in your journal and explore how they operate in your life. Describe in as much detail as you can when these parts come out, what behaviors are connected to them, what feelings you have about yourself and oth-

ers at that moment, whether you "own" these parts for yourself or project them onto others, and who seems to trigger these parts in you: spouse or lover, children, peers, superiors at work, family, the opposite sex, or people of the same sex as your abuser?

2. Ask the trusted people in your life how they see you. Don't react to anything they say immediately. Reflect about their comments for a day or two and see how their remarks compare with the various roles you have identified for yourself.

3. If you haven't done so already, try to record your dreams in your journal so that you can see how the different parts of you are interacting on the unconscious level. Record each dream in story form, with a beginning, a middle, and an end. Develop the details and imagery as you write in the first person. Many people think that they don't dream because they don't remember their dreams. This is inaccurate. Everyone dreams, although your denial and repression may make your dreams unavailable to your conscious awareness. Practice in remembering your dreams will help you remember them. Develop a routine of leaving your journal next to your bed and remember to ask yourself what dreams you had just as you first wake up.

PROFESSIONAL HELP

1. With your therapist, try to give expression to all of these different parts of you. You cannot learn how to strengthen or reduce them without first giving each of them a voice and perhaps even a name. As you experience each part, try to relate it to specific memories, images, and dialogues. What were the conflicts for you in these situations? What about them made you feel good? What part of you comes out most frequently with your therapist? Does that part help you to get what you want from your therapist or not? If not, talk with him or her about it.

2. This is a crucial time in your therapy because it requires special skills to enhance the healthy parts of your personality while increasing your control of the maladaptive parts. Your therapist is best qualified to help you strengthen those parts of yourself that bring promise and hope to your sense of self. Those of you who are aware of antagonistic or aggressive subpersonalities or multiple personalities that are more autonomous than the parts or traits of yourself we have spoken of previously, will need strong guidance from your therapist to decide how best to reduce their impact on your life. The current therapeutic approach is to ask you to speak to the various subpersonalities within

yourself and negotiate a truce, in a sense, that will reduce the power of these persecutory parts and help your new self to regain full control over your primary personality.

STEP 10

I am uncovering my shame and working to transform it into self-acceptance.

Shame is the name for all those bad feelings that survivors have for themselves as well as the psychological source of self-sabotage. Shame is felt as self-blame. Like anger, shame is a normal feeling to have considering what was never provided to you as a child. The problem is that you may have too much of it. Unlike guilt, which has to do with feeling bad about what you do in the external world, shame is feeling like a failure inside: flawed, inferior, contemptible, no good. Shame is the part of you that you can't face because it feels so intolerable. John Bradshaw, the author and television host, has written an excellent book about "toxic shame" as an "emotion that gets internalized as a state of being." Adult survivors begin the process of internalizing shame when they identify with parents who abuse them, abandon them, and fail to validate them as people. The shame gets bundled as a package of self-blaming images, bad feelings, self-destructive thoughts, and self-sabotaging behaviors, which during the childhood years evolve into a major part of the survivors' sense of self. As the child goes through life, this part gets reinforced by other people, external events, and the survivor himself who has learned to defend against the feelings triggered by the abuse by "turning against the self."

Considering how shame is so deeply imbedded in your sense of self, it will take a lot of courageous work to uncover it, face it, and begin to transform it into something else—self acceptance. But it can be done. By working with a caring therapist and sharing these feelings with other people who you trust, you can internalize a different, more accepting message about yourself. To continue self-blaming is to do to yourself as an adult what was done to you as a child. You must sever this legacy by changing what you say to yourself, how you treat yourself, and how you let others treat you.

Jolene

Recently I was having a really rough time in therapy just remembering a lot of things and not being able to talk about stuff that was uncomfortable. Whenever I would talk about my abuse, I started having some physical pain, so I decided to see a masseuse. First of all, I found there's all this tension in my body that had nothing to do with my neck and shoulders, which is where I was feeling it. There were places in my body that would really hurt when this woman would barely touch me. So I walked out of this place more relaxed than I've ever been in my entire life. And I suddenly realized that I'm always sort of holding in my breath and sucking in my belly and thinking that I'm fat and ugly. I have spent my whole life thinking of myself this way and I had never really recognized it. And it got me thinking about a number of things, one of which is that I've always felt so bad about myself, like I'm a worthless, no-good person. I think this feeling is in my bones— I'm so filled with it that I can't even challenge it because I don't know anything different. At that moment, I had a flash of compassion for myself, not self-pity but a feeling of genuine sadness for myself. So I decided at that point that maybe I really could just kind of relax and take care of myself and not be so hard on myself and maybe begin thinking of myself differently.

◆

SELF-HELP

1. Read John Bradshaw's excellent book *Healing the Shame That Binds You* (see Appendix A) for a more complete understanding of shame.
2. Learn to identify the feeling of shame when it occurs in your daily life and write in your journal about situations that trigger shame.
3. Get support from other people on how to act differently in situations that trigger shame. Assertively expressing affirmations about your strengths and admitting your weaknesses will counteract internal shame and arrest the shaming experience in your everyday life.
4. Recall the people in your childhood who had something good to say about you. What words did they use to describe your best qualities? How did you feel when you were around them? Revive these important people in your past by writing about them in your journal and what they meant to you then and now.
5. Those of you who are religious or spiritual can turn to your Higher Power to cleanse yourself of the shame and unworthiness that you so deeply feel. Religion and spirituality can be a tremendous source of inner sustenance and can provide an ideal

vision with which to identify that can replace the negative role models of the past.

PROFESSIONAL HELP

1. In order to resolve shame, you need to have an ongoing, reparative relationship with another person who will help you challenge your internal voice of shame and replace it with a healthier dialogue. Your therapist is an important source for helping to transform the shame into self-acceptance. Talk about your shame with him and share how you experience shame in your life and in therapy.
2. Identify with your therapist how you cover up your shame by adopting a role or a false self that you project to others, which keeps you from feeling the shame. Share this false self with your therapist and try to understand what it gives you that you don't feel you have inside.

STEP 11

I am able to grieve for my childhood and mourn the parents who failed me.

Grieving your childhood losses and mourning the loss of the ideal parents will require a great deal of patience and compassion for yourself. This is a step that asks you to recognize your losses and helps you to resolve them once and for all. Be prepared for this step to take time: You can't be rushed into healing these deepest wounds of your childhood. More often, you heal the wounds in layers, throughout recovery, and come back again and again as new healing covers the old wounds. You may always have a scar there, but the scab covering your painful loss will eventually disappear.

Many survivors tend to avoid this stage after one pass or so, preferring to avoid the dreadful pain. After working through some of it in Stage One, it may be possible to feel much better than before without fully resolving the grief. You may have found your life to be improved but now feel the changes have plateaued. This step can be resolved by sharing the most vulnerable parts of yourself with others, thus turning your fear of being hurt into the building of trust. Ask yourself if you can allow yourself to be comforted by your spouse, lover, or friends. Healthy dependency means letting other people take care of you at times like these.

Richard

I was able to really grieve for my childhood when I finally gave up the hope of getting something from my parents. I think what happens is you're held hostage to the hope that your parents will change, and that they will finally give you what you've been deprived of. You have to reexamine all these premises for your behavior with them because you realize that it is useless. You're never going to get "it," and that sucks. Part of me couldn't really believe it—that little part of me that held on to my sense of specialness. To accept that you aren't going to get it is like facing the abyss. I mean, you hear about old ladies who get their life savings swindled from them—this is far worse because I was only a kid and parental love—not money—is the primary currency of life. Your sense of loss cuts all the way down to your soul, the center of your being. You start to assess the depth of your deprivation, like how much you have not gotten from both parents. And you stay there for a while facing this hole inside you. You dwell on this in therapy, seeing all their inadequacies, and what they failed to do, and how they ripped you off. It's dramatic because I've had to give up my false hopes. Then after a while you learn to start to turn elsewhere. My therapist and I started in 1981 and worked on this on and off until 1983. It takes a long time, but it allows you to start functioning as an adult.

◆

SELF-HELP

1. This step really requires a lot of support and a self-help group or group therapy for survivors can provide you with generous support, validation, and encouragement. You need to be around people who have gone through what you are going through and can be the positive role models that you never had. Sponsors and mentors and therapists are very important people to the grieving survivor because they can symbolize the light at the end of the tunnel.

PROFESSIONAL HELP

1. Your therapist's job is to help you ventilate these feelings of loss and give up the fantasy of getting something that is not available. Expect to receive support, understanding, and compassion during this difficult and painful step. If you are stuck and cannot

resolve these wounds or give up the hope for the ideal parents,
consider doing some guided visualization exercises with your
therapist. These use a trance induction technique to fully and
deeply relax you followed by an imaginary experience that met-
aphorically captures your dilemma as a child. If your therapist
is not trained or comfortable using these techniques, discuss the
value of attending a workshop that specializes in healing childhood traumas. These techniques can unblock the grieving process and help you transform the inner emptiness you feel into
an evolving process that leads to resolution.

2. Your therapist will be skilled in dream analysis and sharing your
dreams in therapy can open an exciting venue for personal exploration. You can bring in your journal and read the dreams
to your therapist and then explore together what the various
meanings and interpretations might be suggesting. Dreams can
be especially vivid and informative during the grieving process,
illuminating conflicts and resistances that are beyond your conscious awareness.

STEP 12

I can challenge faulty beliefs and distorted perceptions, adopting
more healthy attitudes and expectations about myself.

This step is focused on changing the faulty thinking, attitudes, and
beliefs about yourself and your past that go on dictating your view of
the world. Considering how your childhood thoughts or attitudes born
of the past abuse will never really favor you, it is essential that you
challenge these internal tapes that may still be playing themselves out
in your head, often without you being aware of it. Because of the ex-
tremeness of their childhood experience, many survivors become victims of their own misconceptions. A few examples are (1) splitting
everything into good and bad, "thinking in black and white"; (2) dis-
qualifying the positives about yourself or your efforts: "If it isn't perfect,
then its nothing"; (3) magical thinking—attributing some outcome to
factors that are not related: "I was born under the wrong stars, so
nothing will ever change" or "I got lucky once doing this so all I need
to do is repeat myself"; (4) reasoning based on initial impressions or
circumstantial evidence rather than balanced objectivity: "I don't know
why I did it, I thought this guy had it in for me"; (5) personalization—
taking responsibility for something caused by other people; (6) mag-
nification and minimization—either making something catastrophic or
overly diminishing its importance.

First, familiarize yourself with the patterns that you use and then
practice identifying them when they occur. The next step is to catch

them with your newly developed self-awareness so that you can short-circuit them before they can do their damage to you. Devise techniques with your therapist to internalize corrected attitudes about yourself.

Susan

One of the biggest things I learned was that when I got that cloudy feeling in my head—like when your head is in the ozone—and I was about to make some decision that I would regret, instead of following through on it, to just take some time and consider all the options. That was a real eye opener for me. It was like, "You mean I actually could say no to this? I could actually make choices not everyone would agree with?" I realize I was always working from the premise that I couldn't make somebody mad or that no one could see me as less than perfect. I had a real awakening in therapy about considering choices and giving myself "second chances" with situations that I reacted to in the old way. All of this has given me the skill to avoid or at least minimize the number of crises that I have—no more bounced checks, no more buying into other's bad ideas. I still have a lot of self-doubt about my decision making, but I am also learning to trust my judgment a lot more. I tell myself that I can be really conscious in my life, that my ideas can be really valuable if I take the time to think them through clearly and objectively.

◆

SELF-HELP

1. Read over your journal and see what distortions in thinking, perceptions, and attitudes you have had about yourself. Notice the obvious patterns. What are the common results of these kinds of distortions in terms of behaviors and feelings?
2. The most basic skill for you to learn is the ability to stand back and view events and situations from a broader perspective, allowing yourself to be more objective in your perceptions, beliefs, and judgments. This skill is essential because your analytical ability is called into play in virtually all aspects of your life and can make the difference between repeating old mental habits and choosing new ways of looking at things.

   Whenever you uncover some distortion in thinking, attitude, or belief, try to find out the reality of it and then use this as a standard for judging your piece of thinking. Don't assume you know something when you really don't. You may have to make a particular effort or engage in some activity to get the information you need. By educating yourself about what is really true, you can determine the validity of your previously held belief and then substitute the updated version.

PROFESSIONAL HELP

1. What kind of distortions has your therapist pointed out to you in the past? Share your ideas and discuss with your therapist which ones are still a problem for you.
2. Use psychotherapy to help you strengthen your thinking and decision-making style. You can do this by discussing specific situations that are giving you problems in your present life. Take these situations apart with your therapist and see what kind of perceptions, attitudes, and beliefs they may reveal. Considering how feelings may disrupt this process, you may need to work very slowly and deliberately with good follow-up to accurately figure out what is happening.

STEP 13

I accept that I alone have the right to be the way I want to be and to choose how to live my life.

Survivors must ultimately accept and protect their right to self-determination: to be the person they want to be, to live the life they want to live, and to be treated the way they want to be treated. This step marks the separation of your new self from your parents and family and permits conscious choices to be made in directing your life without the guilt and lack of entitlement that characterized your past. You now feel like you have the right to make these choices that reflect your preferences—what your values are, how you spend your time and money, the people you want to share your life with as well as the person you want to share your body with. Working through the abuse to feel entitled to the right of self-determination means that your true identity is beginning to emerge.

Once this voice of the new you is heard, you will need to protect it as a parent should protect a vulnerable child. In a way, this is a vulnerable child because the wounded child that you reclaimed in Step 7 is now growing up and feeling strong enough to venture into the real world. When someone tries to invalidate you or expects you to behave in the old passive or aggressive or maladaptive ways, you can assert your new identity and not allow this new part to be oppressed anymore.

Leigh Anne

O ne of the ways that I have sought to express my independence from my family was to change my name. Being different was always a big deal to me because I always felt my family tried to crush my individuality. So when I became a teenager, I changed the spelling of my name to symbolically show that I was becoming my own person. Recently I've adopted another name that I am beginning to use at the age of thirty-seven. I prefer Leigh Anne. That name feels more like me. It was a name that just flowed out of me and felt right. I think that you need to have a name that feels like your own. And my name was something that my parents gave me. It never felt like mine. In fact, my whole life never felt like mine. The true "me" really felt nameless. And being nameless is the worst thing that can happen to an abused kid — you're afraid to speak, afraid to express yourself and who you really are. So I think that's the reason why the name thing became so important to me. I love Leigh Anne. I feel like it's a little bit of my father—the good part anyway—whose name was Larry, and it's a lot of my grandmother who I dearly love. Her name is Anne. She's the only one in my family who gave me total unconditional love and I wanted to have that represented in my name also. Leigh Anne just sounds like me now. Taking a new name is a sign that I am changing, resolving and letting go of the past and being who I want to be.

♦

SELF-HELP

1. If assertiveness is a problem for you, now is the time to do something about it because you have a lot at stake—the beginning of the new you. People will expect you to be the same old person and may treat you accordingly. Therefore, it is necessary to learn some new skills that will help support the new you. Reading a book on assertiveness training or taking a brief class will give you strategies and encouragement, enabling you to put these new behaviors into practice. The rewards may be immediate: When you start behaving from a position of equality or strength, the world has a way of noticing.

2. Have a friend take a new photograph of you to document your emerging sense of self. Arrange the pose so that the camera is shooting slightly up to you, from an angle that captures your best features. After years of your old self being on the bottom, this picture is going to put you on top. As the picture is taken, try to imagine communicating your new sense of yourself to the camera. Take several shots and experiment with the feelings you want to convey. Choose the picture that expresses this new-found strength and frame it. Put it on your desk or your wall in the bedroom. If a picture is worth a thousand words, then this picture will capture your changes made during the first twelve steps of recovery.

PROFESSIONAL HELP

1. Take some time in your sessions to discuss the progress you have made this far in therapy. Discuss how you feel different than when you first started. What have you accomplished and what remains to be addressed? How is your life better now than before? What does your therapist say about your efforts to date? Are there any areas in your therapy or your relationship with your therapist that you are uncomfortable with or see as a problem? Can you discuss them with your therapist?
2. Not everyone will need to change their name to allow their new sense of self to emerge. Names have important and interesting meanings to people. When a name has a negative significance or meaning it can become psychologically burdensome to someone trying to develop beyond the abuse. Discuss what your name means to you with your therapist to see how comfortable you are with it. Maybe you can find a new meaning or association to it that can help you feel like it represents the new you.

STEP 14

I can control my abusive behavior and find healthy outlets for my aggression.

This step is significant because it represents that fork in the road referred to in previous chapters. Similar to Step 6, in that anger and aggressive or abusive behavior are intricately connected, this step focuses on mastering your control over abusive behavior and relying on tried and true methods for safely discharging aggression. Many survivors, especially men, get stuck at this step because their aggression has such a firm hold on them. Anger may be a natural emotional response to your child abuse, but aggression and abusive behavior directed at others is a repetition of your past and needs to be managed carefully to avoid hurting yourself or someone else. Becoming an abuser would obviously set back your recovery, because in so doing, you would be working against the compassion you are developing for yourself as a child victim. Remember that the feeling of anger doesn't have to find expression in aggressive or abusive behavior.

Aggression is both learned and a product of physiological factors, mostly hormonal. Social roles permit males to express more aggression than females and male survivors are, therefore, more likely to engage in abusive behavior than women. Boys learn aggressive responses to conflict situations very early, which is then reinforced by athletics, military training, and popular culture. If the father is the abuser in the family, boys may be more likely to identify with him because they are the same sex. In actuality, testosterone—the male hormone—may be the biggest culprit in men's aggressive behavior. But what can you do about it? You can't change the hormones in your body, but you can learn some techniques and strategies for controlling this behavior.

Richard

I think of the therapy process as one where you and your guide go into a dark tunnel and shine light where there once was only darkness. Then you try to locate the many time bombs left over from the war and ever so carefully begin to defuse the bombs by tracing all the wiring back to its energy source. Ironically, by locating that connection, you can sever that connection, thereby reducing much of the destructive force of the bomb. But a bomb is still a bomb and it must be treated carefully, even though the danger of instant detonation may have passed. Then you have to neutralize the bomb by gradually draining out its explosive material. This was the longest part of therapy for me— several years in fact—just kind of draining this anger out. Not to switch metaphors, but I felt like a big pustule—full of this angry pus. My therapist's role was sort of being a catalyst for that anger. He would help me bring it to the surface where it could be discharged safely. I'd come in with a tremendous self-loathing—what we call this very harsh inner voice—which was brutal. Then we would gradually take that self-directed hatred and learn to express it verbally. What would happen is that all this anger and hatred came out like a wet firecracker. It's not as large as it feels once you express it. Before you get to it, it's like this incredible dark nightmare and you don't want to spew it out because you're afraid you will become like *The Exorcist*: Your therapist will just fly out the window, the victim of this incredible cosmic rage. Instead it comes out more like a prolonged crackle and hiss.

◆

Self-Help

1. Despite what may have happened to you as child, you are always responsible for your actions as an adult, just as your parents are responsible for what they did to you years ago. Some survivors harbor murderous fantasies about getting revenge or punishing their abusers for what they did. Having these thoughts are one thing, but once you begin to think about putting these thoughts into action you are entering dangerous territory and I suggest you speak to someone about it. Be advised that the courts have dealt with such acts of revenge by adult survivors or battered spouses by finding them guilty and sentencing them to jail.

2. You have a very good reason to be angry. You need to be able to separate your right to have these feelings with your right to act on them. By expressing your feelings *with* people you trust, as opposed to acting out these feelings *against* the abuser, you can dissipate this buildup of aggression without becoming another abuser. For men who are inclined to aggression and violence, this may be one of the most important steps of recovery—and the most difficult to achieve.

3. Make a list of the situations where you lose control of your aggressive behavior. What seems to be the determining factor in losing control? What feelings tend to trigger the abusiveness the most? What do you hope to accomplish by reacting aggressively? Does it work? How do you think the person at whom you are directing your aggression feels? Do you feel optimistic about being able to control this part of you or do you feel hopelessly outmanned? What external factors might be related to losing control—alcohol or drugs? What are your healthiest options for controlling your frustrations and coping with stress? See if you can't find ways of applying them to the typical situations where you lose control.

4. If you are having a very difficult time learning how to control abusive and aggressive behavior, think about joining a group such as Parents Anonymous or Parents United, or take a class in parent effectiveness training or nonviolent alternatives to behavior given at many community colleges. Learning how to short circuit your aggressiveness will take hard work, new in-

formation, and strategies that may need to be tailored to your individual needs and difficulties. Practicing these new behaviors will be essential to incorporating them into your behavioral repertoire.

PROFESSIONAL HELP

1. What kind of aggressive/hostile feelings get stirred up in your therapy sessions? What seems to trigger them? Have you discussed this with your therapist? This is a legitimate topic for your therapy and your therapist should be able to help you without withdrawing her support from you.
2. Be aware that your therapist is bound by law to warn potential victims of any violent intentions you may have, as well as the police. In such a case, confidentiality is broken as the therapist is expected to act to protect both you and your intended victim. You may initially think of this as a betrayal of your confidential relationship, but that is the law and your therapist will not want to support violent actions under any circumstances.

Chapter Fourteen

STAGE THREE
*R*ECOVERY:
STEPS 15 TO 21

Stage Three asks you to build on the gains you have made in the first two stages by putting into action the new behaviors, skills, and attitudes that reflect your newfound psychological health. No longer keyed to defensive reactions to the world, you are now enlivened by the opportunities in life: love, work, parenting, and playing. Integrating the changes into your personality and practicing the new behaviors in your everyday life will result in a new confidence in your emerging sense of self. This is the stage where you will learn to take healthy risks that actually favor you, paying off in some new and positive way. As a result, Stage Three can be a very exciting time because you will finally see the fruits of your labors as you learn to enjoy asserting control of your life.

This stage will ask you to resolve the abuse once and for all by coming to a decision about confronting your parents. Out of this decision and any subsequent contact with your family will flow a revised understanding of why you were abused. Having this new belief system and holding it inside will allow you to let go of the abuse and go beyond to new expressions of your individuality. You will no longer feel comfortable with merely surviving: You will aspire to thrive. Go forward with optimism: Only seven steps remain before your new beginning.

STEP 15

I am strengthening the healthy parts of myself while reducing maladaptive patterns and behaviors

Congratulations—you are now in the home stretch with much of the hard work behind you. This first step of Stage Three recovery continues the process of building up the healthy, adaptive parts of you that developed during childhood and later on during the first two stages of recovery. Your task now is to begin to consolidate, organize, and ultimately integrate these healthy parts into a more positive sense of self—self-image, self-concept, and self-esteem. As you refine this sense of self, you will discover a more flexible, balanced, and adaptive capacity that affects your thinking, your emotions, and your actions—personal strengths that you could live with on a permanent basis!

While strengthening the healthy parts, you will also need to continue to resolve the feelings left from the past, especially those that make you susceptible to resuming old destructive behaviors. You have probably noticed how long these feelings related to the abuse last. Certain situations can still evoke them, although you probably have more resources—internal as well as interpersonal—to deal with them now. Self-sabotage should be an infrequent occurrence by now as your self-awareness catches old tendencies before you can commit them to action. Likewise, aggression is now more easily controlled as you have implemented new skills and learned to avoid or defuse old trigger situations.

Pete

After a few years of therapy, I got to the point where I could see I was moving beyond my parents' limitations. Some parts of them, I could hold on to, such as my dad's sensitivity and my mom's firmness. But most others I have had to create for myself. I can see that I've made progress. I have been able to change my stubbornness into some determination or perserverance, which is really vital in my work and recovery. I work hard and really try to be fair with my customers and it really has started to pay off. I don't do things impulsively as much anymore. I have learned to stop, listen to myself, and think about my options before acting. I am better able to ask my wife for help without judging myself as weak. It's still hard for me to let go of my anger because I still mix it up with giving away my power. One of the big carry-overs from the past that I'm still working on is that I can easily feel betrayed and my reaction to it is usually exaggerated. My wife and I still get into these power struggles. The two big factors here are trust and intimacy. I have a big transference from my feelings about my mom to my wife. Just recognizing it helps to interrupt this merry-go-round. I know that I have to stop it or otherwise it just divides us. So we talk bout the roles we play—I'm the parental one and she's the rebellious one—and what we need to do to break the cycle. I usually have to first apologize and tell her that I felt betrayed or angry by what she did. Sometimes we go to another part of the house for a brief time to calm down and then to talk about it a little bit later. This really works but I must say that the relationship problems are the most entrenched for me.

◆

SELF-HELP

1. In your journal, describe all of the healthy parts of yourself that you want to acknowledge and strengthen over time as well as those tendencies and behaviors from the past that still plague your life today as an adult. Refine your awareness of how these parts play themselves out in your life and what you can do to emphasize some while diminishing others.

2. What novels, magazine profiles, or movies have you seen of characters or people in real life that possess a particular personality trait or way about them that captures some emerging part of you? Write about the similarities or the qualities that you find so appealing.

3. This is a good time to take on roles in your life that will evoke these newly developing healthy parts. Consider becoming a secretary at self-help meetings or signing on for a special committee project at work. If you are a parent, join the Parent-Teachers Association (PTA) or the Boy Scouts or Girl Scouts as a volunteer or leader.

PROFESSIONAL HELP

1. If problems persist in your intimate relationships, this may be the time to consider entering couple's therapy. With all of the changes you have already made, you may greatly benefit from

seeing a couple's therapist, even for a brief period. At this stage, many interpersonal problems are more habitual and reflexive, which can be readily changed with the help of a good referee. Review chapter 11 for more information about couple's therapy.

2. If sexual problems persist, read the helpful book *Incest and Sexuality* listed in Appendix A to give yourself more information about the goals and methods of sex therapy. You can also consider seeing a specialist in sex therapy to resolve the old associations and fears that may have become habitual. Some survivors give up when they reach this last stage because there are so many other positives to fill their lives now. Why limit yourself and your spouse or lover in this area? You can reclaim your sexuality for yourself just as you reclaimed your childhood.

3. Review thoroughly with your therapist your behavior in any new situations that challenges you to draw from the changes you have made. Use the discussion of these situations to carefully pinpoint where you were successful in implementing your changes and where you may have faltered. Look for new situations where you can give it a second chance.

STEP 16

I am entitled to take the initiative in sharing life's riches.

This step resolves the old tendency that many survivors have in not feeling entitled and deserving of the good things in life: success, financial reward, achievement, even luck. Lack of entitlement makes it hard for survivors to bring prosperity into their lives. Prosperity is not limited to financial rewards or material possessions. Prosperity is a state of mind that recognizes your needs, desires, and dreams for a life that bestows emotional and spiritual riches as well as material riches. You know by now how much of this attitude of lack of entitlement is related to the abuse. Nevertheless, knowing you deserve your fair share and feeling it are quite different, to say nothing of enjoying and celebrating it, which is the most fun. This step requires a wholesale change in thought, feeling, and behavior about your terms for success and achievement. This is the step to practice challenging the old attitudes by learning to take healthy risks that offer a better-than-even chance of success.

Taking initiative is a critical step because you are saying that you know something and have something to offer, that you stand behind your actions. You must be feeling stronger and equal to others to be able to push forward with your ideas. You may be asked to lead others, a request that may seem like more of the same to yesterday's caretakers.

For others, being put in a position of authority can be uncomfortable to someone used to being on the bottom. To step away from responsibility, authority, and power is to deny yourself and your talents their full expression, to say nothing of the financial rewards and sense of accomplishment. If you have resolved the previous steps, you are ready to undertake this newest challenge.

Richard

A big step for me was beginning to work part-time for Jim, my next door neighbor, who started this company doing environmental impact studies. For the first time in my life someone I worked for was incredibly positive about me: "God, you're really valuable, really talented," and "Do this and do that. Fix this. Find out about this. Buy that." He really trusted and believed in me. He needed a lot of help with all the work, which was exciting because I had never met anyone who could make things happen like that. His energy and belief in himself was almost contagious. So here I was working in this healthy environment and was valued for being something other than a slave laborer and that was a real awakening. I told myself, "It's not that bad out there, you can get a good idea, develop a good service, and make some money in the bargain." Then Jim offered me a full-time job working for him. It was the moment of truth because I already had this stable job that was going well for me. The old doubts resurfaced about being able to succeed. I talked it out in my therapy and decided to take a leap of faith in myself. So I took it and Jim kept giving me more and more responsibility and more money and more faith. I just kept trying to do the best I possibly could and he was so appreciative. It was really amazing. I felt indispensable. It was like I was growing another part of my self.

◆

SELF-HELP

1. How can you take initiative that would benefit your life? Going for a job promotion, buying a house, going back to school, joining an organization or a church, opening a retirement account are among the million ways that you can help yourself. Remember the basis for taking initiative is feeling entitled to success and prosperity, which grows from within. But eventually you have to put that internal belief in yourself into practice by mak-

ing your move when the time is right. Like Richard, you may be very glad you did.

2. Take a look at yourself in the mirror. Does your appearance reflect this new initiative you feel? Many survivors begin making cosmetic changes to their appearance in the last stage of recovery to reflect their new feelings about themselves. Your self-esteem, long suppressed by the burden of shame, may also be clamoring for a voice in your image to the world. Image and appearance are important in this society, although some people tend to overdo it. And looking good on the outside can go along with feeling good on the inside. Altering your wardrobe, getting a more stylish haircut, or working yourself back into shape are all ways to take initiative in your presentation to the world.

PROFESSIONAL HELP

1. Explore with your therapist how you can take initiative to make your material or personal life better. If problems remain in realizing your goals, try to clarify what seems to hold you back. You may still be struggling with an inner sense of not feeling entitled to success. Go back to Step 9, 10, or 12 and see if you can't find the source of your resistance to success.

STEP 17

I am acquiring the interpersonal skills to adopt new behaviors at home and at work.

This step builds on the tasks of previous steps in challenging you to learn new interpersonal skills to replace the old behaviors. Many survivors never learned the basic skills that are normally taught in a well-functioning, healthy family. You may still be playing catch-up when trying to relate to others in competitive or even cooperative situations at work. Assertiveness, listening, communication, decision making, negotiation, conflict resolution, and leadership skills are just some of the many skills that survivors may need before they can relate more effectively with others at work. Because you didn't acquire these skills in your biological family, you will now have to learn them and then adopt these behaviors as your own. Having these skills available to you as you face the challenges of the future can make each day a little easier and are more likely to produce positive results. With positive results comes more self-confidence in your abilities. Other areas in the more personal realm like parenting, sexuality, and intimacy are also needed to create prosperous relationships at home. Education and skill building are the tools you need to make those dreams a reality.

Susan

I have always been a great believer in taking workshops and seminars and upgrading my computer skills. Of course, in my business, you just don't get ahead if you don't learn the new word processing systems—now its called desktop publishing. They have really helped me get ahead. I've taken classes in time management and stress management. I took this one seminar called "The Human Insult: How to Give It and How to Take It," which was a joke title but very effective in teaching conflict resolution skills with co-workers. I really needed that because now I'm in a supervisory position and responsible for managing other people. I tended to excuse people for things they would do and then sit on my resentment for a few weeks until I slowly killed them with my icicle daggers. They eventually got the message, but it wasn't the best way to deal with it. I learned how to do it differently and it has really helped my job. But I don't do all this just for my business skills; I take a lot of workshops to learn new ways of handling my personal life. The first seminar that made a big impact on my life was called "Women, Sex and Power" and that title really says it all. How to be a woman while taking the power to run your life effectively and successfully. My mother never encouraged us to reach for what we wanted. She was always too concerned with being out of her league. So I have had to resolve this in my therapy and then learn how to be successful in the world. And it really works!

◆

SELF-HELP

1. What skills or knowledge do you still need to realize your life ambitions? How can you go about getting these needs met? Does your company provide for any of these development goals? Have you ever thought of returning to school to get the degree that you once felt was beyond you?
2. There are many books that provide an easy introduction to the type of skill building that you may need. Start by reading these books to get some background information on what your next step in educating yourself might be. Look for them in a good trade book store.

3. Check with your local community college or university extension division for workshops and courses on the topics that you have targeted for yourself.

PROFESSIONAL HELP

1. If you are still unclear about your career interests or goals, consider meeting with a career counselor who may use vocational interest and personality tests to help you narrow down your career and job preferences. Many survivors change jobs and careers as they work through their recovery and find a calling that suits their personality more. Is this you?
2. You can always discuss career options and ideas with your therapist who will be able to help you identify and prioritize your interests and learn how to go about realizing your objectives. Since values, interests, and job preferences are so connected to your identity and personality, it may have taken this long for you to recognize what you like doing and how you like to work.

STEP 18

I have resolved the abuse with my parents or offenders to the extent that it is acceptable for me.

This step involves making a decision about resolving the differences left over from your child abuse with those who abused you or failed to protect you—your parents. The focus of this step and the question many survivors have about confronting their parents with the abuse will be addressed in depth in chapter 15. The important task in this step is to resolve the abuse with your family in a way that is acceptable to you. You have the right to choose how to do this. It is not mandatory to confront your parents or family, although many survivors find value in doing so if they are fully prepared for whatever response or consequence may result. Many of you will need to do something if you want to maintain a relationship with your parents without hiding your efforts to overcome the abuse or denying your new identity as a recovered survivor. They will need to accept you as you now desire to be accepted: with respect, consideration, and hopefully, with an acknowledgment of the burdens you have surmounted.

Recognize that since you are dealing with other people who may have never faced or changed their own abusive behavior, any sense of resolution will be dependent on how far they can go in acknowledging the abuse with you. For this reason, there is a wide range of possible resolutions that ultimately will determine whether you can still have some kind of relationship with them. In some cases, they may not want to accept who you are now becoming, which raises the question of whether it will be healthy for you to have contact with them.

A big question that arises in this step has to do with the decision to forgive your parents or offender. In a sense, resolving the abuse means coming to terms with what was done to you and accepting the feelings you have toward the people who did it. Sometimes this means forgiveness, but not necessarily for everyone. For some people who were too sadistically abused, it may never be possible to forgive someone for what was done. Acceptance that it happened and a desire to put it behind you once and for all may be the only resolution that makes sense and feels right. Deciding to forgive or accept is your choice alone.

Pete

This recent trip back home had a magical quality about it. It was a long time coming, that's for sure. All those letters I wrote to my mom and hers back to me really provided the foundation for a sense of resolution that is probably the only realistic possibility she and I will ever have. A lot of different pieces of the puzzle just slipped into place with this visit. I called her after we got in and she answered the phone drunk—no surprise there. So I just told her I didn't want to talk to her when she was drinking and asked when I could call her when I would find her sober. She started to deny it, but I quickly told her I would call tomorrow morning. The next day she called first and I said, "Listen, we want to see you. I want you to see the kids. But it's only going to happen if you're clean and sober. If I don't feel that you are, I'm going to decide to leave." This is something that I had worked out with my therapist before the visit because I knew she was still drinking and I didn't want to have my kids see her that way. So she agreed to these conditions and the next day we met for breakfast and fortunately she was sober. It turned out to be a wholesome hour with my mom—the way she could be at times when she wasn't drinking. She was in bad shape though—shaking and in physical pain. I think she might have a pill problem as well. Her skin was mottled and her teeth were in bad shape. She looked like an aging, broken-down alcoholic, which made me real sad. I didn't hate her anymore; I had pity for her, and at the end of the visit, I even felt close to her. As we were getting ready to leave, I told her I loved her and I gave her a hug and it felt real good— a wholesome expression of affection. I didn't feel violated or intruded upon and I thanked her for being sober. I told her that I know it was hard for her but that I have such bad memories of her drinking when

I was a kid. She said that she didn't want to hurt me, which felt good to hear, and we actually laughed a bit. When I got back to the car, I felt this outpouring of grief and I cried for half an hour or so. I just felt so much sadness about my mom and her plight in life, her alcoholism, what I didn't get, what happened to our family. And I realized that some glorious resolution wasn't in the cards for me and my mom—not with her still drinking. Our resolution would be bittersweet at best, but a resolution nonetheless.

◆

SELF-HELP

1. Read chapter 15 for a full accounting of all the issues involved in this complicated question.
2. Practice writing some letters to your parents or abusers in your journal and then reread them a few weeks later to develop your sense of what you may someday want to say to them. These letters are a working statement of your message to them, which may continue to evolve until you actually face them.

PROFESSIONAL HELP

1. Confronting your parents is one issue that will require the strong involvement of your therapist to help you sort out what you want to do and how you want to do it. Planning any kind of confrontation, meeting, or simple discussion with your parents about the abuse should include a complete airing of feelings, doubts, expectations, and hopes beforehand between you and your therapist. You will need the outside perspective of your therapist in order for you to make the best decision.
2. Sometimes it is helpful to invite your parents or family into your individual therapy for one or more sessions to discuss and work out selected conflicts with the help of your therapist. This is changing the format of your individual therapy temporarily, although you and your therapist would have an established alliance. If more extensive family work is needed or possible, it may be better to find a separate family therapist who could be more neutral than your individual therapist. Family therapy is not always advisable, nor is it always possible, depending on the circumstances and attitudes of your parents. Obviously, consideration of such a plan will start with your desire for it and your belief that it would be productive. Your therapist will also

have to be in agreement that it could offer benefits to you that would outweigh the possible detractions. Such an undertaking will require a lot of preliminary planning as to what you want to say, what your goals are, and how you will deal with potential challenges to your point of view. In general, this strategy is most likely to be successful when your parents have done some work on themselves or at least have admitted that they made a mistake.

3. Discuss with your therapist what you think and feel about the issue of forgiveness. Explore what feels right to you and your reasons for feeling that way. Be aware that feelings about forgiveness or any other symbol for resolution will shift and refine themselves over time.

STEP 19

I have developed my own meaning about the abuse that releases me from the legacy of the past.

This is the last step that focuses directly on your abuse, but it is nevertheless a critical step in this long process of putting the abuse behind you once and for all. After all your hard work on the previous eighteen steps, your last task is to arrive at your own philosophical understanding of why the abuse happened to you. After growing up thinking it had something to do with you, the person, it is now important to replace this meaning with an idea that rings true based on what you now know and who you now are during the last stage of recovery. In a sense, this step asks you to reflect on how and why things happen the way they do and what it means for the person who is caught up in events beyond her control. Your answer to this question will be highly individualized, just as the development of your new self will be. You may ask yourself about the nature of good and evil: why bad things happen to good people, in this case, innocent children. It may call into consideration your notions about God or it may reinforce your faith in a Higher Power. You need to organize your thoughts and feelings and information gathered during your recovery into a consistent and unified concept that you will stay with you for the rest of your life, and when old doubts arise, you can return to this question to explain once again for yourself what the abuse really meant. As such, it will become an anchor, something that will hold your new understanding in place, while buffeted by the inevitable challenges and opinions voiced by those around you.

Richard

So what does it all mean? Basically I was unlucky in the draw. That's about the extent of it, I guess. I don't have a real strong spiritual part that says, "This all happened for some divine reason." I had a parent who never received anywhere near enough stuff from her parents. Her own human and emotional capabilities didn't reach the level where they could be turned around and given back without causing her extreme deprivation. That was the basic problem with my mother—this howling void of emotional deprivation. My father really wasn't much better because he was never really there for me, and if he was, I imagine his limitations as a person would also leave me high and dry. I think I was lucky in terms of what their genes gave me but not in terms of them being wonderful, richly emotional and giving parents who validated the hell out of their kid. That just didn't happen. They are people who were into themselves and didn't have much for anyone else. For a child to be born into this family with the circumstances that were operating at that time was truly unfortunate for me, to say the least.

♦

SELF-HELP

1. This step will probably evolve within you as you proceed through the steps of recovery. But it is important to acknowledge what your final thoughts on this subject are. Write about it in your journal to develop your ideas further.
2. Raise the question in your self-help group and see how other people think about it. You may hear conceptualizations that capture a feeling you had but were unable to put into words. Continue to refine your thinking on this topic.
3. Have you had any dreams that might reflect this new level of resolution regarding the abuse? Often at major milestones in recovery you can have a dream that captures the essence of your achievement in a way that words cannot.

PROFESSIONAL HELP

1. Your therapist can be an important sounding board on this complicated and philosophical question. Remember that this step is about what you think about the meaning of the abuse, not what your therapist thinks. This can be among the most poignant

moments in your therapy as you finally settle into an acceptance of your past and share your feelings about it with someone without being ashamed or defensive.

STEP 20

I see myself not only as a survivor but as a thriver in all aspects of life: love, work, parenting, and play.

Your journey on the road to recovery is about over. You have gone beyond being a survivor of the abuse to a thriver—someone who finds joy and satisfaction in many aspects of life. By now you have created a new family or support system for yourself that breaks through the isolation and shame of the past. You can readily give of yourself to others while accepting nurturance and consideration in return. This is the step where your new self comes together and fuses into a personality that best expresses your essence in the world.

Intimate relationships are now infused with trust, sexual sharing, and mutual self-reliance. You can communicate your needs, allow mutual dependency, and resolve conflicts without the mind games of the past. Your new self-acceptance allows you to be less critical of others while your new self awareness helps you identify hurtful situations *before* they can do any damage. You can share your feelings with others appropriate to the situation without losing control of them.

By now you are able to avoid exploitive job situations and can stand up for your fair share of promotion opportunities. You no longer get mired in office politics or oppressed by bosses or authority figures. You can promote your career in a way that develops your interests and talents while accepting the financial and emotional rewards. If you find yourself facing a dead end in your career track, you can make the changes necessary to satisfy your new interests. Instead of your work life being a strain, you now feel challenged and satisfied by doing your job.

With your new sense of self comes a new identity as a loving, caring parent who accepts his child and raises the child to respect himself and others. You can build self-esteem by giving your child appropriate amounts of power and control while protecting him from harm by setting clear and consistent limits. You are able to discipline him by using the positives alive in your relationship with him and yet hold him accountable when he falls short of the family values. You need to acknowledge that your family's intergenerational chain of abuse stopped with you. You and your child are living testimony to this formidable achievement. You can continue to grow together into the future, allowing your relationship to mature into a seasoned, adult to adult friendship that can provide joy and affiliation for the rest of your lives.

Susan

Being in therapy enabled me to have more awareness of how I was parenting Sam. I learned how to catch myself when I was becoming my mother all over again—ignoring him, snapping at him, controlling him. I learned to back off and take a few minutes for myself in my room and sort out what I was feeling. Then I would go back and talk with Sam about what had happened. I let him know that it was sometimes hard for me to control myself when I got so mad. He could hear it and understand it and work with me on it. He is always relieved. We are a lot closer now and I know this has helped him trust me more. I'm really proud of him. After years of being an underacheiver at school, he recently has started to blossom and is now a leader both academically and socially at school. At home he has learned how to speak up and tell me when he doesn't think I'm treating him fairly. His therapist told me when we terminated his sessions that the reasons for Sam's positive change had a lot to do with the changes I had made as a parent. That made me feel proud of Sam and myself.

◆

Finally, your new self begins to express itself in one area that may have always been difficult—play. Play may be the most neglected area of expression, but now, with the confidence of thriving in other aspects of your life, you may be ready to explore this exciting domain. Hobbies, sports, creative arts, traveling, and music are just some of the many ways you can play as an adult. The ability to play not only keeps you involved with your inner child but also can be a shared experience with your children. Playing revives us and recharges out emotional batteries, improving our outlook on life and rewarding us for our hard work. Don't deprive yourself of this important element of life. Find new ways of playing that fill you up inside and fuel your new love affair with life.

Many survivors wonder how they will know when recovery has been completed. That moment is very personal and may or may not be related to some external event in your life. It is the moment when the healing on the inside and the change on the outside merge into a unified sense of self and accomplishment in the world. This moment may be a mystical experience when you feel at one with the world, or it may be the moment when you realize you have attained some achievement that symbolizes success. It will be different things to different people. You will know it when you feel it.

Pete

It took a long time, but after several years of working on myself, I'm almost finished. I never used to think I could do it. I so wanted to be a healthy person and have a healthy life—everything that my family was not. You struggle to face the past, you endure the pain, you get the help you need to heal yourself. Then one day you have the opportunity to do something that truly represents health and success. You finally get the rewards that recovery has always promised. For me it was being able to buy a house. Having my own house has always been my dream but there were so many things in the way of it. I needed a good job to make enough money and I needed to get to the point where I believed I deserved it. I remember being so anxious the day escrow closed. I thought some evil power was going to snap it away from me at the last moment. But I survived that day just as I have survived so many other challenges. The day we moved in, I just cried. I knew I had done it.

◆

SELF-HELP

1. Have a celebration or perform some personal ritual to formally mark your achievement in recovery. The possibilities abound for how to acknowledge this important rite of passage. You could bring together all of the people who have supported you in this endeavor and let them know what they have meant to you. You could take the vacation of your dreams to celebrate your hard work. If you are like Pete, you could have a housewarming party. Think of something that would reflect what your recovery has meant to you and find a way of expressing it that celebrates this enormous achievement and affirms the person who did it—you!

2. How long has it been since you marked the date of birth of your recovery? Go back and reread the entry in your journal marking this date. What feelings do you have reading your words that inaugurated your departure on the road to recovery? How many years ago was this? Was it worth it? Do you like where you are today relative to yesterday? Mark down today's date and acknowledge your reactions to coming to the end of recovery. What future directions would you like to explore now with your new self firmly in place?

3. If you are still in a self-help group, this may be the step where you reach out to others to share your recovery experiences and

encourage them with theirs. Being a sponsor for someone just entering recovery is a way to deepen your sense of resolution while supporting his efforts to heal and change. You can get involved with a community hotline that reaches out to parents at risk for abusing their children. You may be interested in running for the local school board to try your hand at social change by exercising a healthy expression of power and authority. All of these activities will affirm the changes you have made in recovery. Your horizon is as broad as you want to make it.

4. This is the last self-help step you will need in this recovery program. By Step 20, helping yourself will be almost second nature! Now you can do this for yourself.

PROFESSIONAL HELP

1. By this step, you are probably thinking about terminating your therapy. The idea of being on your own may raise all sorts of feelings of self-doubt, insecurity, and possibly even loss. Don't worry: This is normal, even at the lofty height of Step 21! Reread chapter 11 to review how to terminate in the best possible way. You have greatly benefitted from this most unusual professional relationship and the idea of not having it available may be difficult to accept. You may have grown really fond of your therapist who has become so much more than the person who listens to your problems. Many survivors prefer a gradual reduction in sessions over an extended period of time with yearly check-in sessions to reinforce all the positive changes they have introduced into their lives. Survivors often have a resurfacing of old feelings and reactions during the major milestones of life and want to return to therapy for a brief time to further resolve or deepen their changes. In most cases, this will be possible. Again, as I've said so many times, discuss it with your therapist and negotiate an acceptable agreement.

STEP 21

I am resolved in the reunion of my new self and my eternal soul.

Step 21 represents the last step of this recovery model—a step that not everyone necessarily reaches. It is the step that we all strive for as we continue in our lives. If you keep working on your recovery beyond what you need to survive the world or even thrive in it, you can reach a state of self-acceptance and satisfaction that registers a unique synchrony between the soul—your spiritual essence—and your new self born of your hard work in recovery. Bringing your new self in sync with the aspirations of your soul is the ultimate step because it allows you to express your essence as a person in your daily life, in perfect harmony with your conscious, unconscious, and spiritual essences.

Shirley

I think I would have gone on for years without realizing to what extent my childhood affected me. I was once so good at denial. And I think a lot of people who have experienced the kind of traumatic childhood I had, never imagined how devastated we were as children and how deeply affected we were as adults. I probably could have gone on longer being ill, killing myself at my job, trying to be superwoman—I could have gone on longer—but I would have died an early death. The quality of my life today is so rich because I have chosen to face the past. It's not easy. It takes a tremendous amount of work, courage, and determination to stick with it. I tell people to hang in there when the going gets rough: Reach out to others and hold on for dear life. The end result is something so much richer. I have a satisfying life with an abundance of possibilities and opportunities in front of me—things that I never would have known about, explored, or considered. People who were abused need to hear this message: If you want to instill hope, believe that change is truly possible.

Chapter Fifteen

CONFRONTING
Your PARENTS WITH
THE ABUSE

There may come a time when you want to confront your parents or your abuser with what they did to you as a child. Disclosing the abuse and sharing your story with friends and loved ones may not have lessened the righteous indignation you still feel even after working through the steps of recovery. You may have any number of reasons to confront your abuser: to express your outrage, to seek revenge, to challenge the family denial and secrecy, or to relieve yourself of your own burden of shame. Some survivors confront their families to demand financial support to pay for the costs of an extended therapy while others simply hope the abusers will acknowledge what they did. Confronting your family may represent some therapeutic goal considered important by you and your therapist. Finally, as many survivors have discovered, you may not have been the only one abused in your family. A more public confrontation with the abuser may be the only way you can intervene to protect a younger sibling from being abused.

Realistically speaking, the idea of confronting your abuser, whether it was a parent, sibling, or someone outside the family, is a controversial one and deserves careful consideration. It is certainly not imperative to confront your abuser or your family in order to heal from the abuse. Such a decision is not right for everyone. But if you decide that you are strong enough in your recovery and prepared for any response or consequence that may result, it may be therapeutic and help you to go forward with your life.

In cases where you were abused by someone outside of your family with whom you no longer have contact, the issue of confrontation is very different than when the abuse occurred within your immediate or extended family. The abuser may no longer be available to you and will likely have far less motivation to hear you out than a family member. Confronting such an offender poses particular dangers, and in most cases, offers little chance for a positive outcome. If you are steadfast in your desire to confront this type of offender, it may be best to focus your energies on reporting him or her to the county child protective services agency where he or she resides, or consult an attorney about the possibility of filing a personal injury lawsuit. The statute of limitations for child abuse cases is being challenged in the courts right now, which means you may still have some legal recourse even if it has been years since the abuse was perpetrated. If you happen to know that your offender is still in contact with children, making a report to the child protection authorities is appropriate because your action may protect other children. Because intrafamilial abuse usually has greater impact, this chapter will focus on confronting your parents or family.

Since child abuse has so much to do with power and control, and survivors generally have a hard time with self-esteem and self-protection, the idea of confronting your abuser can make sense especially if it can rectify, symbolically at least, the imbalances of the past. Confronting your family can be one of the most meaningful experiences a survivor can have during recovery or it can be one of the most destructive. If the abuser was a parent, you may not have given up on mending the rift that the abuse created, hoping you can maintain some kind of relationship with your family. Using your adult faculties, you can marshall the facts about the abuse and demand some kind of accountability that was never possible when you were a child. When the abuser accepts responsibility and apologizes for what he or she did, even offering to pay for therapy, the survivor often feels vindicated from the abuse and experiences a rush of empowerment, validation, and self-acceptance. Out of the successful confrontation can grow a different way of relating to and being treated by your family. It can truly become a turning point in your recovery, if not your life.

If you decide that it would be beneficial to challenge your abuser, the next question concerns the mechanics of the confrontation—the timing, the strategy, the various methods available, and the likely outcomes. The options available on addressing your abuse with your parents or family are both varied and personal. Besides confronting your parent through the aforementioned civil lawsuits that ask for financial compensation for damages incurred during your abusive childhood, there are a range of other, less extreme measures you can also consider. At the other end of the spectrum, many survivors take a more personal approach and seek to challenge the abuser's past actions by confronting him or her on the telephone, or through a series of letters, or in planned family meetings with or without the presence of a therapist.

Whatever you decide, you will need to be prepared for any possible reaction from your family. What you don't want under any circumstances is to have the confrontation be a replay of your abuse. In simple terms, if the potential benefits of the confrontation do not clearly outweigh the possible drawbacks, then you must seriously ask yourself why you are doing it. Consider the issues and dilemmas highlighted in this chapter before going ahead with a plan to confront your parents.

POTENTIAL TRAPS AND PITFALLS

The biggest risk in undertaking either a direct or indirect confrontation is that the abuser's response will undermine your own recovery. Usually this happens when the timing of the confrontation is premature—when you are not fully prepared for all possible reactions. Many abusive families will still be in denial about what was done and their disavowals about the abuse may shatter your own newly formed understanding of the past. In this way, the confrontation may become another repetition of your parents' invalidation of your experience and raise the specter of your buying into the old family myth again—the myth that holds you responsible for what your parents did to you. This would be truly tragic after all the work you have done to reconstruct the past and to build an understanding of yourself and how the abuse affected you.

There are some situations where confrontation may actually be a bad or even dangerous idea. Families that have the potential for violence or retaliation may be better off left alone. Not all abusers are emotionally capable of taking responsibility for their past actions and will resort to their old methods of blaming the victim, manipulating others to support them, or when totally desperate, behaving abusively once again. Clearly, anything that could put you or someone else in physical or psychological danger is not a good idea, however compelling the urge to confront may be. In some cases, survivors have felt a renewed sense of guilt and responsibility for the abuse, which can trigger the old self-destructive behaviors and feelings. In families with aged or ill parents, confronting them with the past may trigger a medical crisis or precipitate a breakup of the family. While you need not take responsibility for other peoples' problems, it is important that you consider whether you could emotionally handle such a negative outcome. Although you are in recovery, the old shame and self-blaming dies hard, especially when it comes to dealing with your family.

THE VALUE OF SEPARATIONS

The theme of separations—temporary or permanent—from your family of origin figures prominently in the recovery process and needs to be fully understood for the adult survivor to use it therapeutically. If your parents or family have not significantly changed in their attitude or treatment of you, then what was true during childhood may still prevail to some degree in adulthood. Consequently during the first two stages of recovery when you are developing your own thinking about the abuse and forging your new sense of self, it may help to control, restrict, and in some instances, temporarily sever contact with parents or family members who may impede your recovery. Many survivors go through a period when being on their own outside of their family's range of influence has helped them to see things more clearly and objectively, without the old pressures to perceive and distort reality in ways that favor your parents—and disfavor you.

Pete

I felt like I had to pull back from my mother for a number of reasons. First of all, she is still an active alcoholic and I am a recovering alcoholic. Being around people who are drinking alcoholically is just not good for me and my mother is no exception. Second, whenever I am with her, she has a way of making me feel that directly or indirectly I'm responsible for taking care of her needs. This was the trap that I was in as her son, and even though I can see it now, I am still susceptible to feeling guilty for not being responsible for her. She also treats me in a way that I am made to feel more important than I should be. This goes right back to the incest—it's not wholesome and it's inappropriate. Not being in direct contact with her over the past few years has set a safe boundary for me that has given me strength to discover who I am as a person—separate from her.

◆

Using separations not only allows you to protect yourself from your parents' abusive treatment but also gives you more power and control in dealing with them. If they do something that is upsetting or abusive to you, and will not try to resolve it with words, then staying in contact with them becomes another form of abuse—self-abuse. Separations can be a powerful message to parents, which say, in effect "There are some minimum conditions for our contact. If you do not wish to honor these then that tells me that it is healthier for me to be apart from you." As you have learned only too well, actions speak louder than words in abusive families. If your family still will not listen to you, you may need to communicate in a way they can understand.

Separations should be accompanied with a message explaining why you are withdrawing from them and what needs to change in order for you to resume contact. For some survivors these conditions may rest on being able to talk about what happened, or receiving a formal apology from the parents or maybe just some acknowledgment that the abuse occurred. As you go through recovery, these needs may change as you get stronger and more confident in how you feel and who you are as a person. Consequently there may be less of a need for a total "no-contact rule" as the issues between you and your family get resolved.

FEELING GUILTY
FOR TAKING CARE OF YOURSELF

One way the effects of abuse can still undermine your needs during the course of recovery is to feel guilty for doing what you need to protect yourself from your family or to heal from the abuse. Since you rarely came first in your family, it is a major step forward for you to put yourself first for once. Your family may revert to their old attitudes that the parents should come first and may attempt to instill guilt in you. Remember that as a family member you have every right to speak your mind and ask others to join in challenging the unhealthy family patterns. If your parents don't like what you are doing, they can tell you and you will listen to them. If they don't want to participate in a family meeting where the abuse will be discussed, that is their choice. But you too have rights and one of your basic rights is to talk about what happened in the past in a way that will help you heal. If the guilt and shame resurfaces, discuss it with your therapist. Don't fall behind your parents' misguided wishes.

USING THERAPISTS
TO TROUBLESHOOT MOTIVATIONS

One of the best ways to protect yourself from making a bad decision about confronting your parents is to thoroughly explore all the issues with your therapist. Some therapists are uniformly against such confrontations because it may take the focus away from resolving the conflicts within yourself. However, among therapists who work with adult survivors, there is an appreciation of the possible benefits of confrontation when the timing and planning are carefully thought out and deemed constructive. Remember that it is always your decision on how to proceed with your recovery, but it can never hurt to listen to a trained professional's point of view, especially if you are about to do something that might not be in your best interests.

Therapists may be more helpful in understanding what is best for you than members of your support group because the therapist's only goal is to help you recover from the effects of the abuse, unlike fellow survivors who may be looking to justify their own decision on the matter. In the same vein, some self-help groups that routinely encourage you to forgive your parents before you fully explore your feelings about the abuse will be against any kind of confrontation. Their ideology may not take into account your personal needs and situation and may fail to understand the complex issues that recovery from child abuse evokes.

How can you use your therapy to sort out what is best for you? For starters, review the following Journal Questions to explore any thoughts, feelings, motivations, and apprehensions about undertaking such a confrontation. Let the questions stimulate other questions and concerns. How have you felt when you disclosed the abuse to someone you trust? What feelings did you recognize in anticipation of their response? How do you think you might feel when confronting your parents? You will need to be aware of how your family typically deals with conflict. Are they likely to get violent? Or do they passively withdraw from each other? Is their denial still incredibly strong or will they be more likely to listen and then avoid the subject in the future?

You will also need to have resolved many of the feelings left over from the abuse. The rage that so many survivors feel during the early stages of recovery will have to be discharged before you will be able to face your parents with calm but forceful determination. You will need to have resolved the feelings of personal responsibility for what your parents did as well as your feelings of guilt and shame that may still incriminate you in your mind. Any misgivings about what you did to cope or about having a sense of complicity, including your guilt about feeling pleasure (in the case of sexual abuse) or acknowledging other gratifying aspects of the abuse, will need to be worked through. Finally you will need to be at a place in Stage Three of recovery where you have acquired sufficient self-esteem and psychological defenses to protect you from virtually any reaction your parents might have. Fantasy expectations will need to be replaced by realistic expectations in terms of how your parents will be capable of responding. In short, there is much work that needs to be accomplished in therapy before confrontation should be considered. You will get there eventually; just be patient and trust your recovery process.

Confronting your family is part of a strategy of externalizing power to change the fundamentals of your life: the way you conduct yourself at work, how you negotiate in your best interests, how you let people treat you, and what you expect to get out of your personal relationships. In essence, you will have to have changed from the inside before you will be ready to change on the outside. In some cases, confronting your family may need to be delayed until recovery is almost completed, with the confrontation representing the icing on the cake—in effect, highlighting the body of work that you have already created. In the majority of cases I have seen, the negative outcomes have occurred more frequently when the confrontation was premature, not when it was delayed.

Journal Questions

1. *What past attempts, if any, have you made to address the abuse with your family, and how did they turn out?*

2. *Who in your family do you think will be the most open to hearing what you have to say?*

3. *Do you suspect that anyone else in your family might have been abused? If so, what reaction would you expect them to have if you asked them about it directly?*

4. *What are your reasons and motivations for confronting your family with the abuse?*

5. *What do you hope to get out of it?*

6. *How do you want your abuser to react to you?*

7. *Based on what you know about your parent or abuser, how would you expect this person to react to your confrontation?*

8. *What specific outcome, if any, would make you regret your decision to confront your abuser?*

9. *In what type of situation do you imagine confronting your parents or abusers?*

10. *Have you thoroughly discussed the idea with a friend, therapist, sponsor, or other family member and prepared for any and all possible family reactions?*

STRATEGIES FOR CONFRONTING YOUR PARENTS

Basically there are two ways to proceed. The first, an indirect confrontation, requires no face-to-face contact with your abuser and is limited to phone calls, letters, and audiotape messages. This indirect strategy will provide you with some controls over the contact and protect you from possible negative responses or retaliation. Often the indirect method is preliminary to the direct method, which calls for face-to-face encounters with the abuser.

It is not even necessary to be in indirect contact with your parent or abuser to confront him in a meaningful way. Many survivors choose to confront their abuser through more symbolic means in psychotherapy or psychodrama groups and workshops. Therapy techniques such as the "empty chair" used by Gestalt therapists allow you to imagine your parent sitting in front of you while you deliver what you have to say. Psychodrama provides for a most dramatic experience in which the survivor selects group members to play the roles of the family members and the therapist "directs" the unfolding of the family drama using a loosely defined script. These techniques can either reenact an old situation of abuse, allowing for a different resolution, or can model the type of confrontation the survivor would like to have but for some reason—death of a parent for instance—is not possible.

Pete

Pete's experience in confronting his mother through letters about the incest illustrates many of the issues, considerations, and strategies, previously discussed. Pete's story also underscores the limitations that exist when dealing with a parent who has a long-standing drinking problem or who is still in denial over her role in the abuse. His story points out how much time it may take to allow a complete unfolding of issues and reactions. Like many survivors, Pete felt it necessary to temporarily sever contact with this mother because it was undermining his work in therapy. In Pete's case, the separation spanned several years during which time he went through the early stages of recovery before initiating limited contact through letters. As his letters will show, he and his mother embarked on a process characterized by anger, confrontation, denial, distortion, acknowledgment, and finally, a degree of resolution. Pete's letters are included here in their entirety. For privacy reasons, his mother's return letters have been paraphrased to give a sense of her reactions to his charges as well as the nature of their relationship.

◆

Pete's First Letter To His Mother

Mom,

I've started this letter many times in my head. The fact is until just now, I've been too scared to confront the issue about which I'm writing you. I want to preface this by saying that I've been in therapy for about four years dealing with the incest that happened between you and me. This letter is about the incest between us and what happened to me as a result.

I sought out professional help after my stay in the alcohol recovery program because I was in pain and was having self-destructive thoughts that were driving me crazy. Very slowly in therapy, I realized the obvious connection between the pain I was experiencing and our relationship when I was growing up. Just admitting and beginning to talk with another human being about the incest was very difficult. I slowly began to unravel the guilt and shame and self-hate and feeling of being evil and perverted and responsible for what went on between us.

As a result of my therapy, I now understand that as a 13-14-15-year-old boy, it wasn't my fault that sexual contact happened with you. You, as an adult and as my mother, had the responsibility to make sure what happened wouldn't happen. But it did. I really didn't accept this for a long while. I wanted to, but I wouldn't let myself. I thought special circumstances made me responsible. It was not until about one and a half years ago that I began to really believe that maybe I wasn't as sick and evil as I felt. As that shift in my thinking happened, all the self hate and guilt turned into rage and a deep, deep hurt. Since I began feeling this rage, I haven't wanted to speak with you. In fact, I have had a lot of anger at you for a long time, but I didn't know it. I had turned it on myself because I dared not be angry at you. I felt disloyal and guilty to feel anger and rage toward you.

Over the last year in therapy I've begun to accept that it is OK to be angry at you in light of all the circumstances of our relationship. In addition to incest I've come to see you were violent and physically abusive and took out your rage on me. I was terrified of you. You hurt me physically and emotionally with your rage. I've come to see that what I thought was normal discipline was not normal at all. Getting kicked in the rectum with a pointed shoe isn't appropriate. Having welts and bruises from whippings isn't healthy discipline. This is what you did to me.

I've come to see that our relationship was sick in many ways and that you were never able to accept me for who I was. You never respected my boundaries even as a young child and insisted that I be your "little man" or your personal possession and your refuge from the realities of your life. When I entered puberty, the stage was set. I was vulnerable to biological changes—hormones—that are part of puberty. Exposed to you in baby dolls pajamas or bra and panties was not appropriate. Because I was having sexual fantasies, this was another reason to indict and convict myself as sick. In fact there were intense sexual urges and fantasies as a result of our relationship. It was eventually played out with my inviting your masturbation which you willingly performed. I thought that it was totally my fault and that I was a pervert. I now understand that our relationship was probably seductive from the very beginning, although it was couched in mother/child closeness. The fact that you masturbated me and that it felt good has haunted me so terribly I can't tell you. I denied it ever happened for years until it came up in therapy. The incest created conflicts in me that have negatively controlled me—my self-esteem, my personhood, and my manhood. Those conflicts have created obstacles to healthy relationships of all kinds, particularly with women where intimacy, trust, and love are supposed to be natural and wholesome. With other people, I'm always ready to feel bad and wrong at every turn and to feel like I have to protect myself. I don't let much affection in.

I felt like I betrayed Dad—I ripped him off at a very deep level to have sexual contact with his wife. I also knew that mothers and sons do not engage in sexual activity normally and I felt ashamed and guilty and hateful of my sexuality and my sexual urges. I came to hate and despise myself completely on so many different levels.

When you asked me that Sunday morning if I came inside you because you couldn't remember and your period was late, I was totally mortified and repulsed—by your questions, by what was happening, and by myself. Unconsciously at that time, I vowed to stop it and I did. From that time on, for you to touch me in any way or to be affectionate became a reminder of a violation of morals so deep inside me that it made me sick. In a way from that time on, I wouldn't accept you as my mother. I have no word better than evil to describe the intensity of hate for myself that was created.

I am investing all that I am in becoming healthy and able to live in a sober and sane way. This issue has got to be confronted directly by

me to you as a part of growing and healing the conflicts. I have made
a firm decision that I'm not willing to have any kind of relationship
with you in light of the facts I've discussed and your continuing choice
to not accept recovery.

If there is any chance of reconciliation, it has to start with the truth
and as long as you are in denial, being in touch with you is a setup for
me to be hurt, angry, frustrated, and depressed. You see, for me to
continue that setup is sick. It is a sickness like alcoholism is a sickness.
It is the sickness that arises from growing up in an alcoholic home.
Believing that if you weren't happy then I had to suffer as well is really
sick. In spite of the distance between us, I felt so guilty and responsible
for your unhappiness that I felt I must either destroy myself or just
suffer an unfilfilling life. This was the unconscious script I've been
playing for most of my adult life, until now.

I've had to make a choice. I've made the choice to recover from the
untruths that have operated in me. I want to be a nurturing, sober, and
sane parent. The facts are that I may repeat the same parenting I received unless I continue my own self-vigilance against these tendencies. It is not that I am blind to your emotions and your well-being or
insensitive to you that motivates me to write this. Your reaction to this
letter is your responsibility, not mine. Although a part of me feels mean
and uncaring for confronting you with this, I now recognize that I must
do this out of love for myself. I also believe it would be good for you
to confront these things in yourself. Regardless of your reaction, I know
this had to be written for me to heal. In the deepest way I hope this is
a springboard for healing not just for me but our relationship. But I
know that whatever your rection may be, I will be OK and able to deal
with it. I'm getting help, support, and love to see me through this.

I am going to conclude now.

Sincerely,

Pete

♦

Pete's mother responded three weeks later in her not-so-subtle way of
discounting his experience, while justifing her refusal to directly address what happened between them. On the surface, the tone of her
letter seemed motherly and somewhat revelatory, but between the
lines, the implicit message revealed the pathos of their relationship.
She began by thanking him for the letter while initially admitting that
she was shocked and stunned by its contents. She wrote that before
addressing his allegations directly, she was glad to know that he was
still alive and well and hoped that he and his family had had a nice
Thanksgiving holiday. This comment was an apparent reference to the

lack of contact over the previous year and a half. She used the message of the Thanksgiving spirit to acknowledge how much they both have to be thankful for despite the little bumps along the road of life—an oblique criticism of the purpose of Pete's letter.

Abruptly abandoning this stoic tone, she then admitted that she often felt like life was a living hell, something so bad that she need not fear whatever hell may come later. Then, in a manner further reinforcing her self-sacrifice, she inquired about the various gifts she had sent over the past year and admonished Pete for not having acknowledged receiving them, however small they might be, while wistfully adding that he had once been so good about writing thank-you notes.

What came next was essentially a global apology for all of the physical and emotional hurt which Pete "claimed" to have been a victim of and in the same sentence asked that he find it within himself to forgive her. She stated that she refused to be judged for her past, for that is the responsibility of her Heavenly Father. She asked him to not take these comments as an excuse or cop-out, although she appeared to be doing just that.

Then she embarked on a lengthy explanation of her immaturity as a young mother and the difficulty in raising a child without the full love and support of her husband. Like any mother, she described with pride how cute Pete was as a child and how important it was for her that she give him the very best. She revealed her massive disappointment with her marriage which illustrated how Pete was the only bright spot in an otherwise dreary life. The theme of substituting her male child for her husband was heavily implied here.

She described about how much she had changed in the last year and a half with the help of AA but did not talk at all about her own problems with alcohol. Rather, she distorted some of the AA philosophy to justify her refusal to be manipulated or made to feel guilty by others. While she avoided mentioning people directly, the unavoidable implication was that Pete and his allegations of sexual abuse were the culprit here.

In closing, she continued the strategy of appearing motherly and supportive of Pete and stated that she was happy that his therapy was working, but again discounted his need of professional help by implying that it might not be necessary. She asserted that his horrible feelings were his problem, not hers. She gave a full apology for the rambling tone of her letter and acknowledged that she could not compete with his eloquent style, reinforcing her self-image of the poor, unfortunate mother. She reiterated once again how much she loved him and then in what may be her closest admission of guilt for what she did, wrote that whatever she did was done out of motherly love. Her final sentence asked him for a reconciliation, but in a challenging tone asserted that it must be a two-way street

Pete's Second Letter, Two Weeks Later

Dear "Mom,"

What I have to say in response to your letter isn't pretty and it isn't "nice" but what I feel inside is the truth. I'm sick with rage and hurt from your letter. Let me start with the worst.

What you did out of "motherly love" was not only immoral it was illegal. Your sense of motherly love which was alluding to the incest is the crux of the reason why I'm livid and feel so betrayed. Do you have any idea of what was and is wrong with our relationship? The fact that it was unwholesome and possessive and controlling and selfish and immoral is what you call "motherly love"? That's sick and it almost cost me my sanity. And today I'm so full of anger at you that it makes me sick. And you persist with the illusion that it was, you thought, "out of motherly love"?

Your apology means nothing to me because you invalidated my perceptions with two words—"you claim"—implying that you don't accept the responsibility of your actions in the same sentence that you are apologizing for them. Do you think I'm an idiot and don't notice that disclaimer? I don't feel in my heart and mind to forgive you in any way on the basis of your qualified apology. It's not good enough. It's the same old game. To let yourself off the hook and placate me into forgiving and forgetting. Sorry!

Do you know what it did to me as a male and as a young man for you to constantly criticize and belittle my father in your drunken stupors? It killed me that's what it did. It hurt me so deeply. It hurt my sense of myself so deeply. I just can't tell you the agony it caused. You don't know how close I came to just flooring you when you were drunk and insane because of your rage. It took everything inside me not to do that. I grabbed your arms instead one time and then you pleaded in your self-pitying way. How could I do such a thing you asked. You provoked it with your insane, drunken, and seductive behavior, that's how.

Onward. What you gave to me in material possessions, especially when I was a little boy, you gave to make me something for your pleasure—in your words "my very own precious little doll." I was a little person. I don't think you were ever willing to let me be a little person or a big person without your hand of control and possession and manipulation.

You spoke in your letter of no more being manipulated and used, etc. While that may be important maybe you ought to think about your own using and manipulating of other people—specifically me when I couldn't see what you were doing to me. I don't know where you get off about AA teaching you to be selfish. Try page 62 in The Big Book.

"Selfishness—self-centeredness!—that we think is the root of our troubles." Are you an exception? I'm sure in some ways learning to say "No" is important. I don't mean to invalidate that. But AA teaching you to be selfish—I don't think I can accept that. Sorry. Quite frankly, I don't trust you or anything you say until you recover from your alcoholism. Your legacy of lying is so long that you must think I'm stupid. You are only fooling yourself. I can't be duped or fooled or manipulated anymore and when you try I'm going to point it out.

Finally, as I said before, reconciliation has to start with the truth and as long as you are in denial, I find your version of the truth lacking in responsibility, honesty, and remorse. So if we are going to communicate it has to begin with the truth. What else can I say?

I close this hoping you will hear what I'm saying and respect my hurt and rage and respond with the truth.

For now,

Pete

◆

Pete's mother responded approximately two months later in a far more brief letter than her first one. She admitted that what had transpired between them had caused both of them extreme emotional distress, but again refused to comment directly on the sexual abuse, instead offering to pray for him that he would not continue to immerse himself in the painful past. She strongly encouraged him to bury his negative thoughts so that he could go forward. Once again she invoked the name of God to describe how rich his life was now that he was blessed with a wife and a child and implored him to be a caring and loyal husband and father, the implication being that his current focus on the past could only get in the way of that pursuit. She signed off with another offer to pray to God that he continue to enjoy good health—the most important asset anyone can have.

Pete's Third Letter, One Week Later

"Mom,"

As I wrote you before, trying to bury the past almost cost me my sanity. If there is one thing I'm sure of it's that I'm no longer willing to bury the past including the bitterness, resentments, hurt, etc. In order to go forward I am looking at the past honestly and with the guidance of professional help.

You obviously are not able to deal with the reality of the past now. If that's where you are, I can't force you. However, we can have virtually no relationship as long as the past isn't addressed. You didn't respond in your letter to any of what I know to be important for my mental, emotional, and physical health, which as you say, are the greatest of gifts.

Incest buried is often repeated, or ends up as insanity or chronic alcoholism. You see, I'm trying to live sober and sane and not repeat incest with my children so it's not going to be buried by me. If you want to bury it then we can have no reconciliations from my point of view. If we are to reconcile you will have to see your responsibility and own up to it without disclaimers and qualifications or blame or rationalizations.

That's all for now.

Pete

♦

Pete's mother's next letter arrived about two weeks later and graphically illustrated the dark side of her personality that emerged when under the influence of alcohol. Right from the opening sentence, she unleashed a torrent of verbal abuse, describing his mental state as "debilitated" due to the influence of professional help and affecting a sarcastic wonderment at how perfect he could turn out considering how horrible she was supposed to have been to him. What followed was a succession of negatively descriptive adjectives that carried on for several lines and provided further proof of the inebriated state she was in while she wrote the letter. Some of the adjectives were taken from Pete's letters while many were of her own making, perhaps indicating how badly she felt about herself deep down inside, but was unable to acknowledge while sober. Her intent, it appeared, was to take Pete's charges to the extreme thereby undermining their credibility. She then threatened him with future legal action by stating that his letters were now in the hands of her attorney. She continued to take the offensive by denying ever kicking him in the rectum with pointy-toed shoes, but adding that if she had, she only wished she had kicked the "holy shit" out of him. Finally, she did address a specific point Pete made in a previous letter concerning the emotional demands she had made of him in return for her love. She denied ever asking him for anything and then in a confused manner justified this position by pointing out how mothers lose their sons when they marry, seeming to imply that she held his marriage accountable for his current anger at her. She then challenged him to stop wallowing in his own pain for the sake of his daughter.

Suddenly, she switched gears, focusing on the rapidly deteriorating health of her father, Pete's grandfather, blaming Pete and his father's family for never caring about her father, as indicated by the lack of cards or flowers in his room. Besides the alcohol, her distress over the impending loss of her father seemed to be fueling this written tirade as she described how wonderful he was and how uncaring everyone else was. She employed the famous line spoken by Clark Gable in *Gone With the Wind* to describe her lack of feelings about ever seeing or talking to Pete or his wife again, while jabbing them for their self-righteous perfection. The letter ended with a post-script informing Pete he would never receive her house upon her death as she contended he had mentioned to her once. Then, she referred to the enclosed picture of Pete's doctor who treated him for a fractured skull when he was young. Wistfully, she reminisced about almost losing Pete as a child only to finally lose him when he got married.

Two days later, Pete received a brief note from her which showed a complete reversal in tone and intent from the previous one. She immediately apologized for the last letter as well as for all transgressions of the past and any that might come in the future. Again, the credibility of her apology was undercut by the absence of any real indication that she might change. One is left with the impression that she was either implying that such past transgressions will be on the same par as those she may unwittingly commit in the future, or that she was simply incapable of controlling herself and her actions and was asking for additional understanding. At the same time, in giving a reason for her apology that no two wrongs make a right, she again implied that Pete was wrong for bringing up the incest. Another reason for her letter, she stated, was her distress over her father's condition which continued to worsen. In closing, she said that the world as well as their lives was filled with too much pain and anguish and that she did not need to contribute more of that. The implication again was to challenge Pete to call a truce to this upsetting matter so that they could both go forward with their lives. While conciliatory in tone, she continued to be unwilling to address the specifics of the incest while in a more subtle way attempting to nudge Pete in the direction of forgiving and forgetting, the latter being her primary mode of psychological defense.

Pete's Fourth Letter, Three Weeks Later

"Mom,"

I want to respond to your last two letters. When I read the first letter—the one that begins "It's always exciting . . ." I was absolutely horrified and shocked. It took me a few days to sort out all my feelings. I was and still am so deeply hurt that you said the things you did. I was also terrified and angered. I need to go through it here because it was absolutely vicious and evil and untrue.

I obviously did not turn out so completely perfect, and I recognize that jab as way of lashing out at me for bringing up to you the painful facts. If you really believe that what I've written to you are "libelous accusations," it just points out your denial as far as I'm concerned. It further breaches my trust in your view of reality.

Your comments about kicking me in the rectum and your statement that you're sorry you didn't kick the holy shit out of me really horrified me. It made me cry that my "mother" wrote that. Let me tell you that you did kick "the holy shit" out of me and it was at an age well before alcohol and drugs were a part of my life. In fact the rage in your letter was just like the rage you had when I was a child. But it was more than that. Sometimes it was just the look in your eyes of absolute vicious rage. It terrified me and left me so lost and alone and confused about whether you were justified to treat me this way. It was very harmful to me. As for your statement that you never asked anything of me—I just hope you don't really believe that. You asked and demanded that I be your possession, that I be as you saw fit. You eventually asked that I be an emotional support for you, rather than you an emotional support for me as a mother should be for her child. As well, you asked that I be your "man" emotionally and sexually.

Regarding your implication that I am confronting you because I now have a wife and no longer need a mother—this is totally untrue and discounts the fact that I have been in therapy for the incest for over four and a half years. My being able to confront you has been the result of me getting well and strong enough to separate your version of reality, as this letter points out, from what I'm finding out is reality. I lost you long before I realized it, I assure you. It's interesting that you equate your role in my life with that of a wife in the first place.

Further, as you state that we don't give a damn about your father— "a tinker's damn." Well, in fact I am sorry that he is so sick and I was truly remiss in not sending a card. I had spoken to your aunt and knew that he probably wouldn't know the difference, but I should have sent a card anyway.

Finally, as you created this idea about getting your house when you died, I just have a news flash back to you—if I so wanted your house, do you think I'd be so stupid as to risk it confronting you? Don't you think I would choose to keep the peace with you and stay sick and suicidal and depressed, if I really wanted your house? This is more of the emotional blackmail that you did to me as a kid. The part that really hurts me is understanding that if that's your game now, then it was obviously your game of control when I was young and vulnerable and really needing to trust you. I got something very different.

Now regarding your second letter that just arrived. I was shocked to read your apology in what seemed to me a sincere way. I was both moved by your sincerity and at the same time, because of your first letter, I was too hurt to ever want to give you a chance to apologize. I know that is what I have asked of you to begin reconciliation, yet I felt untrusting and unsure of it. I want to believe that you are sincere. The dichotomy of your letters was hard to reconcile because of the sharp change in their tone and point of view. In fact I have now realized that it is just that dichotomy in your response to me that was so hard for me when I was young. For you to go from insane rage back to normal left me just as I am feeling today—confused, unsure, untrusting, and seduced and wanting to see and believe there would be no more violence in your personality. I never knew which part of you to believe, and perhaps, I still don't. I want to trust your second letter and use it to convince me that you never wrote the first letter. But that is what I did as a kid and that was unhealthy!!! But just as it happened over and over when I was young, I have to recognize that you did write the first letter and that is a part of you also. What I'm saying is that I appreciate your apology and I temper the opening of my heart with the knowledge that you are both of these parts.

Please understand that if someone you loved and needed and trusted became a different person—violent and rageful and terribly frightening—and then back to a trustworthy person again, and this went on, back and forth, it would leave you devastated. That's what I feel happened to me with you.

I thank you for loving me and caring for me when I was very young and Dad was drunk all the time. I know you were also betrayed and hurt by his sickness—quite frankly, I hate his sickness too. But you left me—I don't know exactly when—but I know I couldn't trust who you were going to be from one day to the next and eventually from one morning to that afternoon. That little boy or young man needed stability and security and the protection of consistency—but it began to disappear and as it did, so did my trust—that's why I lost you long ago. I didn't know who you were going to be—sometimes you were great but other times just horrific—just as your letters demonstrate—and I just shut down after a while. I still need the same things from you as I did when I was young for trust to be there between us.

I hope you have a sense of where I come from. I don't know what else to say. I've said plenty I know.

For now,

Pete

Pete's Fifth Letter, Three Months Later

Mom,

I am drawn to write to you now.

Our second baby girl was born yesterday morning, and mother and daughter are doing wonderfully. In witnessing the beauty of her birth, I thought of you and how you, like me and now our new daughter, were all so innocent and vulnerable when we were born.

Whatever happened to you and me to contribute to our loss of innocence, I am sorry for and sad about tonight. Just as I wrote you last about being sad for your pain, I am sad about that which contributed to your pain as a child. However it happened, it must have been awful because what was passed onto me was awful. May God help me not to continue to pass on my violence to my children.

The healing for me to not do that requires you to hear and know exactly what my point of view is, and I am not distracted now. So, I am continuing on this road—not to punish you—but to heal myself and pass on my wholeness to the highest gift in life, my children. Tonight that means that I will share how very sad I am because I cannot help but see you as the infant child before me— but without the rage and hurt and disease that has since clouded your life.

To close, I'm not sorry about Grampa's passing—it was certainly time for him to go. But I am sorry for your pain that I know you must feel. I hope God is with you as the death of your parent must be your most painful loss. I hope that you are well enough to let the pain just be, rather than blot it out with alcohol.

For now,

Pete

P.S. We don't have a name for her yet.

♦

This last letter marked a turning point in the feelings expressed by Pete and his mother. Although contact was still limited thereafter, the exchange of letters and phone calls became less acrimonious and more accepting of each other's feelings, limitations, and points of view. Some two years later, when Pete's second child was just a toddler, Pete decided to visit his mother, giving her the chance to meet her two granddaughters for the first time. As described in his story contained in Step 18, this visit gave him a measure of resolution that was built on the indirect confrontation expressed in the series of letters.

DIRECT
METHODS OF
CONFRONTATION

Directly confronting your abuser calls for a more thorough preparation than the indirect method and raises many other considerations in terms of personal safety, the expression of strong emotions, and the unpredictable reactions of other family members. In cases where there was widespread sexual abuse involving more than one of the children, the other siblings' reactions may be quite varied, with some preferring to continue the family denial and others seeing it as an opportunity for growth. You will need to determine if you want to speak alone with your parent or want other people to be present including therapists, sponsors, or clergy. There are many options available here but recognize that your plans may be limited by what your parents are willing to do. Not all parents who physically or sexually abused their children will want to face what they did or participate in a family meeting where the abuse is openly acknowledged and discussed.

One option is to convene your family meeting without telling the abuser what the focus of the meeting will be beforehand. The element of surprise is often necessary when the abuser's denial is still very strong. This can be the most dramatic intervention available; however, it is also likely to trigger the most extreme reactions: good or bad, and in some cases violent and destructive. For this reason, it is not recommended to undertake this type of confrontation if your family is prone to violent outbursts. Let me reiterate that this extreme strategy must be carefully thought out and used only in last-ditch efforts to challenge the abuser's denial.

Because direct confrontations are so complex and risky, it is essential that you not attempt one without first working with a therapist to sort out the issues and prepare you for the range of outcomes. Other family members need to be briefed on what will transpire and discussions about how to handle the dialogue with the abuser will be necessary to create a workable plan of action.

Jolene

The idea for a family intervention came from Beth, my foster sister from the Adventist home that I was in. I was twenty-six and in my first year of therapy when she called one day and asked if she could visit because she had something to discuss. We hadn't been that close when I was in the family because I was four years older than she was so we were in different crowds at school. We had never talked about her father, and as far as I knew, she had no idea that he had molested me. And so I said sure and when she came, we went out for a drive and then just parked for a few hours and talked.

Beth told me angrily that after I'd moved out, her father started molesting her. Now she thought he was starting with her younger sister, Alice, and she wanted to do something to stop him. She said she had been in therapy for the last few years, doing a lot of work around the incest, and we talked about the family and how it screwed us up. It turned out that she always thought there was something funny about her dad and me and that his attention to me had caused her some jealousy when she was around twelve and thirteen.

Then she revealed that she'd been working on setting up a therapy session with her whole family and wanted to know if I would be part of it since I had also been part of the family. She had written to her brothers and told them what he had done to her and asked for their support in getting the secret out in the open. They all agreed, although they weren't necessarily clear about what it would involve. Beth kept the exact details pretty vague with them because she didn't know whether they would tell her parents or not, but she was open with me about what she had worked out with her therapist and the family counseling agency where the session was going to take place. She had wanted to do the intervention ever since she met with some of the church elders and told them about her father molesting her. They advised her to let them handle it within the church. They didn't want any outside therapists involved, and in fact, had discouraged her from seeking therapy or getting outside help. But a year went by and no action was taken by the church, and she suspected her father was now molesting Alice, so she decided to arrange a family meeting.

Beth's therapist felt it would be best to do it at the agency with two therapists present because of the tremendous manipulative aspect of her father's personality. It was her therapist's judgment that if Beth confronted him alone, he would turn on her and persuade the whole family and church to turn against her. This is what he has always done—I could see that myself just from living in that house for a few years. He's always twisted things around to his own advantage. I told Beth that I wanted to discuss it with my therapist first and then get back to her.

My therapist and I agreed I could benefit from participating, but that I wasn't going to be taking the lead in dealing with Beth's father—it was her decision and she was going to do the talking. If it felt right for me, I was going to say something, but I guess I felt like I was the foster kid again, not really having as much right to challenge the father because I wasn't really one of them. I guess this feeling of never being a part of a family is still with me. Anyway, I told her that I wanted to be involved to support her and that maybe I would talk if I felt like it, but that I didn't want any pressure to say anything.

The meeting was this real big deal because the agency was prepared for just about any situation that developed. They had video cameras and everything and the other staff observed the session behind one-way mirrors. Beth's therapist was one of two cotherapists, the other being an expert on religious families, someone who could help the father deal with issues of loyalty to the Adventist Church.

First, we had a session in the morning with the therapists, and Beth and me and her brothers and sister—without her parents present. Beth started by telling everyone why we were doing this and asked everyone to say how they were feeling about it. Then she told everyone again what her father had done to her and how it made her feel. Her brothers didn't want to believe it and suggested that Beth was her father's favorite so how could he do something like that. The atmosphere in the room was like a rising tide: Their denial got stronger and I thought it was going to wash away everything that Beth had set up. I decided to tell them what he did to me. This shut them up pretty fast. I told them he started molesting me soon after I was placed in the family and that it developed into intercourse by the time I moved out. There was this long pause when no one said anything and just sat there. Then Alice, who hadn't said anything, just started shaking and then burst out in tears and went to Beth. She and Beth were really crying and then I started to cry a little bit too. I'm not a big crier usually. Fortunately for Alice, it hadn't progressed to the intercourse stage as it had with Beth and me.

Then in the afternoon session with the father and mother and the entire family and me and the two therapists, Beth again told everyone what he did and how it affected her, asking that he respond to what she was saying. He didn't say a lot except that he really loved all of the children and the girls—even me—were really special to him and that he was trying to be the best father that God would allow him to be. But when Beth started confronting him with specific situations and times, he got real uncomfortable and denied he did anything other than love his children, although in a really weak, unconvincing way. He turned to the religious expert and asked how the Lord could help him with this situation and the guy just told him to accept what he had done as another sin that he needs to ask God for repentence for. All the mother said was that she was surprised and hurt if he really did this. She knew that Beth was his favorite daughter and thought they had a good, close relationship but she never suspected or saw anything go on that made her question anything.

Beth looked at me to see if I wanted to say anything. I was real scared, but I felt things were going in our favor after I spoke up in the morning session. So I took a deep breath and told the therapists that I had something to say. At first, I felt choked up like I wasn't going to be able to squeeze the words out. I also felt kind of spacy, and my heart was beating real hard. I just told him that he had molested me and that he had said the same things to me that he said to Beth. Then I told him about the time he took me to a motel on the way back from this church conference and he had intercourse with me there. I gave all these details of the trip so nobody would think I was making it up. As I talked, I started feeling this rage building up inside me and I told him how I really hated him for being such a hypocrite—trying to act so religious and pure and then behind the scenes having sex with kids and now denying it to our face. He got real agitated at this point and said he didn't need to hear this garbage anymore and got up to leave. The therapists both stood up and asked him to sit down because they had something to tell him. He reluctantly sat down and then Beth's therapist told him that they understand that he has also been molesting Alice. He denied that one as well. Beth's therapist told him and the mother that they would have to report it to the authorities and that some decisions would have to be made right now about protecting Alice. The father got really angry again and accused them of setting him up. They agreed that the other therapist and the father would meet in a separate room while the rest of us and the mother continued talking with Beth's therapist.

The therapist just told the mother that either Alice would have to go to a temporary shelter for a few days or that the father would have to move out until everything was settled with the child abuse investigation. This got the mother upset because she really didn't know what to do. Beth's therapist was real good at helping the mother see that it wasn't safe for her child to be around the father, especially with his lying about the abuse. The mother was worried about where he would go and who would pay the bills. The therapist agreed that there were real problems that would have to be solved, but that to go on as before would be sacrificing Alice's welfare. Beth was pretty quiet during this time, and in fact, looked furious at her mother for not going along with what her therapist was saying. Finally Beth reminded her mother that Dad could stay at his sister's for a few weeks until things settle down.

I thought it was productive to get all that out in the open and everything, but it didn't work as well as I'd have liked because neither of the parents really took responsibility for what Beth and I were saying. But the therapists did make an abuse report, which finally brought the county authorities in. The father and the mother were also encouraged to get therapy—individual and group therapy—to get support for what was happening in their family and to learn about how they could make changes for the better. I guess it fell on deaf ears because they never really got any therapy. Fortunately the court put the father on probation and made him attend some groups for a brief period. The problem is that the church basically runs the community and they have stepped in to tell the county people that they will deal with it themselves. I guess the county people backed off and now I don't really know where it's at.

Beth told me she was kind of disappointed with how it turned out except she feels good about protecting her sister since her mother apparently wasn't going to do it. She can talk about it with her brothers, but her father doesn't want to deal with it. Her mother is somewhat supportive, but acts like she doesn't understand what really happened, which is exactly the way she has always been. She certainly hasn't made any move to leave the father.

Beth has kind of pulled back from the family. I guess she feels like she has done what she could and now its up to them. She told me that if she finds out that her dad started molesting her sister again, she would sue the church for letting it happen. As for me, I guess it was helpful to do this. I didn't have very high expectations for anything good happening so I wasn't disappointed. Actually, I felt kind of proud about speaking up and I've felt better about myself since the meeting. My therapist thinks it was real courageous and I think she may even be right!

◆

GOING FORWARD

Coming to a decision about what your family may or may not have to offer will allow you to go forward, unencumbered with false hopes or unrealistic expectations. In a sense, it may open the possibilities for the future because at last you know the score from the past.

FAMILY RECONSTRUCTION

If the outcome of your confrontation with your family is essentially positive, it may be possible to undertake some reconstructive work with your family or selected family members to forge a new relationship based on respect and trust. Often, if other family members enter their own therapy and resolve their feelings about what happened, there may come a time when they may be open to entering family therapy with the survivor. This can be very productive for you and aid in your healing in ways not possible without your family or parents present. It can also sow the seeds for change throughout the family and offer a major restructuring of how the family functions, how they communicate with each other, and most important, how they treat each other.

Working on family issues in family therapy may be the most hopeful sign that a true resolution of the child abuse is possible. For you, the survivor, it may mean finally getting the family that you never had.

KNOWING WHEN TO
LET GO OF YOUR FAMILY

Perhaps more often than not, the opposite scenario is true. The confrontation teaches you something you didn't want to face as a child and still don't as a survivor in recovery—that your parents will never change, their denial will remain forever in place, and their treatment of you will always be emotionally abusive, if not physically or sexually abusive. You must realize that you are never going to get what you want and perhaps still need from them. It is time to accept their limitations and give up hope for things ever being different. When being with your family is harmful, you really only have one choice to make that is healthy for you—to let go of them to the extent necessary to protect yourself, and to get on with your life.

Pete

Several things would have to happen to make me feel like there was some hope for my relationship with my mother. The first step would be for her to give me a real strong indication that she is looking at the past and looking at her life and our relationship in a way that is different—with some openness, honesty, and a willingness to discuss the incest. It would be nice but not necessarily essential if she would admit she was wrong. But it would be essential that she recognize what happened as wrong and unhealthy. That would be a starting point for some kind of rebuilding of our relationship. But I just don't think she is likely to do that. She is in her early sixties now and I'd like to say that all things are possible, but realistically I believe she would have to gain sobriety first, and at this point, that doesn't seem likely. I see people every week in AA meetings who are sober and working the Steps who don't choose to look at their stuff. So, realistically speaking, I'm not holding my breath waiting for my mother to change.

◆

Letting go of your family means loosening your emotional and physical ties to them. When you determine that being in touch with your family is not good for you, you can limit your contact with them and restrict their contact with you in such a way as to protect you from being hurt by them. At the extreme, the conditions for contact are nil: You tell them that under no circumstances do you want to have anything to do with them. More commonly, you can partially let go of them without permanently severing all contact with them. Instead of spending holidays with them, you spend the time with people who really care about you. Instead of calling them for support or sharing the joys and hardships of your life, you wait for them to call you, and even then, you are careful to stick to "safe" topics. Instead of sharing your vulnerabilities with them, you give them only the plain facts of your life. In some cases, when they are still openly hostile to you, you don't have to give them anything at all. You can say good-bye to the parents and family that you never had and feel relieved that they can't hurt you anymore.

GETTING WHAT YOU CAN FROM YOUR FAMILY

Many survivors are not able or do not wish to permanently and completely sever all contact with their parents or family when the chance for maltreatment still exists. What should you do? Look for whatever "positive pieces" your family may be capable of offering and focus your relationship on getting what you can. For example, some parents are able to rise to the occasion when their child is sick. So, when you are sick, this may be the time to give your parents a call and let them know what is happening to you. Maybe this situation will bring out the best in them as it did in the past. The result is that they may help you feel better. Or maybe your family has a history of changing for the better around certain times of the year such as birthdays, holidays, anniversaries, or summer vacations. This might be the time to call them or visit them to catch them at their best. You can be prepared to make a hasty exit when the emotional winds start to shift. The basic premise of this strategy is to be selective in choosing when to contact them, how the contact should be organized, and perhaps who in the family you should contact. You may not get everything you want, but when you have decided that something is better than nothing, this plan may be the best for you.

FORGIVENESS

Many survivors are confused about if and when to forgive their abuser. As addressed in Step 18, the question of forgiveness is part of your resolution with your family. Organized religions, as well as the various 12-Step self-help groups such as Alcoholics Anonymous, directly urge survivors to forgive those who have hurt them in the past. But forgiveness is a personal matter, one that should be decided only by you in consideration of what you feel in your heart. In most cases, people do not forgive someone who has hurt them until the issue has been mostly resolved with the feelings of anger, resentment, and pain greatly reduced.

Considering how severely abused many of you were, you may never get to the point where your hurt feelings are sufficiently resolved to forgive your abuser. If your family is still in denial about the abuse or refuses to apologize or accept responsibility for what they did, it is understandable that you may have no desire to forgive them. Forgiveness does imply a higher level of resolution, but it must be sincere, genuine, and a true reflection of your feelings if you are to offer it. Remember that self-forgiveness, not forgiveness of your abuser, is your most important goal.

Leigh Anne

My father and I were never able to talk about his battering me—in his mind, he never hurt me; he denied until his death that the verbal and physical abuse ever damaged me—after all, no bones were broken. But I think I finally understood that he was just as much a victim as I was. He felt trapped just like I did and was facing a lot of the same torments with my mother that I was. I think the biggest reason why I can forgive him is that he came through for me when I really needed him. He got me off to college and out of the house. When he was away from my mother, he treated me with love and respect. We became almost like peers in a way. I really got a lot from him after he divorced my mom. And I still needed him to be a father to me, even though I was in my late twenties. I got some good stuff from him and I want to remember him that way. When he passed away, I wrote this song and it's called "Raise Me High," and it's just a beautiful letting go of my anguish over what he did to me. I can forgive him now.

◆

WHEN ACCEPTANCE IS
THE ONLY RESOLUTION AVAILABLE

You may ask what options are available to you when you do not feel forgiveness. The answer has to do with acceptance—the kind of acceptance that comes after grieving the loss of something very important like your childhood or the wish for more loving parents. Acceptance means recognizing that the abuse happened and that it hurt you and that your parents or abuser was responsible. It also means that you have accepted how the abuse affected you and that you are powerless to change anything in the past. Acceptance means putting the abuse behind you, not in the sense of forgetting, but in not letting it continue to dominate your life. True acceptance, like true forgiveness, can be very liberating, which is the real goal in your recovery: to allow the soul of your existence to be liberated from the shackles of the past.

Shirley

When I confronted my mother, I told her that I was mad at her for not protecting me, but that was about it. I was just honest. I told her what I experienced and what I'm going through now as a result of it. I didn't tie everything together for her, though I let her read some of my papers I've written for school that describe my feelings about the abuse. But she didn't want to hear it. She cut me off and changed the subject. It was a disappointment for me, but that's her choice. I can't change her, but I can change myself. I don't have the expectation anymore that she will be different. That's where my progress has been. I've finally let go of the expectation and the hope, and now it's being filled with acceptance. She did the best she could at the time, with what she had to work with.

I don't know if I necessarily need to forgive her or not, as long as I let go of my expectations. I know they no longer have power over me. I know that I can be around my dad now and not be afraid. I know that I am in control. I have a personal power that I never possessed before. Now that I am personally powerful, and by that I mean feeling strong and secure in myself and who I am and what I'm doing, he never approaches me in the way he did in the past. I don't have a bitterness. I'm almost thankful because I know that all this has shaped who I am now, and I know I'm a good person. I have taken a look at myself in a way that a lot of people never do. I know that I have courage, I know that I have hope, and I know I have perseverance. I think any resolution with your parents or your family begins and ends with accepting yourself. That's the only resolution you really need. It has much more to do with you than with them.

◆

CREATING A NEW FAMILY

If family reconstruction is not an option, it need not dash your hope for having a family experience that gives you love, affiliation, commitment, and sharing. You have the opportunity to create a new family with people who will give you what you want.

Many survivors develop a new family composed of the important people in their lives: brothers and sisters or other biological family members who support their efforts to heal, families of close friends or partners who they have grown to love and trust, even friends of their parents who showed them care and consideration while growing up under siege. Others bond with members of their support groups and share parenting responsibilities for each other's children. For those of you who got yourself "adopted" by a friend's family during childhood, you may still have those old warm feelings for your "surrogate" mother or father. Who are the people in your life that have been there for you through thick and thin? These are the people who may make the best alternative family for you.

You will need to create some new rituals that capture the family feeling that you want to convey to your chosen family. Holidays, birthdays, and anniversaries of relationships born and relationships reaffirmed are all part of creating a family legacy that will endure. It will affirm your power as a person and underscore the notion that you need not be defeated by the family you never had.

SALVATION
AND FUTURE CALLINGS

We have come to the end of our personal journey together. What began with reading this book and learning about child abuse has developed into a new awareness of your childhood ordeal and the steps that you must take to overcome it. For those of you who have read this book as an introduction to initiating your recovery, I hope the information provided here will make the road ahead less rocky and more illuminated with hope and the possibilities of change. Recognize that you will not start your recovery completely from scratch. Reading this book is an achievement in its own right, considering how difficult it may have been for you to face this particular subject. You now possess a foundation upon which you can build your own recovery.

For those readers who are now well along in recovery, congratulations are in order for you have made formidable changes that would never have been possible without a great deal of courage and perseverance. I hope you will acknowledge these efforts each year when you celebrate the birthday of your recovery. You are now poised at the conclusion of this book, ready to take the first step in your new beginning. As a recovered survivor, you can exult in your new life, affirming your new sense of self in your work, relationships, and play as you continue to fortify and expand upon the resolutions you worked so hard to achieve. As you move forward in your postrecovery years, these new changes, resolutions, and attitudes will infuse your spirit, perhaps leading you to higher levels of consciousness, allowing you to be reborn, in a sense, in the image of your reclaimed soul.

I would love to hear from those of you who wish to share with me your experiences in recovery and reactions to reading this book, which I might incorporate into future editions of *Soul Survivors*. We are still in a period of discovery about the effects of child abuse and your thoughtful comments will aid in our continued understanding of this important subject. To that end, I have included a series of survey questions in Appendix F that you can answer anonymously and return to me at the address shown. I would greatly appreciate your feedback.

It is also time to bid farewell to the six survivors whose experiences as children, adults, and in recovery enlivened this book. Their stories were inspirational for me as I hope they were for you. Their lives are a testimony to the power of recovery and the opportunities in life that follow it. Let me give you one final update on each of them. Pete is continuing to prosper in his own business specializing in home renovations and is busy sharing parenting of his second daughter who is now a feisty three-year-old. He still attends ACA groups, although his formal recovery program is now finished. Susan is continuing her success in the computer field while learning to play baseball with her son, who is now the top student in his class after years of low achievement. She is in her fourth year of therapy and has recently joined a new psychotherapy group. Shirley is continuing her undergraduate studies in human relations while juggling the demands of working and parenting three teenagers. Although mostly finished with her recovery, Shirley returns to her therapy as needed when issues arise in her primary relationship or parenting that are still tied to her abuse.

Jolene is now entering Stage Two of recovery, having continued in individual therapy for the last eighteen months. She is better able to reach out to others, make new friendships, and develop romantic relationships. Recently she contacted her first foster family who took such loving care of her until the age of six. To her great disappointment, she discovered that her foster mother had recently died, but her foster father not only remembered her with warm feelings (some twenty-two years later) but told her that she must visit to look over his house that he was willing to her. She is on her way! Richard is also continuing his successful involvement creating environment reports in the company he was working for and now teaches a well-regarded course on the subject at the university level. Still working in therapy after eight years, he and his wife recently bought a house and are busy making it into a home. Leigh Anne informed me in a Christmas card that she is only months away from finishing her therapy and has lost fifty pounds in preparation for her new beginning! Although work issues still need to be resolved, she is going forward armed with her infectious enthusiasm for life.

All of these survivors made it despite the horrible abuse each of them suffered as children. Let their examples inspire you to go forward with your recovery and beyond. You too may be looking back and appreciating the enormous changes that you made. I want to underscore one final thought taken from Shirley's last comment that is too important not to be repeated: "If you want to instill hope, believe that change is truly possible."

FUTURE CALLINGS

The twenty-first step of recovery recognizes that we all possess the innate human capacity to continue evolving in the image of our chosen spiritual or personal vision. Your future calling may remind you to continue reworking some of the steps as you go through the life cycle. Marriage, the birth of your children, the death of your parents, the growth of your children who will eventually leave home, the birth of your first grandchild, your retirement, and the ensuing twilight years— all of the natural milestones in the life cycle will resonate with the work you have already done, at the same time perhaps revealing the need for an even deeper resolution. Personal growth beyond recovery means periodically returning to the healing and changing processes you have learned. Like the seasonal planting of crops, the changes that you have cultivated may need to be strengthened, replenished, and occasionally reseeded. Retracing some steps will never require the total dedication, energy, and perseverance that marked your recovery in the past. However, having tasted the rich flavors of a healthy life, it may never again be acceptable for you to live life halfway. You owe it to yourself to keep these changes alive and still evolving.

ENDING CHILD ABUSE
AND DOMESTIC VIOLENCE

Family violence including child abuse is an increasing social problem in our country today with estimates as high as one out of every four families being victimized by some kind of abuse according to a report from the Surgeon General. We know that the majority of children who grow up in these families will not become tomorrow's abusers, just as the majority of adult survivors today do not continue this intergenerational link in their parenting. However, the evidence suggests that anywhere from a quarter to a third of all child victims—past and present—will engage in abusive relationships as adults. Just as you have faced this truth in your recovery, our society needs to face this dark reality.

As a culture struggling to evolve socially and psychologically to meet the increasing demands of an expanding population with ever-diminishing resources, it is essential that we learn to coexist peacefully and respectfully. With all the outcry about crime in the streets, our society still denies the physical, emotional, and sexual violence that occurs in American homes. Although social stresses and economic hardship are significant factors in family violence, we can't wait for our government to come up with solutions before facing this problem. It is killing us in the meantime. Eliminating violence and exploitation needs to start in our families before we can expect our society and ultimately our world to be free of it. Although few of us can change this problem on a societal level, we can take control of the way we treat ourselves and our children. Like the philosophy underlying the 21-Step recovery program, healing within brings out the change in the world.

History has revealed that children, our most vulnerable citizens, have always been the recipient of our most punitive and aggressive actions. What was done to children centuries ago would horrify the average citizen today. But each of you who succeeds in recovering from child abuse are helping our civilization to resolve its own violent roots. Ending violence in our world is a developmental milestone just as working your recovery from abuse represents a milestone in your adult life. As more survivors choose a different life made possible by recovery, you will become part of a growing revolution in consciousness that will some day, perhaps in the twenty-first century, brand domestic violence and child abuse as intolerable.

We have made some gains in our society's consciousness about childhood and parenting. While our understanding of child development is much more sophisticated, and child abuse reporting laws now give children greater legal protection, children are still at the bottom of the totem pole in a society that endorses financial, military, and physical might. And contemporary economic and social forces in our society raise new risks for children today. Children are still being abused due to a whole new set of factors alive in our society: lack of adequate jobs, housing, and day care; the invasion of drugs, especially crack and cocaine, into our communities; the demise of the traditional nuclear family and the growth in single-parent and stepfamilies. Children do not have their own power base and must rely on others to bestow protection and respect upon them. In many, many ways, our "enlightened" society still has difficulty putting children first, and due to this limitation, we risk crippling the life blood of future generations.

There is a role here for recovered survivors that can redress the lack of power you felt as a child, and at the same time, help society understand that if children are once victimized, they may later grow up to offend. As in the twelfth step of AA, many survivors find great satisfaction and meaning in reaching out to others who are in desperate need of recovery to provide the type of encouragement and support that may have helped you years ago. Reaching out to others still in denial about their abuse as children or the abuse of their own children as parents offers a higher purpose—helping to break the chain of intergenerational abuse and domestic violence. Your efforts are part of this higher purpose that challenges our society to recognize its own inherent aggression and to resolve it just like you did—to face the underlying hurt and anger and redirect it into healthy behaviors instead of repeating the horrors of the past. This higher purpose may be the final challenge in your recovery, empowering you to take a stand against the abuse and exploitation of children, and in so doing, to help society resolve its own tendency to sacrifice its young. With this hope, I will bid you good-bye.

Appendixes

Appendix A

CHAPTER NOTES

CHAPTER ONE:
HOW TO DETERMINE IF YOU WERE
ABUSED AS A CHILD

de Mause, Lloyd ed. *The History of Childhood: The Untold Story of Child Abuse.* New York: Peter Bedrick Books, 1988.

Garbarino, J.; Guttmann, E.; and Seeley, J. W. *The Psychologically Battered Child.* San Francisco: Jossey-Bass Publishers, 1987.

Helfer, R. E., and Kempe, R. S. *The Battered Child,* 4th ed. Chicago: University of Chicago Press, 1987.

CHAPTER TWO:
UNDERSTANDING YOUR DYSFUNCTIONAL
FAMILY

Finkelhor, D. *Child Sexual Abuse: New Theory and Research.* New York: The Free Press, 1984.

Leroi, D. "The Silent Partner: An Investigation of the Familial Background, Personality Structure, Sexual Behavior and Relationships of the Mothers of Incestuous Families." Doctoral dissertation, California School of Professional Psychology, Berkeley, 1984.

CHAPTER THREE:
DISCOVERING YOUR INNER CHILD

Fraiberg, S. *The Magic Years.* New York: Charles Scribner's Sons, 1959.
Freud, A. *The Ego and the Mechanisms of Defense: The Writings of Anna Freud.* Vol. 2, London: International University Press, 1966.
Kernberg, O. *Internal World and External Reality: Object Relations Theory Applied.* New York: Jason Aronson, 1980.
Russell, D. *The Secret Trauma: Incest in the Lives of Girls and Women.* New York: Basic Books, 1986.
Silbert, M., and Pines, A. "Sexual Abuse As an Antecedent to Prostitution." *Journal of Child Abuse and Neglect* 5 (1981): 407–411.
Summit, R. C. "The Child Sexual Abuse Accommodation Syndrome." *Child Abuse and Neglect* 7 (1983) 177–193.

CHAPTER FOUR:
COMMON PROBLEMS OF
ADULT SURVIVORS

Bellak, L., and Goldsmith, L. A. *The Broad Scope of Ego Function Assessment.* New York: John Wiley & Sons, 1984.
Furst, S., ed. *Psychic Trauma.* New York: Basic Books, 1967.
Gannon, J. P. "Clinical and Group Process Issues in the Treatment of Adults Abused As Children." Paper presented at the 1986 California State Psychological Association Convention, San Francisco, March 1986.
Maltz, W., and Holman, B. *Incest and Sexuality: A Guide to Understanding and Healing.* Lexington, Mass: D. C. Heath & Co., 1987.

CHAPTER FIVE:
OVERCOMING
YOUR ADDICTIONS

Bennett, W. I. "Patterns of Addictions." *The New York Times Magazine,* April 10, 1988, 60.

Covington, S. "Alcohol and Family Violence." Unpublished paper, 1988.

Milkman, H., and Sunderwirth, S. "The Chemistry of Craving." *Psychology Today*. October 1983, 83.

Peoples, K. "The Trauma of Incest: Threats to the Consolidation of the Female Self." Unpublished paper, 1988.

CHAPTER SIX:
SURVIVING ON THE JOB

Woititz, J. G. *Home Away from Home: The Art of Self-Sabotage for Adult Children of Alcoholics in the Workplace*. Deerfield Beach, Fla.: Health Communications, Inc., 1987.

CHAPTER SEVEN:
THE CHALLENGE OF PARENTING

Coopersmith, S. *The Antecedents of Self-Esteem*. Palo Alto, Calif: Consulting Psychologists Press, 1981.

Durphy, M., and Sonkin, D. *Learning to Live Without Violence*. San Francisco: Volcano Press, 1982.

Finkelhor, D.; Williams, L. M.; and Burns, N. "Sexual Abuse in Day Care: A National Study." Durham: Family Research Laboratory, University of New Hampshire, March 1988.

Fraiberg, S.; Addleson, E.; and Shaperio, V. "Ghosts in the Nursery: A Psychoanalytic Approach to Impaired Infant-Mother Relations." *Journal of the American Academy of Child Psychiatry* 14 (1975): 387–421.

Miller, A. *For Your Own Good: Hidden Cruelty in Childrearing and the Roots of Violence*. New York: Farrar, Straus and Giroux, 1983.

CHAPTER EIGHT:
SOUL MATES: FOR FRIENDS, LOVERS,
AND SPOUSES

Bass, E., and Davis, L. *The Courage to Heal: A Guide for Women Survivors of Child Sexual Abuse*. New York: Harper and Row, 1988.

CHAPTER TEN:
SELF-HELP

Hurley, D. "Getting Help from Helping." *Psychology Today* Jan. 1988, 63.

Giarretto, H. *Integrated Treatment of Child Sexual Abuse: A Treatment and Training Manual.* Palo Alto, Calif.: Science and Behavior Books, Inc., 1982.

Taylor, Mary Catherine. "Alcoholics Anonymous: How It Works; Recovery Processes in a Self-Help Group." Doctoral dissertation, University of California, San Francisco, 1974.

Yao, Richard. *There Is a Way Out.* 4th ed. New York: FA Communications, 1987.

CHAPTER ELEVEN:
PROFESSIONAL HELP

Ehrenberg, O., and Ehrenberg, M. *The Psychotherapy Maze: A Consumer's Guide to Getting In and Out of Therapy.* New York: Simon & Schuster, Inc., 1986.

Lanning, K. *Child Molesters: A Behavioral Analysis.* Paper published for the National Center for Missing and Exploited Children by the Federal Bureau of Investigation. February 1986.

Regier, D. A.; Boyd, J. H.; Burke, J. D.; et al. "One Month Prevalence of Mental Disorders in the United States." *Archives of General Psychiatry* 45 (11) (November 1988): 977–986.

CHAPTER TWELVE:
STAGE ONE RECOVERY:
STEPS 1 TO 7

Blum, H. P. "The Role of Identification in the Resolution of Trauma." *Psychoanalytic Quarterly* (1987)

Courtois, C. A. *Healing the Incest Wound.* New York: W. W. Norton & Co., 1988.

Gil, E. *Treatment of Adult Survivors of Childhood Abuse.* Walnut Creek, Calif.: Launch Press, 1988.

Horowitz, M. J. *Stress Response Syndromes.* New York: Jason Aronson, 1976.

Rieker, P., and Carmen, E. "The Victim-to-Patient Process: The Disconfirmation and Transformation of Abuse." *American Journal of Orthopsychiatry* 56 (3): 360–370.

CHAPTER THIRTEEN:
STAGE TWO RECOVERY:
STEPS 8 TO 14

Bradshaw, J. *Healing the Shame That Binds You.* Deerfield Beach, Fla.: Health Communications, Inc., 1988.

Groth, A. N. *Men Who Rape: The Psychology of the Offender.* New York: Plenum Press, 1979.

Kohut, H. *Restoration of the Self.* New York: International Universities Press, 1977.

CHAPTER FOURTEEN:
STAGE THREE RECOVERY:
STEPS 15 TO 21

Ulman, R., and Brothers, D. *The Shattered Self.* New York: The Analytic Press, 1988.

CHAPTER FIFTEEN:
CONFRONTING YOUR PARENTS WITH
THE ABUSE

Bass, E., and Davis, L. *The Courage to Heal: A Guide for Women Survivors of Child Sexual Abuse.* New York: Harper and Row, 1988.

EPILOGUE:
SALVATION AND FUTURE CALLINGS

Daro, D., and Mitchel, L. "Deaths Due to Maltreatment Soar: The Results of the 1986 Annual Fifty State Survey," Working Paper 8. Published by the National Committee for Prevention of Child Abuse.

Gelles, R. J., and Straus, M. A. *Intimate Violence: The Cause and Consequence of Abuse in the American Family.* New York: Simon & Schuster, 1988.

Appendix B

RESOURCE DIRECTORY

INFORMATIONAL CLEARINGHOUSES

American Anorexia/Bulimia Association, Inc. 133 Cedar Lane, Teaneck, NJ 07666 (201) 836-1800

American Human Association 9725 E. Hampden Avenue, Denver, CO 80231 (303) 695-0811

American Professional Society on the Abuse of Children P.O. Box 34028, Los Angeles, CA 90034-0028 (213) 836-2471

California Consortium of Child Abuse Councils 1401 Third Street, Sacramento, CA 95678 (916) 448-9143

California Professional Society on the Abuse of Children (CAPSAC) C/O 171 Mayhew Way, Suite 213, Pleasant Hill, CA 94523

C. Henry Kempe National Center for the Prevention & Treatment of Child Abuse and Neglect, 1205 Oneida Street, Denver, CO 80220 (303) 321-3963

National Center of Child Abuse and Neglect (NCCAN) Department of Health and Human Services, P.O. Box 1182, Washington, DC 20013 (202) 245-2856

NCCAN Child Abuse Clearinghouse P.O. Box 1182, Washington, DC 20013 (310) 251-5157

National Center for Missing and Exploited Children 1835 K St., N.W. Suite 700, Washington, DC 20006 (2020 634-9821). Center assists law enforcement personnel and families in locating missing children. Toll-free number for information about missing children (800) 843-5678

National Clearinghouse for Alcohol Information (NCALI) P.O. Box 234, Rockville, MD 20852 (301) 468-2600

National Clearinghouse for Information National Institute of Drug Abuse, P.O. Box 416, Kensington, MD 20895

National Coalition Against Sexual Assault 8787 State Street, East St. Louis, ILL 62203 (618) 398-7764

National Committee for the Prevention of Child Abuse
332 S. Michigan Ave., Suite 1250, Chicago, IL 60604 (312) 663-3520 Resource and clearinghouse for current information about all topics involving child abuse. Ask for research associate to determine what information is available for no charge. Booklet: "Emotional Abuse: Words Can Hurt" by Stuart Hart and Marla Brassard. Written for parents. Send $2.50

National Institute on Alcohol Abuse and Alcoholism (NIAAA) Parklawn Building, 5600 Fishers Lane, Rockville, MD 20852 (301) 468 2600

PLEA (Prevention, Leadership, Education and Assitance) Hank Astrada, Founder and Director, P.O. Box 291182, Los Angeles, CA 90029 (213) 254-9962 Nonprofit organization of professionals and nonprofessionals serving male survivors.

Survivors of Incest International P.O. Box 21817, Baltimore, MD 21222-6817 (301) 282-3400

VOICES (Victims of Incest Can Emerge Survivors) in Action, Inc. P.O. Box 148309, Chicago, IL 60614 (312) 327-1500 National network that offers a referral service for therapists, agencies, and self-help groups, Resource material, newsletters, and group leader training are available.

SELF-HELP RESOURCES

California Self-Help Center UCLA, 2349 Franz Hall, 405 Hilgard Avenue, Los Angeles, Calif. 90024 Provides a referral service that links individuals with ongoing support groups with other individuals who want to form such groups. A statewide toll-free number is available to the public: 1-800 222-LINK. Also publishes a quarterly newsletter called *Self-Helper*, training materials, consultation and public education to mutual aid groups.

Children of Alcoholics Foundation, 200 Park Avenue, 31st Floor, New York, NY 10166 (212) 949-1404

Children's Defense Fund (CDF) 122 C St., Suite 400, N.W., Washington, DC 20001 (202) 628-8787 Legal advocacy services for class action suits and litigation favoring children. Does not handle individual cases. Call toll-free number for information about federal legislation and regulations concerning children (800) 424-9602.

National Alliance for the Mentally Ill 1901 North Fort Meyer Drive, Suite 500, Arlington, VA 22209. Write for free information on self-help groups.

National Organization for Victim Assistance, 717 D Street, N.W., Washington DC 20004

National Self-Help Clearinghouse City University of New York, 33 W. 42nd Street, #12222, New York, NY 10036 (212) 840-1259

Self-Help Organizations and Professional Practice T. J. Powell. National Association of Social Workers, 7981 Eastern Avenue, Silver Spring, MD 20910, 1987 paper, $16.95 plus $1.70 shipping.

The Self-Help Sourcebook: Finding and Forming mutual Aid Self-Help Groups E. J. Madera and A. Meese, eds. Self-Help Clearinghouse, Saint Clares-Riverside Medical Center, Denville, NJ 07834, 1986, $9.

SELF-HELP GROUPS

Al-Anon Family Group Headquarters. 1372 Broadway, 7th Floor, New York, NY 10018 (800) 245-4656 or (212) 302-7240

Alcoholics Anonymous—General Service Office (AA). 468 Park Avenue South, New York, NY 10016 (212) 686-1100

Cocaine Anonymous—National Office. P.O. Box 1367, Culver City, CA 90232 (213) 559-5833

Fundamentalists Anonymous. P.O. Box 20324, Greeley Square Station, New York, NY 10001-9992 (212) 696-0420 A booklet titled "There Is a Way Out" by cofounder Richard Yao is available for $3 at the above address.

Gamblers Anonymous—National Council on Compulsive Gambling 444 West 56th Street, Room 3207S, New York, NY 10019 (212) 765-3833 Distributes informational material on gambling that defines a compulsive addiction and offers references to therapy groups. Publishes a quarterly *Journal of Gambling Behavior*. $34 per year for individuals.

Incest Survivors Anonymous. P.O. Box 5613, Long Beach, CA 90805-0613 (213) 422-1632

Nar-Anon. Holds meetings for family members involved in drug abuse. Check local listings.

Narcotics Anonymous—World Service Office (NA). P.O. Box 9999, Van
    Nuys, CA 91409 (818) 780-3951
National Association for Children of Alcoholics (NACOA). 31706 Coast
    Highway, #301, So. Laguna, CA 92677 (714) 499-3889
Overeaters Anonymous—National Office. 4025 Spencer Street, Suite
    203, Torrance, CA 90504 (213) 542-8363
Parents Anonymous. 6733 South Sepulveda Blvd., Suite #270, Los An-
    geles, CA 90045 For people not in California call (800) 421-0353 and
    for people in California call (213) 410-9732
Parent Effectiveness Training 531 Stevens Ave. Solana Beach, CA 92075
    (619) 481-8121   Call or write for information about instructors en-
    rolling in new parent education classes in your area. Fee charged
    for groups.
Parents United/Sons and Daughters United (sexual abuse treatment).
    P.O. Box 952, San Jose, CA 95108 (408) 280-5055
Survivors of Physical and Emotional Abuse As Kids (SPEAKS) c/o Par-
    ents Anonymous, 7120 Franklin Ave., Los Angeles, CA 90046 For
    those not in California call (213) 876-0933. For people in California
    call (800) 352-0386.

TELEPHONE HOTLINES

Child Help National Child Abuse Hotline. P.O. Box 630, Hollywood,
    CA 90028 (800) 422-4453
National Cocaine-Abuse Hotline. 800-COCAINE (800-262-2463)
National Institute of Drug Abuse Hotline. (800) 662-HELP (800-662-
    4357). Referrals to treatment centers, 12-Step groups, and infor-
    mation on drugs.
National Institute of Drug Abuse Employers Hotline. (800) 843-4971
    Informational hotline for employers; 9 A.M. to 8 P.M.
Parents Anonymous—National Office. 6733 South Sepulveda Blvd.,
    Suite 270, Los Angeles, CA 90045 (800) 421-0353

VIDEOS AND FILMS

"Breaking Silence," 58 minutes, color, 16 mm or video. Rent: $100.
    Sale—VHS video: $250. Distributed by The Film Distribution Cen-
    ter, 1028 Industry Dr., Seattle, WA 98188 (206) 575-1575. Through
    the presentation of interviews with adult victims of child sexual
    abuse, "Breaking Silence" reveals some of the issues and dynamics
    of incest and sexual abuse that survivors need to overcome to heal
    their childhood pain.

"The Inner Voice of Child Abuse," 47-minute color video (available in VHS, Beta, and U-Matic) produced by Psychological and Educational Films (714) 494-5079. Purchase or rental. Exploration of the psychological dynamics underlying the physical and emotional abuse of children demonstrated through interviews with parents who abuse their children. Narrated by Dr. Robert Firestone, he illustrates how self-destructive feelings and attitudes toward oneself are unconsciously extended to one's children through parenting attitudes and behaviors learned from the parents' own abusive childhoods.

"To a Safer Place," 48 minutes. Canadian Broadcasting Group. An excellent account of a female survivor's recovery as she returns home to face her sexual abuse as a child. Interviews with her family are especially interesting as are her comments about overcoming the abuse and the help that she received along the way. Well produced by Canadian Broadcasting Group.

BOOKS: NONFICTION/SELF-HELP

ABOUT SEXUAL ABUSE

Butler, Sandra. *Conspiracy of Silence: The Trauma of Incest.* San Francisco: Volcano Press, 1985.

Fortune, Marie M. *Sexual Violence: The Unmentionable Sin: An Ethical and Pastoral Perspective.* New York: The Pilgram Press, 1983.

Forward, Dr. Susan, and Buck, Craig. *Betrayal of Innocence: Incest and Its Devastation.* New York: Penguin Books, 1988.

Herman, Judith. *Father-Daughter Incest.* Cambridge: Harvard University Press, 1981.

Masson, Jeffrey Moussaieff. *The Assault on Truth: Freud's Supression of the Seduction Theory.* New York: Farrar, Straus, & Giroux, 1984.

Miller, Alice. *Thou Shalt Not Be Aware: Society's Betrayal of the Child.* New York: New American Library, 1986.

Rush, Florence. *The Best Kept Secret: Sexual Abuse of Children.* Englewood Cliffs, NJ: Prentice-Hall, 1980.

Russell, Diana. *The Secret Trauma: Incest in the Lives of Girls and Women.* New York: Basic Books, 1986.

SURVIVORS SPEAK OUT

Bass, Ellen, and Thornton, Louise, eds. *I Never Told Anyone: Writings by Women Survivors of Child Sexual Abuse.* New York: Harper & Row, 1983.

Brady, Katherine. *Father's Days: A True Story of Incest*. New York: Dell, 1979.

Morris, Michelle. *If I Should Die Before I Wake*. New York: Dell, 1982.

Sisk, Sheila, and Hoffman, Charlotte Foster. *Inside Scars: Incest Recovery As Told by a Survivor and Her Therapist*. Gainesville, Florida: Pandora Press, 1987.

ABOUT HEALING

Bass, Ellen, and Davis, Laura. *The Courage to Heal: A Guide for Women Survivors of Child Sexual Abuse*. New York: Harper & Row, 1988.

Bear, E., and Dimock, P. T. *Adults Molested As Children: A Survivor's Manual for Women and Men*. Orwell, Vt.: The Safer Society Press.

Evert, Kathy, and Bijkerk, Inie. *When You're Ready: A Woman's Healing from Childhood Physical and Sexual Abuse by Her Mother*. Walnut Creek, Calif.: Launch Press, 1988.

Gil, Eliana. *I Told My Secret: A Book for Kids Who Were Abused*. Walnut Creek, Calif.: Launch Press, 1988.

Gil, Eliana. *Outgrowing the Pain: A Book for and about Adults Abused As Children*. San Francisco: Launch Press, 1983.

Ledray, Linda. *Recovering from Rape*. New York: Henry Holt, 1986.

Lew, Mike. *Victims No Longer: Men Recovering from Incest*. New York: Nevraumont Publishing Co., 1988.

Maltz, Wendy, and Holman, Beverly. *Incest and Sexuality: A Guide to Understanding and Healing*. Lexington, Mass., Lexington Books, 1987. An information and self-help book designed to help adult survivors overcome the repercussions of child sexual abuse.

Wynne, Carrie Elizabeth. *That Looks Like a Nice House: A Survivors Story of Recovery and Healing*. Walnut Creek, Calif.: Launch Press, 1988.

COUNSELING AND SUPPORT GROUPS

Ernst, Sheila, and Goodwin, Lucy. *In Our Own Hands: A Woman's Book of Self-Help Therapy*. Los Angeles: J. P. Tarcher, 1981.

Freeman-Longo, R., and Bays, Laren. *Who Am I and Why Am I in Treatment: A Guided Workbook for Clients in Evaluation and Treatment for Sex Offenses*. Orwell, Vt.: The Safer Society Press.

Gangi, Barbara; Bruckner-Gordon, Fredda; and Wallman, Gerry. *Making Therapy Work*. New York: Harper & Row, 1987.

Hall, Marny. *The Lavender Couch: A Consumer's Guide to Psychotherapy for Lesbians and Gay Men*. Boston: Alyson Publications, 1985.

NiCarthy, Ginny; Merriam, Karen; and Coffman, Sandra. *Talking It Out: A Guide to Groups for Abused Women*. Seattle: Seal Press, 1984.

Wyckoff, Hogie. *Solving Women's Problems through Awareness, Action and Contact*. New York: Grove Press, 1980.

Scheffler, L. W. *Help Thy Neighbor*. New York: Grove Press, 1984, hardcover $22.50; paperback, $7.95. Discussion of social support network for members of Overeaters Anonymous.

FOR SUPPORTERS OF SURVIVORS

Beneke, Timothy. *Men on Rape: What They Have to Say about Sexual Violence*. New York: St. Martin's Press, 1982.
McEnvoy, Alan, and Brookings, Jeff. *If She Is Raped: A Book for Husbands, Fathers, and Male Friends*. Holmes Beach, Fla.: Learning Publications, 1984.
Sonkin, Daniel Jay, and Durphy, Michael. *Learning to Live Without Violence: A Handbook for Men*. San Francisco: Volcano Press, 1985.

PARENTING

Bettelheim, Bruno. *The Good Enough Parent*. New York: Alfred A. Knopf, 1987.
Gordon, Thomas. *Parent Effectiveness Training*. New York: Peter H. Wyden, 1970.
Miller, Alice. *For Your Own Good*. New York: Farrar, Straus, Giroux, 1979.
Sears, William, M.D. *Creative Parenting*. New York: Everest House, 1982.

TEACHING CHILDREN ABOUT SAFETY AND SELF-PROTECTION

Adams, Caren, and Fay, Jennifer. *No More Secrets: Protecting Your Child from Sexual Assault*. San Luis Obispo: Impact Publishers, 1981.
Byerly, Carolyn. *The Mother's Book: How to Survive the Incest of Your Child*. Dubuque, Ia.: Kendall/Hunt Publishing, 1985.
Child Assault Prevention Project. *Strategies for Free Children: A Leader's Guide to Child Assault Prevention*. Columbus: Child Assault Prevention Project, 1985.
Colao, Flora, and Hosansky, Tamar. *Your Children Should Know*. New York: Harper & Row, 1987.
Fay, Jennifer, et al. *He Told Me Not to Tell*. Renton, Wash.: King County Rape Relief, 1979.
Gil, Eliana. *Children Who Molest: A Guide for Parents of Young Sex Offenders*. Walnut Creek, Calif.: Launch Press, 1988.
Nelson, Mary, and Clark, Kay. *The Educator's Guide to Preventing Child Sexual Abuse*. Santa Cruz: Network Publications of ETR Associates, 1987.
Sanford, Linda. *The Silent Children: A Parent's Guide to the Prevention of Child Sexual Abuse*. New York: McGraw-Hill, 1980.

Smith, Hon. Sandra Butler. *Children's Story: Sexually Molested Children in Criminal Court.* Walnut Creek, Calif.: Launch Press, 1988.

ADULT CHILDREN OF ALCOHOLICS

Ackerman, Robert J. *Children of Alcoholics.* Holmes Beach, Fla.: Learning Publications, 1983.

Black, Claudia. *It Will Never Happen to Me!* Denver: M.A.C. Printing and Publications Division, 1981.

Gravitz, Herbert L., and Bowden, Julie D. *Guide to Recovery—A Book for ACOAs.* Holmes Beach, Florida: Learning Publications, 1985.

Marlin, Emily. *HOPE: New Choices and Recovery Strategies for Adult Children of Alcoholics.* New York: Harper & Row, 1988.

McConnell, Patty. *A Workbook for Healing: Adult Children of Alcoholics.* New York: Harper & Row, 1986.

Seixas, Judith S., and Youcha, Geraldine. *Children of Alcoholism: A Survivor's Manual.* New York: Harper & Row, 1985.

Wegscheider-Cruse, Sharon. *Choicemaking.* Pompano Beach, Florida: Health Communications, 1985.

Woitiz, Janet Geringer. *Adult Children of Alcoholics.* Pompano Beach, Florida: Health Communications, 1983.

EATING DISORDERS

Bruch, Hilde, M.D. *The Golden Cage.* Cambridge: Harvard University Press, 1978.

Siegal, Michelle, and Brisman, Judith. *Surviving an Eating Disorder.* New York: Harper & Row, 1988.

FAMILY SYSTEMS

Kubler-Ross, Elizabeth. *On Death and Dying.* New York: Macmillan, 1969.

McGoldrick, Monica, and Gerson, Randy. *Genograms in Family Assessment.* New York: W. W. Norton, 1985.

Satir, Virginia. *Peoplemaking.* California: Science & Behavior Books, 1972.

Zimmerman, William. *How to Tape Instant Oral Biographies.* New York: Guarionex Press, 1979.

BOOKS:
NONFICTION/RESOURCE

Crewdson, John. *By Silence Betrayed: Sexual Abuse of Children in America.* Boston: Little, Brown and Company, 1988.

deMause, Lloyd, ed. *The History of Childhood: The Untold Story of Child Abuse*. New York: Peter Bedrick Books, 1988.

Finkelhor, David, *Child Sexual Abuse: New Theory & Research*. New York: The Free Press, 1984.

Finkelhor, David, and associates. *A Sourcebook on Child Sexual Abuse*. Beverly Hills: Sage Publications, Inc., 1986.

Garbarino, James; Guttmann, Edna; and Seeley, Janis Wilson. *The Psychologically Battered Child: Strategies for Identification, Assessment, and Intervention*. San Francisco: Jossey-Bass Inc., Publishers, 1986.

Gelles, Richard J. and Straus, Murray A. *Intimate Violence: The Definitive Study of the Causes and Consequences of Abuse in the American Family*. New York: Simon and Schuster, 1988.

Gil, Eliana. *Treatment of Adult Survivors*. Walnut Creek, Calif.: Launch Press, 1988.

Gordon, Linda. *Heroes of Their Own Lives: The Politics and History of Family Violence*. New York: Viking, 1988.

Helfer, Ray E., and Kempe, Ruth S. *The Battered Child*. Chicago: University of Chicago Press, 1987.

McCormack, Hartman, Burgess and Janus. *Adolescent Runaways: Causes and Consequences*. Lexington, Mass.: Lexington Books, 1987.

Miller, Alice. *For Your Own Good: Hidden Cruelty in Child-Rearing and the Roots of Violence*. New York: Farrar-Straus-Giroux, 1983.

Sagan, Eli, *Freud, Women, and Morality: The Psychology of Good and Evil*. New York: Basic Books, Inc., 1988.

Woititz, Janet Geringer. *Home Away from Home: The Art of Self Sabotage*. Pompano Beach, Florida: Health Communications, Inc., 1987.

BOOKS: FICTION

Conroy, Pat. *The Prince of Tides*. New York: Bantam Books, 1987. An extremely well-written novel about a southern family torn apart by physical abuse and wife battering from the point of view of one of the sons.

Miller, Sue. *The Good Mother*. New York: Harper and Row, 1986. A novel exploring how child custody issues and sexual politics can result in allegations of child abuse.

PERIODICALS AND NEWSLETTERS

Incest Survivor Information Exchange, P.O. Box 3399, New Haven, CT 06515.

Self-Help Reporter. Quarterly newsletter published by the National Self-Help Clearinghouse, 33 West 42nd Street, New York, NY 10036; subscriptions $10 per year.

The "Looking Up" Times, RFD #1, Box 2620, Mt. Vernon, ME 04352 (207) 293-2750.

The Newsy Letter, published by Voices in Action, Inc., P.O. Box 148309, Chicago, IL 60614 (314) 327-1500.

The Pun, Official newsletter of the Santa Clara County Chapter of Parents and Daughters and Sons United. P.O. Box 952, San Jose, CA 95108; tel: (408) 280-5055.

Appendix C

A NOTE TO THERAPISTS

Soul Survivors is intended for adult survivors of child abuse—men as well as women—who are either in recovery or contemplating entering recovery. As defined in chapter 1, this population would include adults who were raised in virtually any kind of dysfunctional family—parents who are chemically dependent, parents with chronic physical or mental disorders, neglectful or criminal/violent families, compulsively addicted or extreme religious and cult families. The paradigm underlying the focus in the first three chapters suggests that the concept of abuse—physical, sexual, or emotional (including neglect)—be viewed on a continuum of severity determined by several factors: type, severity, and duration of abuse; age of onset; and multiple- or single-parent offenders. The term *abuse* is being used specifically and generally to describe a range of pathological parent–child relations that may or may not include episodes of extreme trauma. In this way, the abuse *context* in terms of the ongoing relationships with parents and the typical family atmosphere can be recognized as a separate factor from the abuse *episodes*, which must be separately assessed for traumatic reactions and dissociative splitting. The treatment philosophy underlying the 21-Step recovery program attempts to integrate popular addiction recovery concepts promulgated by Alcoholics Anonymous with a modified object relations/self-psychology approach that emphasizes trauma resolution, building ego functions, and a positive self-concept.

This book has several purposes besides simply educating the reader about child abuse and the issues, problems, and recovery strategies for adult survivors. "Bibliotherapy" as the reading of self-help books is now often identified, can be of particular help to adult survivors of child abuse who feel so stigmatized and isolated by their past. However, in no way is the reading of the book intended to be a substitute for the survivors' involvement in a comprehensive program of self-help and professional help as described in chapters 10 and 11. Rather, the reading and journaling activities suggested can be an adjunct to the therapy program, an extension of the fifty-minute session. Reading about how other survivors have overcome their abuse can help those just beginning in recovery to manage their anxiety about re-experiencing the trauma. For survivors who are currently in therapy, reading can augment the development of self-awareness and insight produced in the therapy while keeping the therapy material fresh in mind between sessions. Reworking the memories of the abuse on their own may also help survivors take better advantage of their therapy sessions, considering how formidable their defenses can be. Reading and writing can help uncover memories while developing secondary ego functions to help clients resolve the material coming into consciousness. Repression is reduced, reality testing is reinforced, and higher-level defenses are supported. For survivors who were severely affected by the abuse, the book can function as a transitional object between sessions, something survivors can hold onto until they return.

The book is also intended to function as an outreach tool for those survivors, especially men and those prone to aggressive behavior, who have yet to identify themselves as victims of child abuse or begun to get professional help. *Soul Survivors* may help them figure out what occurred in their relationship with their parents and family members that could be considered abusive and how it might have contributed to the problems that seem to repeat in their current lives. Additionally, *Soul Survivors* is for the many survivors who attend 12-Step groups or parent education classes who have yet to receive professional help, despite some indication that they might benefit from it. Hopefully reading this book with its strong emphasis on professional long-term psychotherapy will serve as a "bridge into treatment" for those willing and interested to go beyond the 12-Step approach.

Besides the purpose of informing readers and helping them make intelligent recovery decisions, *Soul Survivors* is organized to help educate clients about the use of the psychotherapeutic process in all of its many modalities and orientations in the service of their recovery. The 21-Step recovery program outlined in the last section of the book can be used to trigger discussion and reactions for clients who may still have difficulty organizing their past memories and emotions into words. The survivors' syndrome in fact can include many problems and concerns that are well beyond the boundaries of individual psychotherapy. The reader is introduced to the various treatment options, which will address many of their recovery needs while continuing in their individual therapy. The emphasis in this book is on empowering the survivors to take charge of their recovery. Educating them about their treatment options offers a sense of power and control over their recovery that is consistent with this approach.

Introducing the idea of reading this book to your clients raises a few issues that need to be discussed. Some therapists may be reluctant to suggest a book to their clients due to their theoretical orientation. Clients vary in terms of whether they can derive benefits from reading about a problem they are facing. Some survivors who are just beginning to understand their abuse may feel overwhelmed at being introduced to all of this information, some of it graphic and technical. For these clients, the book can be offered after much of the work has been done to provide some extra validation for their experiences. Others may feel in the dark about child abuse and may be desperate for accurate information that can build their knowledge base and offer some control over a subject matter that is still intimidating. On the other hand, some clients who tend to overrely on intellectual defenses may use the information garnered from their reading as yet another defense against the feelings about the abuse. In this case, the compulsive reading of this and other books may not be indicated if it doesn't make more accessible the emotional material they need to face.

If you would like a professional bibliography appropriate for therapists, refer to Appendix A, which lists background references and rationale for some of the information presented in the book.

If you have any response to the material in this book or ideas about using the book in psychotherapy with adult survivors, please write your comments using the address listed on the top of Appendix F.

Appendix D

A PARENTS GUIDE FOR
SCREENING DAY-CARE CENTERS

Here is a five-point procedure for selecting a quality daycare center. Use it as a guide or starting point for your own personal screening checklist. If, during your visits to programs, you notice other factors that need to be considered, add them to your list. Many of the ideas will be applicable in the selection of a babysitter as well, although a less formal screening process may be sufficient. Remember, it will take time, patience and effort to sift through what is available in your community in terms of quality daycare and babysitting services. Use your intuition as well as the facts to make the right choice for your child.

Get recommendations from local child-care resource organizations about quality, licensed day-care centers.

Contact these centers and ask for references. Contact the references and talk with the parents of children who have used the center in the past. Ask directly about any concerns they or their children had and how the day-care center staff responded to these concerns. My recommendation is to not consider using an unlicensed day-care center.

Visit several centers that have been recommended without your child and make notes about the quality of the program and facility.

Ask to see the license of the center. Large day-care centers as well as in-home, family day care for children must be licensed in most states. Most licensing bureaus operate out of the state Department of Social Services and offer a variety of information to parents who are seeking quality day care for their children. However, these licensing bureaus often do not offer recommendations for specific day-care programs. They can, in many cases, tell the parents if a particular day-care center or provider has had any complaints registered against them. Some states such as California maintain a Child Abuse Index of people who have been charged with child abuse related crimes. Parents can cross-check the names of potential child-care providers with the names on this list. However, this method does not provide any real safeguards because in the vast majority of cases the offender will not have been previously charged with a sexual offense.

During your visit, monitor the activities of the staff, children, and overall program. Compare what you see with the following checklist:

1. Is the facility clean and safe? Does it provide a stimulating environment for children of the age being served?
2. Is there enough room inside and outside for all the children attending at a particular time?
3. Is the staff adequate in numbers and trained in child development and early childhood education?
4. What are the personal characteristics of the staff? Are they warm, sensitive, caring adults who are truly interested in the Children? Can they engage individual children in the various activities that allow for a give and take between child and adult? Or are they overconcerned with "managing" the children as a collective entity with an emphasis on "keeping the peace"? If you have questions or concerns about anything, ask the appropriate person and expect your question to be handled in a responsible manner. If the staff seems confused or uninformed, ask the director about staff turnover. The better programs usually keep usually staff longer, although unfortunately the pay for childcare workers is so low that frequent turnover is common.
5. Is the program sufficiently structured with planned activities or is there an out-of-control and chaotic quality? Does the program offer a variety of activities and experiences for the child under the direction of the staff including art, music, athletics, social development activities, and reading circles? Or are the children left to amuse themselves with the available toys with only min-

imal involvement of the staff? Are there adequate toys, books, and recreational equipment? Are children watching television? If so, how much television time is permitted? Ask the program coordinator or director about her philosophy of child care. Ask her to describe how the program attempts to implement this philosophy.

6. Ask for a list of procedures and policies that are used to address common situations in the care of children. For example, how are the children assisted to use the bathroom? Is there a nap time provided, and if so, where do the children lie down? Are snacks and lunches served, and if so, who does the food preparation and what thought is given to providing a nutritious diet? How are the children disciplined? Corporal punishment is not allowed in licensed homes in most states and *should not be permitted under any circumstances.* Does staff use a "time-out" system that is effective without being punitive or humiliating to the child? Are the children ever taken outside of the center? If so, how are parents notified and what kind of transportation is used and what level of staffing is provided for each child? What kind of emergency medical services are used and what are the procedures for contacting the parent?

7. Does the program permit unannounced "drop-ins" by the parent? In most states, parents have the legal right to "drop in" at any time care is being provided. Ask the director how he feels about parents dropping in unannounced. If you sense that he is uncomfortable or discouraging about this practice, beware of the program. Ask what expectations there are for parent involvement. In most cases, the better programs have a strong parent involvement. While this may be difficult for you considering your busy schedule, be ready to commit to at least some token involvement. It will be helpful to your child to have you involved and it will be helpful to you to see how your child is playing and interacting with others.

Narrow down your choices to two or three programs and make another visit, this time with your child.

Allow your child to participate in some of the activities and meet the staff for an hour or two with you present. Notice what your child likes to do and how he or she interacts with the children and the staff. Does your child look lost and uninterested in the activities, children, and toys? Or does he or she gradually fit in with the flow of play? Look at how your child is being treated by staff and children alike. Is she placed with other children of a similar age group? Are there other children who your child feels comfortable playing with? Do the other children generally seem to be a positive influence on your child? Again, feel free to discuss whatever concerns you have with the appropriate staff member and expect your concerns to be addressed responsibly. After the visit, ask your child how she felt about the various programs. Take into strong consideration which program she liked best, but compare it to your choice as well. Use your intuititon and the facts you have accumulated to make your decision. Let your child know what you will do and set a date for starting the program. Prepare your child for the starting date by talking about it and asking what feelings she has about her first day.

   After deciding on a particular center, and enrolling your child, take some time during the first week to observe how your child is adjusting.

During the first few weeks, in particular, ask your child how he feels about his new program. Listen carefully to what your child says and doesn't say. What is the feeling being communicated between his words? Do you sense that your child is happy and excited to attend the center or is he unenthusiastic and listless about going? Sometimes a child will initially be resistant to going to a new program and being separated from his parents for the first time. Frequently this has nothing to do with the quality of the program, but rather indicates your child is having trouble making the transition. Transitions are generally difficult for young children and frequently can stir up strong emotional issues having to do with safety, separation, and being dependent on the parent. Handling the first situation involving the separation of child and parent will make most future transitions all the more easier for your child.

   In some cases, a child's difficulty in making the transition to a new program may signal that something is not right. It may take some time and effort to sift out the cause of your child's uncomfortable feelings about attending the program. You may need to consult with the program staff members about how they see your child adjusting to the new environment during the transitional phase. If the behavior continues, consider getting a professional opinion to help you deal best with the situation. In cases where your child can articulate a reason for his uncomfortableness, take it seriously. If his concerns cannot be resolved, think about trying another program that might be more comfortable for him.

Appendix E

21-STEP RECOVERY PROGRAM

STAGE ONE:

1. I have resolved the breakthrough crisis, regaining some control of my life.
2. I have determined, intuitively or objectively, that I was physically, sexually, or emotionally abused as a child.
3. I have made a commitment to recover from my abuse.
4. I shall reexperience each set of memories of the abuse as they surface in my mind.
5. I accept that I was powerless over my parents' actions, which makes them, not me, responsible for the abuse.
6. I respect my anger as a natural reaction to the abuse and am learning to not turn it against myself or others.
7. I have reconnected with my inner child whose efforts to survive can now be appreciated.

STAGE TWO

8. I have made an inventory of the problem areas in my life.
9. I have identified the parts of myself connected to self-sabotage.
10. I am uncovering my shame and working to transform it into self-acceptance.
11. I am able to grieve my childhood and mourn the parents who failed me.
12. I can challenge faulty beliefs and distorted perceptions, adopting more healthy attitudes and expectations about myself.
13. I accept that I alone have the right to be the way I want to be and to choose how to live my life.
14. I can control my abusive behavior and find healthy outlets for my aggression.

STAGE THREE

15. I am strengthening the healthy parts of myself while reducing maladaptive patterns and behaviors.
16. I am entitled to take the initiative to share in life's riches.
17. I am acquiring the interpersonal skills to adopt new behaviors at home and at work.
18. I have resolved the abuse with my parents or offenders to the extent that is acceptable to me.
19. I have developed my own meaning about the abuse that releases me from the legacy of the past.
20. I see myself not only as a survivor but as a thriver in all aspects of life: love, work, parenting, and play.
21. I am resolved in the reunion of my new self and my eternal soul.

Appendix F

READER QUESTIONAIRE

The following survey is intended to give you a chance to respond about the particulars of your abuse as well as any reactions to the material presented in this book. We are still discovering more about how child abuse impacts the lives of adult survivors and your story may add to our developing knowledge base. This information will be incorporated into future editions of this book. Please don't put your name on it. I do need some demographic information about you to organize the information. It is your ideas and thoughts that I am interested in, not your identity as a person. Send the survey back to: Dr. J. Patrick Gannon, c/o The Philip Lief Group, Inc., 6 West 20th Street, New York, N.Y. 10011.

Date of Birth: Sex:

Marital Status: Children:

Occupation: Religion (if any):

Ethnic Background: Educational Level:

1. Describe the family that raised you—the members, their ages, personalities, family problems, significant experiences in your parents' childhoods, family myths, roles that everyone played, and the type of family, using the typology in chapter 2.

2. Describe the abuse you suffered as a child by identifying what type(s) of abuse, who did it, when it started, degree of severity, how long it lasted, how it ended, the response of the non-abusing parent, and how it affected your relationships with family members. Did anyone ever report it? Did anyone outside the family know about it? Also, describe in detail from beginning to end, one episode of each type of abuse that typifies the pattern of each episode.

3. Describe how you coped with the reality of the abuse as a child. What did you do that helped you survive? What defenses did you employ based on those described in chapter 3? What role or mixture of roles did you take on during childhood? What was the immediate impact of the abuse on your childhood? What were your feelings about the abuse and how did you feel about yourself as you were growing up?

4. Describe the long-term effects of your child abuse on your adult life before recovery and prioritize them by listing them in *decreasing* order of importance. Make sure to address the effects on social functioning, emotional life, physical reactions, sexual response, family relations, sense of self, and relations to the same sex and opposite sex. Describe in detail, with a particular emphasis on any problem that is not mentioned in this book.

5. Describe the impact of the abuse on parenting and work issues, particularly since little research is currently available in this area. Describe if and how your feelings left over from the abuse shape your parenting style. Again describe in detail using examples to illustrate the issues.

6. What impact has the abuse had on your personal adult relationships? What feelings get stirred up in your intimate relationships that seem connected to the abuse? Describe in detail any examples that might illustrate the conflicts that you have with your spouse or partner. How has your spouse or partner reacted to the effects of the abuse on your relationship? What does your spouse or partner say about the hardships of living with a survivor in recovery?

7. Describe how you got help for yourself and the kind of help you have received to date: self-help or professional help or

both. What type of help has benefitted you and what kinds didn't? How long have you been in recovery? When did you start seeing results in the form of feeling better and making changes in your life? Specifically, what issue or resolution of some issue seemed to give you the biggest boost? If you were to add to the list of twenty-one Steps described in *Soul Survivors*, what new steps were important to you based on your experience?

8. What self-help ideas have you discovered that might help others who are also in recovery from child abuse? What self-help groups have you attended and what did you get out of them that has not been mentioned in this book? Describe any experiences that you have had in self-help groups that illustrate either their positive impact or their limitations.

9. What has been your experience in professional therapy to date? What has your therapist done to make the sessions more productive in dealing with the long-term impact of the abuse? Do you have any suggestions to add to the process of selecting a therapist? What examples can you give of bad experiences that you have had with therapists? What limitations of professional help need to be recognized, especially as they affect recovery from child abuse? What additional issues about using professional therapy would you like to see in future editions of *Soul Survivors*?

10. What have you done by way of confronting your parents, abuser, or family members with your abuse as a child? What kind of confrontation—direct or indirect—did you employ? Describe in detail what you did, when you initiated it, what actually occurred, and how it turned out. How did the confrontation help or hinder your efforts to resolve the abuse? How did the confrontation affect your relationship with your family members? What issues about confronting your family that were not included in chapter 15 should be addressed in future editions based on your experience?

11. Describe your reactions to reading *Soul Survivors*. How did you hear of the book and what was your initial reaction to reading it? What did you like about the book? What did you not like about the book? Would you recommend the book to others? How do you think it might be changed in future editions to make it more valuable to recovering survivors like yourself?

12. What other comments, reactions, observations, or suggestions would you like to share with me? Use as much space as you like.

    I am very interested in receiving your comments. Thank you for your time and effort in responding to these questions. Good luck in your recovery efforts.

J. PATRICK GANNON, PH.D. is a clinical psychologist in private practice in San Francisco. For the last ten years he has worked with children and adults who have been abused as well as with parents accused of child abuse. He lectures widely on child abuse issues and the need for new strategies of prevention. He also trains mental health professionals in the treatment of abused children and adults.

Dr. Gannon graduated from Boston College with a B.A. in psychology and philosophy and received an M.A. and Ph.D. from the California School of Professional Psychology. He is married and lives in Berkeley, California.